T0100189

Designing Deep Learning Systems

A GUIDE FOR SOFTWARE ENGINEERS

CHI WANG
AND DONALD SZETO
CODE LAB BY YAN XUE
FOREWORD BY SILVIO SAVARESE AND CAIMING XIONG

MANNING

SHELTER ISLAND

For online information and ordering of this and other Manning books, please visit
www.manning.com. The publisher offers discounts on this book when ordered in quantity.
For more information, please contact

> Special Sales Department
> Manning Publications Co.
> 20 Baldwin Road
> PO Box 761
> Shelter Island, NY 11964
> Email: orders@manning.com

©2023 by Manning Publications Co. All rights reserved.

No part of this publication may be reproduced, stored in a retrieval system, or transmitted, in
any form or by means electronic, mechanical, photocopying, or otherwise, without prior written
permission of the publisher.

Many of the designations used by manufacturers and sellers to distinguish their products are
claimed as trademarks. Where those designations appear in the book, and Manning Publications
was aware of a trademark claim, the designations have been printed in initial caps or all caps.

⊖ Recognizing the importance of preserving what has been written, it is Manning's policy to have
the books we publish printed on acid-free paper, and we exert our best efforts to that end.
Recognizing also our responsibility to conserve the resources of our planet, Manning books
are printed on paper that is at least 15 percent recycled and processed without the use of
elemental chlorine.

The author and publisher have made every effort to ensure that the information in this book
was correct at press time. The author and publisher do not assume and hereby disclaim any
liability to any party for any loss, damage, or disruption caused by errors or omissions, whether
such errors or omissions result from negligence, accident, or any other cause, or from any usage
of the information herein.

Manning Publications Co.
20 Baldwin Road
PO Box 761
Shelter Island, NY 11964

Development editor:	Frances Lefkowitz
Technical development editor:	Ninoslav Čerkez
Review editor:	Adriana Sabo
Production editor:	Andy Marinkovich
Copy editor:	Kristen Bettcher
Proofreader:	Alisa Larson
Technical proofreader:	Al Krinker
Typesetter:	Dennis Dalinnik
Cover designer:	Marija Tudor

ISBN: 9781633439863
Printed in the United States of America

Get the eBook FREE!

(PDF, ePub, Kindle, and liveBook all included)

We believe that once you buy a book from us, you should be able to read it in any format we have available. To get electronic versions of this book at no additional cost to you, purchase and then register this book at the Manning website.

Go to https://www.manning.com/freebook and follow the instructions to complete your pBook registration.

That's it!
Thanks from Manning!

brief contents

contents

foreword

A deep learning system can be assumed to be efficient if it can bridge two different worlds—research and prototyping with production operations. Teams who design such systems must be able to communicate with practitioners across these two worlds and work with the different sets of requirements and constraints that come from each. This requires a principled understanding of how the components in deep learning systems are designed and how they are expected to work in tandem. Very little of the existing literature covers this aspect of deep learning engineering. This information gap becomes an issue when junior software engineers are onboarded and expected to become effective deep learning engineers.

Over the years, engineering teams have filled this void by using their acquired experience and ferreting out what they need to know from the literature. Their work has helped traditional software engineers build, design, and extend deep learning systems in a relatively short amount of time. So it was with great excitement that I learned that Chi and Donald, both of whom have led deep learning engineering teams, have taken the very important initiative of consolidating this knowledge and sharing it in the form of a book.

We are long overdue for a comprehensive book on building systems that support bringing deep learning from research and prototyping to production. *Designing Deep Learning Systems* finally fills this need.

The book starts with a high-level introduction describing what a deep learning system is and does. Subsequent chapters discuss each system component in detail and provide motivation and insights about the pros and cons of various design choices.

Each chapter ends with an analysis that helps readers assess the most appropriate and relevant options for their own use cases. The authors conclude with an in-depth discussion, pulling from all previous chapters, on the challenging path of going from research and prototyping to production. And to help engineers put all these ideas into practice, they have created a sample deep learning system, with fully functional code, to illustrate core concepts and offer a taste to those who are just entering the field.

Overall, readers will find this book easy to read and navigate while bringing their understanding of how to orchestrate, design, and implement deep learning systems to a whole new level. Practitioners at all levels of expertise who are interested in designing effective deep learning systems will appreciate this book as an invaluable resource and reference. They will read it once to get the big picture and then return to it again and again when building their systems, designing their components, and making crucial choices to satisfy all the teams that use the systems.

—SILVIO SAVARESE, EVP, Chief Scientist, Salesforce
—CAIMING XIONG, VP, Salesforce

preface

A little more than a decade ago, we had the privilege of building some early end user–facing product features that were powered by artificial intelligence. It was a huge undertaking. Collecting and organizing data that would be fit for model training was not a usual practice at that time. Few machine learning algorithms were packaged as ready-to-use libraries. Performing experiments required running management manually and building out custom workflows and visualizations. Custom servers were made to serve each type of model. Outside of resource-intensive tech companies, almost every single new AI-powered product feature was built from scratch. It was a far-reaching dream that intelligent applications would one day become a commodity.

After working with a few AI applications, we realized that we had been repeating a similar ritual each time, and it seemed to us that it made more sense to design a systematic way, with prototyping, for delivering AI product features to production. The fruit of this effort was PredictionIO, an open source suite of framework software that put together state-of-the-art software components for data collection and retrieval, model training, and model serving. Fully customizable through its APIs and deployable as services with just a few commands, it helped shorten the time required at every stage, from running data science experiments to training and deploying production-ready models. We were thrilled to learn that developers around the world were able to use PredictionIO to make their own AI-powered applications, resulting in some amazing boosts to their businesses. PredictionIO was later acquired by Salesforce to tackle a similar problem on an even larger scale.

By the time we decided to write this book, the industry was thriving with a healthy AI software ecosystem. Many algorithms and tools have become available to tackle different use cases. Some cloud vendors such as Amazon, Google, and Microsoft even provide complete, hosted systems that make it possible for teams to collaborate on experimentation, prototyping, and production deployments at one centralized location. No matter what your goal is, you now have many choices and numerous ways to put them together.

Still, as we work with teams to deliver deep learning–powered product features, there have been some recurring questions. Why is our deep learning system designed the way it is? Is this the best design for other specific use cases? We noticed that junior software engineers were the ones most often asking these questions, and we interviewed a few of them to find out why. They revealed that their conventional software engineering training did not prepare them to work effectively with deep learning systems. And when they looked for learning resources, they found only scant and scattered information on specific system components, with hardly any resources discussing the fundamentals of the software components, why they were put together the way they were, and how they worked together to form a complete system.

To address this problem, we started building a knowledge base, which eventually evolved into manual-like learning material explaining the design principles of each system component, the pros and cons of the design decisions, and the rationale from both technical and product perspectives. We were told that our material helped to quickly ramp up new teammates and allowed traditional software engineers with no prior experience in building deep learning systems to get up to speed. We decided to share this learning material with a much larger audience, in the form of a book. We contacted Manning, and the rest was history.

acknowledgments

Writing a book indeed takes a lot of solitary effort, but this book would not have been possible without the help of the following individuals.

Working with different teams at the Salesforce Einstein groups (Einstein platform, E.ai, Hawking) formed the basis of a large part of this book. These brilliant and influential teammates include (in alphabetical order) Sara Asher, Jimmy Au, John Ball, Anya Bida, Gene Becker, Yateesh Bhagavan, Jackson Chung, Himay Desai, Mehmet Ezbiderli, Vitaly Gordon, Indira Iyer, Arpeet Kale, Sriram Krishnan, Annie Lange, Chan Lee, Eli Levine, Daphne Liu, Leah McGuire, Ivaylo Mihov, Richard Pack, Henry Saputra, Raghu Setty, Shaun Senecal, Karl Skucha, Magnus Thorne, Ted Tuttle, Ian Varley, Yan Yang, Marcin Zieminski, and Leo Zhu.

We also want to take this opportunity to thank our development editor, Frances Lefkowitz. She is not only an excellent editor who provides great writing guidance and inline editing but also a great mentor who guided us throughout the entire book-writing process. This book wouldn't be of its current quality or completed as planned without her.

Our thanks go out to the Manning team for their guidance throughout the book's writing process. We really appreciate the opportunity to have readers' opinions in the early stages of the book's writing through Manning Early Access Program (MEAP).

To all the reviewers—Alex Blanc, Amit Kumar, Ayush Tomar, Bhagvan Kommadi, Dinkar Juyal, Esref Durna, Gaurav Sood, Guillaume Alleon, Hammad Arshad, Jamie Shaffer, Japneet Singh, Jeremy Chen, João Dinis Ferreira, Katia Patkin, Keith Kim, Larry Cai, Maria Ana, Mikael Dautrey, Nick Decroos, Nicole Königstein, Noah Flynn,

Oliver Korten, Omar El Malak, Pranjal Ranjan, Ravi Suresh Mashru, Said Ech-Chadi, Sandeep D., Sanket Sharma, Satej Kumar Sahu, Sayak Paul, Shweta Joshi, Simone Sguazza, Sriram Macharla, Sumit Bhattacharyya, Ursin Stauss, Vidhya Vinay, and Wei Luo—your suggestions helped make this a better book.

I would like to thank my wife Pei Wu for her unconditional love and tremendous support throughout the process of writing this book. During the tough times of the Covid pandemic, Pei remained a peaceful and quiet corner that allowed the book to be composed amid a busy family with two lovely young children—Catherine and Tiancheng.

Also, I would like to extend my gratitude to Yan Xue, a talented 10X developer who wrote nearly the entire code lab. His help makes the code lab not only high quality but also easy to learn. Yan's wife, Dong, supported him wholeheartedly so Yan could concentrate on the book lab.

The other person I want to thank is Dianne Siebold, a talented and experienced tech writer at Salesforce. Dianne inspired me with her own writing experiences and encouraged me to begin writing.

— Chi Wang

Co-founding PredictionIO (later acquired by Salesforce) has taught me invaluable lessons about building open source machine learning developer products. This adventurous and rewarding journey would not be possible without courageous souls who placed immense trust in one another. They are (in alphabetical order) Kenneth Chan, Tom Chan, Pat Ferrel, Isabelle Lee, Paul Li, Alex Merritt, Thomas Stone, Marco Vivero, and Justin Yip.

Simon Chan deserves a special mention. Chan co-founded PredictionIO, and I also had the honor to work with and learn from him in his previous entrepreneurial endeavors. He was the first person who officially introduced programming to me when we were both attending the same secondary school (Wah Yan College, Kowloon) in Hong Kong. Other inspiring figures from the school include (in alphabetical order) Donald Chan, Jason Chan, Hamlet Chu, Kah Kuen Fu, Jeffrey Hau, Francis Kong, Eric Lau, Kam Lau, Raylex Lee, Kevin Lei, Danny Shing, Norman So, Steven Tung, and Lobo Wong.

I am extremely grateful to my parents and my brother Ronald. They provided me with early exposure to computers. Their perpetual support played a vital role in my formative years as I aspired to become a computer engineer.

My son, Spencer, is the walking proof of why biological deep neural networks are the most amazing things in the world. He is a wonderful gift who shows me every day that I can always grow and become better.

Words cannot express how much my wife, Vicky, means to me. She can always bring out the best in me so that I can keep moving forward during difficult moments. She is the best companion that I could ever ask for.

— Donald Szeto

about this book

This book aims to equip engineers to design, build, or set up effective machine learning systems and to tailor those systems to whatever needs and situations they may encounter. The systems they develop will facilitate, automate, and expedite the development of machine learning (deep learning, in particular) projects across a variety of domains.

In the deep learning field, it is the models that get all the attention. Perhaps rightly so, when you consider that new applications developed from those models are coming onto the market regularly—applications that make consumers excited, such as human-detecting security cameras, virtual characters in internet video games who behave like real humans, a program that can write code to solve arbitrary problems posed to it, and advanced driver assistance systems that can one day lead to fully autonomous and self-driving cars. Within a very short period of time, the deep learning field is filled with immense excitement and promising potential waiting to be fully realized.

But the model does not act alone. To bring a product or service to fruition, a model needs to be situated within a system or platform (we use these terms interchangeably) that supports the model with various services and stores. It needs, for instance, an API, a dataset manager, and storage for artifacts and metadata, among others. So behind every team of deep learning model developers is a team of non–deep learning developers creating the infrastructure that holds the model and all the other components.

The problem we have observed in the industry is that often the developers tasked with designing the deep learning system and components have only a cursory knowledge of deep learning. They do not understand the specific requirements that deep learning needs from system engineering, so they tend to follow generic approaches when building the system. For example, they might choose to abstract out all work related to deep learning model development to the data scientist and only focus on automation. So the system they build relies on a traditional job scheduling system or business intelligence data analysis system, which is not optimized for how deep learning training jobs are run, nor for deep learning-specific data access patterns. As a result, the system is hard to use for model development, and model shipping velocity is slow. Essentially, engineers who lack a profound understanding of deep learning are being asked to build systems to support deep learning models. As a consequence, these engineering systems are inefficient and inappropriate for deep learning systems.

Much has been written about deep learning model development from the data scientist's point of view, covering data collection and dataset augmentation, writing training algorithms, and the like. But very few books, or even blogs, deal with the system and services that support all these deep learning activities.

In this book, we discuss building and designing deep learning systems from a software developer perspective. The approach is to first describe a typical deep learning system as a whole, including its major components and how they are connected; then we dive deep into each of the main components in a separate chapter. We begin every component chapter by discussing requirements. We then introduce design principles and sample services/code and, finally, evaluate open source solutions.

Because we cannot cover every existing deep learning system (vendor or open source), we focus on discussing requirements and design principles (with examples) in the book. After learning these principles, trying the book's sample services, and reading our discussion of open source options, we hope readers can conduct their own research to find what suits them best.

Who should read this book?

The primary audience of this book is software engineers (including recently graduated CS students) who want to quickly transition into deep learning system engineering, such as those who want to work on deep learning platforms or integrate some AI functionality—for example, model serving—into their products.

Data scientists, researchers, managers, and anyone else who uses machine learning to solve real-world problems will also find this book useful. Upon understanding the underlying infrastructure (or system), they will be equipped to provide precise feedback to the engineering team for improving the efficiency of the model development process.

This is an engineering book, and you don't need a background in machine learning, but you should be familiar with basic computer science concepts and coding tools, such as microservices, gRPC, and Docker, to run the lab and understand the technical material. No matter your background, you can still benefit from the book's nontechnical material to help you better understand how machine learning and deep learning systems work to bring products and services from ideas into production.

By reading this book, you will be able to understand how deep learning systems work and how to develop each component. You will also understand when to gather requirements from users, translate requirements into system component design choices, and integrate components to create a cohesive system that helps your users quickly develop and deliver deep learning features.

How this book is organized: A roadmap

There are 10 chapters and three appendixes (including one lab appendix) in this book. The first chapter explains what a deep learning project development cycle is and what a basic deep learning system looks like. The next chapters dive into each functional component of the reference deep learning system. Finally, the last chapter discusses how models are shipped to production. The appendix contains a lab session to allow readers to try out the sample deep learning system.

Chapter 1 describes what a deep learning system is, the different stakeholders of the system, and how they interact with it to deliver deep learning features. We call this interaction the deep learning development cycle. Additionally, you will conceptualize a deep learning system, called a reference architecture, that contains all essential elements and can be adapted based on your requirements.

Chapters 2 to 9 cover each core component of the reference deep learning system architecture, such as dataset management service, model training service, auto hyperparameter optimization service, and workflow orchestration service.

Chapter 10 describes how to take a final product from the research or prototyping stage to make it ready to be released to the public. Appendix A introduces the sample deep learning system and demonstrates the lab exercise, appendix B surveys existing solutions, and appendix C discusses Kubeflow Katib.

About the code

We believe the best way to learn is by doing, practicing, and experimenting. To demo the design principles explained in this book and provide hands-on experience, we created a sample deep learning system and code lab. All the source code, set-up instructions, and lab scripts of the sample deep learning system are available on GitHub (https://github.com/orca3/MiniAutoML). You can also obtain executable snippets of code from the liveBook (online) version of this book at https://livebook .manning.com/book/designing-deep-learning-systems and from the Manning website (www.manning.com).

The "hello world" lab (in appendix A) contains a complete, though simplified, mini deep learning system with the most essential components (dataset management, model training and serving). We suggest you try out the "hello world" lab after reading the first chapter of the book or do it before trying our sample services in this book. This lab also provides shell scripts and links to all the resources you need to get started.

Besides the code lab, this book contains many examples of source code in numbered listings and in line with normal text. In both cases, the source code is formatted in a `fixed-width font like this` to separate it from ordinary text. Sometimes code is also **in bold** to highlight code that has changed from previous steps in the chapter, such as when a new feature adds to an existing line of code.

In many cases, the original source code has been reformatted; we've added line breaks and reworked indentation to accommodate the available page space in the book. In rare cases, even this was not enough, and listings include line-continuation markers (➥). Additionally, comments in the source code have often been removed from the listings when the code is described in the text. Code annotations accompany many of the listings, highlighting important concepts.

liveBook discussion forum

Purchase of *Designing Deep Learning Systems* includes free access to liveBook, Manning's online reading platform. Using liveBook's exclusive discussion features, you can attach comments to the book globally or to specific sections or paragraphs. It's a snap to make notes for yourself, ask and answer technical questions, and receive help from the author and other users. To access the forum, go to https://livebook .manning.com/book/designing-deep-learning-systems/discussion. You can also learn more about Manning's forums and the rules of conduct at https://livebook.manning .com/discussion.

Manning's commitment to our readers is to provide a venue where a meaningful dialogue between individual readers and between readers and the author can take place. It is not a commitment to any specific amount of participation on the part of the author, whose contribution to the forum remains voluntary (and unpaid). We suggest you try asking the authors some challenging questions lest their interest stray! The forum and the archives of previous discussions will be accessible from the publisher's website as long as the book is in print.

about the authors

CHI WANG is a principal software developer in the Salesforce Einstein group, where he builds the deep learning platform used by millions of Salesforce customers. Previously, he worked at Microsoft Bing and Azure, building large-scale distributed systems. Chi has filed six patents, mostly related to deep learning systems, and recently completed Stanford's AI graduate certificate program.

DONALD SZETO was the co-founder and CTO of PredictionIO, a startup that aimed to help democratize and accelerate the adoption of machine learning. PredictionIO was acquired by Salesforce, where he continued his work on machine learning and deep learning systems. Donald is the founder of Aftermint, whose goal is to bridge Web2 and Web3. He is also investing in, advising on, and mentoring technology startups.

about the cover illustration

The figure on the cover of *Designing Deep Learning Systems* is "Homme de la Foret Noire," or "Man of the Black Forest," taken from a collection by Jacques Grasset de Saint-Sauveur, published in 1797. Each illustration is finely drawn and colored by hand.

   In those days, it was easy to identify where people lived and what their trade or station in life was just by their dress. Manning celebrates the inventiveness and initiative of the computer business with book covers based on the rich diversity of regional culture centuries ago, brought back to life by pictures from collections such as this one.

An introduction
to deep learning systems

This chapter covers

- Defining a deep learning system
- The product development cycle and how a deep learning system supports it
- An overview of a basic deep learning system and its components
- Differences between building a deep learning system and developing models

This chapter will prepare you with a big-picture mental model of a deep learning system. We will review some definitions and provide a reference system architecture design and a complete sample implementation of the architecture. We hope this mental model will prime you to see how the rest of the chapters, which address each system component in detail, fit into the whole picture.

To begin this chapter, we will discuss an even bigger picture beyond the deep learning system: something we call *the deep learning development cycle*. This cycle outlines the various roles and stages involved in bringing products based on deep learning to market. The model and the platform do not exist in a vacuum; they affect and are affected by product management, market research, production, and other stages. We believe that engineers design better systems when they understand this cycle and know what each team does and what it needs to do its job.

In section 1.2, we start our discussion of deep learning system design with a sample architecture of a typical system that can be adapted for designing your own deep learning system. The components described in this section will be explored in greater detail in their own chapters. Finally, we will emphasize the differences between developing a model and developing a deep learning system. This distinction is often a point of confusion, so we want to clear it up right away.

After reading this introductory chapter, you will have a solid understanding of the deep learning landscape. You will also be able to start creating your own deep learning system design, as well as understand existing designs and how to use and extend them, so you don't have to build everything from scratch. As you continue reading this book, you will see how everything connects and works together as a deep learning system.

Terminology

Before we proceed with the rest of the chapter (and the rest of the book), let's define and clarify a few terms that we use throughout the book.

Deep learning vs. machine learning

Deep learning is machine learning, but it is considered an evolution of machine learning. Machine learning, by definition, is an application of artificial intelligence that includes algorithms that parse data, learn from that data, and then apply what it has learned to make informed decisions. Deep learning is a special form of machine learning that uses a programmable neural network as the algorithm to learn from data and make accurate decisions.

Although this book primarily focuses on teaching you how to build the system or infrastructure to facilitate deep learning development (all the examples are neural network algorithms), the design and project development concepts we discuss are all applicable to machine learning as well. So, in this book we use the terms *deep learning* and *machine learning* somewhat interchangeably. For example, the deep learning development cycle introduced in this chapter and the data management service introduced in chapter 2 work in the machine learning context, too.

Deep learning use case

A deep learning use case refers to a scenario that utilizes deep learning technology—in other words, a problem that you want to solve using deep learning. Examples include

- *Chatbot*—A user can initiate a text-based conversation with a virtual agent on a customer support website. The virtual agent uses a deep learning model to understand sentences that the user enters and carries on a conversation with the user like a real human.
- *Self-driving car*—A driver can put a car into an assistive driving mode that automatically steers itself according to road markings. Markings are captured by multiple cameras on board the car to form a perception of the road using deep learning–based computer vision technology.

Model, prediction and inference, and model serving

These three terms are described as follows:

- *Model*—A deep learning model can be seen as an executable program that contains an algorithm (model architecture) and required data to make a prediction.
- *Prediction and inference*—Both model prediction and model inference refer to executing the model with given data to get a set of outputs. As prediction and inference are used widely in the context of model serving, they are used interchangeably in this book.
- *Model serving* (prediction service)—This book describes model serving as hosting machine learning models in a web application (on the cloud or on premises) and allowing deep learning applications to integrate the model functionality into their systems through an API. The model serving web program is usually referred to as the prediction service or model serving service.

Deep learning application

A deep learning application is a piece of software that utilizes deep learning technologies to solve problems. It usually does not perform any computationally intensive tasks, such as data crunching, deep learning model training, and model serving (with the exception of hosting models at the edge, such as an autonomous vehicle). Examples include:

- A *chatbot application* that provides a UI or APIs to take natural sentences as input from a user, interprets them, takes actions, and provides a meaningful response to the user. Based on the model output calculated in the deep learning system (from model serving service), the chatbot responds and takes action.
- *Self-driving software* that takes input from multiple sensors, such as video cameras, proximity sensors, and LiDAR, to form a perception of a car's surroundings with the help of deep learning models and drives the car accordingly.

Platform vs. system vs. infrastructure

In this book, the terms *deep learning platform*, *deep learning system*, and *deep learning infrastructure* all share the same meaning: an underlying system that provides all necessary support for building deep learning applications efficiently and to scale. We tend to use *system* most commonly, but in the context of this book, all three terms have the same meaning.

Now that we're all on the same page about the terms, let's get started!

1.1 The deep learning development cycle

As we've said, deep learning systems are the infrastructure necessary for deep learning *project development* to progress efficiently. So, before we dive into the structure of a deep learning system, it's prudent to look at the development paradigm that a deep learning system enables. We call this paradigm the *deep learning development cycle*.

You may wonder why, in a technical book, we want to emphasize something that is as nontechnical as product development. The fact is that the goal of most deep learning work is, in the end, to bring a product or service to market. Yet many engineers are not familiar with the other stages of product development, just as many product developers do not know about engineering or modeling. From our experience in building deep learning systems, we have learned that persuading people in multiple roles in a company to adopt a system largely depends on whether the system will actually fix their particular problems. We believe that outlining the various stages and roles in the deep learning development cycle helps to articulate, address, communicate, and eventually solve everyone's pain points.

Understanding this cycle solves a few other problems, as well. In the last decade, many new deep learning software packages have been developed to address different areas. Some of them tackle model training and serving, whereas others handle model performance tracking and experimentation. Data scientists and engineers would piece these tools together each time they needed to solve a specific application or use case; this is called MLOps (machine learning operations). As the number of these applications grows, piecing these tools together every time from scratch for a new application becomes repetitive and time-consuming. At the same time, as the importance of these applications grows, so do the expectations for their quality. Both of these concerns call for a consistent approach to developing and delivering deep learning features quickly and reliably. This consistent approach starts with everyone working under the same deep learning development paradigm or cycle.

How does the deep learning *system* fit into the deep learning *cycle*? A well-built deep learning system would support the product development cycle and make performing the cycle easy, quick, and reliable. Ideally, data scientists can use a deep learning system as the infrastructure to complete the entire deep learning cycle without learning all the engineering details of the underlying complex systems.

Because every product and organization is unique, it is crucial for system builders to understand the unique requirements of the various roles to build a successful system. By "successful," we mean one that helps stakeholders collaborate productively to deliver deep learning features quickly. Throughout this book, as we go through the design principles of deep learning systems and look at how each component works, your understanding of your stakeholder requirements will help you adapt this knowledge to form your own system design. As we discuss the technical details, we will point out when you need to pay attention to certain types of stakeholders during the design of the system. The deep learning development cycle will serve as the guiding framework when we consider the design requirements of each component of a deep learning system.

Let's start with a picture. Figure 1.1 illustrates what a typical cycle looks like. It shows the machine learning (especially deep learning) development progress phase by phase. As you can see, cross-functional collaboration happens at almost every step. We will discuss each phase and role involved in this diagram in the following two sections.

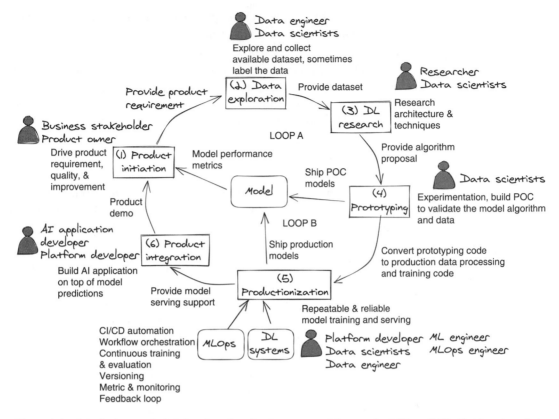

Figure 1.1 A typical scenario to bring deep learning from research to a product. We call this *the deep learning development cycle.*

1.1.1 *Phases in the deep learning product development cycle*

The deep learning development cycle typically begins with a business opportunity and is driven by a product plan and its management. After that, the cycle normally goes through four phases: data exploration, prototyping, productionization (shipping to production), and application integration. Let's look at these phases one at a time. Then we'll look at all the roles involved (denoted by the icon of a person in figure 1.1).

NOTE   The number in parentheses next to each following subsection corresponds to the same number in figure 1.1.

PRODUCT INITIATION (1)

First, the business stakeholder (product owner or project manager) analyzes the business and identifies a potential business opportunity or problem that can be addressed with machine learning.

DATA EXPLORATION (2)

When data scientists have a clear understanding of business requirements, they begin to work with data engineers to collect as much data as possible, label it, and build datasets. Data collection can include searching publicly available data and exploring internal sources. Data cleaning may also occur. Data labeling can either be outsourced or performed in-house.

Compared to the following phases, this early phase of data exploration is unstructured and often done casually. It might be a Python script or shell script, or even a manual copy of data. Data scientists often use web-based data analysis applications, such as Jupyter Notebook (open source; https://jupyter.org), Amazon SageMaker Data Wrangler (https://aws.amazon.com/sagemaker/data-wrangler), and Databricks (www.databricks.com), to analyze data. There is no formal data collection pipeline that needs to be built.

Data exploration is not only important but also critical to the success of a deep learning project. The more relevant data is available, the higher the likelihood of building effective and efficient deep learning models.

RESEARCH AND PROTOTYPING (3, 4)

The goal of prototyping is to find the most feasible algorithm/approach to address the business requirement (from product owner) with the given data. In this phase, data scientists can work with AI researchers to propose and evaluate different training algorithms with datasets built from the previous data exploration phase. Data scientists usually pilot multiple ideas in this phase and build proof-of-concept (POC) models to evaluate them.

Although newly published algorithms are often considered, most of them will not be adopted. The accuracy of an algorithm is not the only factor to be considered; one also must consider computing resource requirements, data volume, and algorithm implementation cost when evaluating an algorithm. The most practical approach is usually the winner.

Note that due to resource constraints, researchers are not always involved in the prototyping phase. Frequently, data scientists do the research work as well as build the POC.

You may also notice that in figure 1.1, there is an inner loop (loop A) in the big development cycle: Product Initiation > Data Exploration > Deep Learning Research > Prototyping > Model > Product Initiation. The purpose of this loop is to obtain product feedback in the early phase by building a POC model. We may run through this loop multiple times until all stakeholders (data scientists, product owners) arrive at a consensus on the algorithms and data that will be used to address the business requirement.

Multiple hard lessons finally taught us that we must vet the solution with the product team or the customer (even better) before starting the expensive process of productionization—building production data and training pipelines and hosting models. The purpose of a deep learning project is no different from any other software development project: to solve a business need. Vetting the approach with the product team in the early stage will prevent the expensive and demoralizing process of reworking it in later stages.

Productionization aka MLOps (5)

Productionization, also called "shipping to production," is the process of making a product production worthy and ready to be consumed by its users. Production worthiness is commonly defined as being able to serve customer requests, withstand a certain level of request load, and gracefully handle adverse situations such as malformed input and request overload. Production worthiness also includes postproduction efforts, such as continuous model metric monitoring and evaluation, feedback gathering, and model retraining.

Productionization is the most engineering-intensive part of the development cycle because we'll be converting prototyping experiments into serious production processes. A nonexhaustive to-do list of productionization can include

- Building a data pipeline to pull data from different data sources repeatedly and keep the dataset versioned and updated.
- Building a data pipeline to preprocess dataset, such as data enhancement or enrichment and integrating with external labeling tools.
- Refactoring and dockerizing the prototyping code to production-quality model training code.
- Making the result of training and serving codes reproducible by versioning and tracking the inputs and outputs. For example, we could enable the training code to report the training metadata (training date and time, duration, hyperparameters) and model metadata (performance metrics, data, and code used) to ensure the full traceability of every model training run.
- Setting up continuous integration (Jenkins, GitLab CI) and continuous deployment to automate the code building, validation, and deployment.
- Building a continuous model training and evaluation pipeline so the model training can automatically consume the latest dataset and produce models in a repeatable, auditable, and reliable manner.
- Building a model deployment pipeline that automatically releases models that have passed the quality gate, so the model serving component can access them; `async` or real-time model prediction can be performed depending on the business requirements. The model serving component hosts the model and exposes it via a web API.
- Building continuous-monitoring pipelines that periodically assess the dataset, model, and model serving performance to detect potential feature drift (data distribution change) in dataset or model performance degradation (concept drifting) and alert developers or retrain the model.

These days, the productionization step has a new alias with buzz: MLOps (machine learning operation), which is a vague term, and its definition is ambiguous for researchers and professionals. We interpret MLOps to mean bridging the gap between model development (experimentation) and operations in production environments (Ops) to facilitate productionization of machine learning projects. An example might be streamlining the process of taking machine learning models to production and then monitoring and maintaining them.

MLOps is a paradigm rooted in the application of similar principles that DevOps has to software development. It leverages three disciplines: machine learning, software engineering (especially the operation), and data engineering. See figure 1.2 for a look at deep learning through the lens of MLOps.

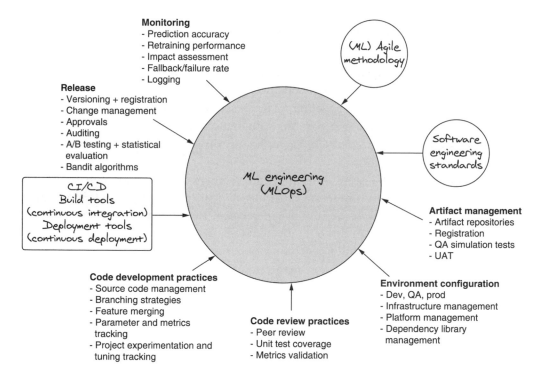

Figure 1.2   MLOps applies DevOps approaches to deep learning for the productionization phase, when models get shipped to production. (Source: *Machine Learning Engineering in Action*, **by Ben Wilson, Manning, 2022, figure 2.7)**

Because this book is about building machine learning systems that support ML operations, we won't go into details about the practices shown in figure 1.2. But, as you can see, the engineering effort that supports the development of machine learning models in production is huge. Compared to what data scientists used to do during the previous phase of data exploration and model prototyping, the tooling (software), engineering standards, and processes have dramatically changed and become much more complex.

Why is shipping models to production difficult?

The massive underlying infrastructure (tools, services, servers) and heavy cross-team collaboration are the two biggest hurdles for shipping models to production. This section on productionization (aka MLOps) establishes that data scientists need to work with data engineers, platform developers, DevOps engineers, and machine learning engineers, as well as learn a massive infrastructure (deep learning system), to ship an algorithm/model from prototype to production. It's no wonder that productionizing a model takes so much time.

To solve these challenges, we need to abstract away the complexity from data scientists when designing and building a deep learning system. As with building a car, we want to put data scientists behind the wheel but without asking them to know much about the car itself.

Now, returning to the development cycle, you may notice there is *another* inner loop (loop B) in figure 1.1 that goes from Productionization (box 5) and Model to Product Initiation (box 1). This is the second vet with the product team before we integrate the model inference with an AI application.

Our second vet (loop B) compares the model and data between prototyping and production. We want to ensure the model performance and scalability (for example, model serving capacity) match business requirements.

NOTE The following two papers are recommended; if you want to learn more about MLOps, they are great starting points: "Operationalizing Machine Learning: An Interview Study" (arXiv:2209.09125) and "Machine Learning Operations (MLOps): Overview, Definition, and Architecture" (arXiv:2205.02302).

APPLICATION INTEGRATION (6)

The last step of the product development cycle is to integrate the model prediction to the AI application. The common pattern is to host the models in the model serving service (which will be discussed in section 1.2.2) of the deep learning system and integrate the business application logic with the model by sending model prediction requests over the internet.

As a sample user scenario, a chatbot user interacts with the chatbot user interface by typing or voicing questions. When the chatbot application receives input from the customer, it calls the remote model serving service to run a model prediction and then takes action or responds to the customer based on the model prediction result.

Along with integrating model serving with application logic, this phase also involves evaluating metrics important to the product, such as clickthrough rate and churn rate. Nice ML-specific metrics (good precision–recall curve) do not always guarantee the business requirement is met. So the business stakeholders often perform customer interviews and product metric evaluation at this stage.

1.1.2   *Roles in the development cycle*

Because you now have a clear idea of each step in a typical development cycle, let's look at the key roles that collaborate in this cycle. The definitions, job titles, and responsibilities of each role may vary across organizations. So make sure you clarify who does what in your organization and adjust your system's design appropriately.

BUSINESS STAKEHOLDERS (PRODUCT OWNER)

Many organizations assign the stakeholder role to multiple positions, such as product managers, engineering managers, and senior developers. Business stakeholders define the business goal of a product and are responsible for communication and execution of the product development cycle. The following are their responsibilities:

- Getting inspiration from deep learning research, discussing potential application of deep learning features in products, and driving product requirements that in turn drive model development
- Owning the product! Communicating with customers and making sure the engineering solution meets the business requirement and delivers the results
- Coordinating cross-functional collaborations between different roles and teams
- Running project development execution; providing guidance or feedback during the entire development cycle to ensure the deep learning features offer real value to the customers of the product
- Evaluating the product metrics (such as user churn rate and feature usage)— not the model metrics (precision or accuracy)—and driving improvement of model development, productionization, or product integration

RESEARCHERS

Machine learning researchers research and develop new and novel neural network architectures. They also develop techniques for improving model accuracy and efficiency in training models. These architectures and techniques can be used during model development.

> **NOTE**   The machine learning researcher role is often associated with big tech companies like Google, Microsoft, and Salesforce. In many other companies, data scientists fulfill the same role.

DATA SCIENTISTS

Data scientists may wear a research hat, but most of the time, they translate a business problem into a machine learning problem and implement it using machine learning methods. Data scientists are motivated by the product's need and apply research techniques to production data rather than standard benchmark datasets. Besides researching model algorithms, a data scientist's responsibilities may also include

- Combining multiple deep learning neural network architectures and/or techniques from different research into a solution. Sometimes they apply additional machine learning techniques besides pure deep learning.

- Exploring available data, determining what data is useful, and deciding on how to preprocess it before supplying it for training.
- Prototyping different approaches (writing experimental code) to tackle the business problem.
- Converting model prototyping code into production code with workflow automation.
- Following the engineering process to ship models to production by using the deep learning system.
- Iterating on the need for any additional data that may help with model development.
- Continuously monitoring and evaluating data and model performance in production.
- Troubleshooting model-related problems, such as model degradation.

DATA ENGINEERS

Data engineers help collect data and set up data pipelines for continuous data ingestion and processing, including data transformation, enrichment, and labeling.

MLOPS ENGINEER/ML ENGINEER

An MLOps engineer fulfills a number of roles across multiple domains, including that of data engineer, DevOps (operation) engineer, data scientist, and platform engineer. As well as setting up and operating the machine learning infrastructure (both systems and hardware), they manage automation pipelines to create datasets and train and deploy models. ML infrastructures and user activities, such as training and serving, are also monitored by MLOps engineers.

As you can see, MLOps is hard, because it requires people to master a set of practices across software development, operation, maintenance, and machine learning development. MLOps engineers' goal is to ensure the creation, deployment, monitoring, and maintenance of machine learning models are efficient and reliable.

DEEP LEARNING SYSTEM/PLATFORM ENGINEER

Deep learning system engineers build and maintain the general pieces of the machine learning infrastructure—the primary focus of this book—to support all the machine learning development activities for data scientists, data engineers, MLOps engineers, and AI applications. Among the components of the machine learning system are data warehouses, compute platforms, workflow orchestration services, model metadata and artifact stores, model training services, model serving services, and more.

APPLICATION ENGINEER

Application engineers build customer-facing applications (both frontend and backend) to address given business requirements. The application logic will make decisions or take actions based on the model prediction for a given customer request.

NOTE In the future, as machine learning systems (infrastructure) mature, the roles involved in deep learning development cycle will merge into fewer and fewer. Eventually, data scientists will be able to complete the entire cycle on their own.

1.1.3   *Deep learning development cycle walk-through*

By giving an example, we can demonstrate the roles and the process in a more concrete manner. Suppose you have been assigned the task of building a customer support system that answers questions automatically about the company's product lines. The following steps will guide you through the process of bringing that product to market:

1   The product requirement is to build a customer support application that presents a menu, so customers can navigate to find answers to commonly asked questions. As the number of questions grows, the menu becomes larger, with many layers of navigation. Analytics has shown that many customers are confused by the navigation system and drop off from navigating the menu while trying to find answers.

2   The product manager (PM) who owns the product is motivated to improve the user retention rate and experience (finding the answers quickly). After conducting some research with customers, the PM finds that a majority of customers would like to obtain answers without a complex menu system, preferably as simple as asking questions in their natural language.

3   The PM reaches out to machine learning researchers for a potential solution. It turns out that deep learning may help. Experts think the technology is mature enough for this use case and suggest a few approaches based on deep learning models.

4   The PM writes a product spec indicating that the application should take one question from a customer at a time, recognize intent from the question, and match it with relevant answers.

5   Data scientists receive product requirements and start to prototype deep learning models that fit the need. They first start data exploration to collect available training data and consult with researchers for the choices of algorithms. And then data scientists start to build prototyping code to produce experimental models. Eventually, they arrive at some datasets, a few training algorithms, and several models. After careful evaluation, one natural language process model is selected from various experiments.

6   Then the PM assembles a team of platform engineers, MLOps engineers, and data engineers to work with the data scientist to onboard the prototyping code, made in step 5, to production. The work includes building a continuous data processing pipeline and a continuous model training, deployment, and evaluation pipeline, as well as setting up the model serving functionality. The PM also specifies the number of predictions per second and the latency required.

7   Once a production setup is complete, the application engineers integrate the customer support service's backend with the model serving service (built in step

6), so when a user types in a question, the service will return answers based on the model prediction. The PM also defines product metrics, such as average time spent finding an answer, to evaluate the end result and use it to drive the next round of improvement.

1.1.4 *Scaling project development*

As you saw in section 1.1.2, we need to fill seven different roles to complete a deep learning project. The cross-functional collaboration between these roles happens at almost every step. For example, data engineers, platform developers, and data scientists work together to productionize a project. Anyone who has been involved in a project that requires many stakeholders knows how much communication and coordination are required to keep a project like this moving forward.

These challenges make deep learning development hard to scale because we either don't have the resources to fill all the required roles or we can't meet the product timeline due to the communication costs and slowdowns. To reduce the enormous amount of operational work, communication, and cross-team coordination costs, companies are investing in machine learning infrastructure and reducing the number of people and the scope of knowledge required to build a machine learning project. The goal of a deep learning infrastructure stack is not only to automate model building and data processing but also to make it possible to merge the technical roles so that the data scientist is empowered to take care of all these functions autonomously within a project.

A key success indicator of a deep learning system is to see how smooth the model productionization process can be. With a good infrastructure, the data scientist, who is not expected to suddenly become an expert DevOps or data engineer, should be able to implement models in a scalable manner, set up data pipelines, and deploy and monitor models in production independently.

By using an efficient deep learning system, data scientists will be able to complete the development cycle with minimal additional overhead—less communication required and less time wasted waiting by others—and focus on the most important data science tasks, such as understanding the data and experimenting with algorithms. The ability to scale deep learning project development is the true value proposition of a deep learning system.

1.2 *Deep learning system design overview*

With the context of section 1.1 in mind, let's dive into the focus of this book: the deep learning system itself. Designing a system—any system—is the art of achieving goals under a set of constraints that are unique to your situation. This is also true for deep learning systems. For instance, let's say you have a few deep learning models that need to be served at the same time, but your budget does not allow you to operate a machine that has enough memory to fit all of them at the same time. You may need to design a caching mechanism to swap models between memory and disk. Swapping, however, will increase inference latency. Whether this solution is feasible will depend on latency requirements. Another possibility is to operate multiple smaller machines for each model, if your model sizes and budget will allow it.

Or, for another example, imagine your company's product must comply with certain certification standards. It may mandate data access policies that pose significant limitations to anyone who wants to gain access to data collected by the company's product. You may need to design a framework to allow data access in a compliant fashion so that researchers, data scientists, and data engineers can troubleshoot problems and develop new models that require such data access in your deep learning system.

As you can see, there are many knobs that can be turned. It will certainly be an iterative process to arrive at a design that will satisfy as many requirements as possible. But to shorten the iterative process, it is desirable to start with a design that is as close to the end state as possible.

In this section, we first propose a deep learning system design with only essential components and then explain the responsibility of each of the components and user workflows. In our experience of designing and tailoring deep learning systems, a few key components are common across different designs. We think that they can be used as a reasonable starting point for your design. We call this the *reference system architecture.*

You can make a copy of this reference for your design project, go through your list of goals and constraints, and start by identifying knobs in each component that you can adjust to your needs. Because this isn't an authoritative architecture, you should also assess whether all components are really necessary and add or remove components as you see fit.

1.2.1   *Reference system architecture*

Figure 1.3 shows the high-level overview of the reference deep learning system. The deep learning system has two major parts. The first is the application programming interface (API; box A) for the system, located in the middle of the diagram. The second is the collection of components of the deep learning system, which is represented by all the rectangular boxes located within the large box, outlined in a dotted line and taking up the lower half of the diagram. These boxes each represent a system component:

- API (box A)
- Dataset manager (box B)
- Model trainer (box C)
- Model serving (box D)
- Metadata and artifacts store (box E)
- Workflow orchestration (box F)
- Interactive data science environment (box G)

In this book, we assume that these system components are *microservices.*

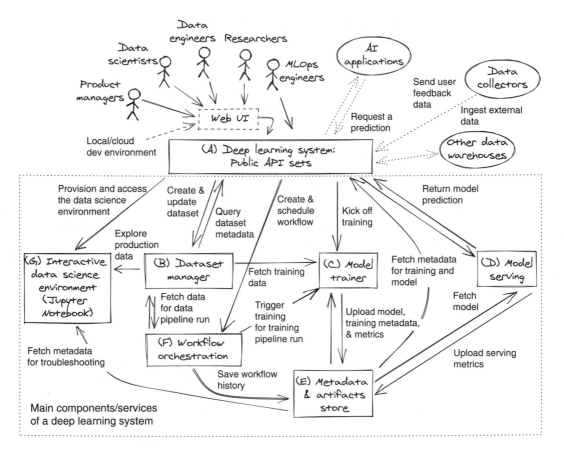

Figure 1.3 An overview of a typical deep learning system that includes basic components to support a deep learning development cycle. This reference architecture can be used as a starting point and further tailored. In later chapters, we discuss each component in detail and explain how it fits into this big picture.

DEFINITION There is no single definition for microservices. Here, we will use the term to mean processes that communicate over a network with the HTTP or the gRPC protocol.

This assumption means we can expect these components to reasonably support multiple users with different roles securely and are readily accessible over a network or the internet. (This book, however, will not cover all engineering aspects of how microservices are designed or built. We will focus our discussion on specifics that are relevant to deep learning systems.)

NOTE You may wonder whether you need to design, build, and host all deep learning system components on your own. Indeed, there are open source (Kubeflow) and hosted alternatives (Amazon SageMaker) for them. We hope that after you have learned the fundamentals of each component, how they fit in the big picture, and how they are used by different roles, you will make the best decision for your use case.

1.2.2   Key components

Now let's walk through the key components that we consider essential to a basic deep learning system, as shown in figure 1.3. You may want to add additional components or simplify them further as you see fit for your requirements.

APPLICATION PROGRAMMING INTERFACE

The entry point (box A in figure 1.3) of our deep learning system is an API that is accessible over a network. We opted for an API because the system needs to support not only graphical user interfaces that will be used by researchers, data scientists, data engineers, and the like but also applications and possibly other systems—for example, a data warehouse from a partner organization.

Although conceptually the API is the single point of entry of the system, it is entirely possible that the API is defined as the sum of all APIs provided by each component, without an extra layer that aggregates everything under a single-service endpoint. Throughout this book, we will use the sum of all APIs provided by each component directly and skip the aggregation for simplicity.

> **NOTE**   Should you use a centralized or distributed deep learning system API? In the reference architecture (figure 1.3), the deep learning system API is shown as a single box. It should be interpreted as a logical container for the complete set of your deep learning system API, regardless of whether it is implemented on single (e.g., an API gateway that proxies for all components) or multiple service endpoints (direct interaction with each component). Each implementation has its own merits and shortcomings, and you should work with your team to figure out what functions best. Direct interaction with each component may be easier if you start with a small use case and team.

DATASET MANAGER

Deep learning is based on data. There is no doubt that the data management component is a central piece of a deep learning system. Every learning system is a garbage-in, garbage-out system, so ensuring good data quality for learning is of paramount importance. A good data management component should provide the solution to this problem. It enables collecting, organizing, describing, and storing data, which in turn makes it possible for data to be explored, labeled, and used for training models.

In figure 1.3, we can see at least four relationships of the dataset manager (box B) with other parties:

- Data collectors push raw data to the dataset manager to create or update datasets.
- The workflow orchestration service (box F) executes the data process pipeline, which pulls data from the dataset manager to enhance the training dataset or transform the data format and pushes the result back.

- Data scientists, researchers, and data engineers use Jupyter Notebook (box G) to pull data from the data manager for data exploration and examination.
- The model training service (box C) pulls training data from the data manger for model training.

In chapter 2, we will discuss dataset management in depth. Throughout the book, we use the term *dataset* as a unit of collected data that may be related.

MODEL TRAINER

Model trainer (aka, model training service; box C) responds to provide foundational computation resources, such as CPUs, RAM, and GPUs, and job management logics to run the model training code and produce model files. In figure 1.3, we can see that the workflow orchestration service (box F) tells the model trainer to execute a model training code. The trainer takes input training data from the dataset manager (box B) and produces a model. Then it uploads the model with training metrics and metadata to the metadata and artifacts store (box E).

It is usually necessary to perform intense computation on a large dataset to produce high-quality deep learning models that can make accurate predictions. Adoption of new algorithms and training libraries/frameworks is also a critical requirement. These requirements produce challenges on several levels:

- *Capability of reducing model training time*—Despite the growing size of training data and complexity of model architecture, training systems must keep training times reasonable.
- *Horizontal scalability*—An effective production training system should be able to support multiple training requests from different applications and users simultaneously.
- *Cost of adopting new technologies*—The deep learning community is a vigorous one, with constant updates and improvements to algorithms and tooling (SDK, framework). The training system should be flexible enough to accommodate new innovations easily without interfering with the existing workload.

In chapter 3, we will investigate different approaches to solving the aforementioned problems. We will not go deep into the theoretical aspect of training algorithms in this book, as they do not affect how we design the system. In chapter 4, we will look at how we can distribute training to accelerate the process. In chapter 5, we will explore a few different approaches for optimizing training hyperparameters.

MODEL SERVING

Models can be used in various settings, such as online inference for real-time predictions or offline inference for batch predictions using large volumes of input data. This is where model serving surfaces—when a system hosts the model, takes input prediction requests, runs model prediction, and returns the prediction to users. There are a few key questions to be answered:

- Are your inference requests coming from over the network? Or are they coming from sensors that need to be served locally?
- What is an acceptable latency? Are inference requests ad hoc or streaming?
- How many models are being served? Is each model individually serving a type of inference request, or is an ensemble of models doing so?
- How large are model sizes? How much memory capacity do you need to budget?
- What model architectures need to be supported? Does it require a GPU? How much computing resources do you need to produce inferences? Are there other supporting serving components—for example, embeddings, normalization, aggregation, etc.?
- Are there sufficient resources to keep models online? Or is a swapping (such as moving models between memory and disk) strategy needed?

From figure 1.3, the main input and output of the model serving (box D) are inference requests and the prediction returned, respectively. To produce inferences, models are retrieved from the metadata and artifacts store (box E). Some requests and their responses may be logged and sent to the model monitoring and evaluation service (not shown in figure 1.3 or covered in this book), which detects anomalies from this data and produces alerts. In chapters 6 and 7, we will go deeper into model serving architecture, explore these key aspects, and discuss their solutions.

METADATA AND ARTIFACTS STORE

Imagine working on a simple deep learning application as a one-person team, where you have to work with only a few datasets and train and deploy only one type of model. You can probably keep track of how datasets, training codes, models, inference codes, and inferences are related to one another. These relationships are essential for model development and troubleshooting as you need to be able to trace certain observations back to the cause.

Now imagine adding more applications, more people, and more model types. The number of these relationships will grow exponentially. In a deep learning system that is designed to support multiple types of users working on multiple datasets, code, and models at various stages, there is a need for a component that keeps track of the web of relationships. The metadata and artifacts store in a deep learning system does just that. Artifacts include code that trains models and produces inferences, as well as any generated data such as trained models, inferences, and metrics. Metadata is any data that describes an artifact or the relationship between artifacts. Some concrete examples are

- The author and version of a piece of training code
- A reference of the input training dataset and the training environment of a trained model
- Training metrics of a trained model, such as training date and time, duration, and the owner of the training job

- Model-specific metrics, such as model version, model lineage (data and code used in training), and performance metrics
- The model, request, and inference code that produce a certain inference
- Workflow history, tracking each step of the model training and data process pipeline runs

These are just a few examples of what a baseline metadata and artifacts store would help track. You should tailor the component to the needs of your team or organization.

Every other component that generates metadata and artifacts in figure 1.3 would flow into the metadata and artifacts store (box E). The store also plays an important role in model serving because it provides model files and their metadata to the model serving service (box D). Although not shown in the figure, custom tools for trace lineage and troubleshooting are usually built at the user interface layer, powered by the metadata and artifacts store.

As we proceed through chapter 8, we will look at a baseline metadata and artifacts store. This store is usually the central component of a deep learning system's user interface.

WORKFLOW ORCHESTRATION

Workflow orchestration (figure 1.3, box F) is ubiquitous in many systems, where it helps to automatically launch computation tasks triggered by programmatic conditions. In the context of a machine learning system, the workflow orchestration is the driving force behind all the automations running in a deep learning system. It allows people to define workflows or pipelines—directed acyclic graphs (DAGs)—to glue individual tasks together with an execution order. The workflow orchestration component orchestrates the task executions of these workflows. Some typical examples are

- Launching model training whenever a new dataset is built
- Monitoring upstream data sources, augmenting new data, transferring its format, notifying external labelers, and merging the new data into existing datasets
- Deploying the trained model to the model server if it passes some accepted criteria
- Continually monitoring model performance metrics and alerting developers when degradation is detected

You will learn how to build or set up a workflow orchestration system in chapter 9.

INTERACTIVE DATA SCIENCE ENVIRONMENT

Customer data and models cannot be downloaded to a local workstation from production for compliance and security reasons. For data scientists to interactively explore data, troubleshoot pipeline execution in workflow orchestration, and debug models, a remote interactive data science environment (figure 1.3, box G) located inside the deep learning system is required.

It is common for companies to set up their own trusted data science environment by using open source Jupyter Notebooks (https://jupyter.org/) or by utilizing cloud

vendors' JupyterLab-based solutions, such as Amazon SageMaker Studio (https://aws
.amazon.com/sagemaker/studio/).

A typical interactive data science environment should provide the following
functionalities:

- *Data exploration*—Offers data scientists easy access to customer data but keeps it
  secure and compliant; there are no data leaks, and any unauthorized data
  access will be rejected.
- *Model prototyping*—Provides the much-needed tooling for data scientists to develop
  quick POC models inside the deep learning system.
- *Troubleshooting*—Enables engineers to debug any activity happening inside the
  deep learning system, such as downloading the model and playing with it to
  analyze its behavior or checking all the input/output artifacts (intermediate
  datasets or configurations) from a failed pipeline.

1.2.3   *Key user scenarios*

To better understand how deep learning systems can be used during the development
cycle (figure 1.1), we prepared sample scenarios that illustrate how they could be
used. Let's start with programmatic consumers, shown in figure 1.4. Data collectors
that push data to the system will usually end up at the data management service via the
API, which collects and organizes raw data for model training.

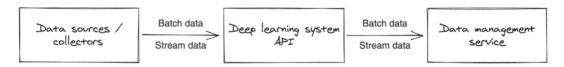

**Figure 1.4   Data is pushed from sources or collectors, through the API to the data management service, where
the data is further organized and stored in formats that are more friendly for model training.**

Deep learning applications will usually hit the model inference service to obtain inferences from a trained model, which is used to power deep learning features that end
users will consume. Figure 1.5 shows the sequence of this interaction. Scripts, or even
full-fledged management services, can be programmatic consumers, too. Because they
are optional, we omitted them from the figure for simplicity.

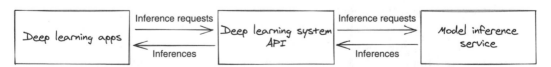

**Figure 1.5   Deep learning applications request inferences through the API. The model inference service
accepts and processes these requests against trained models and produces inferences that are returned
back to applications.**

Between human consumers and the API usually lies an extra layer—the user interface. The interface can be web based or command-line based. Some power users may even skip this interface and consume the API directly. Let's walk through each persona one by one.

A typical scenario of researchers using the system is illustrated in figure 1.6. Researchers can look up available data to try out their new modeling technique. They access the user interface and visit the data exploration and visualization section, which pulls data from the data management service. A great deal of manual data processing might be involved in massaging it into forms that can be consumed by new training techniques. Once researchers settle with a technique, they can package it as a library for others' consumption.

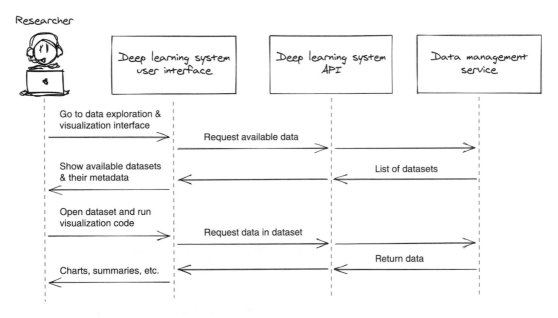

Figure 1.6 A usage sequence of a researcher who is interested in seeing what data is available for researching and developing a new modeling technique. The researcher interacts with a user interface that is supported by the API and data management behind the scenes.

Data scientists and engineers can work on use cases by first looking at what data is available, similar to what researchers would initially do in the previous paragraph. This would be supported by the data management service. They make hypotheses and put together data processing and training techniques as code. These steps can be combined to form a workflow using the workflow management service.

When the workflow management service performs a run of the workflow, it contacts the data management service and the model training service to perform actual duties and track their progress. Hyperparameters, code versions, model training metrics, and test results are all stored to the metadata and artifacts store by each service and training code.

Through the user interface, data scientists and engineers can compare experimental runs and deduce the best way to train models. This aforementioned scenario is shown in figure 1.7.

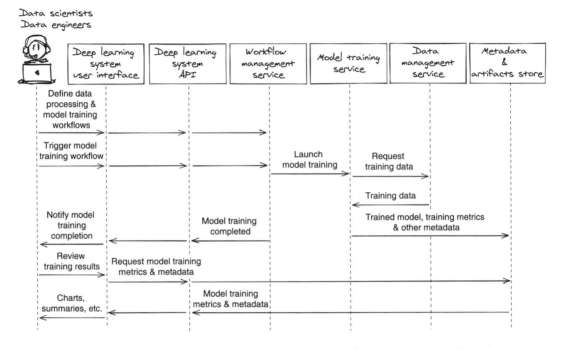

Figure 1.7   A usage sequence of a data scientist defining model training workflow, running it, and reviewing results

Product managers can also look at and query all kinds of metrics throughout the system through the user interface. The metrics data can be supplied by the metadata and artifacts store.

1.2.4   *Derive your own design*

Now that we have gone over all aspects of the reference system architecture, let's discuss some guidelines for customizing your own version.

GATHERING GOALS AND REQUIREMENTS

The first step to designing any successful system design is to have a set of clear goals and requirements with which to work. These should ideally come from users of your system, either directly or indirectly through the product management team or engineering management. This short list of goals and requirements will help you form a vision of what your system will look like. This vision, in turn, should be the guideline that drives you throughout the design and development phases of your system.

> **NOTE** Sometimes engineers are asked to develop a system to support one or more deep learning applications that already exist. In this case, you may instead start with identifying the set of common requirements among these applications and how your system can be designed to help bring innovation quickly to these applications.

To collect the system goals and requirements, you need to identify the different types of users and stakeholders, or *personas*, of the system. (This is a general concept that can be applied to most system design problems.) It is the users, after all, who will help you articulate the goals and requirements of the system.

Our recommendation is to start with use cases or application requirements if you are not sure of a good starting point. Here are some example questions that you can ask your users:

- *To data engineers and product managers*—Does the system allow applications to collect data for training? Does the system need to handle streaming input data? How much data is being collected?
- *To data scientists and engineers*—How do we process and label the data? Does the system need to provide labeling tools for external vendors? How do we evaluate the model? How do we handle the test dataset? Is an interactive notebooking user interface needed for data science work?
- *To researchers and data scientists*—How large of a volume of data is needed for training models? What's the average time of model training runs? How much computing and data capacity is needed for research and data science? What kind of experiments should the system support? What metadata and metrics need to be collected to evaluate different experiments?
- *To product managers and software engineers*—Is model serving done on the remote server or on the client? Is it a real-time model inference or offline batch prediction? Is there a latency requirement?
- *To product managers*—What problems are we trying to solve at our organization? What is our business model? How are we going to gauge the effectiveness of our implementations?
- *To security teams*—What level of security is needed in your system? Is data access wide open or strictly restricted/isolated? Is there an audit requirement? Is there a certain level of compliance or certification (e.g., General Data Protection Regulation, System and Organization Controls 2, etc.) that the system needs to achieve?

CUSTOMIZING THE REFERENCE ARCHITECTURE

Once the design requirement and scope are clear, we can start to customize the reference architecture in figure 1.3. First, we can decide whether we need to add or remove any components. For example, if the requirement is purely managing model training in a remote server farm, we could remove the workflow management component. If data scientists want to evaluate model performance effectively with production data, they could also add an experiment management component. This component allows data scientists to perform training and validation using full-scale data that already exists in the system and conduct online A/B testing against production traffic with previously unseen data.

The second step is to design and implement each key component suite to your specific needs. Depending on the requirement, you might exclude the data streaming API from the dataset management service and add distributed training support if training speed is a concern. You can either build each key component from scratch or use open source software. In the rest of the book, we cover both options for each key component to ensure you know what to do.

> **TIP** Keep the system design simple and user friendly. The purpose of creating such a large deep learning system is to improve the productivity of deep learning development, so please keep this in mind when designing it. We want to make it easy for data scientists to build high-quality models without the need to learn what's going on in the underlying system.

1.2.5 *Building components on top of Kubernetes*

We have introduced a list of key components that are implemented as services. With this number of services, you may want to manage them with a sophisticated system at the infrastructure level, such as Kubernetes.

Kubernetes is an open source system for automating deployment, scaling, and management of containerized applications, which are applications that run in isolated runtime environments—for example, docker containers. We have seen a number of deep learning systems that are built on top of Kubernetes. Some people learn how to use Kubernetes without ever knowing why it is used to run deep learning services, so we want to explain the thinking behind it. If you are familiar with Kubernetes, please feel free to skip this section.

> **NOTE** Kubernetes is a complex platform that would require a book-length of material to teach, so we are only discussing its merits for a deep learning system. If you want to learn Kubernetes, we highly recommend you check out *Kubernetes in Action* (Manning, 2018), by Marko Luksa.

CHALLENGES FOR MANAGING COMPUTING RESOURCES

Executing one docker container on a remote server seems to be a simple task, but running 200 containers on 30 different servers is a different story. There are many challenges, such as monitoring all remote servers to determine on which one to run the container, needing to failover a container to a healthy server, restarting a container when it's stuck, following up each container run and getting notified when it completes, etc. To address these challenges, we must monitor the hardware, OS processes, and networking ourselves. Not only is it technically challenging, but it is also a huge amount of work.

How Kubernetes helps

Kubernetes is an open source container orchestration platform for scheduling and automating the deployment, management, and scaling of containerized applications. Once you set up a Kubernetes cluster, your server groups' operation (deployment, patching, updates) and resources become manageable. Here is a deployment example: you can tell Kubernetes to run a docker image with 16 GB memory and 1 GPU with a command; Kubernetes will allocate the resource to run this docker image for you.

This is a huge benefit for software developers because not every one of them has extensive experience with hardware and deployment. With Kubernetes, we only need to declare the end state of our cluster, and Kubernetes will do the actual job to meet our goals.

Besides container deployment benefits, the following are some other key Kubernetes functionalities that are crucial for managing our training containers:

- *Autoscaling features*—Kubernetes automatically resizes the number of nodes in the cluster based on the workload. This means if there is a sudden burst of user requests, Kubernetes will add the capacity automatically, which is called *elastic compute management.*
- *Self-healing capabilities*—Kubernetes restarts, replaces, or reschedules pods when they fail or when nodes die. It also kills pods that do not respond to user-defined health checks.
- *Resource utilization and isolation*—Kubernetes takes care of computing resource saturation; it ensures every server is fully utilized. Internally, Kubernetes launches application containers in *pods*. Each pod is an isolated environment with a computing resource guarantee, and it runs a function unit. In Kubernetes, multiple pods can be in one node (server) as long as their combined resource requirements (CPU, memory, disk) don't exceed the node's limitations, so servers can be shared by different function units easily with guaranteed isolation.
- *Namespaces*—Kubernetes supports splitting a physical cluster into different virtual clusters. These virtual clusters are called *namespaces.* You can define resource quota per namespace, which allows you to isolate resources for different teams by assigning them to different namespaces.

On the flip side, these benefits come at a cost—they consume resources as well. When you run a Kubernetes pod, the pod itself takes some amount of system resources (CPU, memory). These resources are consumed on top of those that are needed to run containers inside pods. Kubernetes's overhead seems reasonable in many situations; for example, from an experiment published in the article "How We Minimized the Overhead of Kubernetes in Our Job System" (http://mng.bz/DZBV) by Lally Singh and Ashwin Venkatesan (February 2021), the CPU overhead per pod was about 10 ms per second.

NOTE   We recommend you check out appendix B to see how existing deep learning systems relate to the concepts presented in this chapter. In that appendix, we compare the reference architecture described in section 1.2.1 with Amazon SageMaker, Google Vertex AI, Microsoft Azure Machine Learning, and Kubeflow.

1.3   *Building a deep learning system vs. developing a model*

A final piece of groundwork before we begin: we think it is crucial to call out the differences between *building a deep learning system* and *developing a deep learning model*. In this book, we define *the practice of developing a deep learning model* to solve a problem as the process of

- Exploring available data and how it can be transformed for training
- Determining the effective training algorithm(s) to use for the problem
- Training models and developing inference code to test against unseen data

Recall that a deep learning system should support not only all tasks required by model development but also those that need to be performed by other roles and make collaboration between these roles seamless. When building a deep learning system, you are not developing deep learning models; you are building a system that supports the development of deep learning models, making that process more efficient and scalable.

We have found an abundance of material published about building the models. But we have seen precious little written about designing and building the platforms or systems that support those models. And that is why we wrote this book.

Summary

- A typical machine learning project development goes through the following cycle: product initiation, data exploration, model prototyping, productionization, and production integration.
- There are seven different roles involved in deep learning project development: a product manager, researchers, data scientists, data engineers, MLOps engineers, machine learning system engineers, and application engineers.
- A deep learning system should reduce complexity in the deep learning development cycle.
- With the help of deep learning systems, the data scientist, who is not expected to suddenly become an expert DevOps or data engineer, should be able to implement models in a scalable manner, set up data pipelines, and deploy and monitor models in production independently.
- An efficient deep learning system should allow data scientists to focus on interesting and important data science tasks.

- A high-level reference architecture like the one we present in figure 1.3 can help you quickly start a new design. First, make your own copy and then collect goals and requirements. Finally, add, modify, or subtract components and their relationships as you see fit.

- A basic deep learning system consists of the following key components: dataset manager, model trainer, model serving, metadata and artifacts store, workflow orchestration, and data science environment.

- The data management component helps collect, organize, describe, and store data as datasets that can be used as training input. It also supports data exploration activities and tracks lineage between datasets. Chapter 2 will discuss data management in detail.

- The model training component is responsible for handling multiple training requests and running them efficiently provided a given, limited set of computing resources. Chapters 3 and 4 will review the model training component.

- The model serving component handles incoming inference requests, produces inferences with models, and returns them to requesters. It will be covered in chapters 6 and 7.

- The metadata and artifacts store component records metadata and stores artifacts from the rest of the system. Any data produced by the system can be treated as artifacts. Most of them would be models, which come with metadata that will be stored in the same component. This provides complete lineage information to support experimentation and troubleshooting. We will talk about this component in chapter 8.

- The workflow management component stores workflow definitions that chain together different steps in data processing and model training. It is responsible for triggering periodic workflow runs and tracking the progress of each run step that is being executed on other components—for instance, a model training step being executed on the model training service. In chapter 9, we will provide a walk-through of this component.

- A deep learning system should support the deep learning development cycle and make collaboration between multiple roles easy.

- Building a deep learning system is different from developing a deep learning model. The system is the infrastructure to support deep learning model development.

2

Dataset management service

This chapter covers

- Understanding dataset management
- Using design principles to build a dataset management service
- Building a sample dataset management service
- Using open source approaches to dataset management

After our general discussion of deep learning systems, we are ready for the rest of the chapters, which focus on specific components in those systems. We present dataset management first not only because deep learning projects are data-driven but also because we want to remind you how important it is to think about data management before building other services.

Dataset management (DM) often gets overlooked in the deep learning model development process, whereas data processing and model training and serving attract the most attention. A common thought in data engineering is that good data processing pipelines, such as ETL (extract, transform, and load) pipelines, are all we need. But if you avoid managing your datasets as your project proceeds, your data collection and dataset consumption logic become more and more complicated, model performance improvement becomes difficult, and eventually, the entire project slows down. A good DM system can expedite model development by decoupling training data collection and consumption; it also enables model reproducibility by versioning the training data.

We guarantee that you will appreciate your wise decision to build or at least set up a dataset management component in addition to your existing data processing pipelines. And build it before working on the training and serving components. Your deep learning project development will go faster and can produce better results and simpler models in the long run. Because the DM component shields the upstream data complexity from your model training code, your model algorithm development and data development can run parallel.

This chapter is about building dataset management functionality for your deep learning project. Because of the variety of deep learning algorithms, data pipelines, and data sources, dataset management is an often-discussed topic in the deep learning industry. There is no unified approach, and it seems there will never be one. To be beneficial to you in practice, therefore, we will focus on teaching the design principles instead of advocating one single approach. The sample dataset management service we build in this chapter demonstrates one possible way to implement these principles.

In section 2.1, you will learn why dataset management is needed, the challenges it should address, and the crucial role it plays in a deep learning system. We will also introduce its key design principles to prepare you for the concrete examples in the next section.

In section 2.2, we will demonstrate a dataset management service based on the concepts and design principles introduced in section 2.1. First, we will set up the service on your local machine and experiment with it. Second, we will discuss the internal dataset storage and data schema, user scenarios, data ingestion API, and dataset fetching API, as well as provide an overview of design and user scenarios. During the tour, we will also discuss the pros and cons of some important decisions we made in the service design.

In section 2.3, we will look at two open source approaches. If you don't want a DIY dataset management service, you can use the components that are already built, available, and adaptable. For instance, you can use Delta Lake with Petastorm for dataset management if your existing data pipeline is built on top of Apache Spark. Or you can adopt Pachyderm if your data comes directly from a cloud object storage such as AWS Simple Storage Service (S3) or Azure Blob. We use image dataset preparation as an example to show how these two approaches can work with unstructured data in practice. By the end of this chapter, you will have a deep understanding of the intrinsic characteristics of dataset management and its design principles, so you can either build a dataset management service on your own or improve an existing system in your work.

2.1   Understanding dataset management service

A dataset management component or service is a specialized data store for organizing data in favor of model training and model performance troubleshooting. It processes raw data fed from upstream data sources and returns training data in a well-defined structure—a dataset—for use in model training. Figure 2.1 shows the core value a dataset management service delivers. In the figure, we see that a dataset management component converts the raw data into a consistent data format that favors model training, so downstream model training applications can just focus on algorithm development.

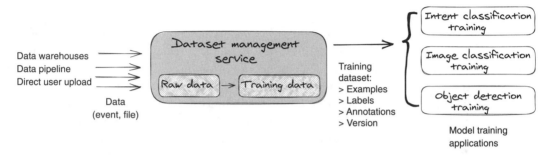

Figure 2.1   A dataset management service is a specialized data store; it ingests data into its internal storage with its own raw data format. During training, it converts the raw data into training data in a consistent data format that favors model training.

2.1.1   Why deep learning systems need dataset management

Let's take a moment to explain why DM is a crucial part of any deep learning system before we start looking at the sample dataset management service. This section is important because, from our experience, it is impossible to design a system that solves a real problem unless you fully understand the *why*.

There are two answers to the why question. First, DM can help to expedite model development by decoupling the *collection* of training data from the *consumption* of that data. Second, a well-designed DM service supports model reproducibility by having version tracking on training datasets. Let's look at both of these points in detail.

DECOUPLING THE TRAINING DATA COLLECTION AND CONSUMPTION

If you work on a deep learning project completely by yourself, the project development workflow is an iterative loop of the following steps: data collection, dataset preprocess, training, and evaluation (see figure 2.2). Although you can break the downstream dataset preprocess code or training code if you change the data format in the data collection component, it's not a big problem. Because you are the single code owner, you make free changes; no other people are affected.

When we are building a serious deep learning platform catering to tens of different deep learning projects and opening it to multiple people and teams, the simple data flow chart will dilate quickly to a bewildering 3D diagram (figure 2.3).

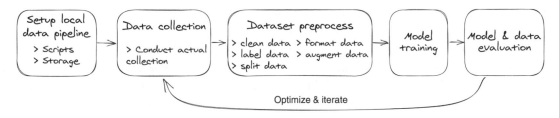

Figure 2.2   The workflow for a single-person deep learning project development is an iterative loop of linear steps.

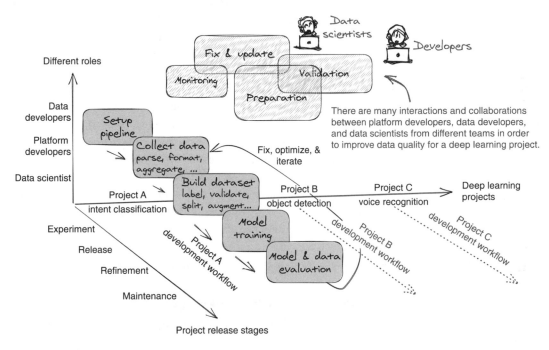

Figure 2.3   Deep learning model development in enterprise runs in multidimensions. Multiple teams of people work together to ship a project in different phases. Each team focuses on one step of the workflow and also works on multiple projects in parallel.

Figure 2.3 shows the complexity of an enterprise deep learning development environment. In this setting, each person only works on a single step instead of the entire workflow, and they develop their work for multiple projects. Ideally, this process is efficient because people build their expertise by focusing on one particular problem. But here is the catch: the communication cost is often ignored.

When we divide the steps of a workflow (figure 2.2) between multiple teams, data schemas are needed for the handshake. Without a data contract, the downstream team doesn't know how to read the data sent from the upstream team. Let's go back to figure 2.3. Imagine how many data schemas we need to communicate between teams if there are 10 projects developed by four teams in parallel, especially if every team handles different steps of the workflow.

Now, if we want to add a new feature or attribute (such as text language) to a training dataset, we need to gather every team, obtain a consensus on the new data format, and implement the change. This is a huge effort because cross-team collaboration in corporations is complicated. It often takes months to make a small change; because each team has its own priority, you have to wait on its to-do list.

To make the situation worse, deep learning model development is an iterative process. It demands constantly tuning the training dataset (including the upstream data pipelines) to improve model accuracy. This requires data scientists, data developers, and platform developers to interact at a high frequency, but because of the cross-team workflow setting, the data iteration happens slowly, which is one of the reasons why model development is so slow in a production environment.

Another problem is that when we have multiple types of projects (image, video, and text) developing in parallel, the number of data schemas will explode. If we let each team define new data schemas freely and don't manage them properly, keeping the system backward compatible is almost impossible. The new data updates will become more and more difficult because we have to spend extra time to make sure the new data update doesn't break the projects built in the past. As a consequence, the project development velocity will slow down significantly.

To address the slow iteration and data schema management problem, we can build a dataset management service. Let's look at figure 2.4 to help determine the changes in the project development workflow after introducing the dataset management service.

In figure 2.4, we see a dataset management service that splits the model development workflow into two separate spaces: data developer space and data scientist space.

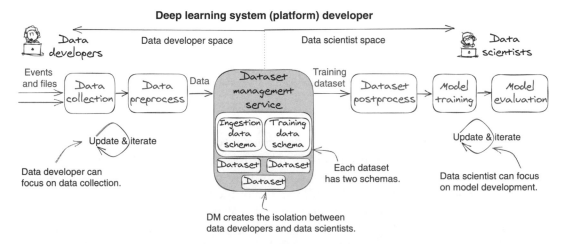

Figure 2.4   A dataset management component creates a good separation between training data collection and consumption by defining strongly typed schemas for both, which allows data development and model algorithm development to iterate in their own loop, thus expediting the project development.

The long iteration loop (figure 2.2) is now divided into two small loops (figure 2.4), and each loop is owned by a single team, so the data developer and data scientist can iterate on data collection and model training separately; therefore, the deep learning project can iterate much faster.

You may also notice that we now have all data schemas in one place: a dataset management service, which manages two strongly typed data schemas—the ingestion data schema and the training data schema—for each type of dataset. By having two separate data schemas for data ingestion and training while doing data transformation inside DM, you ensure that the data changes in the upstream data collection won't break the downstream model training. Because the data schemas are strongly typed, future data upgrades can easily be made backward compatible.

Defining a strongly typed dataset may not be a good idea for projects in the beginning or experimental phase because we are still exploring all kinds of data options. Therefore, we also recommend defining a special schema-free dataset type, such as GENERIC type, which has no strong schema restriction. For data in this dataset type, DM just accepts the data as is and does not perform data validation and transformation (for a detailed example, see section 2.2.6). The data collected from the data processing pipeline can be consumed directly by the training process. Although the whole workflow would be fragile, a free dataset type addresses the need to be flexible for projects in the early phase. Once the project matures, we can create strongly typed schemas and define a dataset type for them.

To summarize this section, managing two data schemas of a dataset type is the secret sauce that decouples data scientists and data developers. In section 2.2.6, we will show how these schemas can be implemented in our sample dataset management service.

ENABLING MODEL REPRODUCIBILITY

A well-designed dataset management service supports model reproducibility by having version tracking on training datasets—for example, using a version string to obtain the exact training files used in previous model training runs. The advantage of model reproducibility with respect to the data scientist (model algorithm development) is that you can repeatedly run a deep learning algorithm (such as the self-attention transformer in NLP) on a certain dataset and gain the same or similar quality of results. This is called *algorithm reproducibility*.

From the view of a deep learning system developer, model reproducibility is the superset of algorithm reproducibility. It requires the dataset management system to be able to reproduce its output artifacts (datasets). For example, we need to obtain the exact training data and training configuration to reproduce models that were trained in the past.

Model reproducibility is crucial to machine learning projects for two main reasons. The first is trust. Reproducibility creates trust and credibility for the system that produces the model. For any system, if the output can't be reproduced, people simply won't trust the system. This is extremely relevant to machine learning projects because applications will make decisions based on model output—for example, a chatbot will transfer a user call to proper service departments according to the user intent prediction. If we can't reproduce a model, the applications built on top of the model are nondeterministic and untrustworthy.

The second reason is that model reproducibility facilitates performance troubleshooting. When detecting a model performance regression, people first want to find out what has changed in the training dataset and training algorithm code. If model reproducibility is not supported, performance troubleshooting will be very difficult.

2.1.2 Dataset management design principles

We want to outline five design principles for DM before we start building one.

> **NOTE**   We consider these five principles to be the most important elements in this chapter. For data applications, the principles we follow in design are more important than the actual design. Because data could be anything in any form, there is no paradigm for data storage, in general, and there is no standard design that suits all kinds of data processing use cases. So, in practice, we build our own data application by following certain general principles. Therefore, these principles are critical.

The five principles here will give you clear design targets for building a new DM service or improving your existing DM service.

PRINCIPLE 1: SUPPORT DATASET REPRODUCIBILITY FOR REPRODUCING MODELS

Dataset reproducibility means that the DM always returns the same exact training examples it has returned in the past. For instance, when the training team starts training a model, the DM provides a dataset with a version string. Anytime the training team—or any other team—needs to retrieve the same training data, it can use this version string to query DM to retrieve the same training data.

We believe all DM systems should support dataset reproducibility. Even better would be to also offer data diff functionally, so we can see the data difference between two different dataset versions easily. This is very convenient for troubleshooting.

PRINCIPLE 2: PROVIDE UNIFIED API ACROSS DIFFERENT TYPES OF DATASETS

A dataset of deep learning might be structured (text, such as sales records or the transcript of a user conversation) or unstructured (image, voice recording file). No matter how a DM system processes and stores these different forms of data internally, it should provide a unified API interface for uploading and fetching different types of datasets. The API interface also abstracts away the data source from the data consumer; no matter what happens under the hood, such as data parsing changes and internal storage format changes, downstream consumers shouldn't be affected.

Therefore, our users, both data scientists and data developers, only need to learn one API to work with all the different types of datasets. This makes the system simple and easy to use. Also, the code maintenance cost will be greatly reduced because we only expose one public API.

PRINCIPLE 3: ADOPT A STRONGLY TYPED DATA SCHEMA

A strongly typed data schema is the key to avoiding unexpected failures caused by data changes. With data schema enforcement, the DM service can guarantee that the raw data it ingests and the training data it produces are consistent with our specs.

The strongly typed data schema acts as a safety guard to ensure the downstream model training code does not get affected by the upstream data collection changes, and it also ensures backward compatibility for both upstream and downstream clients of DM. Without data schema protection, the dataset consumer—the downstream model training code—can easily be broken by upstream data changes.

Data schemas can be versioned as well, but this will add another layer of complexity to management. An additional option is to only have one schema per dataset. When introducing new data changes, make sure that the schema update is backward compatible. If a new data requirement requires a breaking change, create a new dataset type with a new schema instead of updating the existing one.

PRINCIPLE 4: ENSURE API CONSISTENCY AND HANDLE SCALING INTERNALLY

The current trend in the deep learning field is model architecture that keeps getting bigger as datasets continue to grow larger. For example, GPT-3 (a generative pretrained transformer language model for language understanding) uses more than 250 TB of text materials with hundreds of billions of words; in Tesla, the autonomous driving model consumes an immense amount of data at the petabyte level. On the other hand, we still use small datasets (around 50 MB) for some easy tasks in narrow domains, such as customer support ticket classification. Dataset management systems should handle the data scaling challenges internally, and the API exposed to users (data developers and data scientists) should be consistent for both large- and small-sized datasets.

PRINCIPLE 5: GUARANTEE DATA PERSISTENCY

Ideally, datasets used for deep learning training should be stored immutably to reproduce training data and troubleshoot. Data removal should be soft deletions with only a few exceptions for hard deletions, such as deleting customer data permanently when a customer chooses to opt out of or cancel their account.

2.1.3 The paradoxical character of datasets

To close out our conceptual discussion on dataset management, we would like to clarify an ambiguous aspect of datasets. We have seen dozens of poorly designed dataset management systems fail on this point.

A dataset has a paradoxical trait: it is both dynamic and static. From a data scientist's point of view, a dataset is static: it is a fixed set of files with annotations (also known as labels). From a data developer's point of view, a dataset is dynamic: it is a file-saving destination in a remote storage to which we keep adding data.

So, from a DM perspective, a dataset should be a logic file group and satisfy both data collection and data training needs. To help you get a concrete understanding of how to accommodate both the dynamic and static nature of datasets, let's look at figure 2.5.

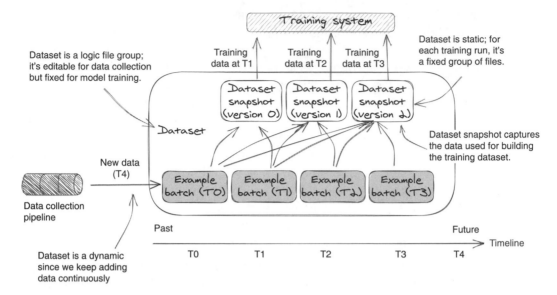

Figure 2.5   A dataset is a logic file group: it's both dynamic and static, and it's editable for data collection but fixed for model training.

We can read figure 2.5 from two angles: data ingestion and data fetching. First, from the data ingestion side, we see that the data collection pipeline (from the left of the graph) keeps pumping in new data, such as text utterances and labels. For example, at time T0, an example data batch (example batch T0) is created in the dataset—the same for time T1, T2, and T3; we have a total of four data batches created over time. So, from the data developer's view, this dataset is mutable, because the pipeline keeps adding data to it.

Second, on the training data fetching side (from the top of the graph), we see that when fetching training data, the DM reads all the current data from the dataset at the same time point. We see that the data is returned as a static versioned snapshot, which has a version string to uniquely identify the actual data it picked from a dataset. For example, when we fetch training data from the dataset at time T2, the dataset has three data batches (batch T0, batch T1, and batch T2). We package these three data batches into a snapshot, assign a version string ("version1"), and return it as training data.

From a model training perspective, the dataset fetched from DM is a static snapshot of the dataset—a time-filtered plus customer logic-filtered dataset. The static snapshot is crucial to model reproducibility because it represents the exact training files used in a training run. When we need to rebuild the model, we can use the snapshot version string to find the snapshot that was used in the past model training.

Our theoretical introductions have been thoroughly covered, and you should be able to grasp the needs, goals, and unique characteristics of the dataset management component. The next section is a concrete example of how to design a dataset management service.

2.2 Touring a sample dataset management service

In this section, we will walk you through a sample DM service. We built this sample to give you an idea of how the principles presented in section 2.1.2 can be implemented. We will first run the service locally, play with it, and then look at its API design and internal implementation.

2.2.1 Playing with the sample service

To make this easy for you, we built seven shell scripts to automate the entire DM lab. These shell scripts are the recommended way to experience the demo scenarios in this section because they not only automate services' local setup but also take care of setting the environment variables, preparing sample data, and initializing the local network.

You can find these scripts at https://github.com/orca3/MiniAutoML/tree/main/scripts, starting with the search: "dm". The "function demo" doc in our GitHub repo (https://github.com/orca3/MiniAutoML/tree/main/data-management) provides detailed instructions for how to complete the lab and sample outputs of these scripts.

> **NOTE** Before running the function demo, the system requirement should be met first. Please refer to https://github.com/orca3/MiniAutoML#system-requirements.

This lab consists of three sections: first, run the sample dataset management service; second, create a dataset and upload data to it; and third, fetch training data from the dataset just created.

SETTING UP SERVICE LOCALLY

The sample service is written in Java 11. It uses MinIO as the file blob server to mimic cloud object storage (such as Amazon S3), so we can run everything locally without any remote dependency. If you have set up the lab in appendix A, you can run the following commands (listing 2.1) in your terminal at the root of the scripts folder to start the service.

> **NOTE** Starting with a clean setup is highly recommended before running DM demo scripts. You can execute `./scripts/lab-999-tear-down.sh` to clean up previous labs.

Listing 2.1 Starting the service locally

```
# (1) Start minio server
./scripts/dm-001-start-minio.sh

# (2) start dataset management service, it will build
➥ the dm image and run the container.
./scripts/dm-002-start-server.sh
```

NOTE   To keep the service setup to a bare minimum, we maintain all the dataset records in memory to avoid using databases. Please be aware that you will lose all datasets if you restart the dataset management service.

CREATING AND UPDATING A LANGUAGE INTENT DATASET

Our sample DM service offers three API methods for users to create/update a dataset and check the result. These API methods are `CreateDataset`, `UpdateDataset`, and `GetDatasetSummary`. We will discuss them in detail in the next few sections.

In this example scenario, first we call the `CreateDataset` API method on the data management service to create a new language intent dataset; then we use the `UpdateDataset` API method to append more data to the dataset. Finally, we use the `GetDatasetSummary` API method to obtain the dataset's statistics and commit (data change) history.

NOTE   The scripts dm-003-create-dataset.sh and dm-004-add-commits.sh automate the previous steps. Please use them to run the demo scenario. Please note that the following code listings are only for illustration purposes.

Let's run the lab now. First, we'll create a dataset using the following listing.

Listing 2.2   Creating a language intent dataset

```
mc -q cp data-management/src/test/resources/datasets/test.csv       ◁
⮡ myminio/"${MINIO_DM_BUCKET}"/upload/001.csv
                                                              Uploads raw data
                                                              (upload/001.csv)
                                                              to cloud storage
grpcurl -v -plaintext \            ◁──┐ gRPC request to
  -d '{"name": "dataset-1", \          │ create a dataset
Dataset ┌─▷   "dataset_type": "LANGUAGE_INTENT", \
type    │     "bucket": "mini-automl", \           Data URL of the raw data in MinIO,
        └     "path": "{DATA_URL_IN_MINIO}"}' \     for example, upload/001.csv
${DM_SERVER}:${DM_PORT} \
  data_management.DataManagementService/CreateDataset      ◁──┐ API name
```

It should be noted that the `CreateDataset` API expects users to provide a downloadable URL in the gRPC request, not the actual data, which is why we first upload the 001.csv file to the local MinIO server. After the dataset is created, the `CreateDataset` API will return a JSON object that contains a data summary and commits the history of the dataset. See a sample result as follows:

```
{
  "datasetId": "1",
  "name": "dataset-1",
  "dataset_type": "TEXT_INTENT",                      Commits are the
  "last_updated_at": "2021-10-09T23:44:00",           snapshot dataset
  "commits": [                                         updates.
    {
      "dataset_id": "1",
```

```
    "commit_id": "1",
    "created_at": "2021-10-09T23:44",          Commit ID; this commit
    "commit_message": "Initial commit",        captures the data from
                                                upload/001.csv.
    "tags": [
      {                                         Commit tags are used to
        "tag_key": "category",                  filter commits when building
        "tag_value": "test set"                 a training dataset.
      }
    ],
    "path": "dataset/1/commit/1",
    "statistics": {                             Data
      "numExamples": "5500",                    summary of
      "numLabels": "151"                        the commit
    }
  }
 ]
}
```

After creating a dataset, you can keep updating it by appending more data; see the
dataset update gRPC request as follows.

Listing 2.3   Updating a language intent dataset

Replace the dataset ID with   Uploads raw data
the value returned from the   (upload/002.csv)
CreateDataset API.   to cloud storage

```
mc -q cp data-management/src/test/resources/datasets/train.csv
      myminio/"${MINIO_DM_BUCKET}"/upload/002.csv

grpcurl -v -plaintext \                     A request to append more
  -d '{"dataset_id": "1", \                 data (upload/002.csv)
      "commit_message": "More training data", \
      "bucket": "mini-automl", \
      "path": "upload/002.csv", \           The data URL of raw data,
      "tags": [{ \                          created by raw data upload
        "tag_key": "category", \
        "tag_value": "training set\"}]}' \
${DM_SERVER}:${DM_PORT} \
data_management.DataManagementService/UpdateDataset    Updates the
                                                       dataset API name
```

Once the dataset update completes, the UpdateDataset API returns a data summary
JSON object in the same way as the CreateDataset API does; see a sample responsible
object as follows:

```
{
  "datasetId": "1",
  "name": "dataset-1",
  "dataset_type": "TEXT_INTENT",
  "last_updated_at": "2021-10-09T23",
  "commits": [
    {
```

```
    "commit_id": "1",          ◁────  The commit created by the
    .. .. ..                          create dataset request
  },
  {
    "dataset_id": "1",
    "commit_id": "2",          ◁────  Commit ID; this commit
    "created_at": "2021-10-09T23:59:17",    captures the data from
    "commit_message": "More training data",  upload/002.csv.
    "tags": [
      {
        "tag_key": "category",
        "tag_value": "training set"
      }
    ],
    "path": "dataset/1/commit/2",
    "statistics": {
      "numExamples": "7600",
      "numLabels": "151"
    }
  }
 ]
}
```

You can also fetch the data summary and commit history of a dataset by using the Get-DatasetSummary API. See the following sample gRPC request:

```
grpcurl -v -plaintext
  -d '{"datasetId": "1"}' \        ◁──  The ID of the
${DM_SERVER}:${DM_PORT} \               dataset to query
data_management.DataManagementService/GetDatasetSummary
```

FETCH TRAINING DATASET

Now we have a dataset (ID = 1) created with raw data; let's try to build a training dataset from it. In our sample service, it's a two-step process.

We first call the PrepareTrainingDataset API to start the dataset-building process. And then we use the FetchTrainingDataset API to query the dataset preparation progress until the request completes.

> **NOTE** Scripts dm-005-prepare-dataset.sh, dm-006-prepare-partial-dataset.sh, and dm-007-fetch-dataset-version.sh automate the steps that follow. Please try to use them to run the sample dataset fetching demo in code listings 2.4 and 2.5.

To use the PrepareTrainingDataset API, we only need to provide a dataset ID. If you just want a portion of data to be in the training dataset, you can use tag as a filter in the request. See a sample request as follows.

Listing 2.4   Preparing a training dataset

```
grpcurl -plaintext \
  -d "{"dataset_id": "1"}" \        A request to prepare the training
  ${DM_SERVER}:${DM_PORT} \         dataset with all data commits
data_management.DataManagementService/PrepareTrainingDataset
```

```
                grpcurl -plaintext \                    A request to prepare the training
                -d "{"dataset_id": "1", \               dataset with partial data commits
                "Tags":[ \                              by defining filter tags
    Data          {"tag_key":"category", \
    filters         "tag_value":"training set"}]}" \
                ${DM_SERVER}:${DM_PORT}
                    data_management.DataManagementService/PrepareTrainingDataset
```

Once the data preparation gRPC request succeeds, it returns a JSON object as follows:

```
{
  "dataset_id": "1",
  "name": "dataset-1",
  "dataset_type": "TEXT_INTENT",
  "last_updated_at": "2021-10-09T23:44:00",
  "version_hash": "hashDg==",          ◁──┐  ID of the training
  "commits": [                                dataset snapshot
    {
      "commit_id": "1",
      .. .. ..                          The selected
    },                                  data commits of
    {                                   the raw dataset
      "commit_id": "2",
      .. .. ..
    }
  ]
}
```

Among the data that the `PrepareTrainingDataset` API returns is the `"version_hash"` string. It is used to identify the data snapshot produced by the API. Using this hash as an ID, we can call the `FetchTrainingDatasetc` API to track the progress of building the training dataset; see the following example.

Listing 2.5 Checking dataset prepare progress

```
grpcurl -plaintext \
 -d "{"dataset_id": "1", \
      "version_hash":          ID of the training
      "hashDg=="}" \           dataset snapshot
${DM_SERVER}:${DM_PORT}
data_management.DataManagementService/FetchTrainingDataset
```

The `FetchTrainingDatasetc` API returns a JSON object that describes the training dataset. It tells us the status of the background dataset-building process: RUNNING, READY, or FAILED. If the training data is ready for consumption, the response object will display a list of downloadable URLs for the training data. In this demo, the URLs point to the local MinIO server. See a sample response as follows:

```
{
  "dataset_id": "1",            Status of
  "version_hash": "hashDg==",   the training
  "state": "READY",      ◁──┘   dataset
```

```
  "parts": [
    {
      "name": "examples.csv",
      "bucket": "mini-automl-dm",
      "path": "versionedDatasets/1/hashDg==/examples.csv"
    },
    {
      "name": "labels.csv",
      "bucket": "mini-automl-dm",
      "path": "versionedDatasets/1/hashDg==/labels.csv"
    }
  ],
  "statistics": {
    "numExamples": "16200",
    "numLabels": "151"
  }
}
```

Data URLs of the training data

Good job! You just experienced all the major data APIs offered by our sample dataset management service. By trying to upload data and build training datasets by yourself, we hope you have gained a feeling for how this service can be used. In the next few sections, we will look at user scenarios, service architecture overview, and code implementation of our sample dataset management services.

NOTE   If you encounter any problems when running the mentioned scripts, please refer to the instructions in the "function demo" doc of our GitHub repo. Also, if you want to try the labs in chapters 3 and 4, please keep the containers running because they are the prerequisites for the model training labs.

2.2.2   *Users, user scenarios, and the big picture*

When designing backend services, the method we found very useful is thinking from the outside in. First, figure out who the users are, what value the service will provide, and how customers will interact with the service. Then the inner logic and storage layout should come naturally to you. For touring this sample DM service, we will show you using the same approach. So let's look at our users and user scenario first.

NOTE   The reason we look at the use cases first is that we believe any system design should consider the user the most. Our approach to efficiency and scalability will come up naturally if we identify how customers use the system. If the design is taken in the reverse order (consider technology first and usability second), the system often is clumsy to use because it's designed for technology and not for customers.

USERS AND USER SCENARIOS

Our sample DM service is built for two fictional users: Jianguo, a data engineer, and Julia, a data scientist. They work together to train a language-intent classification model.

Jianguo works on training data collection. He continuously collects data from different data sources (such as parsing user activity logs and conducting customer surveys) and labels them. Jianguo uses a DM data ingestion API to create datasets, append new data to existing datasets, and query datasets' summary and status.

Julia uses the dataset built by Jianguo to train intent classification models (usually written in PyTorch or Tensorflow). At the training time, Julia's training code will first call the DM service's fetch training data API to get the training dataset from the DM and then start the training process.

THE SERVICE'S OVERALL ARCHITECTURE

Our sample DM service is built in three layers: the data ingestion layer, dataset fetching layer, and dataset internal storage layer. The data ingestion API set is built so that Jianguo can upload new training data and query dataset status. The dataset fetching API is built so that Julia can obtain the training dataset. See figures 2.6 and 2.7 for the whole picture.

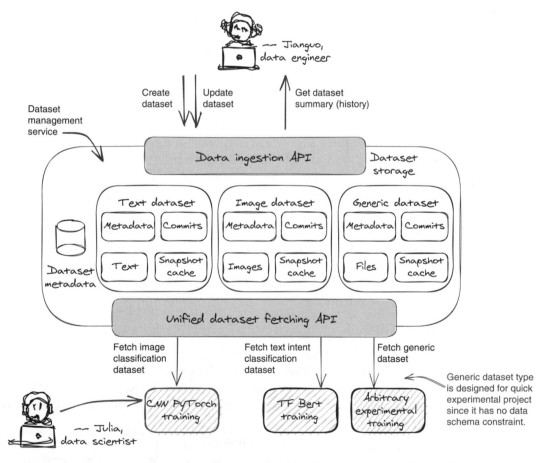

Figure 2.6   System overview of the sample dataset management service. The sample service contains three main components, a data ingestion API, internal storage, and a dataset fetching API.

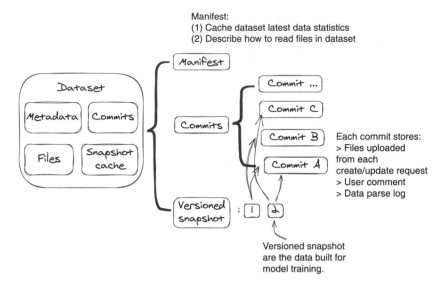

Figure 2.7   The internal storage structure for storing a dataset

The central big box in figure 2.6 shows the overall design of our sample dataset management service. It has an internal dataset storage system and two public-facing interfaces: a data ingestion API and a dataset fetching API—one for data ingestion and another for dataset fetching. The system supports both strongly typed schema datasets (text and image types) and nonschema datasets (GENERIC type).

Figure 2.7 displays the overall data structure the sample DM service uses to store a dataset. The commits are created by the data ingestion API, and versioned snapshots are created by the data fetching API. The concepts of commit and versioned snapshot are introduced to address the dynamic and static nature of a dataset. We will discuss storage in detail in section 2.2.5.

In the remaining subsections, we will walk you through every detail of the previous two diagrams, component by component. We first start with the API and then move to the internal storage and data schema.

2.2.3   *Data ingestion API*

The data ingestion API allows creating, updating, and querying datasets in the sample dataset management service. The gray box in figure 2.8 shows the definition of four service methods in the data ingestion layer that support ingesting data into DM. Their names are self-explanatory; let's look at their gRPC method definition in listing 2.6.

> **NOTE**   To reduce boilerplate code, we chose gRPC to implement the public interface for our sample DM service. This doesn't mean gRPC is the best approach for a dataset management service, but compared to the RESTful interface, gRPC's concise coding style is perfect for demonstrating our idea without exposing you to unnecessary Spring Framework details.

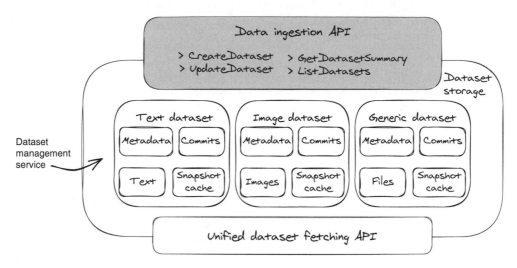

Figure 2.8   Four methods to support data ingestion: create the dataset, update the dataset, get the dataset summary, and list the datasets

DEFINITION OF DATA INGESTION METHODS

Let's take a look at what our sample data ingestion API looks like.

Listing 2.6   Data ingestion API service definition

```
# create a new dataset and save data into it
rpc CreateDataset (CreateDatasetRequest) returns (DatasetSummary);

# add new data to an existing dataset
rpc UpdateDataset (CreateCommitRequest) returns (DatasetSummary);

# get summary and history of a given dataset
rpc GetDatasetSummary (DatasetPointer) returns (DatasetSummary);

# list all existing datasets' summary
rpc ListDatasets (ListQueryOptions) returns (stream DatasetSummary);

message CreateDatasetRequest {
  string name = 1;
  string description = 2;
  DatasetType dataset_type = 3;
  string bucket = 4;
  string path = 5;
  repeated Tag tags = 6;
}
```

**Defines dataset type,
"TEXT_INTENT" or
"GENERIC"**

**Defines the file URL of the
uploading data in MinIO server**

**Sets data filter
by using tags**

> **NOTE**   The topic of data deletion and modification is not covered in this sample service, but the service can be easily extended to support them.

DATA URL VS. DATA STREAMING

You may notice in our API design that we require users to provide data URLs as raw data input instead of uploading files directly to our service. In section 2.2.4, we also choose to return data URLs as a training dataset instead of returning files directly via a streaming endpoint. The main reason is that we want to offload the file-transferring work to a cloud object storage service, such as Amazon S3 or Azure Blob. Doing this has two benefits: first, it saves network bandwidth because there are no actual files passed between client and service, and second, it reduces code complexity because keeping data streaming working with high availability can be complicated when files are large and API usage is high.

CREATING A NEW DATASET

Let's look at how the gRPC `CreateDataset` method is implemented. Before calling the DM (`createDataset` API) to create a dataset, the user (Jianguo) needs to prepare a downloadable URL for the data they want to upload (steps 1 and 2); the URL can be a downloadable link in a cloud object storage service, like Amazon S3 or Azure Blob. In our sample service, we use the MinIO server to run on your local to mock Amazon S3. Jianguo also can name the dataset and assign tags in the dataset creation request. Listing 2.7 highlights the key pieces of code (`dataManagement/DataManagementService` `.java`) that implement the workflow pictured in figure 2.9.

Listing 2.7   New dataset creation implementation

```
public void createDataset(CreateDatasetRequest request) {          Receives dataset
                                                                    creation request
  int datasetId = store.datasetIdSeed.incrementAndGet();    ◁      (step 3)

  Dataset dataset = new Dataset(
    datasetId, request.getName(),
    request.getDescription(),                               Creates a dataset object
    request.getDatasetType());                              with metadata from user
  int commitId = dataset.getNextCommitId();                 request (step 4a)


  CommitInfo.Builder builder = DatasetIngestion              Downloads data from
    .ingest(minioClient, datasetId, commitId,                URL and uploads it to
    request.getDatasetType(), request.getBucket(),           DM's cloud storage
    request.getPath(), config.minioBucketName);              (step 4b)

  store.datasets.put(Integer.toString(datasetId), dataset);  Saves the dataset
  dataset.commits.put(commitId, builder                      with downloaded
    .setCommitMessage("Initial commit")                      data as the initial
    .addAllTags(request.getTagsList()).build());             commit (step 5)


  responseObserver.onNext(dataset.toDatasetSummary());       Returns the dataset summary
  responseObserver.onCompleted();                            to the client (steps 6 and 7)
}
```

The implementation details of `DatasetIngestion.ingest()` will be discussed in section 2.2.5.

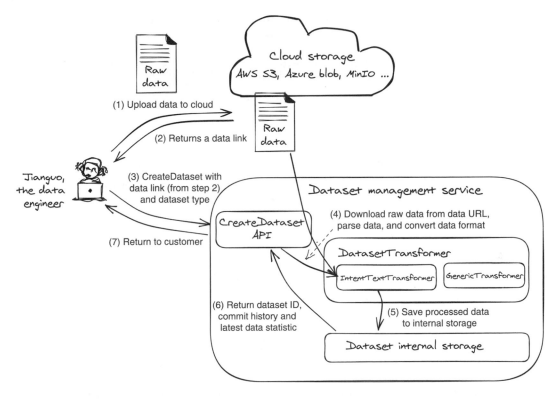

Figure 2.9   A high-level overview of the seven steps to creating a new dataset: (1) upload data to the cloud object storage; (2) get a data link; (3) call `createDataset` API with a data link as the payload; (4) DM first downloads data from the data link and then finds the right dataset transformer (`IntentTextTransformer`) to do data parsing and conversion; (5) DM saves the transformed data; and (6 and 7) DM returns the dataset summary (ID, commit history, data statistics) to the user.

UPDATING AN EXISTING DATASET

Deep learning model development is a continuous process. Once we create a dataset for a model training project, data engineers (like Jianguo) will keep adding data to it. To accommodate this need, we provide the `UpdateDataset` API.

To use the `UpdateDataset` API, we need to prepare a data URL for the new data. We can also pass in a commit message and some customer tags to describe the data change; these metadata are useful for data history tracking and data filtering.

The dataset update workflow is almost identical to the dataset creation workflow (figure 2.9). It creates a new commit with the given data and appends the commit to the dataset's commit list. The only difference is that the dataset update workflow won't create a new dataset but will work on an existing dataset. See the following code listing.

NOTE   Because every dataset update is saved as a commit, we could easily remove or soft delete those commits with some dataset management API if

Jianguo mistakenly uploads some mislabeled data to a dataset. Because of space limitations, these management APIs are not discussed.

Listing 2.8   Dataset update implementation

```
public void updateDataset(CreateCommitRequest request) {

    String datasetId = request.getDatasetId();          ◄──  Receives dataset
                                                             creation request (step 3)

    Dataset dataset = store.datasets
      .get(datasetId);                                   Finds the existing dataset
    String commitId = Integer.toString(dataset          and creates a new commit
      .getNextCommitId());                               object (step 4a)

    // the rest code are the same as listing 2.7
    .. .. ..
}
```

We will talk more about the concept of commits in section 2.2.3. For now, you just need to be aware that every dataset update request creates a new commit object.

NOTE   Why save data updates in commits? Can we merge the new data with the current data so we only store the latest state? In our update dataset implementation, we create a new commit every time the UpdateDataset API is called. There are two reasons we want to avoid an in-place data merge: first, an in-place data merge can cause irreversible data modification and silent data loss. Second, to reproduce the training dataset used in the past, we need to make sure the data batches DM receives are stored immutably because they are the source data we used to create the training dataset at any time.

LIST DATASETS AND GET DATASETS SUMMARY

Besides CreateDataset and UpdateDataset API, our users need methods to list existing datasets and query the overview of a dataset, such as the number of a dataset's examples and labels and its audit history. To accommodate these needs, we build two APIs: ListDatasets and GetDatasetSummary. The first one can list all the existing datasets, and the second one provides detailed information about a dataset, such as commit history, example and label count, and dataset ID and type. The implementation for these two APIs is straightforward; you can find them in our Git repo (mini-AutoML/DataManagementService.java).

2.2.4   *Training dataset fetching API*

In this section, we will look at the dataset fetching layer, which is highlighted as a gray box in figure 2.10. To build training data, we designed two APIs. The data scientist (Julia) first calls the PrepareTrainingDataset API to issue a training data preparation request; our DM service will kick off a background thread to start building the training data and return a version string as a reference handle for the training data. Next,

Julia can call the FetchTrainingDataset API to obtain the training data if the background thread is completed.

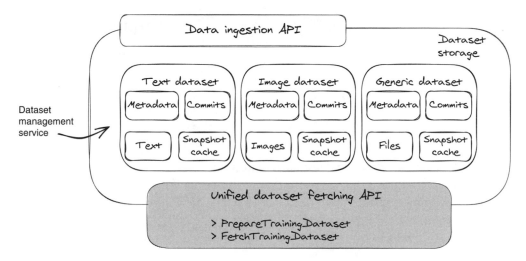

Figure 2.10 **Two methods in the dataset fetching layer to support dataset fetching:** **PrepareTrainingDataset and FetchTrainingDataset**

DEFINITION OF DATASET FETCHING METHODS
First, let's see the gRPC service method definition (grpc-contract/src/main/proto/data_management.proto) for the two dataset fetching methods—PrepareTrainingDataset and FetchTrainingDataset.

Listing 2.9 Training dataset fetching service definition

```
rpc PrepareTrainingDataset (DatasetQuery)          Prepares training
  returns (DatasetVersionHash);                     dataset API

rpc FetchTrainingDataset (VersionHashQuery)         Fetches training
  returns (VersionHashDataset);                      dataset API

message DatasetQuery {           ◁        The payload of dataset
  string dataset_id = 1;        ◁         preparation API
  string commit_id = 2;         ◁
  repeated Tag tags = 3;        ◁         Specifies which dataset
}                                          to build training data

                                           Specifies which commit of a
message VersionHashQuery {                  dataset to build training
  string dataset_id = 1;                    data, optional
  string version_hash = 2;     ◁
}                                           Filters data by
                                            commit tags,
              Version hash                  optional
The payload of the    string represents
training dataset      the training
fetch API             dataset snapshot.
```

> ## Why we need two APIs (two steps) to fetch a dataset
>
> If we only publish one API for acquiring training data, the caller needs to wait on the API call until the backend data preparation completes to obtain the final training data. If the data preparation takes a long time, this request will time out.
>
> A deep learning dataset is normally big (at the gigabyte level); it can take minutes or hours to complete the network I/O data transfer and local data aggregation. So the common solution to acquiring large data is to offer two APIs—one for submitting data preparation requests and another for querying the data status—and pull down the result when the request is complete. In this way, the dataset fetching API performs consistently regardless of the size of the dataset.

SENDING THE PREPARE TRAINING DATASET REQUEST

Now let's look at the code workflow of the `PrepareTrainingDataset` API. Figure 2.11 shows how our sample service handles Julia's preparation training dataset request.

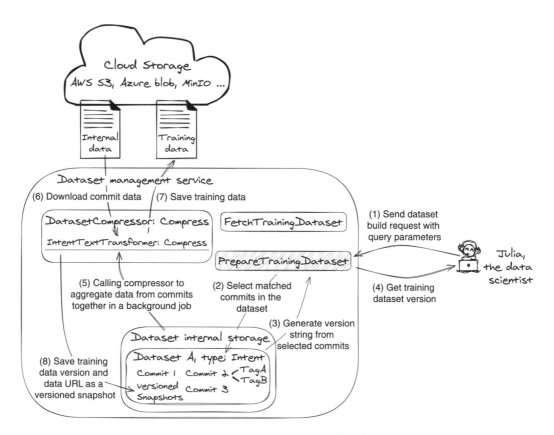

Figure 2.11   A high-level overview of the eight steps to responding to a dataset build request: (1) the user submits a dataset preparation request with data filters; (2) DM selects data from commits that satisfy the data filters; (3 and 4) DM generates a version string to represent the training data; and (5–8) DM starts a background job to produce the training data.

When DM receives a dataset preparation request (figure 2.11, step 1), it carries out three acts:

- Tries to find the dataset in its storage with the given dataset ID.
- Applies the given data filter to select commits from the dataset.
- Creates a `versionedSnapshot` object to track training data in its internal storage (`versionHashRegistry`). The ID of the `versionedSnapshot` object is a hash string generated from the selected commits' ID list.

The `versionedSnapshot` object is the training dataset Julia wants; it is a group of immutable static files from the selected commits. Julia could use the hash string (snapshot ID) returned at step 3 to query the dataset preparation status and get the data-downloadable URL when the training dataset is ready. With this version string, Julia can always obtain the same training data (`versionedSnapshot`) from any time in the future, which is how dataset reproducibility is supported.

A side benefit of `versionedSnapshot` is that it can be used as a cache across different `PrepareTrainingDataset` API calls. If the snapshot ID—a hash string of a list of commits—already exists, we return the existing `versionedSnapshot` without rebuilding the same data, which can save computation time and network bandwidth.

> **NOTE**   In our design, the data filtering happens at the commit level, not at the individual example level; for example, having a filter tag `"DataType=Training"` in the preparation request indicates that the user only wants data from the commits that are labeled `"DataType=Training"`.

After step 3, DM will spawn a background thread to build the training dataset. In the background job, DM will download the files of each dataset commit from the MinIO server to the local, aggregate and compress them into one file in a predefined format, and upload them back to the MinIO server in a different bucket (steps 6 and 7). Next, DM will put the data URL of the actual training data in the `versionedSnapshot` object and update its status to `"READY"` (step 8). Now Julia can find the data URLs from the returned `versionedSnapshot` object and start to download the training data.

What we haven't covered is the data schema. In the dataset management service, we save the ingested data (`commit`) and the generated training data (`versionedSnapshot`) in two different data formats. A data merge operation (figure 2.11, steps 6 and 7) aggregates the raw ingested data (the selected commits) and converts it into training data in an intent classification training data schema. We will discuss data schemas in detail in section 2.2.6. Listing 2.10 highlights the code implemented for figure 2.11.

Listing 2.10   Preparing training data request API

```
public void prepareTrainingDataset(DatasetQuery request) {
  # step 1, receive dataset preparation request
  Dataset dataset = store.datasets.get(datasetId);
  String commitId;
  .. .. ..
```

```
# step 2, select data commits by checking tag filter
BitSet pickedCommits = new BitSet();
List<DatasetPart> parts = Lists.newArrayList();
List<CommitInfo> commitInfoList = Lists.newLinkedList();
for (int i = 1; i <= Integer.parseInt(commitId); i++) {
  CommitInfo commit = dataset.commits.get(Integer.toString(i));
  boolean matched = true;
  for (Tag tag : request.getTagsList()) {
    matched &= commit.getTagsList().stream().anyMatch(k -> k.equals(tag));
  }
  if (!matched) {
    continue;
  }
  pickedCommits.set(i);
  commitInfoList.add(commit);
  .. .. ..
}

# step 3, generate version hash from the selected commits list
String versionHash = String.format("hash%s",
  Base64.getEncoder().encodeToString(pickedCommits.toByteArray()));

if (!dataset.versionHashRegistry.containsKey(versionHash)) {
  dataset.versionHashRegistry.put(versionHash,
    VersionedSnapshot.newBuilder()
      .setDatasetId(datasetId)
      .setVersionHash(versionHash)
      .setState(SnapshotState.RUNNING).build());
```

Creates VersionedSnapshot object to represent the training dataset

```
  # step 5,6,7,8, start a background thread to aggregate data
  # from commits to the training dataset
  threadPool.submit(
    new DatasetCompressor(minioClient, store, datasetId,
      dataset.getDatasetType(), parts, versionHash,
    config.minioBucketName));
  }

# step 4, return hash version string to customer
responseObserver.onNext(responseBuilder.build());
responseObserver.onCompleted();
}
```

FETCHING THE TRAINING DATASET

Once the DM service receives a training dataset preparation request on the prepare-
TrainingDataset API, it will spawn a background job to build the training data and
return a version_hash string for tracking purposes. Julia can use the FetchTraining-
Dataset API and the version_hash string to query the dataset-building progress and
eventually get the training dataset. Figure 2.12 shows how dataset fetching requests
are handled in DM.

The fetch training dataset is essentially querying the training data preparation
request status. For each dataset, the DM service creates a versionedSnapshot object
to track each training dataset produced by the prepareTrainingDataset request.

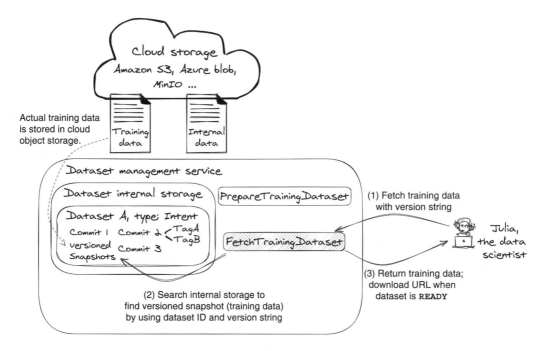

Figure 2.12 A high-level overview of the three steps to serving a dataset fetching request: (1) the user calls the `FetchTrainingDataset` API with a dataset ID and a version string; (2) DM will search the `versionHashRegistry` of the dataset in its internal storage and return a `versionedSnapshot` object; and (3) the `versionedSnapshot` object will have a download URL when the data preparation job is completed.

When a user sends a fetch dataset query, we simply use the hash string in the request to search its corresponding `versionedSnapshot` object in the dataset's training snapshots (`versionHashRegistry`) and return it to the user if it exists. The `versionedSnapshot` object will keep being updated by the background training data process job (figure 2.11, steps 5–8). When the job completes, it will write the training data URL to the `versionedSnapshot` object; therefore, the user gets the training data at the end. See the code implementation in the following listing.

Listing 2.11 Preparing the training data request API

```
public void fetchTrainingDataset(VersionQuery request) {
  String datasetId = request.getDatasetId();
  Dataset dataset = store.datasets.get(datasetId);

  if (dataset.versionHashRegistry.containsKey(        // Searches versionedSnapshot in
      request.getVersionHash())) {                    // a dataset's training snapshots

    responseObserver.onNext(

      dataset.versionHashRegistry.get(                // Returns versionedSnapshot; it
      request.getVersionHash()));                     // contains the latest progress of
    responseObserver.onCompleted();                   // dataset preparation.
```

```
    }
    .. .. ..
}
```

2.2.5   *Internal dataset storage*

The internal storage of the sample service is simply a list of in-memory dataset objects. Earlier we talked about how a dataset can be both dynamic and static. On one hand, a dataset is a logical file group, changing dynamically as it continuously absorbs new data from a variety of sources. On the other hand, it's static and reproducible for training.

   To showcase this concept, we design each dataset containing a list of commits and a list of versioned snapshots. A commit represents the dynamically ingested data: data added by a data ingestion call (`CreateDataset` or `UpdateDataset`); a commit also has tags and messages for annotation purposes. A versioned snapshot represents the static training data, which, produced by the prepare training dataset request (`Prepare-TrainingDataset`), is converted from a list of selected commits. Each snapshot is associated with a version; once the training dataset is built, you can use this version string to fetch the corresponding training data (`FetchTrainingDataset`) at any time to reuse. Figure 2.13 visualizes the internal storage structure of a dataset.

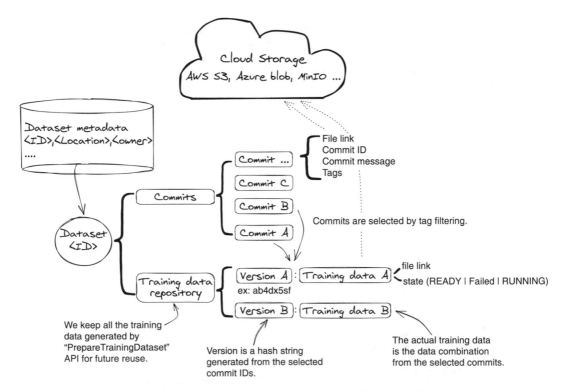

Figure 2.13   An internal dataset storage overview. A dataset stores two types of data: commits for the ingested raw data and versioned snapshots for the training dataset. The dataset metadata and data URLs are stored in the dataset management service, and the actual data is stored in the cloud object storage service.

NOTE Although the individual training examples of different types of datasets can be in different forms, such as images, audios, and text sentences, the dataset's operations (creating, updating, and querying dataset summary) and its dynamic/static characters are the same. Because we designed a unified API set across all dataset types, we can use one uniformed storage structure to store all different kinds of datasets.

In our storage, the actual files (commit data, snapshot data) are stored in cloud object storage (such as Amazon S3), and we only keep dataset metadata (see explanation later) in our DM system. By offloading file storage work and only tracking the file links, we can focus on organizing the datasets and tracking their metadata, such as edit history, data statistics, training snapshots, and ownership.

Dataset metadata

We define dataset metadata as everything except actual data files, such as the dataset ID, data owner, change history (audits), training snapshots, commits, data statistics, and so on.

For demonstration purposes, we store the datasets' metadata in a memory dictionary with the ID as key and put all data files into the MinIO server. But you can extend it to use a database or NoSQL database to store the dataset's metadata.

So far, we have talked about dataset storage concepts, but how do the actual dataset writing and reading work? How do we serialize commits and snapshots for different dataset types, such as `GENERIC` and `TEXT_INTENT` types?

In the storage backend implementation, we use a simple inheritance concept to handle file operations for different dataset types. We define a `DatasetTransformer` interface as follows: the `ingest()` function saves input data into internal storage as a commit, and the `compress()` function merges data from selected commits into a version snapshot (training data).

More specifically, for the `"TEXT_INTENT"` type dataset, we have `IntentText-Transformer` to apply the strong type of file schema on file conversion. For a `"GENERIC"` type dataset, we have `GenericTransformer` to save data in the original format without any checks or format conversions. Figure 2.14 illustrates these.

From figure 2.14, we see that the raw intent classification data from data ingestion API (section 2.2.3) is saved as a commit by `IntentTextTransformer:Ingest()`; the intent classification training data produced by training dataset fetching API (section 2.2.4) is saved as a versioned snapshot by `IntentTextTransformer:Compress()`. Because they are plain Java code, we leave it for your own discovery; you can find the implementation code at our Git repo (org/orca3/miniAutoML/dataManagement/transformers/IntentTextTransformer.java).

DatasetTransformer applies file
schema to commit and snapshot data

DatasetTransformer

Create & update dataset

IntentTextTransformer   GenericTransformer

Create new commit

> **Ingest()**

Prepare
training data

> **Compress()**

(1) Match commits

(2) Create version string

(3) Merge data into one snapshot

New version snapshot
for training

Figure 2.14   Implement `DatasetTransformer` **interface to handle different dataset types; implement ingest function to save raw input data as commit; and implement compress function to aggregate commit data to training data.**

2.2.6   *Data schemas*

So far, we have seen all the APIs, workflows, and internal storage structures. Now let's consider what the data looks like in the DM service. For each kind of strongly typed dataset, such as a "TEXT_INTENT" dataset, we defined two data schemas: one for data ingestion and one for training data fetching (figure 2.15).

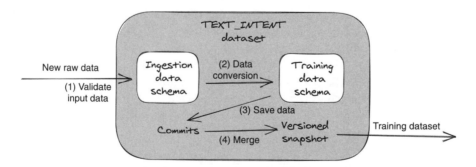

Figure 2.15   Each type of dataset has two data schemas: ingestion data schema and training data schema. These two schemas will ensure that the data we accept and the data we produce follow our data spec.

Figure 2.15 shows how the DM service uses two data schemas to implement its data contract. Step 1 uses the ingestion data schema to validate the raw input data; step 2 uses the training data schema to convert the raw data to the training data format; step 3 saves the converted data as a commit; and step 4 merges the selected commits into one versioned snapshot when building a training dataset but still obeys the training data schema.

These two different data schemas are the data contract that DM service provides to our two different users: Jianguo and Julia. No matter how Jianguo collects the data, it needs to be converted to the ingestion data format to insert into DM. Alternatively, because DM guarantees that the output training data follows the training data schema, Julia feels comfortable consuming the dataset without worrying about being affected by the data collection changes made by Jianguo.

A DATA INGESTION SCHEMA

We have seen the data schema concept; now let's look at the ingestion data schema we defined for the TEXT_INTENT dataset:

```
>> TEXT_INTENT dataset ingestion data schema
<text utterance>, <label>,<label>,<label>, ...
```

For simplicity, our ingestion data schema requires that all the input data for the TEXT_INTENT dataset must be in a CSV file format. The first column is text utterance, and the remainder of the columns are labels. See a sample CSV file as follows:

```
"I am still waiting on my credit card", activate_my_card      | Labels
➡ ;card_arrival
"I couldn't purchase gas in Costco", card_not_working
```

A TRAINING DATASET SCHEMA

For TEXT_INTENT training data, our schema defines the output data as a zip file that contains two files: examples.csv and labels.csv. Labels.csv defines a label name to a label ID mapping, and the examples.csv defines training text (utterance) to label ID mapping. See the following examples:

```
examples.csv: <text utterance>, <label_id>,<label_id>, ...
"I am still waiting on my credit card", 0;1
"I couldn't purchase gas in Costco", 2

Labels.csv: <label_id>, <label_name>
0, activate_my_card
1, card_arrival
2, card_not_working
```

> ## Why we use a self-defined data structure
> We build TEXT_INTENT with the self-defined data schema instead of using the PyTorch or Tensorflow dataset format (like TFRecordDataset) to create abstraction from model training frameworks.

> **(continued)**
>
> By choosing a framework-specific dataset format, your training code will also need to be written in the framework, which is not ideal. Introducing a self-defined intermediate dataset format can make the DM framework-neutral, so no framework-specific training codes are required.

THE BENEFIT OF HAVING TWO STRONGLY TYPED DATA SCHEMAS IN ONE DATASET

By having two strongly typed data schemas in a dataset and letting DM do the data transformation from the ingestion data format to the training data format, we could parallelize data collection development and training code development. For example, when Jianguo wants to add a new feature—"text language"—to the TEXT_INTENT dataset, he can work with the DM service developers to update the data ingestion schema to add a new data field.

Julia won't be affected because the training data schema is not changed. Julia may come to us later to update the training data schema when she has the bandwidth to consume the new feature in her training code. The key point is that Jianguo and Julia don't have to work synchronously to introduce a new dataset enhancement; they can work independently.

> **NOTE**   For simplicity and demo purpose, we choose to use a CSV file to store data. The problem with using plain CSV files is their lack of backward compatibility support and data-type validation support. In production, we recommend using Parquet, Google protobuf, or Avro to define data schemas and store data. They come with a set of libraries for data validation, data serialization, and schema backward-compatible support.

A GENERIC DATASET: A DATASET WITH NO SCHEMA

Although we emphasize at multiple places that defining strongly typed dataset schemas is fundamental to dataset management service, we will make an exception here by adding a free format dataset type—the GENERIC dataset. Unlike the strongly typed TEXT_ INENT dataset, a GENERIC-type dataset has no data schema validation. Our service will save any raw input data as is, and when building training data, the service simply packs all the raw data together in its original format into a training dataset.

A GENERIC dataset type may sound like a bad idea because we basically pass whatever data we receive from upstream data sources to the downstream training application, which can break the data parsing logic in the training code easily. This is definitely not an option for production, but it provides the agility necessary for experimental projects.

Although a strongly typed data schema offers good data type safety protection, it comes at the cost of maintaining it. It is quite annoying when you have to make frequent schema changes in the DM service to adopt the new data format required by a new experimentation.

At the beginning of a deep learning project, a lot of things are uncertain, such as which deep learning algorithm works the best, what kind of data we can collect, and what data schema we should choose. To move forward with all these uncertainties, we need a flexible way to handle arbitrary data to enable model training experimentations. This is what GENERIC dataset type designs are for.

Once the business value is proven and the deep learning algorithm is chosen, we are now clear about how the training data looks; then it's time for us to define a strongly typed dataset in the dataset management service. In the next section, we will discuss how to add a new strongly typed dataset.

2.2.7   Adding new dataset type (IMAGE_CLASS)

Let's imagine one day Julia asks us (the platform developers) to promote her experimental image classification project to a formal project. Julia and her team is developing an image classification model by using a GENERIC dataset, and because they get good results, they now want to define a strongly typed dataset (IMAGE_CLASS) to stabilize the data schema for raw data collection and training data consumption. This will protect the training code from future dataset updates.

To add a new dataset type—IMAGE_CLASS—we can follow three steps. First, we must define the training data format. After discussing with Julia, we decide the training data produced by FetchTrainingDataset API will be a zip file; it will contain these three files:

```
>> examples.csv: <image filename>,<label id>
"imageA.jpg", 0
"imageB.jpg", 1
"imageC.jpg", 0

>> labels.csv: <label id>,<label name>
0, cat
1, dog

>> examples/ - folder
imageA.jpg
imageB.jpg
imageC.jpg
```

The examples.csv and labels.csv files are manifest files that define labels for each training image. The actual image files are stored in the examples folder.

Second, define the ingestion data format. We need to discuss the ingestion data schema with Jianguo, the data engineer who collects images and labels them. We agree that the payload data for each CreateDataset and UpdateDataset request is also a zip file; its directory looks as follows: the zip file should be a folder with only subdirectories. Each subdirectory under the root folder represents a label; the images under it belong to this label. The subdirectory should only contain images and not any nested directories:

```
├── cat
│   ├── catA.jpg
│   ├── catB.jpg
│   └── catC.jpg
```

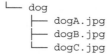

```
└── dog
    ├── dogA.jpg
    ├── dogB.jpg
    └── dogC.jpg
```

The last step is the code change. After having two data schemas in mind, we need to create an `ImageClassTransformer` class that implements the `DatasetTransformer` interface to build the data reads and writes logic.

We first implement the `ImageClassTransformer.ingest()` function. The logic needs to use the input data format—defined in step 2—to parse the input data in the dataset creation and update requests and then convert the input data to a training data format and save it as a commit of the dataset.

We then implement the `ImageClassTransformer.compress()` function, which first selects commits by matching data filters and then merges the matched commits into a single training snapshot. As the last step, we register the `ImageClassTransformer` `.ingest()` function to the `DatasetIngestion.ingestion()` function with an **IMAGE_ CLASS** type and register `ImageClassTransformer.compress()` to `DatasetCompressor` `.run()` with an `IMAGE_CLASS` type.

As you can see, with proper dataset structure, we can support new dataset types by just adding a few new code snippets. The existing types of datasets and the public data ingestion and fetching APIs are not affected.

2.2.8   Service design recap

Let's recap how this sample dataset management service addresses the five design principles introduced in section 2.1.2:

- *Principle 1*—Support dataset reproducibility. Our sample DM service saves all the generated training data as a versioned snapshot with a version hash string as key. Users can apply this version string to obtain the training data snapshot at any time.

- *Principle 2*—Provide a unified experience across different dataset types. The data ingestion API and training data fetching API work the same way for all dataset types and sizes.

- *Principle 3*—Adopt strongly typed data schema. Our sample TEXT_INENT type and IMAGE_CLASS type datasets apply a self-defined data schema to both raw ingestion data and training data.

- *Principle 4*—Ensure API consistency and handle scaling internally. Although we save all datasets' metadata in memory in our sample code (for simplicity), we can easily implement the dataset storage structure in cloud object storage; in theory, it has infinite capacity. Also, we require data URLs to send data and return data, so no matter how large a dataset is, our API remains consistent.

- *Principle 5*—Guarantee data persistency. Every dataset creation request and update request creates a new commit; every training data prepare request creates a versioned snapshot. Both commit and snapshot are immutable and persist with no data expiration limits.

NOTE We have trimmed many important features from the sample dataset management service to keep it simple. Management APIs, for example, allow you to delete data, revert data commits, and view data audit history. Feel free to fork the repo and try to implement them.

2.3 Open source approaches

If you are interested in employing open source approaches to set up dataset management functionality, we select two approaches for you: Delta Lake and Pachyderm. Let's look at them individually.

2.3.1 Delta Lake and Petastorm with Apache Spark family

In this approach, we propose to save data in a Delta Lake table and use the Petastorm library to convert the table data to PyTorch and Tensorflow dataset objects. The dataset can be consumed in training code seamlessly.

DELTA LAKE

Delta Lake is a storage layer that brings scalable, ACID (atomicity, consistency, isolation, durability) transactions to Apache Spark and other cloud object stores (e.g., Amazon S3). Delta Lake is developed as open source by Databricks, a respected data and AI company.

Cloud storage services, such as Amazon S3, are some of the most scalable and cost-effective storage systems in the IT industry. They are ideal places to build large data warehouses, but their key-values store design makes it difficult to achieve ACID transactions and high performance. The metadata operations such as listing objects are expensive, and consistency guarantees are limited.

Delta Lake is designed to fill the previously discussed gaps. It works as a file system that stores batch and streaming data in object storage (such as Amazon S3). In addition, Delta Lake manages metadata, caching, and indexing for its table structure and schema enforcement. It provides ACID properties, time travel, and significantly faster metadata operations for large tabular datasets. See figure 2.16 for the Delta Lake concept graph.

The Delta Lake table is the core concept of the system. When working with Delta Lake, you are usually dealing with Delta Lake tables. They are like SQL tables; you can query, insert, update, and merge table content. Schema protection in Delta Lake is one of its advantages. It supports schema validation on table writing, which prevents data pollution. It also tracks table history, so you can roll back a table to any of its past stages (known as time travel).

For building data processing pipelines, Delta Lake recommends naming your tables in three categories: bronze, silver, and gold. First, we use bronze tables to keep the raw input from different sources (some of which are not so clean). Then the data flows constantly from bronze tables to silver tables with data cleaning and transformation (ETL).

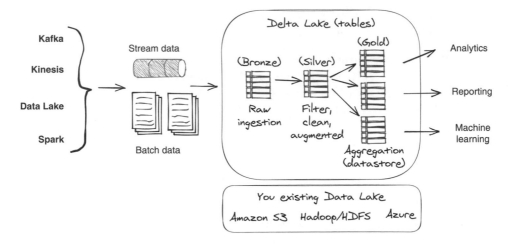

Figure 2.16 Delta Lake data ingestion and processing workflow. Both stream data and batch data can be saved as Delta Lake tables, and the Delta Lake tables are stored in the cloud object storage, such as Amazon S3.

Finally, we perform data filtering and purification and save the results to gold tables. Each table is in a machine learningstate; they are reproducible and type-safe.

WHY DELTA LAKE IS A GOOD OPTION FOR DEEP LEARNING DATASET MANAGEMENT

The following are three features that make Delta Lake a good option for managing datasets for deep learning projects.

First, Delta Lake supports dataset reproducibility. It has a "time travel" feature that has the ability to query the data as it existed at a certain point in time using data versioning. Imagine you have set up a continuously running ETL pipeline to keep your training dataset (gold table) up to date. Because Delta Lake tracks table updates as snapshots, every operation is automatically versioned as the pipeline writes into the dataset. This means all the training data snapshots are kept for free, and you can browse table update history and roll back to past stages easily. The following listing provides a few sample commands.

Listing 2.12 Delta Lake time travel commands

```
pathToTable = "/my/sample/text/intent/dataset/A"          Finds the dataset
                                                           in Delta Lake
deltaTable = DeltaTable.forPath(spark, pathToTable)
fullHistoryDF = deltaTable.history()              Lists the full
lastOperationDF = deltaTable.history(1)           history of the data

df = spark.read.format("delta")          Gets the last
      .option("timestampAsOf", "2021-07-01")   operation on
      .load(pathToTable)                        the dataset
```

Rolls back
the dataset
by time stamp

```
df = spark.read.format("delta")
    .option("versionAsOf", "12")
    .load(pathToTable)
```
| **Rolls back dataset**
| **by version**

Second, Delta Lake supports continuously streaming data processing. Its tables can handle the continuous flow of data from both historical and real-time streaming sources seamlessly. For example, your data pipeline or stream data source can keep adding data to the Delta Lake table while querying data from the table at the same time. This saves you extra steps when writing code to merge the new data with existing data.

Third, Delta Lake offers schema enforcement and evolution. It applies schema validation on write. It will ensure that new data records match the table's predefined schema; if the new data isn't compatible with the table's schema, Delta Lake will raise an exception. Having data type validation at writing time is better than at reading time because it's difficult to clean data if it's polluted.

Besides strong schema enforcement, Delta Lake also allows you to add new columns to existing data tables without causing breaking changes. The dataset schema enforcement and adjustment (evolvement) capabilities are critical to deep learning projects. These capabilities protect the training data from being polluted by unintended data writes and offer safe data updates.

PETASTORM

Petastorm is an open source data access library developed at Uber ATG (Advanced Technologies Group). It enables single-machine or distributed training and evaluation of deep learning models directly from datasets in the Apache Parquet format (a data file format designed for efficient data storage and retrieval).

Petastorm can convert Delta Lake tables to Tensorflow and PyTorch format datasets easily, and it also supports distributed training data partitions. With Petastorm, the training data from a Delta Lake table can be simply consumed by downstream training applications without worrying about the details of data conversion for a specific training framework. It also creates good isolation between the dataset format and training frameworks (Tensorflow, PyTorch, and PySpark). Figure 2.17 visualizes the data conversion process.

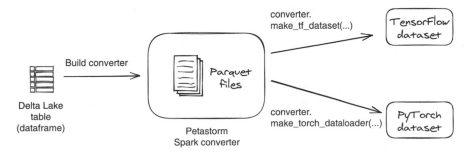

Figure 2.17   Petastorm converts the Delta Lake table to datasets that can be read by the PyTorch or Tensorflow framework.

ED 620 8703

Figure 2.17 depicts the Petastorm data conversion workflow. You can create a Petas-torm spark converter that reads Delta Lake tables into its cache as Parquet files and generates Tensorflow or Pytorch dataset.

EXAMPLE: PREPARING TRAINING DATA FOR A FLOWER IMAGE CLASSIFICATION

Now that we have a general idea of Delta Lake and Petastorm, let's see a concrete model training example. The following code snippets—code listings 2.13 and 2.14—demonstrate an end-to-end image classification model training workflow in two steps. First, they define an image process ETL pipeline that parses a group of image files into the Delta Lake table as an image dataset. Second, they use Petastorm to convert the Delta Lake table to a dataset that can be loaded into the PyTorch framework directly to start model training.

Let's first visit the four-step ETL data processing pipeline in code listing 2.13. You can also find the complete code at http://mng.bz/JVPz.

In the beginning step of the pipeline, we load the images from a folder, `flower_photos`, to spark as binary files. Second, we define the extract functions to obtain metadata from each image file, such as label name, file size, and image size. Third, we construct the data processing pipeline with the extract functions and then pass the image files to the pipeline, which will produce a data frame. Each row of the data frame represents an image file and its metadata, including file content, label name, image size, and file path. In the last step, we save this data frame as a Delta Lake table—gold_table_training_dataset. You can also see this Delta Lake table's data schema at the end of the following code listing.

Listing 2.13   An ETL to create an image dataset in Delta Lake

```
## Step 1: load all raw images files
path_labeled_rawdata = "datacollablab/flower_photos/"

images = spark.read.format("binary")          ┐
 .option("recursiveFileLookup", "true")       │  Reads images
 .option("pathGlobFilter", "*.jpg")           │  as binaryFile
 .load(path_labeled_rawdata)                   │
 .repartition(4)                              ┘

## Step 2: define ETL extract functions
def extract_label(path_col):              ◁─── Extracts labels from the
 """Extract label from file path using built-in SQL functions."""   image's subdirectory name
 return regexp_extract(path_col, "flower_photos/([^/]+)", 1)

def extract_size(content):                ◁─┐
 """Extract image size from its raw content."""   │  Extracts
 image = Image.open(io.BytesIO(content))  │  image
 return image.size                        │  dimensions
                                          │
@pandas_udf("width: int, height: int")    │
def extract_size_udf(content_series):     ◁─┘
 sizes = content_series.apply(extract_size)
 return pd.DataFrame(list(sizes))
```

```
## Step 3: construct and execute ETL to generate a data frame
## contains label, image, image size and path for each image.
df = images.select(
 col("path"),
 extract_size_udf(col("content")).alias("size"),
 extract_label(col("path")).alias("label"),
 col("content"))


## Step 4: save the image dataframe produced
# by ETL to a Delta Lake table
gold_table_training_dataset = "datacollablab.flower_train_binary"
spark.conf.set("spark.sql.parquet.compression.codec", "uncompressed")
df.write.format("delta").mode("overwrite")
  .saveAsTable(gold_table_training_dataset)


>>>
ColumnName: path: string
ColumnName: label: string
ColumnName: labelIndex: bigint
ColumnName: size: struct<width:int, length:int>
ColumnName: content: binary
```

Data schema of the Delta Lake table— gold_table_training_dataset

NOTE The raw data used in the demo is the flowers dataset from the Tensor-Flow team. It contains flower photos stored under five subdirectories, one per class. The subdirectory name is the label name for the images it contains.

Now that we have an image dataset built in a Delta Lake table, we can start to train a PyTorch model by using this dataset with the help of Petastorm. In code listing 2.14, we first read the Delta Lake table gold_table_training_dataset produced by the ETL pipeline defined in code listing 2.13 and then split the data into two data frames: one for training and one for validation. Next, we load these two data frames to two Petastorm spark converters; the data will be converted to Parquet files inside the converter. At the end, we use the Petastorm API make_torch_dataloader to read training examples in PyTorch for model training. See the following code for the entire three-step process. You can also find the full sample code at: http://mng.bz/wy4B.

Listing 2.14 Consuming a Delta Lake image dataset in PyTorch with Petastorm

```
## Step 1: Read dataframe from Delta Lake table
df = spark.read.format("delta")
  .load(gold_table_training_dataset)
 .select(col("content"), col("label_index"))
 .limit(100)
num_classes = df.select("label_index").distinct().count()

df_train, df_val = df
  .randomSplit([0.9, 0.1], seed=12345)
```

Splits Delta Lake table data into two data frames: training and validation

```
## (2) Load dataframes into Petastorm converter
spark.conf.set(SparkDatasetConverter.PARENT_CACHE_DIR_URL_CONF,
  "file:///dbfs/tmp/petastorm/cache")
```

```
converter_train = make_spark_converter(df_train)
converter_val = make_spark_converter(df_val)

## (3) Read training data in PyTorch by using
## Petastorm converter
def train_and_evaluate(lr=0.001):
 device = torch.device("cuda")
  model = get_model(lr=lr)
 .. .. ..

  with converter_train.make_torch_dataloader(
        transform_spec=get_transform_spec(is_train=True),
        batch_size=BATCH_SIZE) as train_dataloader,
      converter_val.make_torch_dataloader(
        transform_spec=get_transform_spec(is_train=False),
        batch_size=BATCH_SIZE) as val_dataloader:

    train_dataloader_iter = iter(train_dataloader)
    steps_per_epoch = len(converter_train) // BATCH_SIZE

    val_dataloader_iter = iter(val_dataloader)
    validation_steps = max(1, len(converter_val) // BATCH_SIZE)

    for epoch in range(NUM_EPOCHS):
      .. ..
      train_loss, train_acc = train_one_epoch(
        model, criterion, optimizer,
        exp_lr_scheduler,
        train_dataloader_iter,
        steps_per_epoch, epoch,device)

      val_loss, val_acc = evaluate(
        model, criterion,
        val_dataloader_iter,
        validation_steps, device)
 return val_loss
```

Creates the PyTorch data loader from the Petastorm converter for training and evaluation

Consumes the training data in the training iterations

WHEN TO USE DELTA LAKE

The common misconception about Delta Lake is that it can only handle structured text data, such as sales records and user profiles. But the previous example shows it can also deal with unstructured data like images and audio files; you can write the file content as a bytes column into a table with other file properties and build datasets from them.

Delta Lake is a great choice for doing dataset management if you already use Apache Spark to build your data pipeline; it supports both structured and unstructured data. It's also cost-effective because Delta Lake keeps data in cloud object storage (e.g., Amazon S3, Azure Blob), and Delta Lake's data schema enforcement and live data updated table support mechanism simplify your ETL pipeline development and maintenance. Last but not least, the time travel function keeps track of all the table updates automatically, so you can feel safe to make data changes and roll back to previous versions of the training dataset.

THE LIMITATIONS OF DELTA LAKE

The biggest risks of using Delta Lake are lock-in technology and its steep learning curve. Delta Lake stores tables in its own mechanism: a combination of Parquet-based storage, a transaction log, and indexes, which means it can only be written/read by a Delta cluster. You need to use Delta ACID API for data ingestion and Delta JDBC to run queries; thus, the data migration cost would be high if you decide to move away from Delta Lake in the future. Also, because Delta Lake goes with Spark, there is a lot of learning ahead of you if you are new to Spark.

Regarding data ingestion performance, Delta Lake stores data to the underlying cloud object store, and it's difficult to achieve low-latency streaming (millisecond scale) when using object store operations, such as table creation and saving. In addition, Delta Lake needs to update indexes for each ACID transaction; it also introduces latency compared with some ETLs performing append-only data writes. But in our opinion, data ingestion latency at the second level is not a problem for deep learning projects. If you are unfamiliar with Spark and don't want the heavy lifting of setting up Spark and Delta Lake clusters, we have another lightweight approach for you—Pachyderm.

2.3.2 *Pachyderm with cloud object storage*

In this section, we want to propose a lightweight, Kubernetes-based tool—Pachyderm—to handle dataset management. We will show you two examples of how to use Pachyderm to accomplish image data processing and labeling. But before that, let's look at what Pachyderm is.

PACHYDERM

Pachyderm is a tool for building version-controlled, automated, end-to-end data pipelines for data science. It runs on Kubernetes and is backed by an object store of your choice (e.g., Amazon S3). You can write your own Docker images for data scraping, ingestion, cleaning, munging, and wrangling and use the Pachyderm pipeline to chain them together. Once you define your pipelines, Pachyderm will handle the pipeline scheduling, executing, and scaling.

Pachyderm offers dataset version control and provenance (data lineage) management. It sees every data update (create, write, delete, etc.) as a commit, and it also tracks the data source that generates the data update. So you not only can see the change history of a dataset, but you can also roll back the dataset to a past version and find the data provenance of the change. Figure 2.18 gives a high-level view of how Pachyderm works.

In Pachyderm, data is version-controlled with a Git style. Each dataset is a repository (repo) in Pachyderm, which is the highest-level data object. A repo contains commits, files, and branches. Pachyderm only keeps metadata (such as audit history and branch) internally and stores the actual files in cloud object storage.

The Pachyderm pipeline performs various data transformations. The pipelines execute a user-defined piece of code—for example, a docker container—to perform

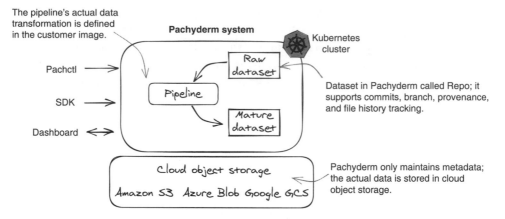

Figure 2.18   The Pachyderm platform runs with two kinds of objects—a pipeline and versioned data. The pipeline is the computational component, and the data is the version-control primitive. A data change in the "raw dataset" can trigger a pipeline job to process the new data and save the result to the "mature dataset."

an operation and process the data. Each of these executions is called a job. Listing 2.15 shows a simple pipeline definition. This "edges" pipeline watches an "images" dataset. When there is a new image added to the images dataset, the pipeline will launch a job to run the "pachyderm/opencv" docker image to parse the image and save its edge picture into the edges dataset.

Listing 2.15   A Pachyderm pipeline definition

```
{
  "pipeline": {                      A Pachyderm
    "name": "edges"           <──┘   pipeline
  },
  "description": "A pipeline that performs image \
     edge detection by using the OpenCV library.",
  "transform": {
    "cmd": [ "python3", "/edges.py" ],
    "image": "pachyderm/opencv"
  },
  "input": {
    "pfs": {                         A Pachyderm
      "repo": "images",       <──┘   dataset
      "glob": "/*"
    }
  }
}
```

VERSION AND DATA PROVENANCE

In Pachyderm, any changes applied to both the dataset and pipeline are versioned automatically, and you can use the Pachyderm command tool `pachctl` to connect to the Pachyderm workspace to check file history and even roll back those changes. See the following example for using the `pachctl` command to check the edges dataset's change history and the change provenance. First, we run the `pachctl list` command to list all the commits in the edges dataset. In our example, there are three changes (commits) applied to the edges dataset:

```
$ pachctl list commit edges #A
REPO   BRANCH COMMIT                             FINISHED
edges master 0547b62a0b6643adb370e80dc5edde9f 3 minutes ago
edges master eb58294a976347abaf06e35fe3b0da5b 3 minutes ago
edges master f06bc52089714f7aa5421f8877f93b9c 7 minutes ago
```

To get the provenance of a data change, we can use pachctl inspect command to check on the commit. For example, we can use the following command to check the data origin of commit.

```
"eb58294a976347abaf06e35fe3b0da5b".
$ pachctl inspect commit edges@eb58294a976347abaf06e35fe3b0da5b \
        --full-timestamps
```

From the following response, we can see the commit eb58294a976347abaf06e35fe3b0da5b of the edges dataset is computed from the images dataset's 66f4ff89a017412090dc4a542d9b1142 commit:

```
Commit: edges@eb58294a976347abaf06e35fe3b0da5b
Original Branch: master
Parent: f06bc52089714f7aa5421f8877f93b9c
Started: 2021-07-19T05:04:23.652132677Z
Finished: 2021-07-19T05:04:26.867797209Z
Size: 59.38KiB
Provenance:  __spec__@91da2f82607b4c40911d48be99fd3031 (edges)
images@66f4ff89a017412090dc4a542d9b1142 (master)
```
Data provenance

The data provenance feature is great for reproducibility and troubleshooting datasets, as you can always find the exact data that was used in the past, along with the data process code that created it.

EXAMPLE: USING PACHYDERM FOR LABELING AND TRAINING AN IMAGE DATASET

Having seen how Pachyderm works, let's see a design proposal for using Pachyderm to build an automated object detection training pipeline. For object detection model training, we first need to prepare the training dataset by labeling the target object with a bounding box on each image and then send the dataset—the bounding box label file and images—to the training code to start the model training. Figure 2.19 shows the process of using Pachyderm to automate this workflow.

In this design, we use two pipelines, the labeling pipeline and the training pipeline, and two datasets to build this training workflow. In step 1, we upload image files to the "raw image dataset." In step 2, we kick off the labeling pipeline to launch a labeling application that opens up a UI for the user to label objects by drawing bounding

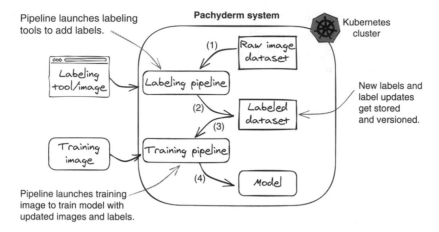

Figure 2.19   Automated object detection model training in Pachyderm. The training process starts automatically when new images are labeled.

boxes on the images; these images are read from the raw image dataset. Once the user finishes the labeling work, the image and the generated label data will be saved to the "labeled dataset." In step 3, we add new training data to the labeled dataset, which will trigger the training pipeline to launch the training container and start the model training. In step 4, we save the model file.

Besides the automation, data including the raw image dataset, the labeled dataset, and the model files are all versioned by Pachyderm automatically. Also, by leveraging the data provenance feature, we can tell with any given model file which version of the labeled dataset is used in its training and from which version of the raw image dataset this training data is made.

WHEN TO USE PACHYDERM

Pachyderm is a lightweight approach to help you build data engineering pipelines easily and offers data versioning support in Git style. It is data scientist–centric and easy to use. Pachyderm is Kubernetes based and uses cloud object storage as a data store, so it's cost-effective, simple to set up, and easy to maintain for small teams. We would suggest using Pachyderm, and not using Spark, for any data science teams that own their infrastructure. Pachyderm works really well with unstructured data, like image and audio files.

LIMITATIONS WITH PACHYDERM

What is missing in Pachyderm are schema protection and data analysis efficiency. Pachyderm sees everything as files; it keeps snapshots for each file version but doesn't care about the file content. There is no data type validation on data writing or reading; it completely depends on the pipeline to protect the data consistency.

Lack of schema awareness and protection introduces a lot of risk for any continuous-running deep learning training pipeline because any code changes in the upstream data processing code might break the downstream data processing or training code. Also, without knowing the schema of the data, dataset comparison is hard to implement.

Summary

- The primary goal of dataset management is to continuously receive fresh data from a variety of data sources and deliver datasets to model training while supporting training reproducibility (data version tracking).

- Having a dataset management component can expedite deep learning project development by parallelizing model algorithm development and data engineering development.

- The principles to validate the design of a dataset management service are as follows: supporting dataset reproducibility; employing strongly typed data schema; designing unified API and keeping API behavior consistent across different dataset types and sizes; and guaranteeing data persistence.

- A dataset management system should at least support (training) dataset versioning, which is crucial for model reproducibility and performance troubleshooting.

- A dataset is a logic file group for a deep learning task; it's static from the model training perspective and dynamic from the data collection perspective.

- The sample dataset management service is made of three layers—the data ingestion layer, internal dataset storage layer, and training dataset fetching layer.

- We define two data schemas for each dataset type in the sample dataset management service, one for data ingestion and one for dataset fetching. Each data update is stored as a commit, and each training dataset is stored as a versioned snapshot. Users can employ a version hash string to fetch the related training data at any time (dataset reproducibility).

- The sample dataset management service supports a special dataset type—a `GENERIC` dataset. A `GENERIC` dataset has no schema and no data validation, and users can upload and download data freely, so it's good for prototyping new algorithms. Once the training code and dataset requirements become mature, the dataset format can be promoted to a strongly typed dataset.

- Delta Lake and Petastorm can work together to set up a dataset management service for Spark-based, deep learning projects.

- Pachyderm is a lightweight, Kubernetes-based data platform that offers data versioning support in Git style and allows easy pipeline setup. A pipeline is made by docker containers; it can be used to automate data process workflow and training workflow for a deep learning project.

Model training service

This chapter covers

- Designing principles for building a training service
- Explaining the deep learning training code pattern
- Touring a sample training service
- Using an open source training service, such as Kubeflow
- Deciding when to use a public cloud training service

The task of model training in machine learning is not the exclusive responsibility of researchers and data scientists. Yes, their work on training the algorithms is crucial because they define the model architecture and the training plan. But just like physicists need a software system to control the electron-positron collider to test their particle theories, data scientists need an effective software system to manage the expensive computation resources, such as GPU, CPU, and memory, to execute the training code. This system of managing compute resources and executing training code is known as the *model training service*.

Building a high-quality model depends not only on the training algorithm but also on the compute resources and the system that executes the training. A good training service can make model training much faster and more reliable and can also reduce the average model-building cost. When the dataset or model architecture is massive, using a training service to manage the distributed computation is your only option.

In this chapter, we first examine the training service's value proposition and design principles, and then we meet our sample training service. This sample service not only shows you how to apply the design principles in practice but also teaches you how the training service interacts with arbitrary training code. Next, we introduce several open source training applications that you can use to set up your own training service quickly. We end with a discussion on when to use a public cloud training system.

This chapter focuses on designing and building effective training services *from a software engineer's perspective, not a data scientist's.* So we don't expect you to be familiar with any deep learning theories or frameworks. Section 3.2, on the deep learning algorithm code pattern, is all the preparation you need to understand the training code in this chapter. The training code is not our main focus here; we wrote it only for demonstration purposes, so we have something on which to demonstrate the sample training service.

Model training topics often intimidate engineers. One common misunderstanding is that model training is all about training algorithms and research. By reading this chapter, I hope you will not only learn how to design and build training services but also absorb this message: the success of model training is built on two pillars, algorithms and system engineering. The model training activities in an organization cannot scale without a good training system. So we, as software engineers, have a lot to contribute to this field.

3.1 Model training service: Design overview

In an enterprise environment, there are two roles involved in deep learning model training: data scientists, who develop model training algorithms (in TensorFlow, PyTorch, or other frameworks), and platform engineers, who build and maintain the system that runs the model training code in remote and shared server farms. We call this system the model training service.

A model training service works as a training infrastructure to execute the model training code (algorithm) in a dedicated environment; it handles both training job scheduling and compute resource management. Figure 3.1 shows a high-level workflow in which the model training service runs a model training code to produce a model.

The most common question asked about this component is why we would need to write a service to do model training. For many people, it seems much easier to write a simple bash script to execute the training code (algorithm) locally or remotely, such as with an Amazon Elastic Cloud Computing (Amazon EC2) instance. The rationale behind building a training service, however, goes beyond just launching a training computation. We will discuss it in detail in the next section.

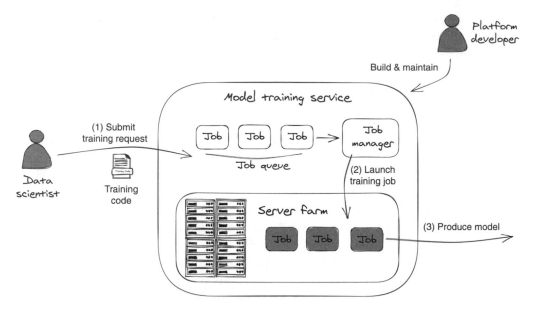

Figure 3.1   A high-level workflow for executing model training via a training service. In step 1, the data scientist submits a training request with training code to the training service, which creates a job in the job queue. In step 2, the model training service allocates compute resources to execute the training job (training code). In step 3, the job produces a model when the training execution completes.

3.1.1   *Why use a service for model training?*

Imagine you lead a data science team, and you need to assign the team's precious compute resources wisely to the team members Alex, Bob, and Kevin. The computing resource needs to be allocated in a way that all team members can complete their model training tasks within a time limit and a budget. Figure 3.2 paints two approaches for allocating the compute resources: dedicated and shared.

The first option, dedicated, is to exclusively assign a powerful workstation to each member of the team. This is the simplest approach but clearly not an economic one because when Alex is not running his training code, his server sits idle and neither Bob nor Kevin can use it. So, in this approach, our budget is underutilized.

Another problem with the dedicated approach is that it cannot scale. When Alex wants to train a large model or a model with a large dataset, he will need multiple machines. And training machines are normally expensive; because of the complexity of the deep learning model architecture, even a decent size neural network requires a GPU with large memory. In this case, we must assign more dedicated servers to Alex, which exacerbates the inefficient resource allocation problem.

The second option, shared compute resources, is to build an elastic server group (the size of the group is adjustable) and share it with all members. This approach is obviously more economical because we use fewer servers to achieve the same result, which maximizes our resource utilization.

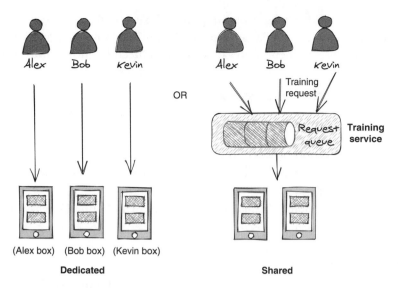

Figure 3.2 Different compute resource allocation strategies: dedicated vs. shared

It's not a hard decision to choose a sharing strategy because it greatly reduces the cost of our training cluster. But the sharing approach requires proper management, such as queuing user requests if there is a sudden burst of training requests, babysitting each training execution and intervening (restarting or aborting) when necessary (training progress is stuck), and scaling up or scaling down our cluster according to the real-time system usage.

SCRIPT VS. SERVICE

Now let's revisit the previous script versus service discussion. In a model training context, *training script* refers to using shell scripts to orchestrate different training activities in a shared server cluster. A training service is a remote process that communicates over the network using HTTP (hypertext transfer protocol) or gRPC (gRPC Remote Procedure Call). As data scientists, Alex and Bob send training requests to the service, and the service orchestrates these requests and manages the training executions on the shared servers.

The script approach may work for a single-person scenario but will prove difficult in a shared-resource environment. Besides executing training code, we need to take care of other important elements, such as setting up the environment, ensuring data compliance, and troubleshooting model performance. For example, environment setup requires that the library dependencies of the training framework and training code are installed properly on the training server before starting model training. Data compliance requires that the sensitive training data (user credit card numbers, payment records) is protected with restricted access. And performance troubleshooting requires that everything used in training, including dataset IDs and versions, training code versions, and hyperparameters, is tracked for model reproduction purposes.

It's hard to imagine addressing these requirements in shell scripts and having the model training executed in a reliable, repeatable, and scalable fashion. This is why most models trained in production nowadays are produced by thoughtfully designed model training services.

BENEFITS OF HAVING A MODEL TRAINING SERVICE

From the previous discussion, we can imagine a model training service's value proposition as follows:

- Saturates computing resources and reduces model training costs
- Expedites model development by building models in a fast (more resources available) and reliable way
- Enforces data compliance by executing training in a confined environment
- Facilitates model performance troubleshooting

3.1.2   *Training service design principles*

Before we look at our sample training service, let's look at the four design principles we can use to evaluate a model training system.

PRINCIPLE 1: PROVIDES A UNIFIED API AND IS AGNOSTIC ABOUT ACTUAL TRAINING CODE

Having only one public API to train models with different kinds of training algorithms makes the training service easy to use. Whether it's object detection training, voice recognition training, or text-intent classification training, we can use sample APIs to trigger the model training execution. Future algorithm performance A/B tests can also be easily implemented by having a single training API.

Training code-agnostic means that the training service defines a clear mechanism or protocol for how it executes a training algorithm (code). It establishes, for instance, how the service passes in variables to the training code/process, how the training code obtains the training dataset, and where the trained model and metrics are uploaded. As long as training code follows this protocol, it doesn't matter how it's implemented, what its model architecture is, or which training libraries it uses.

PRINCIPLE 2: BUILDS A MODEL WITH HIGH PERFORMANCE AND LOW COSTS

A good training service should set cost-effectiveness as a priority. Cost-effectiveness can provide methods to shorten the model training execution time and improve the utilization rate of the compute resources. For instance, a modern training service can reduce time and hardware costs by supporting various distributed training methods, offering good job-schedule management to saturate the server farm, and alerting users when a training process goes off the original plan so it can be terminated early.

PRINCIPLE 3: SUPPORTS MODEL REPRODUCIBILITY

A service should produce the same model if given the same inputs. This is not only important for debugging and performance troubleshooting but also builds trustworthiness in the system. Remember, we will build business logic based on the model prediction result. We might, for instance, employ a classification model to predict a user's credibility and then make loan-approval decisions based on it. We can't trust the entire loan-approval application unless we can repeatedly produce models of the same quality.

PRINCIPLE 4: SUPPORTS ROBUST, ISOLATED, AND ELASTIC COMPUTE MANAGEMENT

Modern deep learning models, such as language understanding models, take a long time to train (more than a week). If the training process is interrupted or gets aborted in the middle for some random OS failures, all the time and computation expenses are wasted. A matured training service should handle the training job robustness (failover, failure recovery), resource isolation, and elastic resource management (ability to adjust the number of resources), so it can make sure its training job execution will complete successfully in a variety of situations.

After discussing all the important abstract concepts, let's tackle how to design and build a model training service. In the next two sections, we will learn a general code pattern for deep learning code and an example of a model training service.

3.2 *Deep learning training code pattern*

Deep learning algorithms can be complicated and often intimidating for engineers. Fortunately, as software engineers designing the platform for deep learning systems, we don't need to master these algorithms for our daily work. We do, however, need to be familiar with the general code pattern of these algorithms. With a high-level understanding of the model training code pattern, we can comfortably treat model training code as a black box. In this section, we'll introduce you to the general pattern.

3.2.1 *Model training workflow*

In a nutshell, most deep learning models are trained through an iterative learning process. The process repeats the same set of computation steps in many iterations, and in every iteration, it tries to update the weights and biases of the neural network to get the algorithm output (prediction result) closer to the training targets in the dataset.

To measure how well a neural network models the given data and uses it to update the weights of the neural network to get better results, a loss function is defined to calculate the deviations of the algorithm output from the actual results. The output of the loss function is named LOSS.

So, you can see the entire iterative training process as a repeating effort to reduce the loss value. Eventually, when the loss value meets our training goal or it can't be reduced any further, then the training completes. The training output is the neural network and its weights, but we generally refer to it simply as a model.

Figure 3.3 illustrates the general model training steps. Because neural networks cannot load the entire dataset at once due to memory limitations, we usually regroup the dataset into small batches (mini-batches) before training begins. In step 1, the mini-batch examples are fed to the neural network, and the network calculates the prediction result for each example. In step 2, we pass in the predicted results and the

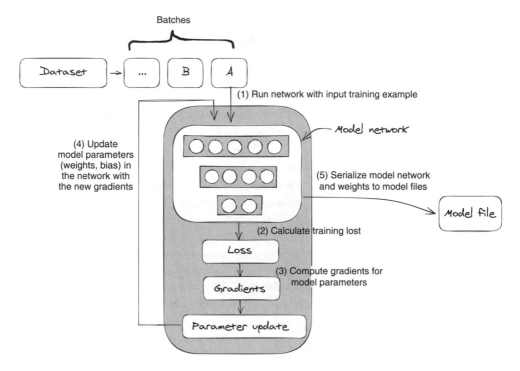

Figure 3.3 General steps of a deep learning model training workflow

expected value (training labels) to the loss function to compute the loss value, which indicates the deviation between the current learning and the target data pattern. In step 3, a process called backpropagation calculates gradients for each of the neural network's parameters with the loss value. These gradients are used to update the model parameters, so the model can get a better prediction accuracy in the next training loop. In step 4, The neural network's parameters (weights and biases) are updated by a selected optimization algorithm, such as stochastic gradient descent and its variants. The gradients (from step 3) and learning rate are the input parameters for the optimization algorithm. The model accuracy is supposed to improve after this model update step. Finally, in step 5, training completes and the network and its parameters are saved as the final model file. The training is completed under either of the two following conditions: finishing the expected training runs or reaching the expected model accuracy.

Although there are different types of model architectures, including recurrent neural networks (RNNs), convolutional neural networks (CNNs), and autoencoders, their model training processes all follow this same pattern; only the model network differs. Also, abstracting model training code to the previously repeated general steps is the foundation for running distributed training. This is because, no matter how the model architecture is different, we can train them in a common training strategy. We will discuss distributed training in detail in the next chapter.

3.2.2 *Dockerize model training code as a black box*

With the previously discussed training pattern in mind, we can view deep learning training code as a black box. No matter what model architecture and training algorithm a training code implements, we can execute it the same way in a training service. To run the training code anywhere in the training cluster and create isolation for each training execution, we can pack the training code and its dependent libraries into a Docker image and run it as a container (figure 3.4).

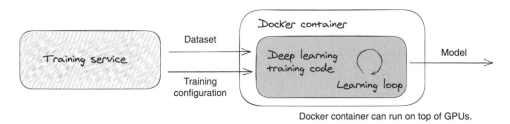

Figure 3.4 A training service launches a Docker container to perform model training instead of running the training code directly as a process.

In figure 3.4, by Dockerizing the training code, the training service can execute a model training by simply launching a Docker container. Because the service is agnostic about what's inside the container, the training service can execute all different code in this standard method. This is much simpler than letting the training service spawn a process to execute model training because the training service needs to set up the various environments and dependent packages for each training code. Another benefit of Dockerization is it decouples the training service and training code, which enables data scientists and platform engineers to focus on model algorithm development and training execution performance, respectively.

You may wonder how a training service communicates with training code if they are agnostic to each other. The key is to define a communication protocol; this protocol delineates which parameters and their data format a training service passes to training code. These parameters include dataset, hyperparameters, model saving location, metrics saving location, and more. We will see a concrete example in the next section.

3.3 *A sample model training service*

As we now know, most deep learning training codes follow the same pattern (figure 3.3), and they can be Dockerized and executed in a unified fashion (figure 3.4). Let's take a closer look at a concrete example.

To demonstrate the concept and design principles we introduced so far, we built a sample service that implements the basic production scenarios of model training—receiving a training request, launching a training execution in a Docker container, and tracking its execution progress. Although the scenarios are quite simple—a few hundred lines of code—they demonstrate the key concepts we discussed in previous sections, including using a unified API, Dockerized training code, and communication protocol between the training service and training container.

> **NOTE**   To show the key pieces clearly, the service is built in a slim fashion. Model training metadata (such as running jobs and waiting jobs) is tracked in memory instead of a database, and the training jobs are executed in the local Docker engine directly. By removing lots of intermediate layers, you will have a straight view of two key areas: training job management and the communication between the training service and training code (Docker container).

3.3.1   *Play with the service*

Before we look at service design and implementation, let's see how we can play with it.

> **NOTE**   Please follow the GitHub instructions to run this lab. We highlight only the major steps and key commands for how to run the sample service to avoid the lengthy pages of code and execution outputs, so the concept can be demonstrated clearly. To run this lab, follow the instructions in the "single trainer demo" doc (training-service/single_trainer_demo.md) in the orca3/MiniAutoML Git repository, which also captures the desired outputs.

First, we start the service with scripts/ts-001-start-server.sh:

```
docker build -t orca3/services:latest -f services.dockerfile .
docker run --name training-service -v
     /var/run/docker.sock:/var/run/docker.sock
     --network orca3 --rm -d -p "${TS_PORT}":51001
     orca3/services:latest training-service.jar
```

After launching the training service Docker container, we can send a gRPC request to kick off a model training execution (scripts/ts-002-start-run.sh <dataset id>). See a sample gRPC request as follows.

Listing 3.1   Calling training service API: Submitting a training job

```
grpcurl -plaintext
 -d "{
   "metadata":
     { "algorithm":"intent-classification",      ⊲─┐ Training algorithm;
       "dataset_id":"1",                             also the name of the
       "name":"test1",                               training Docker image
       "train_data_version_hash":"hashBA==",   ⊲── Version hash of the
       "parameters":                    ⊲─┐           training dataset
         {"LR":"4","EPOCHS":"15",         │ Training
          "BATCH_SIZE":"64",              │ hyperparameters
          "FC_SIZE":"128"}}               
 }"
 "${TS_SERVER}":"${TS_PORT}"
 training.TrainingService/Train
```

Once the job is submitted successfully, we can use the returned job ID from the `train` API to query the progress of the training execution (`scripts/ts-003-check-run.sh <job id>`); see the following example:

```
grpcurl -plaintext \
 -d "{"job_id\": "$job_id"}" \          ◄──┤ Uses the job ID returned
"${TS_SERVER}":"${TS_PORT}"                │ by the train API
training.TrainingService/GetTrainingStatus
```

As you can see, by calling two gRPC APIs, we can kick off deep learning training and track its progress. Now, let's look at the design and implementation of this sample training service.

> **NOTE**   Check out appendix A if you encounter any problems. Scripts in section A.2 automate both dataset preparation and model training. If you want to see a working model training example, read the lab portion of that section.

3.3.2   *Service design overview*

Let's use Alex (a data scientist) and Tang (a developer) to show how the service functions. To use the training service to train a model, Alex needs to write training code (for example, a neural network algorithm) and build the code into a Docker image. This Docker image needs to be published to an artifact repository, so the training service can pull the image and run it as a container. Inside the Docker container, the training code will be executed by a bash script.

   To provide an example, we wrote a sample intent classification training code in PyTorch, built the code into a Docker image, and pushed it to the Docker hub (https://hub.docker.com/u/orca3). We will explain it again in section 3.3.6.

> **NOTE**   In real-world scenarios, the training Docker image creation, publication, and consumption are done automatically. A sample scenario could be as follows: step 1, Alex checks his training code into a Git repository; step 2, a preconfigured program—for example, a Jenkins pipeline—is triggered to build a Docker image from this repo; step 3, the pipeline also publishes the Docker image to a Docker image artifactory, for example, JFrog Artifactory; and step 4, Alex sends a training request, and then the training service pulls the training images from the artifactory and begins model training.

When Alex finishes the training code development, he can start to use the service to run his training code. The entire workflow is as follows: step 1.a, Alex submits a training request to our sample training service. The request defines the training code—a Docker image and tag. When the training service receives a training request, it creates a job in the queue and returns the job ID to Alex for future job tracking; step 1.b, Alex can query the training service to get the training progress in realtime; step 2, the service launches a training job as a Docker container in the local Docker engine to execute the model training; and step 3, the training code in the Docker container uploads training metrics to the metadata store during training and the final model when training completes.

> **NOTE** Model evaluation is the step we did not mention in the aforementioned model training workflow. After the model is trained, Alex (data scientist) will look at the training metrics, reported by the training service, to validate the model's quality. To evaluate the model quality, Alex can check the prediction failure rate, gradients, and loss-value graphs. As model evaluation is usually a data scientist's responsibility, we will not cover it in this book, but we will discuss in chapter 8 how model training metrics are collected and stored.

The entire training workflow is self-serve; Alex can manage the model training entirely by himself. Tang develops the training service and maintains the system, but the system is agnostic about the training code developed by Alex. Tang's focus is not the model's accuracy but the availability and efficiency of the system. See figure 3.5 for the user workflow we just described.

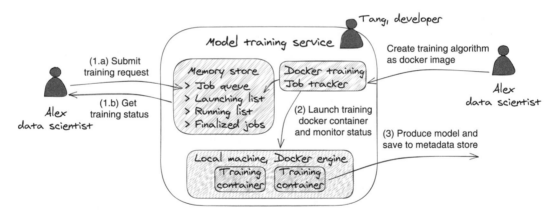

Figure 3.5   A high-level service design and user workflow: user training requests are queued, and the Docker job tracker picks up jobs from the queue and launches Docker containers to run model training.

Having seen the user workflow, let's look at two key components: memory store and Docker job tracker. The memory store uses the following four data structures (maps) to organize requests (jobs): job queue, job launch list, running list, and finalized list. Each of these maps represents jobs in a different running status. We implement the job tracking store in memory just for simplicity; ideally, we should use a database.

The Docker job tracker handles the actual job execution in the Docker engine; it periodically monitors the job queue in the memory store. When there is capacity in the Docker engine, the tracker will launch a Docker container from the job queue and keep monitoring the container execution. In our example, we use the local Docker engine, so the service can run on your local. But it can be easily configured to a remote Docker engine as well.

After launching a training container, based on the execution status, the Docker job tracker moves the job object from the job queue to other job lists, such as the job launching list, running list, and finalizedJobs list. In section 3.4.4, we will discuss this process in detail.

> **NOTE** Consider that a dataset will be split in a training container (at training time). It is valid to split datasets during dataset building or model training, and both processes have pros and cons. But either way, it will not affect the design of the training service significantly. For simplicity, we assume in this sample training service that the algorithm code will split the dataset into train, validate, and test subsets.

3.3.3 Training service API

Having seen the overview, let's dive into the public gRPC APIs (grpc-contract/src/main/proto/training_service.proto) to gain a deeper understanding of the service. There are two APIs in the training service: Train and GetTrainingStatus. The Train API is for submitting training requests, and the GetTrainingStatus API is for fetching the training execution status. See the API definition in the following listing.

Listing 3.2 A model training service gRPC interface

```
service TrainingService {
 rpc Train(TrainRequest) returns (TrainResponse);
 rpc GetTrainingStatus(GetTrainingStatusRequest)
   returns (GetTrainingStatusResponse);
}

message TrainingJobMetadata {
 string algorithm = 1;
 string dataset_id = 2;
 string name = 3;
 string train_data_version_hash = 4;
 map<string, string> parameters = 5;
}
```

Defines the dataset, training algorithm, and extra parameters for the model-building request

```
message GetTrainingStatusResponse {
 TrainingStatus status = 1;
 int32 job_id = 2;
 string message = 3;
 TrainingJobMetadata metadata = 4;
 int32 positionInQueue = 5;
}
```

From the gRPC interface in listing 3.2, to use the Train API, we need to provide the following information as TrainingJobMetadata:

- dataset_id—The dataset ID in the dataset management service
- train_data_version_hash—The hash version of the dataset that is used in training

- name—Training job name
- algorithm—Specify which training algorithm to use to train the dataset. This algorithm string needs to be one of our predefined algorithms. Internally, the training service will find the Docker image associated with this algorithm to execute training.
- parameters—Training hyperparameters that we pass directly to the training container, such as number of epochs, batch size, etc.

Once the Train API receives a training request, the service puts the request to the job queue and returns an ID (job_id) for the caller to reference the job. This job_id can be used with the GetTrainingStatus API to check the training status. Now that we have seen the API definitions, let's look at their implementations in the next two sections.

3.3.4   *Launching a new training job*

When a user calls the Train API, a training request is added to the job queue of the memory store, and then the Docker job tracker handles the actual job execution in another thread. This logic will be explained in the next three listings (3.3–3.5).

RECEIVING TRAINING REQUESTS

First, a new training request will be added to the job-waiting queue and will be assigned a job ID for future reference; see code (training-service/src/main/java/org/orca3/miniAutoML/training/TrainingService.java) as follows.

> **Listing 3.3   Submitting training request implementation**

```
public void train(                        ◁─┐  Implements train API
  TrainRequest request,
  StreamObserver<TrainResponse> responseObserver) {

    int jobId = store.offer(request);      ◁─┐  Enqueues the
    responseObserver.onNext(TrainResponse      training request
      .newBuilder().setJobId(jobId).build());  ◁─┐  Returns
    responseObserver.onCompleted();             the job ID
}

public class MemoryStore {
    // jobs are waiting to pick up
    public SortedMap<Integer, TrainingJobMetadata>
      jobQueue = new TreeMap<>();
    // jobs' docker container is in launching state
    public Map<Integer, ExecutedTrainingJob>
      launchingList = new HashMap<>();          ┐  Four different
    // jobs' docker container is in running state   job lists to track
    public Map<Integer, ExecutedTrainingJob>      job status
      runningList = new HashMap<>();
    // jobs' docker container is completed
    public Map<Integer, ExecutedTrainingJob>
      finalizedJobs = new HashMap<>();
    // .. .. ..
```

```
public int offer(TrainRequest request) {
    int jobId = jobIdSeed.incrementAndGet();        ⟵——|  Generates job ID
    jobQueue.put(jobId, request.getMetadata());     ⟵—   Starts the job at
    return jobId;                                          the waiting queue
}
}
```

LAUNCHING A TRAINING JOB (CONTAINER)

Once the job is in the waiting queue, the Docker job tracker will process it when there are enough system resources. Figure 3.6 shows the entire process. The Docker job tracker monitors the job-waiting queue and picks up the first available job when there is enough capacity in the local Docker engine (step 1 in figure 3.6). Then the Docker job tracker executes the model training the job by launching a Docker container (step 2). After the container launches successfully, the tracker moves the job object from the job queue to the launching list queue (step 3). The code implementation for figure 3.6 (`training-service/src/main/java/org/orca3/miniAutoML/training/tracker/DockerTracker.java`) is highlighted in listing 3.4.

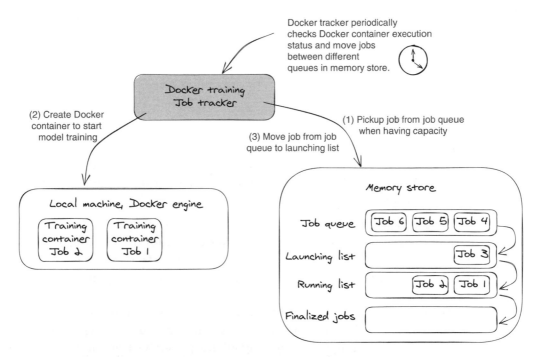

Figure 3.6   The training job launching workflow: the Docker job tracker launches training containers from the job queue when it has the capacity.

Listing 3.4   Launching a training container with DockerTracker

```
public boolean hasCapacity() {        ⟵——|  Checks the system's capacity
    return store.launchingList.size()
```

```
          + store.runningList.size() == 0;
}

public String launch(                              ◁──── Launches the training
    int jobId, TrainingJobMetadata metadata,             Docker container
    VersionedSnapshot versionedSnapshot) {

    Map<String, String> envs = new HashMap<>();
    .. .. ..
    envs.put("TRAINING_DATA_PATH",                       Converts training
    versionedSnapshot.getRoot());                        parameters into
    envs.putAll(metadata.getParametersMap());            environment variables
    List<String> envStrings = envs.entrySet()
            .stream()
            .map(kvp -> String.format("%s=%s",
              kvp.getKey(), kvp.getValue()))
            .collect(Collectors.toList());          Builds the Docker
                                                    launch command
    String containerId = dockerClient          ◁────┘
      .createContainerCmd(metadata.getAlgorithm())    ◁──┐  Sets the Docker image
                                                          name; the value is from the
            .. .. ..                                      algorithm name parameter.
            .withCmd("server", "/data")
            .withEnv(envStrings)
            .withHostConfig(HostConfig.newHostConfig()
              .withNetworkMode(config.network))
            .exec().getId();

    dockerClient.startContainerCmd(containerId).exec();    ◁──┐ Runs the Docker
    jobIdTracker.put(jobId, containerId);                       container
    return containerId;
}
```

Passes the training parameter to the Docker container as environment variables (annotation pointing to `.withEnv(envStrings)`)

It is important to note that the training parameters defined in the train API request are passed to the training container (training code) as environment variables by the launch function in code listing 3.4.

TRACKING TRAINING PROGRESS

During the last step, the Docker job tracker continues tracking each job by monitoring its container's execution status. When it detects a container status change, the job tracker moves the container's job object to the corresponding job list in the memory store.

The job tracker will query the Docker runtime to fetch the container's status. For example, if a job's Docker container starts running, the job tracker will detect the change and put the job in the "running job list"; if a job's Docker container finishes, the job is then moved to the "finalized jobs list" by the job tracker. The job tracker will stop checking the job status once it's placed on the "finalized jobs list," which means the training is completed. Figure 3.7 depicts this job tracking workflow. Code listing 3.5 highlights the implementation of this job tracking process.

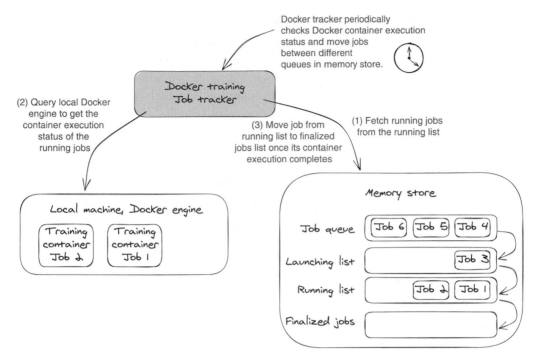

Figure 3.7   The Docker job tracker monitors the Docker container execution status and updates the job queues.

Listing 3.5   DockerTracker monitoring Docker and updating the job status

```
public void updateContainerStatus() {
  Set<Integer> launchingJobs = store.launchingList.keySet();
  Set<Integer> runningJobs = store.runningList.keySet();

  for (Integer jobId : launchingJobs) {          ⟵   Checks container
                                                     status for all jobs in
                                                     the launching job list

    String containerId = jobIdTracker.get(jobId);
    InspectContainerResponse.ContainerState state =      Queries the
        dockerClient.inspectContainerCmd(                container's
          containerId).exec().getState();                execution status
    String containerStatus = state.getStatus();

    // move the launching job to the running
    // queue if the container starts to run.
      .. .. ..
  }
                                                 Checks the container status for
  for (Integer jobId : runningJobs) {   ⟵       all jobs in the running job list
    // move the running job to the finalized
    // queue if it completes (success or fail).
      .. .. ..
  }
}
```

3.3.5   *Updating and fetching job status*

Now that you have seen how a training request is executed in the training service, let's move on to the last stop of the code tour: obtaining the training execution status. After launching a training job, we can query the `GetTrainingStatus` API to get the training status. As a reminder, we are reposting figure 3.5, presented here as figure 3.8, which shows the service's high-level design, as follows.

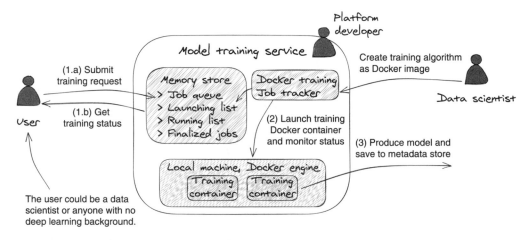

Figure 3.8   A high-level service design and user workflow

Based on figure 3.8, we can see that obtaining the training status needs only one step, 1.b. Also, the latest status of a training job can be determined by finding which job list (in the memory store) contains the `jobId`. See the following code for querying the status of a training job/request (`training-service/src/main/java/org/orca3/mini-AutoML/training/TrainingService.java`).

Listing 3.6   Training status implementation

```
public void getTrainingStatus(GetTrainingStatusRequest request) {
  int jobId = request.getJobId();
  .. .. ..
  if (store.finalizedJobs.containsKey(jobId)) {          ◁── Searches the job in
    job = store.finalizedJobs.get(jobId);                     the finalized job list
    status = job.isSuccess() ? TrainingStatus.succeed
        : TrainingStatus.failure;
                                                         Searches the job in
                                                         the launching job list
  } else if (store.launchingList.containsKey(jobId)) {   ◁──
    job = store.launchingList.get(jobId);
    status = TrainingStatus.launch;
                                                    Searches the job in
                                                    the running job list
  } else if (store.runningList.containsKey(jobId)) {  ◁──
    job = store.runningList.get(jobId);          The job is still in the
    status = TrainingStatus.running;             waiting job queue.
  } else {                              ◁──
```

```
        TrainingJobMetadata metadata = store.jobQueue.get(jobId);
        status = TrainingStatus.waiting;
           .. .. ..
    }
    .. .. ..
}
```

Because the Docker job tracker moves the job to the corresponding job list in real time, we can rely on using the job queue type to determine a training job status.

3.3.6 *The intent classification model training code*

Until now, we have been working with the training service code. Now let's look at the last piece, the model training code. Please do not be intimidated by the deep learning algorithms here. The purpose of this code example is to show you a concrete example of how a training service interacts with the model training code. Figure 3.9 draws the workflow of the sample intent classification training code.

Figure 3.9   The intent classification training code workflow first reads all the input parameters from environment variables and then downloads the dataset, processes it, and starts the training loop. At the end, it uploads the output model file.

Our sample training code trains a three-layer neural network to perform intent classification. It first obtains all the input parameters from environment variables that are passed by our training service (see section 3.3.4). The input parameters include hyperparameters (epoch number, learning rate, etc.), dataset download settings (MinIO server address, dataset ID, version hash), and model upload settings. Next, the training code downloads and parses the dataset and starts the iterative learning process. In the last step, the code uploads the generated model and training metrics to the metadata store. The following code listing highlights the major steps mentioned previously (train-service/text-classification/train.py and train-service/text-classification/Dockerfile).

Listing 3.7   Intent classification model training code and Docker file

```
# 1. read all the input parameters from
# environment variables, these environment
# variables are set by training service - docker job tracker.
```

```
EPOCHS = int_or_default(os.getenv('EPOCHS'), 20)
.. .. ..
TRAINING_DATA_PATH = os.getenv('TRAINING_DATA_PATH')

# 2. download training data from dataset management
client.fget_object(TRAINING_DATA_BUCKET,
  TRAINING_DATA_PATH + "/examples.csv", "examples.csv")
client.fget_object(TRAINING_DATA_BUCKET,
  TRAINING_DATA_PATH + "/labels.csv", "labels.csv")

# 3. prepare dataset
.. .. ..
train_dataloader = DataLoader(split_train_, batch_size=BATCH_SIZE,
                              shuffle=True, collate_fn=collate_batch)
valid_dataloader = DataLoader(split_valid_, batch_size=BATCH_SIZE,
                              shuffle=True, collate_fn=collate_batch)
test_dataloader = DataLoader(split_test_, batch_size=BATCH_SIZE,
                              shuffle=True, collate_fn=collate_batch)

# 4. start model training
for epoch in range(1, EPOCHS + 1):
   epoch_start_time = time.time()
   train(train_dataloader)
   .. .. ..

print('Checking the results of test dataset.')
accu_test = evaluate(test_dataloader)
print('test accuracy {:8.3f}'.format(accu_test))

# 5. save model and upload to metadata store.
.. .. ..
client.fput_object(config.MODEL_BUCKET,
  config.MODEL_OBJECT_NAME, model_local_path)
artifact = orca3_utils.create_artifact(config.MODEL_BUCKET,
  config.MODEL_OBJECT_NAME)
.. .. ..
```

> **NOTE** We hope our sample training code demonstrates how a deep learning training code follows a common pattern. With Dockerization and a clear protocol to pass in parameters, a training service can execute varieties of training code, regardless of the training framework or model architecture.

3.3.7   *Training job management*

In section 3.1.2, we mentioned that a good training service should address computation isolation and provide on-demand computing resources (principle 4). This isolation has two meanings: training process execution isolation and resource consumption isolation. Because we Dockerize the training process, the process execution isolation is guaranteed by the Docker engine. But we still have to handle the resource consumption isolation ourselves.

Imagine three users (A, B, and C) from different teams submitting training requests to our training service. If user A submits 100 training requests and then users

B and C both submit one request each, user B's and C's requests will sit in the waiting job queue for a while until all of user A's training requests complete. This is what happens when we treat the training cluster as a playing field for everyone: one heavy-use case will dominate the job scheduling and resource consumption.

To solve this resource competition problem, we need to set boundaries within the training cluster for different teams and users. We could create machine pools inside the training cluster to create resource consumption isolation. Each team or user can be assigned to a dedicated machine pool, each pool has its own GPU and machines, and the pool size depends on the project needs and training usage. Also, each machine pool can have a dedicated job queue, so the heavy users won't affect other users. Figure 3.9 shows this approach at work.

> **NOTE** The resource segregation approach, like the server pools method we just mentioned, may not be efficient on the resource utilization front. For example, server pool A may be extremely busy, whereas server pool B may be idle. It is possible to define the size of each server pool in a range instead of a fixed number, such as a minimum of 5 servers and a maximum of 10 to improve resource utilization. Additional logic that either shuffles servers between pools or provisions new servers can then be applied.

The ideal approach for implementing figure 3.10 is to use Kubernetes. Kubernetes allows you to create multiple virtual clusters backed by the same physical cluster, which is called a namespace. Kubernetes namespace is a lightweight machine pool that consumes very few system resources.

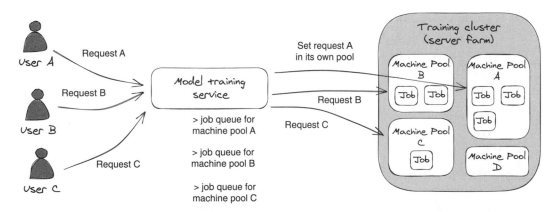

Figure 3.10 Creating machine pools within the training cluster to set up the resource consumption boundary for different users.

If you are using Kubernetes to manage your service environment and your computing cluster, setting up such isolation is fairly easy. First, you create a namespace with a resource quota, such as the number of CPUs, memory size, and GPU counts; then, define the user and its namespace mapping in the training service.

Now, when a user submits a training request, the training service first finds the right namespace for the user by checking the user information from the request and then calls the Kubernetes API to place the training executable in the namespace. Because Kubernetes tracks the system usage in real time, it knows whether a namespace has enough capacity, and it will reject the job launch request if the namespace is fully loaded.

As you can see, by using Kubernetes to manage training clusters, we can offload the resource capacity tracking and resource isolation management from the training service. This is one of the reasons why Kubernetes is a good choice for building training cluster management for deep learning.

3.3.8 *Troubleshooting metrics*

What we didn't demo in this sample service is metrics. In general, metrics are measures of quantitative assessment commonly used for assessing, comparing, and tracking performance or production. For deep learning training specifically, we usually define two types of metrics: model training execution metrics and model performance metrics.

Model training execution metrics include resource saturation rate, training jobs' execution availability, average training job execution time, and job failure rate. We check these metrics to make sure the training service is healthy and functioning and that our user's daily activities are healthy. As an example, we expect service availability to exceed 99.99% and training job failure rate to be less than 0.1%.

Model performance metrics measure the quality of the model learning. It includes a loss value and evaluation score for each training iteration (epoch) and the final model evaluation results, such as accuracy, precision, and F1 score.

For model performance–related metrics, we need to store the metrics in a more organized way, so we can use a unified method to search for information and compare performance between different training runs easily. We will discuss this in more detail in chapter 8.

3.3.9 *Supporting new algorithm or new version*

Now let's discuss how to onboard more training code to our sample training service. In the current implementation, we define a naive mapping between the user training request and the training code, using the `algorithm` variable in the request to find the training image. The underlying rule is the `algorithm` variable must equal a Docker image name; otherwise, the training service can't find the right image to run model training.

Use our intent classification training as an example. First, we need to Dockerize our intent training Python code to a Docker image and name it "intent-classification." Then, when the user sends a training request with the parameter `algorithm='intent-classification'`, the Docker job tracker will use the algorithm name (intent-classification) to search local Docker repository for the "intent-classification" training image and run the image as a training container.

This approach is definitely oversimplified, but it exemplifies how we work with data scientists to define a formal contract for mapping user training requests to the actual training code. In practice, the training service should provide a set of APIs to allow data scientists to register training code in a self-serve manner.

One possible approach is to define an algorithm name and training code mapping in a database and add some API to manage this mapping. The proposed APIs can be

- `createAlgorithmMapping(string algorithmName, string image, string version)`
- `updateAlgorithmVersion(string algorithmName, string image, string version)`

If data scientists want to add a new algorithm type, they would call the `create-AlgorithmMapping` API to register the new training image with a new algorithm name into the training service. Our users just need to use this new algorithm name in the training request to kick off model training with this new algorithm.

If data scientists want to release a newer version of an existing algorithm, they can call the `updateAlgorithmVersion` API to update the mapping. Our users will still have the same algorithm name (such as intent-classification) to send requests, but they won't be aware that the training code has upgraded to a different version behind the scenes. Also, it is worth pointing out that the service's public API won't be affected by adding new training algorithms; only a new parameter value is used.

3.4 *Kubeflow training operators: An open source approach*

After seeing our sample training service, let's look at an open source training service. In this section, we will discuss a set of open source training operators from the Kubeflow project. These training operators work out of the box and can be set up independently in any Kubernetes cluster.

Kubeflow is a mature, open source machine learning system built for production use cases. We briefly discuss it in appendix B.4 along with Amazon SageMaker and Google Vertex AI. We recommend Kubeflow training operators because they are well designed and offer high-quality training that's scalable, distributable, and robust. We will first talk about the high-level system design and then discuss how to integrate these training operators into your own deep learning system.

> **What Is Kubeflow?**
> Kubeflow is an open source machine learning platform (originated from Google) for developing and deploying production-level machine learning models. You can view Kubeflow as the open source version of Amazon SageMaker, but it runs natively on Kubernetes, so it's cloud agnostic. Kubeflow integrates a full list of machine learning features into one system—from notebooks and pipelines to training and serving.

(continued)

I highly recommend that you pay attention to Kubeflow projects, even if you have no interest in using it. Kubeflow is a well-designed and fairly advanced deep learning platform; its feature list covers the entire machine learning life cycle. By reviewing its use cases, design, and code, you will gain a deep understanding of modern deep learning platforms.

Also, because Kubeflow is built natively on top of Kubernetes, you can easily set up the whole system on your local or production environment. If you are not interested in borrowing the entire system, you can also port some of its components—such as training operators or hyperparameter optimization services—which can work by themselves in any Kubernetes environment out of the box.

3.4.1 *Kubeflow training operators*

Kubeflow offers a set of training operators, such as TensorFlow operator, PyTorch operator, MXNet operator, and MPI operator. These operators cover all the major training frameworks. Each operator has the knowledge to launch and monitor the training code (container) written in a specific type of training framework.

If you plan to run model training in Kubernetes cluster and want to set up your own training service to reduce the operation cost, Kubeflow training operators are the perfect choice. Here are the three reasons:

- *Easy install and low maintenance*—Kubeflow operators work out of the box; you can make them work in your cluster by issuing a few lines of Kubernetes commands.
- *Compatible with most training algorithms and frameworks*—As long as you containerize your training code, you can use Kubeflow operators to execute it.
- *Easy integration to existing systems*—Because Kubeflow training operators follow the Kubernetes operator design pattern, you can use Kubernetes's declarative HTTP API to submit the training job request and check the job running status and result. You can also use RESTful queries to interact with these operators.

3.4.2 *Kubernetes operator/controller pattern*

Kubeflow training operators follow the Kubernetes operator (controller) design pattern. If we understand this pattern, running Kubeflow training operators and reading their source code is straightforward. Figure 3.11 shows the controller pattern design graph.

Everything in Kubernetes is built around resource objects and controllers. Kubernetes' resource objects such as Pods, Namespaces, and ConfigMaps are conceptual objects that persist entities (data structures) that represent the state (desired and current) of your cluster. A controller is a control loop that makes changes to the actual

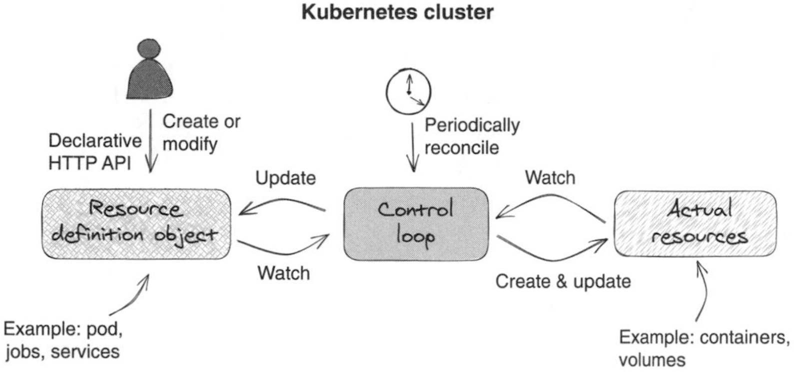

Kubernetes cluster

Figure 3.11 The Kubernetes operator/controller pattern runs an infinite control loop that watches the actual state (on the right) and desired state (on the left) of certain Kubernetes resources and tries to move the actual state to the desired one.

system resources to bring your cluster from the current state closer to the desired one, which is defined in resource objects.

> **NOTE** Kubernetes pods are the smallest deployable units of computing that you can create and manage in Kubernetes. Pods can be viewed as "logical hosts" that run one or more Docker containers. A detailed explanation of the Kubernetes concepts, such as Namespaces and ConfigMaps, can be found at the official website: https://kubernetes.io/docs/concepts/.

For example, when a user applies the Kubernetes command to create a pod, it will create a pod resource object (a data structure) in the cluster, which contains the desired states: two Docker containers and one disk volume. When the controller detects this new resource object, it will provision the actual resource in the cluster and run the two Docker containers and attach the disk. Next, it will update the pod resource object with the latest actual status. Users can query the Kubernetes API to get the updated information from this pod resource object. When the user deletes this pod resource object, the controller will remove the actual Docker containers because the desired state is changed to zero.

To extend Kubernetes easily, Kubernetes allows users to define customer resource definition (CRD) objects and register customized controllers to handle these CRD objects, which are called operators. If you want to learn more about controllers/operators, you can read the "Kubernetes/sample-controller" GitHub repository, which implements a simple controller for watching a CRD object. This sample controller code can help you to understand operator/controller patterns, and this understanding is very useful for reading the Kubeflow training operator source code.

> **NOTE** The terms *controller* and *operator* are used interchangeably in this section.

3.4.3   *Kubeflow training operator design*

Kubeflow training operators (TensorFlow operator, PyTorch operator, MPI operator) follow the Kubernetes operator design. Each training operator watches its own kind of customer resource definition object—such as `TFJob`, `PyTorchJob`, and `MPIJob`—and creates the actual Kubernetes resources to run the training.

For example, the TensorFlow operator processes any `TFJob` CRD object generated in the cluster and creates the actual services/pods based on the `TFJob` spec. It synchronizes `TFJob` objects' resource requests with the actual Kubernetes resources, such as services and pods, and continuously strives to make the observed state match the desired state. See a visual workflow in figure 3.12.

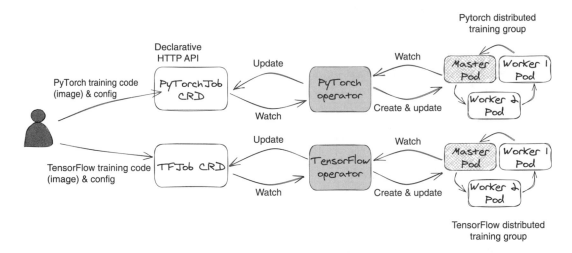

Figure 3.12   The Kubeflow training operator workflow. A user first creates a `TFJob` CRD object that defines a training request, and then the TensorFlow operator detects this object and creates actual pods to execute the TensorFlow training image. The TensorFlow operator also monitors the pod status and updates its status to the `TFJob` CRD object. The same workflow applies to the PyTorch operator.

Each operator can run training pods for its own type of training framework. For example, the TensorFlow operator knows how to set up a distributed training pod group for training code written in TensorFlow. The operator reads the user request from the CRD definition, creates training pods, and passes the correct environment variables and command-line arguments to each training pod/container. You can check out the `reconcileJobs` and `reconcilePods` functions in each operator's code for further details.

Each Kubeflow operator also handles job queue management. Because Kubeflow operators follow the Kubernetes operator pattern and create Kubernetes resources at the pod level, the training pod failover is handled nicely. For example, when a pod fails unexpectedly, the current pod number becomes one less than the desired pod number. In this situation, the `reconcilePods` logic in the operator will create a new pod in the cluster to make sure the actual pod number is equal to the desired number defined in the CRD object, thus addressing failover.

> **NOTE** At the time of writing this book, the TensorFlow operator was becoming the all-in-one Kubeflow operator. It aims to simplify running distributed or nondistributed TensorFlow/PyTorch/MXNet/XGBoost jobs on Kubernetes. No matter how it ends up, it will be built on top of the design we mention here but simply more convenient to use.

3.4.4 How to use Kubeflow training operators

In this section, we will use the PyTorch operator as an example for training a PyTorch model in four steps. Because all Kubeflow training operators follow the same usage pattern, these steps are applicable to other operators as well.

First, install the stand-alone PyTorch operator and `PyTorchJob` CRD in your Kubernetes cluster. You can find detailed instructions in the developer guide from the PyTorch operator Git repository. After installation, you can find a training operator pod running and a CRD definition created in your Kubernetes cluster. See the CRD query command as follows:

```
$ kubectl get crd          ⟵┘  Lists all CRD definitions

NAME                                CREATED AT
...
pytorchjobs.kubeflow.org            2021-09-15T18:33:58Z
...
```
PyTorchJob CRD is created in Kubernetes.

> **NOTE** The training operator installation can be confusing because the README suggests that you install the entire Kubeflow to run these operators, but this isn't necessary. Each training operator can be installed individually, which is how we recommend handling it. Please check the development guide or the setup script at https://github.com/kubeflow/pytorch-operator/blob/master/scripts/setup-pytorch-operator.sh.

Next, update your training container to read the parameter input from environment variables and command-line arguments. You can pass in these parameters later in the CRD object.

Third, create a `PyTorchJob` CRD object to define our training request. You can create this CRD object by first writing a YAML file (e.g., pytorchCRD.yaml) and then running `kubectl create -f pytorchCRD.yaml` in your Kubernetes cluster. The PT-operator will detect this newly created CRD object, put it into the controller's job queue, and try to allocate resources (Kubernetes pods) to run the training. Listing 3.8 shows a sample `PyTorchJob` CRD.

Listing 3.8   A sample PyTorch CRD object

```
kind: PyTorchJob          ◁─┐  The name of the CRD
metadata:
  name: pytorch-demo      ◁─   Trains job name
spec:
  pytorchReplicaSpecs:    ◁─┐  Defines training
    Master:                     group specs
      replicas: 1
      restartPolicy: OnFailure
      containers:
        .. .. ..
    Worker:                    ┌─ Numbers of
      replicas: 1         ◁─   │  worker pods
      .. .. ..
        spec:                  ┌─ Defines training
          containers:     ◁─── │  container
            - name: pytorch    │  configuration
              .. .. ..
              env:
                - name: credentials
                  value: "/etc/secrets/user-gcp-sa.json"
              command:
                - "python3"
                - "-m"
                - "/opt/pytorch-mnist/mnist.py"
                - "--epochs=20"
                - "--batch_size=32"
```

Numbers of master pods → replicas: 1

Numbers of worker pods → replicas: 1

Defines environment variable for each training pod → env:

Defines the command-line parameters → command:

The last step is monitoring. You can obtain the training status by using the `kubectl get -o yaml pytorchjobs` command, which will list the details of all the `pytorchjobs` types of CRD objects. Because the controller of the PyTorch operator will continue updating the latest training information back to the CRD object, we can read the current status from it. For example, the following command will make the `PyTorchJob` type CRD object with the name equal to `pytorch-demo`:

```
kubectl get -o yaml pytorchjobs pytorch-demo -n kubeflow
```

> **NOTE**   In the previous sample, we used the Kubernetes command `kubectl` to interact with the PyTorch operator. But we could also send RESTful requests to the cluster's Kubernetes API to create a training job CRD object and query its status. The newly created CRD object will then trigger training actions in the controller. This means Kubeflow training operators can be easily integrated into other systems.

3.4.5   *How to integrate these operators into an existing system*

From section 3.4.3, we see that the operators' CRD objects act as the gateway APIs to trigger training operations and the source of truth of the training status. Therefore, we can integrate these training operators into any system by building a web service as a wrapper on top of the operator CRD objects. This wrapper service has two responsibilities: first, it converts training requests in your system to the CRUD (create, read, update, and delete) operation on the CRD (training job) objects; second, it queries training status by reading the CRD objects. See the main workflow in figure 3.13.

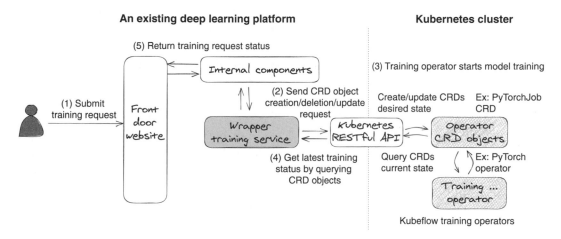

Figure 3.13   Integrating Kubeflow training operators into an existing deep learning system as training backend. The wrapper service can transform training requests to CRD objects and fetch the training status from the CRD objects.

In figure 3.13, the front part of the existing system is untouched—for example, the front door website. At the computation backend, we changed the internal components and talked to the wrapper training service to execute model training. The wrapper service does three things: first, it manages the job queue; second, it translates the training request from the existing format to the Kubeflow training operators' CRD objects; and third, it fetches the training status from CRD objects. With this approach, by adding the wrapper service, we can adopt Kubeflow training operators easily as the training backend for any existing deep learning platform/systems.

Building a production-quality training system from scratch requires a lot of effort. You need to know not only every nuance of different training frameworks but also how to handle the reliability and scalability challenges on the engineering side. Therefore, we highly recommend adopting Kubeflow training operators if you decide to run model training in Kubernetes. It's an out-of-the-box solution and can be ported to an existing system easily.

3.5   When to use the public cloud

Major public cloud vendors like Amazon, Google, and Microsoft provide their deep learning platforms such as Amazon SageMaker, Google Vertex AI, and Azure Machine Learning Studio out of the box. All these systems claim to offer fully managed services that support the entire machine learning workflow to train and deploy machine learning models quickly. In fact, they cover not only model training but also data processing and storage, versioning, troubleshooting, operating, and more.

In this section, we're not going to talk about which cloud solution is the best; instead, we want to share our thoughts on when to use them. When we propose building services inside our company, such as training services or hyperparameter tuning services, we often hear questions like "Can we use SageMaker? I heard they have a feature . . ." or "Can you build a wrapper on top of Google Vertex AI? I heard. . . ." These questions are sometimes valid and sometimes not. What you can afford really depends on the stage of your business.

3.5.1 *When to use a public cloud solution*

If you run a startup or want to validate your business idea quickly, using the public cloud AI platform is a good option. It handles all the underlying infrastructure management and provides a standard workflow for you to follow. As long as the predefined methods work for you, you can focus on developing your business logic, collecting data, and implementing model algorithms. The real benefit is the time saved on building your own infrastructure, so you can "fail early and learn fast."

Another reason to use the public cloud AI platforms is that you have only a few deep learning scenarios, and they fit the public cloud's standard-use case well. In this event, it isn't worth the resources to build a complicated deep learning system for just a few applications.

3.5.2 *When to build your own training service*

Now, let's talk about situations when you need to build your own training approach. If you have any of the following five requirements for your system, building your own training service is the way to go.

BEING CLOUD AGNOSTIC

You can't use Amazon SageMaker or Google Vertex AI platforms if you want your application to be cloud agnostic because these systems are cloud specific. Being cloud agnostic is important when your service stores customer data because some potential customers have specific requirements on which cloud they *don't* want to put their data in. You want your application to have the capability of running on various cloud infrastructures seamlessly.

The common method of building a cloud-agnostic system on public clouds is to *only* use the foundation services, such as virtual machines (VM) and storage, and build your application logic on top of it. Using model training as an example, when using Amazon Web Services, we first set up a Kubernetes cluster (Amazon Elastic Kubernetes Service (Amazon EKS)) by using Amazon EC2 service to manage the computing resources and then build our own training service with the Kubernetes interfaces to launch training jobs. In this way, when we need to migrate to Google Cloud (GCP), we can simply apply our training service to the GCP Kubernetes cluster (Google Kubernetes Engine) instead of Amazon EKS, and most of the service remains unchanged.

REDUCING INFRASTRUCTURE COST

Using the cloud provider's AI platform will charge you premium dollars compared to operating on your own services. You may not care so much about your bill at the prototyping phase, but after the product is released, you certainly should.

Using Amazon SageMaker as an example, at the time this book was written (2022), SageMaker charged $0.461 per hour for an m5.2xlarge type (eight virtual CPUs, 32 GB memory) machine. If you launch an Amazon EC2 instance (VM) on this hardware spec directly, it charges $0.384 per hour. By building your own training service and operating on the Amazon EC2 instances directly, you save nearly 20% on average for model building. If a company has multiple teams doing model training on a daily basis, a self-built training system will give you an edge over your competitors.

CUSTOMIZATION

Although the cloud AI platform gives you a lot of options for the workflow configuration, they are still black-box approaches. Because they are the one-for-all approach, these AI platforms focus on the most common scenarios. But there are always exceptions that you need to customize for your business; it won't be a good experience when there aren't many choices.

Another problem for the cloud AI platform is it always has a delay in adopting new technologies. For example, you have to wait for the SageMaker team's decision on whether to support a training method and when to support it, and sometimes that decision is not agreeable to you. Deep learning is a rapidly developing space. Building your own training service can help you to adopt the latest research and pivot quickly, which will give you an edge over the fierce competition.

PASSING COMPLIANCE AUDITS

To be qualified to run some businesses, you need to obtain certificates for compliance laws and regulations—for example, HIPAA (Healthcare Insurance Portability and Accountability Act) or CCPA (California Consumer Privacy Act). These certifications require that you provide evidence not only that your code meets these requirements but also that the infrastructure on which your application runs is compliant. If your application is built on Amazon SageMaker and Google Vertex AI platforms, they also need to be in compliance. As cloud vendors are a black box, running through compliance checklists and providing evidence is an unpleasant task.

AUTHENTICATION AND AUTHORIZATION

Integrating authentication and authorization functionality into cloud AI platforms and in-house auth services (on-premises) requires a lot of effort. Many companies have their own version of auth services to authenticate and authorize user requests. If we adopt SageMaker as the AI platform and expose it to different internal services for various business purposes, bridging SageMaker auth management with the in-house user auth management services is not going to be easy. Instead, building on-premises training services is a lot easier because we can change our API freely and simply integrate it into existing auth services.

Summary

- The primary goal of the training service is to manage the computing resources and training executions.
- A sophisticated training service follows four principles: it supports all kinds of model training code through a unified interface; it reduces training cost; it supports model reproducibility; and it has high scalability and availability and handles compute isolation.
- Understanding the general model training code pattern allows us to treat the code as a black box from the perspective of the training service.
- Containerization is the key to using a generic method to handle the diversities of deep learning training methods and frameworks.
- By Dockerizing training code and defining clear communication protocol, a training service can treat training code as a black box and execute the training on a single device or distributively. This also benefits data scientists because they can focus on model algorithm development without worrying about training execution.
- Kubeflow training operators are a set of Kubernetes-based open source training applications. These operators work out of the box, and they can be easily integrated into any existing systems as a model training backend. Kubeflow training operators support both distributed and nondistributed training.
- Using public cloud training services can help to build deep learning applications quickly. On the other hand, building your own training services can reduce training operation costs, provide more customized options, and remain cloud agnostic.

Distributed training 4

This chapter covers

- Understanding data parallelism, model parallelism, and pipeline parallelism
- Using a sample training service that supports data parallel training in Kubernetes
- Training large models with multiple GPUs

One obvious trend in the deep learning research field is to improve model performance with larger datasets and bigger models with increasingly more complex architecture. But more data and bulkier models have consequences: they slow down the model training process as well as the model development process. As is often the case in computing, performance is pitted against speed. For example, it can cost several months to train a BERT (Bidirectional Encoder Representations from Transformers) natural language processing model with a single GPU.

To address the problem of ever-growing datasets and model parameter size, researchers have created various distributed training strategies. And major training frameworks, such as TensorFlow and PyTorch, provide SDKs that implement these training strategies. With the help of these training SDKs, data scientists can write training code that runs across multiple devices (CPU or GPU) and in parallel.

In this chapter, we will explore how to support distributed training from a software engineer's perspective. More specifically, we will see how to write a training service to execute different distributed training codes (developed by data scientists) in a group of machines.

After reading this chapter, you will have a holistic view of how distributed training can work from the perspectives of both a data scientist and a developer. You will know several distributed training strategies and distributed training code patterns, as well as how a training service facilitates different distributed training codes.

4.1   *Types of distributed training methods*

There are three major types of distributed training methods: model parallelism, data parallelism, and pipeline parallelism. *Model parallelism* is a strategy to split a neural network into several sequential subnetworks and run each subnetwork on different devices (GPU or CPU). In this way, we can train a large model with a group of GPUs.

Pipeline parallelism is an advanced version of model parallelism. A major problem with model parallelism is that only one GPU is active during training; the others are idle. By dividing each training example batch into small microbatches, pipeline parallelism overlaps computations between layers to maximize GPU performance. This allows different GPUs to work on various microbatches at the same time. The GPUs' training throughput and device utilization improve, resulting in a much faster model training speed than model parallelism.

Data parallelism partitions the dataset into smaller pieces and lets each device train these subdatasets separately. Because each device now trains a smaller dataset, the training speed improves.

Converting a single-device training code to model parallelism or pipeline parallelism training requires lots of code changes, including splitting the neural network into multiple subnetworks, running subnetworks on different GPUs, and copying the subnetworks' compute output on different GPUs. The sheer quantity, as well as the complexity of these changes, makes them problematic and hard to debug. Each model algorithm might have a dramatically different model architecture, so no standardized method exists for splitting a model for model parallelism or pipeline parallelism. Data scientists must build the code case by case.

On the contrary, data parallelism requires only minimal code changes on a single-device training code. And there are standardized patterns for converting a nondistributed training code to data parallelism without changing the model algorithm or architecture. Also, data parallelism code is relatively easy to both understand and debug. These merits make data parallelism our primary choice for distributed training.

Although data parallelism has a lot of advantages, model parallelism and pipeline parallelism have their own strengths and uses as well. When you have large models that can't fit into one GPU, for instance, they are the best-distributed solution. We will talk about them more in section 4.4.

4.2 Data parallelism

In this section, we will look at data parallelism theories and their parallel execution challenges, along with sample training codes in PyTorch, TensorFlow, and Horovod.

4.2.1 Understanding data parallelism

Data parallelism involves a group of training devices working together on a large dataset. By having each device process a subset of the dataset, we can greatly reduce the training time.

Synchronous data parallelism is the most adopted data parallelism method. It replicates the model network to every device in the training group, whether it is a GPU or CPU. The dataset is split into minibatches, and these batches are distributed across all devices (again, either CPU or GPU). The training steps occur simultaneously, using a different minibatch on each of the devices; therefore, the devices act as their own data partition. When calculating gradients to update the neural network, the algorithm calculates the final gradients by aggregating them from each device. Then it dispatches the aggregated gradients back to each device to update their local neural network. Although the training dataset on each device is different, the neural networks local to these devices are the same because they are updated by the same gradients in each training iteration. As a result, this process is called synchronous data parallelism.

You can visualize this process in figure 4.1. The figure compares the process of deep learning training on a single GPU, in graph (a) on the left, with the setup for synchronous data parallel training using three GPUs, in graph (b) on the right.

By comparing graphs (a) and (b), you can see that synchronous data parallelism introduces two extra steps compared with single-device training. The first extra step is to divide one training batch into three minibatches, so each device can work on its own minibatch. The second step is to synchronize the gradients aggregated from all the machines, so they are all operating with the same gradients when updating their local model.

> **NOTE** To aggregate gradients computed by different workers, you can use the algorithm all-reduce. This is a popular algorithm that independently combines arrays of data from all processes into a single array. In "Writing Distributed Applications with PyTorch" (https://pytorch.org/tutorials/intermediate/dist_tuto.html), you can find an example of how PyTorch supports the all-reduce algorithm.

From an implementation perspective, data parallelism requires minimal changes in a single-device model training process. Its main overhead is the added step of synchronizing the gradient aggregation.

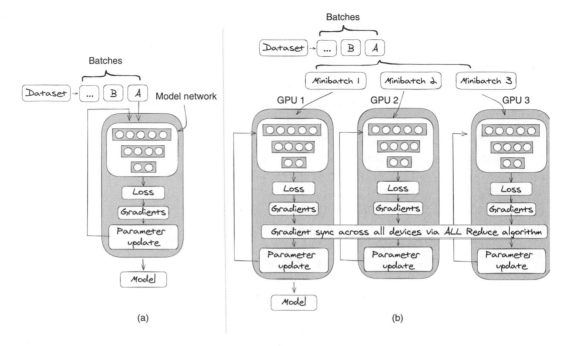

Figure 4.1   A synchronous data parallelism concept graph. (a) Deep learning training on a single GPU. (b) Synchronous data parallel training with three GPUs.

MODEL PARAMETER UPDATES: SYNCHRONOUS VS. ASYNCHRONOUS

There are two schools of thought on aggregating gradients across workers in data parallelism: synchronous updates and asynchronous updates. Let's review how each of these works, along with their advantages and drawbacks, so you can choose for yourself:

- *Synchronous model update*—As demonstrated in figure 4.1, a synchronous model update pauses the training iteration at the gradient sync step until all devices receive the aggregated gradients. Then it proceeds to the next step, updating the model parameters. In this way, all devices get the same gradient updates at the same time, thus ensuring that the model of each worker is on the same page in every training iteration. The problem with synchronous model updates is obvious: the training iteration is blocked while the gradients are being synchronized among the workers, so none of the workers can begin processing the next minibatch of data. If there are some slow machines or network problems, the entire distributed working group is stuck, and the faster workers are idle.

- *Asynchronous model update*—In contrast, the asynchronous model update approach does not force each training device or worker to wait to receive gradients from the other devices. Instead, whenever a device has finished computing the gradients, it immediately updates its local model without checking other devices. Every device works independently, and although its gradients still need to be copied to every other device, synchronization of these updates is not necessary. The asynchronous method may seem very appealing; it's simple and can run more training steps per minute than the synchronous method. A downside to the asynchronous method is that it takes a longer time to train and produces less-accurate models than the synchronous model update method.

When we use the asynchronous method, gradients are calculated independently on different devices. Some machines run faster while others run slower; consequently, these gradients can be produced from different training iterations of each device. So there is no guarantee that the aggregated gradients will point in the optimal direction. For example, say the gradients from a slow machine are calculated from training iteration 5, while other, faster machines have already moved to training iteration 20. When we aggregate the gradients from all the workers, the gradients from the lower iteration are applied to those from the higher iteration; this degrades the gradient quality.

In addition, the asynchronous method often converges slowly and has a higher accuracy loss than the synchronous method. Thus, most data parallelism libraries today are doing synchronous model updates. In this chapter, when we mention data parallelism and its code implementation, we mean synchronous data parallelism.

MEMORY CONSTRAINT FOR DATASET AND MODEL

In deep learning, datasets and models consume the most memory of the compute instance during training. The training process will be terminated by an out-of-memory (OOM) error if the training data or neural network (model) exceeds the memory limits of the local device. Data parallelism is designed to improve training speed but not to solve memory constraint problems.

For OOM caused by loading a dataset, we can reduce the batch size of the training data, so the training process loads a smaller amount of data into local memory in each training loop. In the data parallelism context, we need to make sure the minibatch training data can fit into the memory of every worker device.

For OOM caused by the model size, we need to adopt model parallelism or pipeline parallelism (see section 4.4). Data parallelism simply won't work when the size of a neural network (model) exceeds the memory limits of a single device.

4.2.2 Multiworker training challenges

Fault tolerance and bandwidth saturation are the two challenges we, as software developers, need to address when executing data parallelism code in the training service. Meeting these two challenges is critical to reducing operating costs and improving training performance for data parallelism–distributed training.

FAULT TOLERANCE

We don't want the entire distributed training group to fail just because one of the workers fails unexpectedly. This not only causes a problem for service availability but also increases our training cost because all other workers' efforts are wasted if one fails.

To improve fault tolerance, we can preserve the training state (i.e., the model parameters) of each training step in a remote filesystem for each worker. Then, if one worker fails or takes too long to complete one training iteration, we can restart that worker and load its most recent previous state.

Both TensorFlow and PyTorch frameworks have features to back up and restore. As training service developers, we can set up the remote disk or backup storage system and pass the access configuration to the training container. Then, during the training, the training code can use the external filesystem to backup or restore states.

BANDWIDTH SATURATION

Adding more GPUs and more machines to the distributed training group doesn't always improve performance. Whether we use synchronous or asynchronous model updates, the algorithm must communicate the gradients or model parameters between the training workers at the end of each training iteration. The time spent on moving data in and out of GPU RAM and across the network will eventually outweigh the speedup obtained by splitting the training workload.

Therefore, a cap exists for how many parallel instances can occur before data parallelism reaches its peak performance. This cap is determined by the number of model parameters and the density of the model (how many nonzero values are in model weights). If it's a large, dense model with lots of parameters and gradients to transfer, its saturation is greater than either a smaller model or a large, sparse model.

There are some recommended parallel instance numbers, such as a 6× speedup on 8 GPUs for neural machine translations and a 32× speedup on 50 GPUs for ImageNet models. But we need to determine the sweet spot with our own experiments because both GPU and model architectures evolve rapidly, and standard recommendations will quickly become outdated. As platform developers, besides choosing the perfect number of parallel workers, we have three additional methods for mitigating bandwidth saturation.

First, we can group the parallel workers (i.e., the containers or pods) into fewer machines to reduce the network hops. For example, in Kubernetes, you can set `node-Selector` with affinity and anti-affinity rules (http://mng.bz/qo76) to provision training instances (Kubernetes pods) on a few selected servers that have a better network and more computational power.

A second option is to always upgrade the training image to use the latest version of the training framework. Popular frameworks such as PyTorch, TensorFlow, and others are constantly evolving to reduce the data volume transferred within the network for distributed training. Pay attention to the release note and take advantage of these improvements.

Finally, don't underestimate the gains that can result from doing small tweaks when initializing the distributed group. Consider using PyTorch, for example. The PyTorch data parallel library partitions the neural network parameter gradients into buckets and then sends the buckets around to the workers during the gradient synchronization step. The bucket size determines how much data is transferred between different devices at one time. So by choosing the right bucket size, we can determine a sweet spot between device saturation and network saturation, thus reaching the best training speed. The bucket size can be configured in the constructor of the PyTorch distributed data parallel (DDP) component (http://mng.bz/7ZB7).

4.2.3 Writing distributed training (data parallelism) code for different training frameworks

In this section, you will see some training code snippets for data parallel distributed training in three training frameworks: TensorFlow, PyTorch, and Horovod. Don't worry if the code samples here are difficult to parse. The purpose is to experience how data scientists handle distributed training on their side. This will give you a sense of how training services enable distributed training.

PYTORCH

The PyTorch framework has a DDP library that implements data parallelism at the module level. The DDP wraps the model object so that it can run the object across multiple machines seamlessly. Its training processes can be placed on the same machine or across machines.

To convert a single device/process training code to a data parallel–distributed training code, we need to make the following two modifications. First, we must initialize the training group by allowing each training process to register itself with the master process. One of the processes claims to be the master while the others claim to be the workers. Each training process will be pending at this registration stage until all workers join the distributed group.

To register a process, we need to know the total number of training processes (`world_size`), a unique ID for this process (`rank`), and the master process's address (define `MASTER_ADDR` and `MASTER_PORT` in environment variables). See the code sample as follows:

```
def setup(rank, world_size):
  os.environ['MASTER_ADDR'] = 'xxxx'
  os.environ['MASTER_PORT'] = 'xxx'

  # initialize the process group, "gloo" is one of the communication
  # backends Pytorch supports, it also supports MPI and NCCL.
  # rank is the process's rank, it's a globally unique id
  # for this process. rank=0 means  master process.
  # world_size is the total number of processes in this training group.
  dist.init_process_group("gloo", rank=rank, world_size=world_size)

def cleanup():
  dist.destroy_process_group()
```

Second, we use the DDP class to wrap the model object. The PyTorch DDP class will handle the distributed data communication, gradient aggregation, and local model parameter updates:

```
import torch.distributed as dist
from torch.nn.parallel import DistributedDataParallel as DDP

# create model and move it to GPU
model = DpModel().to(device)

# wrap the model with DDP
ddp_model = DDP(model, device_ids=[rank])
outputs = ddp_model(data)

# compute the loss and sync gradient with other workers.
# when 'backward' function returns, the param.grad already
# contains synchronized gradient tensor
loss_fn(outputs, labels).backward()
```

> **The DDP wrapper takes care of the distributed training execution.**

For advanced use cases, the PyTorch library provides the API so you can implement your own gradient synchronization function at a lower level. You can check the details at the official tutorial, "Writing Distributed Applications with Pytorch" (http://mng .bz/m27W).

TENSORFLOW/KERAS

TensorFlow supports distributed training in a very similar way to PyTorch; it first defines a distributed training strategy (such as MultiWorkerMirroredStrategy) and then initializes the model with this strategy. To let the strategy identify the workers in the distributed group, we need to define a TF_CONFIG environment variable in each training process. TF_CONFIG contains a worker's unique ID and the addresses of all other workers in the group. See the code as follows:

```
# Step 1: define 'TF_CONFIG' environment variable to describe
# the training group and the role for the process.
# The worker array defines the IP addresses and ports of
# all the TensorFlow servers used in this training.
tf_config = {
  'cluster': {
    'worker': ['192.168.4.53:12345', '192.168.4.55:23456']
  },

  # A 'task' provides information of the current task and is
  # different for each worker. It specifies the 'type' and
  # 'index' of that worker.
  'task': {'type': 'worker', 'index': 0}
}

os.environ['TF_CONFIG'] = json.dumps(tf_config)

# Step 2: define distributed training strategy,
# the MultiWorkerMirroredStrategy takes
# care of the synchronous data parallel distributed training.
strategy = tf.distribute.MultiWorkerMirroredStrategy()

global_batch_size = per_worker_batch_size * num_workers
multi_worker_dataset = mnist.mnist_dataset(global_batch_size)
```

```
# Step 3: start the distributed training.
with strategy.scope():
  # Model building/compiling need to be within 'strategy.scope()'.
  multi_worker_model = mnist.build_and_compile_cnn_model()

multi_worker_model.fit(multi_worker_dataset,
  epochs=3, steps_per_epoch=70)
```

HOROVOD

Horovod is a single-purpose distributed framework. Compared to TensorFlow and PyTorch, which can be used across a range of tasks, such as data processing, model training, and model serving, Horovod can only focus on one task: making distributed deep learning training fast and easy to use.

Horovod's greatest advantage is that it works with different training frameworks, such as TensorFlow, Keras, PyTorch, and Apache MXNet. Therefore, we can configure our training cluster in one manner (the Horovod way) to run distributed training for PyTorch, TensorFlow, and other frameworks. Here, we only list two code snippets for using Horovod with TensorFlow and PyTorch, but you can check examples of other frameworks on Horovod's website.

Let's look at the TensorFlow example. To set up data parallelism–distributed training, first we initialize the Horovod training group, which will find other Horovod nodes in your cluster automatically. Next, we broadcast the rank 0's (master worker's) initial variable states to all other processes. This will ensure the consistent initialization of all workers. Then we wrap the gradient tape with distributed gradient tape, which will average gradients on all workers. The remaining code is simply normal TensorFlow training code. As such, please see the code that follows (https://github .com/horovod/horovod/blob/master/examples):

```
hvd.init()        ◁──┐   Initializes
.. .. ..             │   Horovod

@tf.function
def training_step(images, labels, first_batch):
    with tf.GradientTape() as tape:
        probs = mnist_model(images, training=True)
        loss_value = loss(labels, probs)

    # Wrap tape with Horovod Distributed GradientTape.
    # This gradient tape averages gradients from all
    # workers by using allreduce or allgather, and then
    # applies those averaged gradients back to the local model.
    tape = hvd.DistributedGradientTape(tape)

    grads = tape.gradient(loss_value, mnist_model.trainable_variables)
    opt.apply_gradients(zip(grads, mnist_model.trainable_variables))

    # Broadcast initial variable states
    # from rank 0 to all other processes.
    if first_batch:
```

```
      hvd.broadcast_variables(mnist_model.variables, root_rank=0)
      hvd.broadcast_variables(opt.variables(), root_rank=0)

   return loss_value

for batch, (images, labels) in \
   enumerate(dataset.take(10000 / hvd.size())):
   loss_value = training_step(images, labels, batch == 0)
   .. .. ..


# save checkpoints only on worker 0 to
# prevent other workers from corrupting it.
if hvd.rank() == 0:
   checkpoint.save(checkpoint_dir)
```

Adjusts the number of steps based on the number of GPUs

The following code is an example of using Horovod with PyTorch. Some PyTorch Horovod APIs are different than TensorFlow—for example, hvd.DistributedOptimizer versus hvd.DistributedGradientTape. But these APIs are from the same Horovod SDK and share the same interworker mechanism under the hood. Let's look at the PyTorch code snippet:

```
# Horovod: initialize Horovod.
import torch
import horovod.torch as hvd

# Initialize Horovod
hvd.init()
.. .. ..


# Build model...
model = ...
optimizer = optim.SGD(model.parameters())


# Add Horovod Distributed Optimizer, this is equal
# to hvd.DistributedGradientTape(tape)
# for Tensorflow2
optimizer = hvd.DistributedOptimizer(optimizer,
   named_parameters=model.named_parameters())


# Broadcast parameters from rank 0 to
#all other processes.
hvd.broadcast_parameters(model.state_dict(),
   root_rank=0)

for epoch in range(100):
   for batch_idx, (data, target) in enumerate(train_loader):
      optimizer.zero_grad()
      output = model(data)
      loss = F.nll_loss(output, target)
      loss.backward()
      optimizer.step()
   .. .. ..
```

Although the model is defined in two different frameworks—TensorFlow 2 and PyTorch—we can see from these two code snippets that they use the same Horovod SDK to run distributed training. The benefit here is that we can use a standard method (the Horovod way) to set up the distributed worker group in our training cluster, and it can still function for the training code written in different training frameworks.

TWO TAKEAWAYS ON TRAINING CODE

It's fine if you are confused when reading those training code snippets. As a training service developer, you don't need to write these pieces of code. We want to emphasize two points from this discussion:

- Although the code samples in this section implement distributed training in different frameworks with different APIs, the code follows the same data parallelism paradigm described in section 4.2.1. That is, the code always (1) sets up the communication group for each parallel training process and (2) configures the model object to aggregate gradients across all workers. So, as developers, we can use a unified method to set up and manage distributed training processes for different training frameworks.

- The work of extending model training code from single-device training to data parallelism–distributed training is relatively trivial. Nowadays, the distributed training frameworks/SDKs are so powerful that we don't need to implement every detail of data parallelism, such as the gradient synchronization that synchronizes the gradients across the network. The training frameworks and SDKs handle these processes so they run seamlessly. The distributed data parallel training code is almost identical to the single-device training code, except when configuring training groups.

4.2.4 *Engineering effort in data parallel–distributed training*

So what does the work look like for enabling data parallel–distributed training in production? First, it requires a joint engineering effort between data scientists and service developers. For their part, data scientists need to upgrade the single-device training code to run distributedly, using code like the snippets in the previous section. Meanwhile, service developers must enhance the training service to automatically set up distributed worker groups that allow distributed training to happen.

To make the training service user friendly, the service should incorporate the setup details for different distributed training frameworks. Therefore, data scientists have to define only the number of parallel instances they need for the training.

Let's use TensorFlow distributed training as an example. From our discussion in section 4.2.3, the TensorFlow training code on each device must have `tf_config` (see the following example) as an environment variable. So the underlying TensorFlow-distributed library in the training process knows how to communicate with other training processes:

```
tf_config = {
  'cluster': {
    'worker': ['192.168.4.53:12345', '192.168.4.55:23456']
  },

  # A 'task' provides information of the current task
  # and is different for each worker. It specifies
  # the 'type' and 'index' of that worker.
  'task': {'type': 'worker', 'index': 0}
}
```

From a usability perspective, we can't expect data scientists to figure out the setup value—server IP address and task indexes—for every distributed training process, especially if the entire training group is provisioned dynamically. A training service should automatically create the group of compute resources for a distributed training request, initialize the distributed training libraries with the correct IP addresses, and kick off the training process.

Figure 4.2 is a conceptual diagram of a training service that supports distributed training. From the diagram, you can see that Alex, a data scientist, sends a training request to kick off a distributed training run. The service (built by Tang, the service developer) then spawns two worker machines and executes the training code distributedly. Besides preparing the training code, Alex can specify configurations for the training run, such as the number of parallel workers and the type of distributed training framework (TensorFlow, PyTorch, or Horovod).

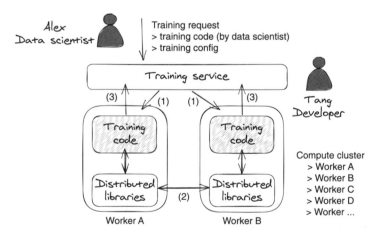

Figure 4.2   An overview of a distributed training system

Let's take a slow walk through this diagram to better understand how the system is set up and who does what job. We see that Tang, as the engineer, needs to make three enhancements—numbered 1, 2, and 3 in figure 4.2—to change the training service from a single-device trainer (as we saw in chapter 3) to a data parallel–distributed trainer.

The first step is to update the training service to build a distributed training group on demand (at the runtime). When the service receives the request for distributed training, it allocates multiple workers from the training cluster for the training job and distributes the training code to each worker.

The second step is to programmatically initialize each training process with the correct server IP, port number, and training process ID. This ensures that the distributed libraries (collectively known as the framework, such as TensorFlow) have enough information to set up interworker communication for the training group. As we saw in the previous section, the setup configuration varies for each distributed training framework. The training service should know how to set up interworker communication for various frameworks, so data scientists can focus only on the algorithm development and not worry about the infrastructure underneath.

The third step is to provide remote storage to back up and restore each worker's training state. In distributed training, if a single worker fails, the entire training group fails, and a great deal of computation is wasted. Thus, giving distributed training groups the capability to recover from a hardware failure or network problem is crucial. By providing remote storage and a backup API, the distributed training processes can save their training state (neural network) after each training iteration. When a training process fails in the middle of the training and can restore its previous state and start over, the entire training group continues.

> **NOTE** If you want to learn more about data parallelism, you can start with the following two articles: a blog post from O'Reilly, "Distributed TensorFlow: Reduce both experimentation time and training time for neural networks by using many GPU servers," by Jim Dowling (www.oreilly.com/content/distributed-tensorflow/), and a paper from Google Brain, "Revisiting Distributed Synchronous SGD," by Chen et al. (https://arxiv.org/pdf/1604.00981.pdf).

4.3   A sample service supporting data parallel–distributed training

In this section, we will extend the sample service introduced in the previous chapter (section 3.3) to support data parallelism–distributed training.

4.3.1   Service overview

Compared to the single-device training discussed in section 3.3, the user workflow remains the same. Alex, the data scientist, first builds the model training code and sends a training request to the training service. Then, the service runs the actual training and produces the model at the end.

However, there are some crucial differences. First, Alex upgrades the intent classification training code to enable it for both a single device and multiple devices. Second, Tang, the service developer, modifies the training service API to offer a new parameter, `PARALLEL_INSTANCES`. This parameter allows Alex to define the size of the worker group for his distributed training run.

To manage a cluster of servers properly, we need help from Kubernetes. Kubernetes can save us a lot of effort on worker resource allocation and interworker communication. So we introduce a new component—the *Kubernetes job tracker*—to manage training jobs in Kubernetes. You can see the updated service design graph and user workflow in figure 4.3.

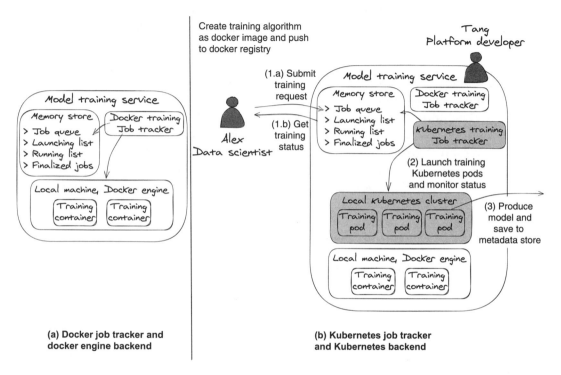

(a) Docker job tracker and
docker engine backend

(b) Kubernetes job tracker
and Kubernetes backend

Figure 4.3   (a) The previous training service design introduced in figure 3.5; (b) the updated service design with distributed training support in Kubernetes

Figure 4.3 (a) repeats the training service's system diagram we discussed in section 3.3, which uses a Docker job tracker to run the training jobs in the Docker engine. Figure 4.3 (b) visualizes the updated training service that now supports distributed training—including both Kubernetes and Docker engine backends. The Kubernetes job tracker is added to run training jobs in the Kubernetes cluster for distributed training jobs. This component executes training jobs by launching Kubernetes pods and monitors and updates the job-execution status in the memory store.

We also made some changes to the intent classification PyTorch training code so it can run distributedly. We'll review this shortly, in section 4.3.5.

One great timesaver is that we don't need to change the service API interface that we've already created (section 3.3.3). Our users can simply work the same API to train models in both Docker engines and Kubernetes clusters. This follows training service principle number one, which we introduced in chapter 3 (section 3.1.2): using unified APIs and keeping them agnostic on the backend implementation.

4.3.2   *Playing with the service*

First, let's run the training service with the Kubernetes backend; see the commands as follows (`scripts/ts-001-start-server-kube.sh`):

```
$ docker build -t orca3/services:latest -f services.dockerfile .
$ docker run --name training-service -v \
    $HOME/.kube/config:/.kube/config --env \        ◄──   Local
    APP_CONFIG=config-kube.properties \                   Kubernetes
    --network orca3 --rm -d -p                            config
  "${TS_PORT}":51001
  orca3/services:latest training-service.jar
```

> **NOTE**   This section contains only the main steps and key commands necessary to run the sample service. As a result, the concept can be demonstrated clearly without lengthy pages of code and execution output. Please follow the instructions in the "Distributed trainer training demo" (github.com/orca3/MiniAutoML/blob/main/training-service/distributed_trainer_demo.md) document at the orca3/MiniAutoML git repository if you want to run the lab in this section.

Once the training service container is running, we can submit a training gRPC request. Although the service is now running on the Kubernetes backend, the training API is still the same. Compared to the training request we sent to the Docker backend demo (see section 3.3.1), only one more parameter—PARALLEL_INSTANCES=3—is added in the request payload. This tells the training service to create a distributed training group with three workers to train the model. If we set this parameter to 1, it will be a single-device training request. See the following code snippet to submit a distributed training request with three parallel instances (`scripts/ts-004-start-parallel-run.sh 1`):

```
# submit a distributed training request
$ grpcurl -plaintext -d "{ "metadata":
  { "algorithm":"intent-classification",
    "dataset_id":"1",
    "Name":"test1",
    "train_data_version_hash":"hashBA==",
    "Parameters":{
      "LR":"4","EPOCHS":"15",
      "PARALLEL_INSTANCES":"3",        ◄──   Requires a training
    "BATCH_SIZE":"64","FC_SIZE":"128"}}          group with three
  }"                                             workers
 ${TS_SERVER}:${TS_PORT}
training.TrainingService/Train
```

EQ 246 3122

To check the progress of the training execution, we can use the `GetTrainingStatus` API:

```
grpcurl -plaintext -d "{"job_id": "$1"}"          Provides job ID
  ${TS_SERVER}:"${TS_PORT}"                        to query status
training.TrainingService/GetTrainingStatus
```

Besides querying the training service API to obtain job-execution status, we can also check the training progress in Kubernetes. By using the Kubernetes command `kubectl get all`, we see three worker pods are created in the local Kubernetes environment. One is the master worker, and the other two are normal workers. A Kubernetes service object `intent-classification-1-master-service` is also created for the master worker/pod, which enables the network connectivity between master pods and worker pods. See the code snippet as follows:

```
# check Kubernetes resources status.
# We could see a distributed training group contains
# with three pods and one service are created in Kubernetes
$ kubectl get all -n orca3
NAME                                      READY    STATUS           One of the
pod/intent-classification-1-1-worker     0/1      Completed        worker pods
pod/intent-classification-1-2-worker     0/1      Completed
pod/intent-classification-1-master       0/1      Completed        Mastering the
                                                                   training pod
NAME                                                 TYPE    .. ..
    service/intent-classification-1-master-service   ClusterIP
                                          The Kubernetes service for
                                          training pods communication
```

4.3.3   Launching training jobs

Now, let's look at the workflow for launching training jobs with the Kubernetes backend. When receiving a training request, the request will be added to the job queue. Meanwhile, the Kubernetes job tracker monitors the job queue. When the tracker finds jobs waiting and the system has available capacity, it will start to process these jobs.

To launch a PyTorch-distributed training job, the tracker first creates the required numbers of Kubernetes pods. Each pod hosts one training process. The tracker also passes separate parameters to each pod, and it then moves the job from the job queue to the launching list (figure 4.4).

In figure 4.4, the Kubernetes job tracker can handle both single-device training and distributed training. It creates one Kubernetes pod for single-device training and multiple pods for distributed training.

A Kubernetes job tracker runs one training pod similarly to a Docker job tracker. It wraps up all the user-defined parameters in the environment variables and passes them to the Kubernetes pod.

To set up PyTorch distributed training with multiple pods, the service handles two more functions. First, it creates a Kubernetes service object to talk to the master pod.

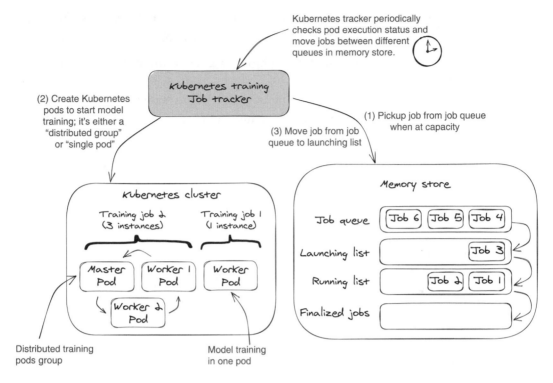

Figure 4.4   The workflow for launching a training job in Kubernetes: step 1, detects the waiting job in the job queue; step 2, creates Kubernetes pods to run training; and step 3, moves the job from the job queue to the launching list.

From the PyTorch distributed training algorithm section (4.2.3), we know that each PyTorch training process needs the IP address of the master process (pod) to initialize the distributed training group. For example, each PyTorch code needs to have the following code snippet before the training logic starts:

```
def setup(rank, world_size):
    os.environ['MASTER_ADDR'] = 'xxx.xxx.xxx.xxx'
    os.environ['MASTER_PORT'] = '12356'
    dist.init_process_group("gloo",          Joins the current process
      rank=rank, world_size=world_size)      to a distributed group by
                                             seeking the master pod
```

But in Kubernetes, a pod is an ephemeral resource, so we can't rely on the pod IP address to locate a pod. Instead, we use the Kubernetes domain name service (DNS) as a permanent address to locate pods. Even if the pod is destroyed and recreated in a different node and the IP is different, we can always use the same DNS to reach it. So, to enable the training group's initialization, we first create a Kubernetes service for the master pod and then pass the DNS to all worker pods as the master pod address.

Second, it passes four environment variables to each pod. The four variables required by each training pod are WORLD_SIZE, RANK, MASTER_ADDR, and MASTER_PORT:

- WORLD_SIZE means the total number of pods of the training group, including master and workers.
- RANK is the unique ID of one training process; the master process's rank must be 0.
- MASTER_ADDR and MASTER_PORT define the host address and port number of the master process, so each worker can use them to reach the master pod.

For example, when running distributed training with three instances, we create three pods (one master, two workers) with the following environment variables for each pod:

```
Master Pod:
  WORLD_SIZE:3; RANK:0,
  MASTER_ADDR: intent-classification-1-master-service,
  MASTER_PORT: 12356
Worker Pod 1:
  WORLD_SIZE:3; RANK:1,
  MASTER_ADDR: intent-classification-1-master-service,
  MASTER_PORT: 12356
Worker Pod 2:
  WORLD_SIZE:3; RANK:2,
  MASTER_ADDR: intent-classification-1-master-service,
  MASTER_PORT: 12356
```

In light of all the explanations, let's take a look at how the actual code is implemented. The following listing highlights how launching distributed training in Kubernetes is implemented.

Listing 4.1   Launching a distributed training job

```
protected List<String> launchTrainingPods(
  int jobId, int worldSize, TrainingJobMetadata metadata, .. ..) {
  .. .. ..


  // It's a distributed training if the worldSize is greater than 1.
  if (worldSize > 1) {
    // .. .. ..
    api.createNamespacedService(              // Creates a Kubernetes
      config.kubeNamespace, serviceBody,      // service and points to
      null, null, null);                      // the master pod

    serviceTracker.add(masterServiceName);
    logger.info(String.format("Launched master service %s",
     masterServiceName));
      .. .. ..
  }


  // create training pods definition
  for (int rank = 0; rank < worldSize; rank++) {
```

World size >1: indicates it's a distributed training (annotation pointing to `if (worldSize > 1) {`)

```
    envs.put("WORLD_SIZE", Integer.toString(worldSize));
    // RANK 0 is master
    envs.put("RANK", Integer.toString(rank));
    envs.put("MASTER_ADDR", masterPodDnsName);
    envs.put("MASTER_PORT", Integer.toString(masterPort));

    V1PodSpec podSpec = new V1PodSpec()
      .restartPolicy("Never")
      .addContainersItem(new V1Container()
        .image(algorithmToImage(
          metadata.getAlgorithm()))
        .env(envVarsToList(envs)) .. .. ..

    String workerPodName = rank == 0 ? masterPodName :
      String.format("job-%d-%d-%s-worker-%d", jobId,
        now, metadata.getName(), rank);
    V1Pod workerPodBody = new V1Pod();
    workerPodBody.apiVersion("v1");
      .. .. ..

    // (3)
    api.createNamespacedPod(config.kubeNamespace,
      workerPodBody, null, null, null);
      .. .. ..
  }
  return podNames;
}
```

> Sets the distributed training–related config as the environment variable

> Defines pod configuration; passes in training parameters as environment variables

> Creates actual training pods

RANK values do not neccesarily map to pods one to one

RANK is a tricky variable in distributed training. Please be aware that RANK is the unique ID of a training process, not a pod. A pod can run multiple training processes if it has multiple GPUs. In the example here, because we run one training process per pod, we assign a different RANK value to each pod.

When we run multiple training processes in one pod, then we need to assign multiple RANK values to a pod. For example, when we run two processes in a pod, this pod needs two RANK values, one for each process.

You may notice that the Kubernetes pods and services created in this sample are customized for PyTorch distributed training library. In fact, the sample service is not limited to PyTorch. To support training code written in other frameworks, such as TensorFlow 2, we can extend the Kubernetes job tracker to support the settings for TensorFlow distributed training.

For example, we can collect all the IPs or DNSs of the worker pods, put them together, and broadcast them back to each worker pod. During the broadcasting, we set worker group information to the TF_CONFIG environment variable in every pod to start the distributed training group. The TF_CONFIG environment variable is a special requirement for the TensorFlow distributed library.

4.3.4   *Updating and fetching the job status*

After creating training pods, the Kubernetes job tracker will continue querying the pod execution status and move the job to other job lists when its status changes. For example, if the pod is created successfully and starts running, the tracker moves the job from the launching list to the running list. If the pod execution is completed, the tracker moves the job from the running list to the finalized jobs list. Figure 4.5 depicts this process.

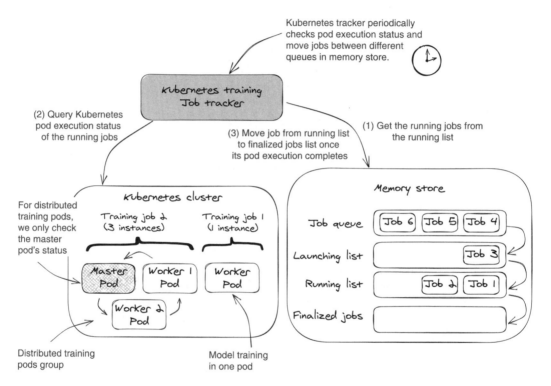

Figure 4.5   Track the Kubernetes training job status: step 1, obtains the jobs in the running list; step 2, queries the pod execution status of each of the jobs running in the Kubernetes cluster; and step 3, moves the job to the finalized job list if the pod execution is complete (success or failure).

When a user submits a job status query, the training service will search the job ID in all four job queues in the memory store and return the job object. Interestingly, although there are multiple training pods, we only need to check the status of the master pod to track the distributed training progress. This is because, for synchronous data parallel training, all workers have to sync with each other in every training cycle, so the master pod can represent the other worker pods.

The code for querying and updating job execution status is very similar to the Docker job tracker that we see in section 3.3.5. The only difference is that we query the Kubernetes cluster instead of the Docker engine to obtain the training status. We leave the code for you to explore; you can find it in the `updateContainerStatus` method of the `KubectlTracker` class.

4.3.5 Converting the training code to run distributedly

We made two changes to our intent classification training code (introduced in the previous chapter, section 3.3.6) to support both distributed mode and single-device mode.

FIRST CHANGE: INITIALIZE THE TRAINING GROUP

We use the `WORLD_SIZE` environment variable to check whether the training code should run in distributed training. If the world size equals 1, then we use the same single-device training code that we saw in section 3.3.6.

But if the value is greater than 1, we initialize the training process to join the distributed group. Please also notice that a unique `RANK` value for each pod is passed from the training service (Kubernetes job tracker), which is needed for distributed group initialization. After self-registering to the distributed group, we declare the model and data sampler to be distributed as well. See the following code for the changes:

```
def should_distribute():
    return dist.is_available() and config.WORLD_SIZE > 1

def is_distributed():
    return dist.is_available() and dist.is_initialized()

if should_distribute():
    # initialize the distributed process group,
    # wait until all works are ready.
    dist.init_process_group("gloo",
      rank=config.RANK, world_size=config.WORLD_SIZE)

if is_distributed():
    # wrap the model with DistributedDataParallel (DDP)
    # package to enable data parallel training.
    model = DDP(model)

if is_distributed():
    # restricts data loading to a subset of the dataset
    # exclusive to the current process
    train_sampler = DistributedSampler(
      dataset=split_train_, num_replicas=config.WORLD_SIZE,
      rank=config.RANK)
```

SECOND CHANGE: ONLY UPLOAD THE FINAL MODEL FROM THE MASTER POD

In the second change, we only allow the master pod (rank = 0) to upload the final model. This is to prevent each worker from uploading the same models multiple times:

```
if config.RANK == 0:                              ◁──┐ Rank 0 is the
    accu_test = evaluate(test_dataloader)            │ master pod.
    .. .. ..
    # upload model to metadata store.
    artifact = orca3_utils.create_artifact(
      config.MODEL_BUCKET, config.MODEL_OBJECT_NAME)
    .. .. ..
```

4.3.6   *Improvements*

If we continue the path to making this sample service production ready, we can follow the thoughts in section 4.2.2 to work on improving fault tolerance and reducing network bandwidth saturation. We can also extend the Kubernetes job tracker to support TensorFlow and Horovod distributed training. From a training service perspective, they are not very different because the configuration that the training service passes to the training code is very generic; this information is needed for all frameworks but with different names. As long as the protocol between the training service and the training code is clear and stable, we can still treat the training code as a black box, even in the distributed setting.

4.4   *Training large models that can't load on one GPU*

The neural network size (defined by the number of parameters) is growing rapidly in the research field, and we cannot ignore this trend. Using the ImageNet challenge as an example, the winner in 2014 (GoogleNet) had 4 million parameters; the winner in 2017 (Squeeze-and-Excitation Networks) had 145.8 million parameters; and the current leading approaches have more than 1 billion parameters.

Although our neural network size grew nearly 300×, GPU memory has only increased 4×. You will see cases more often in the future in which we can't train a model because it can't be loaded onto one GPU.

In this section, we will discuss common strategies for training large models. Unlike the data parallelism strategy described in section 4.2, the method introduced here requires effortful work on training code.

> **NOTE**   Although the methods introduced in this section are normally implemented by data scientists, we hope you can still follow them. Understanding the strategies behind these training techniques is very helpful for designing communication protocols between training services and training codes. It also provides insight into troubleshooting or fine-tuning the training performance in training service. To keep it simple, we will only describe algorithms at the concept level and focus on the necessary work from an engineering perspective.

4.4.1   *Traditional methods: Memory saving*

Let's say your data science team wants to train a model that can load to the largest GPU in your training cluster; for example, they want to train a 24 GB BERT model in a 10 GB memory GPU. There are several memory-saving techniques the team can use to train the model in this situation, including gradient accumulation and memory swap. This work is generally implemented by data scientists. As a platform developer, you just need to be aware of these options. We'll describe them briefly, so you will know when to suggest each of their use.

> **NOTE**   There are several other memory-saving methods, such as OpenAI's gradient checkpointing (https://github.com/cybertronai/gradient-checkpointing)

and NVIDIA's vDNN (https://arxiv.org/abs/1602.08124), but because this book is not about deep learning algorithms, we will leave them for independent study.

GRADIENT ACCUMULATION

In deep learning training, the dataset is split into batches. In each training step, for loss calculation, gradient computation, and model parameter updating, we take the whole batch of examples (training data) into memory and handle the computations all at once.

We can mitigate the memory pressure by reducing the batch size—for example, training 16 examples in a batch rather than 32 examples in a batch. But reducing batch size can cause the model to converge a lot more slowly. And this is where gradient accumulation can be helpful.

Gradient accumulation cuts batch examples into configurable numbers of minibatches and then calculates the loss and gradients after each minibatch. But instead of updating the model parameters, it waits and accumulates the gradients over all the minibatches. And then, ultimately, it updates the model parameters based on the cumulative gradient.

Let's look at an example to see how this speeds up the process. Imagine that, because of GPU memory constraints, we can't run training with a batch size of 32. With gradient accumulation, we can split each batch into four minibatches, each with a size of 8. Because we accumulate the gradients for all four minibatches and only update the model after all four are complete, the process is almost equal to training with a batch size of 32. The difference is that we only compute 8 examples at a time in GPU instead of 32, so the cost is 4× *slower* than it would be with a batch of 32.

MEMORY SWAP (GPU AND CPU)

The memory swap method is very simple: it copies activations between CPU and GPU, back and forth. If you are unaccustomed to deep learning terms, think of *activation* as the computation output from each node of the neural network. The idea is to only keep the necessary data for the current computation step in GPU and swap the compute result out to CPU memory for future steps.

Building on this idea, a new relay-style execution technique called L2L (layer to layer) keeps only the executing layers and transit buffers on the GPU. The whole model and the optimizer—which holds the state—are stored in the CPU space. L2L can greatly increase the GPU throughput and allow us to develop large models on affordable devices. If you are interested in this method, you can check out the paper "Training Large Neural Networks with Constant Memory Using a New Execution Algorithm," by Pudipeddi et al. (https://arxiv.org/abs/2002.05645), which also has a PyTorch implementation in GitHub.

Both gradient accumulation and memory swap are effective ways to train a large model on a smaller GPU. But, like most things, they come with a cost: they tend to slow down the training. Because of this drawback, we normally use them only for prototyping ideas.

To obtain workable training speeds, we really need to train models distributedly on multiple GPUs. So, in the next section, we will introduce a more production-like approach: pipeline parallelism. It can train a large model distributedly with impressive training speed.

4.4.2   *Pipeline model parallelism*

In section 4.2, we discussed the most commonly used distributed training method: data parallelism. This approach keeps a copy of the whole model on each device and partitions data into multiple devices. Then it aggregates the gradients and updates the model in each training step. The whole approach of data parallelism works well, as long as the entire model can be loaded into one GPU. As we see in this section, however, we are not always able to do this. And that is where pipeline parallelism can be useful. In this section, we will learn about pipeline parallelism, a training method that trains large models distributedly on multiple GPUs.

To understand pipeline parallelism, let's first take a brief look at model parallelism. This little detour will make the jump to pipeline parallelism easier.

MODEL PARALLELISM

The idea of model parallelism is to split a neural network into smaller subnets and run each subnet on different GPUs. Figure 4.6 illustrates the model parallelism approach.

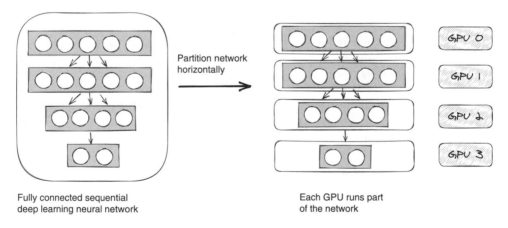

Fully connected sequential
deep learning neural network

Partition network
horizontally

Each GPU runs part
of the network

Figure 4.6   Split a four-layer, fully connected deep learning network into four subgroups; each group has one layer, and each subgroup runs on one GPU.

Figure 4.6 visualizes the model parallel process. It first converts a neural network (four layers) into four sub–neural networks (single layer) and then assigns each single-layer network a dedicated GPU. By doing so, we run a model distributedly on four GPUs.

The concept of model parallelism is straightforward, but the actual implementation can be tricky; it depends on the architecture of the network. To give you an idea, the following listing is a piece of dummy PyTorch code that makes a network run on two GPUs.

Listing 4.2 A sample model parallelism implementation in PyTorch

```
gpu1 = 1
gpu2 = 2

class a_large_model(nn.Module):
  def __init__(self):
    super().__init__()

    # initialize the network as two subnetworks.
    self.subnet1 = ...
    self.subnet2 = ...

    # put subnetwork 1 and 2 to two different GPUs
    self.subnet1.cuda(gpu1)
    self.subnet2.cuda(gpu2)

  def forward(x):
    # load data to GPU 1 and calculate output for
    # subnet 1, GPU 2 is idle at the moment.
    x = x.cuda(gpu1)
    x = self.subnet1(x)

    # move the output of subnet 1 to GPU 2 and calculate
    # output for subnet 2. GPU 1 is idle
    x = x.cuda(gpu2)
    x = self.sub_network2(x)
    return x
```

As you can see in listing 4.2, two subnetworks are initialized and assigned to two GPUs in the __init__ function, and then they are connected in the forward function. Because of the variety of structures of deep learning networks, no general method (paradigm) exists to split the network. We must implement model parallelism case by case.

Another problem with model parallelism is its severe underutilization of GPU resources. Because all the devices in the training group have sequential dependency, only one device can work at a time, which wastes a lot of GPU cycles. Figure 4.7 visualizes the GPU utilization situation for model parallel training with three GPUs.

Let's walk through this figure to see why GPU usage is so low. On the left, in figure 4.7 (a), we see the model parallel design. We split a model network into three subnetworks and let each subnetwork run on a different GPU. In each training iteration, when running the forward pass, we first compute subnet 1 and then subnet 2 and subnet 3; when running the backward pass, the gradient update happens reversely.

In figure 4.7 (b), on the right, you can see the resource utilization of the three GPUs during the training. The time axis is divided into two parts: the forward pass and the backward pass. The forward pass means the computation of the model inference, from GPU 1 to GPU 2 and GPU3, whereas the backward pass means backpropagation for the model weights update, from GPU 3 to GPU 2 and GPU 1.

If you look vertically at the time bar, regardless of whether it's a forward pass or a backward pass, you see only one GPU active at a time. This is because of the sequential

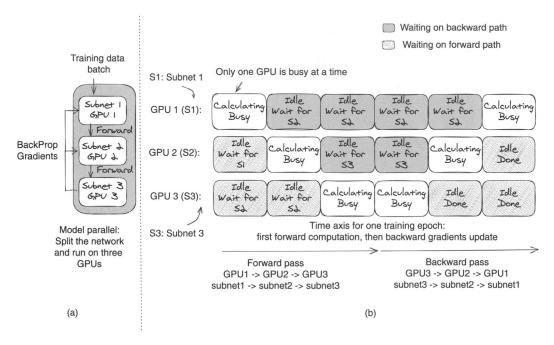

Figure 4.7   Model parallel training can have severely low GPU usage. In this approach, the network is split into three subnets and runs on three GPUs. Because of the sequential dependency among the three GPUs, each GPU is idle 66% of the training time.

dependency between each subnet. For instance, in the forward pass, subnet 2 needs to wait for subnet 1's output to fulfill its own forward calculation, so GPU 2 will be idle in the forward pass until the calculation on GPU 1 completes.

No matter how many GPUs you add, only one GPU can work at one time, which is a huge waste. This is when pipeline parallelism comes in handy. Pipeline parallelism makes model training more efficient by eliminating that waste and fully saturating the GPUs. Let's see how it works.

PIPELINE PARALLELISM

Pipeline parallelism is essentially an improved version of model parallelism. In addition to partitioning a network to different GPUs, it also divides each training example batch into small minibatches and overlaps computations of these minibatches between layers. By doing so, it keeps all GPUs busy most of the time, thus improving GPU utilization.

There are two major implementations of this approach: PipeDream (Microsoft) and GPipe (Google). We use GPipe as the demo example here because it optimizes the gradients' update in each training step and has better training throughput. You can find further details about GPipe from "GPipe: Easy scaling with micro-batch pipeline parallelism," by Huang et al. (https://arxiv.org/abs/1811.06965). Let's look, in figure 4.8, at how GPipe works at a high level.

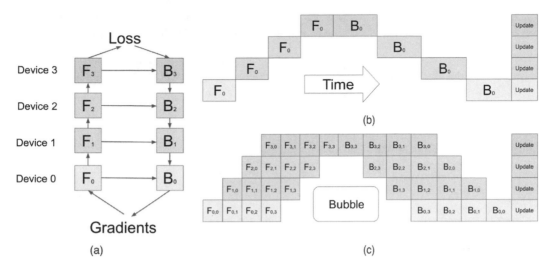

Figure 4.8 **(a) An example neural network with sequential layers is partitioned across four accelerators. F_k is the composite forward computation function of the kth cell. Bk is the backpropagation function, which depends on both B_{k+1}, from the upper layer, and F_k. (b) The naive model parallelism strategy leads to severe under utilization due to the sequential dependency of the network. (c) Pipeline parallelism divides the input minibatch into smaller microbatches, enabling different accelerators to work on different microbatches simultaneously. Gradients are applied synchronously at the end. (Source: figure 2, "GPipe: Easy Scaling with Micro-Batch Pipeline Parallelism," Huang et al., 2019, arXiv:1811.06965)**

Figure 4.8 (a) depicts a neural network made of four subnetworks; each subnetwork is loaded on one GPU. F means forward pass, B means backward pass, and F_k and B_k run on GPUk. The training sequence is first, forward pass, F_0 -> F_1 -> F_2 -> F_3, and second, backward pass, F_3 -> (B_3, F_2) -> (B_2, F_2) -> (B_1, F_1) -> B_0.

Figure 4.8 (b) displays the training flow for naive model parallelism. We can see that the GPU is seriously underutilized; only one GPU is activated in the forward- and backward pass; thus, each GPU is idle 75% of the time.

Figure 4.8 (c) shows the GPipe improvements in the sequence of training operations. GPipe first divides every training example batch into four equal microbatches, which are pipelined through the four GPUs. $F_{(0,2)}$ in the graph means forward pass computation at GPU 0 with minibatch 2. During the backward pass, gradients for each microbatch are computed based on the same model parameters used for the forward pass. The key is that it doesn't update model parameters immediately; instead, it accumulates all the gradients for each microbatch. At the end of each training batch, we use the accumulated gradients from all four microbatches to update the model parameters across all four GPUs.

By comparing figure 4.8 (b) and (c), we see the GPU utilization increase greatly; now each GPU is idle 47% of the time. Let's see a code example using PyTorch GPipe implementation to train a transformer model on two GPUs (see following listing). To demo the idea clearly, we keep only the pipeline-related code and partition them into four parts. You can check out the tutorial "PyTorch: Training transformer models using pipeline parallelism," by Pritam Damania, for the full code (http://mng.bz/5mD8).

Listing 4.3   Training transformer models using pipeline parallelism

```
## Part One: initialize remote communication
# for multiple machines
rpc.init_rpc(
  name="worker",
  # set rank number to this node, rank is the global
  # unique id of a node, 0 is the master,
  # other ranks are observers
  rank=0,

  # set the number of workers in the group
  world_size=1,
    .. .. ..
)


.. .. ..


## Part Two: split model to 2 subnetworks, load
# to different GPUs and initialize the pipeline.

num_gpus = 2
partition_len = ((nlayers - 1) // num_gpus) + 1

# Add all the necessary transformer blocks.
for i in range(nlayers):
  transformer_block = TransformerEncoderLayer(emsize,
    nhead, nhid, dropout)
    .. .. ..

  # Load first half encoder layers to GPU 0 and second hard encoder layers to
    GPU 1.
  device = i // (partition_len)
  tmp_list.append(transformer_block.to(device))

# Load decoder to GPU 1.
tmp_list.append(Decoder(ntokens, emsize).cuda(num_gpus - 1))
module_list.append(nn.Sequential(*tmp_list))

## Part Three: Build up the pipeline.
chunks = 8 # Set micro-batches number to 8.
model = Pipe(torch.nn.Sequential(*module_list), chunks = chunks)


.. .. ..


## Part 4: Train with pipeline
def train():
  model.train() # Turn on the train mode
    .. .. ..
```

```
for batch, i in enumerate(range(0, nbatches, bptt)):
  data, targets = get_batch(train_data, i)
  optimizer.zero_grad()

  # Compute pipeline output,by following the pipeline setup,
  # the Pytorch framework will coordinate the network computation
  # between GPU 0 and GPU 1.
  # Since the Pipe is only within a single host and process the "RRef"
  # returned by forward method is local to this node and can simply
  # retrieved via "RRef.local_value()".
  output = model(data).local_value()

  # Compute the loss on GPU 1.
  # Need to move targets to the device where the output of the
  # pipeline resides.
  loss = criterion(output.view(-1, ntokens), targets.cuda(1))

  # Backprop and model parameters update are the same as single GPU
   training.
  # The Pytorch framework hides all the details of micro-batches
  # computation and model parameters update.
  loss.backward()
  torch.nn.utils.clip_grad_norm_(model.parameters(), 0.5)
  optimizer.step()

.. .. ..
```

As we can see from listing 4.3, pipeline parallelism code is much more complicated than distributed data parallelism. Besides setting up the communication group, we also need to consider how to divide our model network and transfer gradients and activation (model the subnetwork's forward output) in interworker communication.

4.4.3   *How software engineers can support pipeline parallelism*

You may have noticed that all the methods we talk about in this section are techniques for writing training code. Because data scientists normally write the training code, you may be wondering what we, as software developers, can do to support pipeline parallel training.

First, we can work on building the training service to automate the pipeline training execution and improve resource utilization (for example, always keeping the GPU busy). This automation includes matters like allocating worker resources, enabling interworker communication, and distributing the pipeline training code with corresponding initialized parameters to each worker (such as worker IP address, process ID, GPU ID, and worker group size).

Second, we can alert the data scientist team about the new distributed training options. Sometimes the data scientist team isn't aware of the new engineering methods that can improve the model training experience, so communication is key here. We can collaborate with members of the team and lead the conversation about experimenting with the pipeline parallelism method.

Third, we can work on improving the availability of model training. In section 4.2.4, we discussed that distributed training is fragile; it requires every worker to perform consistently. If one worker fails, the entire training group fails, which is a huge waste of time and budget. The effort spent on training-process monitoring, failover, and failure recovery would be much appreciated by data scientists.

Data parallelism or pipeline parallelism?

Now we know that there are two major strategies for distributed training: data parallelism and pipeline parallelism. You might understand these concepts, but you might still be uncertain about when to use them.

We would suggest always starting with model training on a single machine. If you have a large dataset and the training takes a long time, then consider distributed training. We always prefer data parallelism over pipeline parallelism merely because data parallelism is simpler to implement and we can obtain results quicker. If the model is so big that it can't load on one GPU, then pipeline parallelism is the right choice.

Summary

- Distributed training has two schools of thought: data parallelism and model parallelism. Pipeline parallelism is an improved version of model parallelism.
- If a model can be loaded into one GPU, data parallelism is the primary method to implement distributed training; it's simple to use and provides great speed improvements.
- Using Kubernetes to manage the computing cluster can greatly reduce the complexity of compute resource management.
- Although each training framework (TensorFlow, PyTorch) offers different configurations and APIs to write distributed training code, their code pattern and execution workflow are very similar. Thus, a training service can support the various distributed training codes with a unified approach.
- After encapsulating the setup configuration of various training frameworks, a training service can still treat training code as a black box, even in the distributed training setting.
- To obtain data parallelism training progress/status, you only need to check the master worker because all workers are always in sync with each other. Also, to avoid saving duplicated models from all workers when their training jobs complete, you can set the training code to persist model and checkpoint files only when the code is executed by the master worker.
- Horovod is a great distributed training framework. It offers a unified method to run distributed training for code written in various frameworks: PyTorch, TensorFlow, MXNet, and PySpark. If a training code uses Horovod to implement

distributed training, a training service can use a single method (the Horovod method) to execute it, regardless of the training frame with which it's written.

- Availability, resilience, and failure recovery are important engineering concerns for distributed training.

- There are two strategies for training a model that does not fit into one GPU: the memory-saving method and the model parallelism method.

- The memory-saving method loads only a portion of the model or a small data batch to GPU at a time—for instance, gradient accumulation and memory swap. These methods are easy to implement but slow down the model training process.

- The model parallelism method divides a large model into a group of sub–neural networks and distributes them onto multiple GPUs. The downside of this approach is low GPU utilization. To overcome that, pipeline model parallelism was invented.

5

Hyperparameter optimization service

This chapter covers

- Hyperparameters and why they are important
- Two common approaches to hyperparameter optimization (HPO)
- Designing an HPO service
- Three popular HPO libraries: Hyperopt, Optuna, and Ray Tune

In the previous two chapters, we saw how models are trained: a training service manages training processes in a remote compute cluster with given model algorithms. But model algorithms and training services aren't all there is to model training. There's one more component we haven't discussed yet—hyperparameter optimization (HPO). Data scientists often overlook the fact that hyperparameter choices can influence model training results significantly, especially when these decisions can be automated using engineering methods.

Hyperparameters are parameters whose value must be set before the model training process starts. Learning rate, batch size, and number of hidden layers are all examples of hyperparameters. Unlike the value of *model parameters*—weights and bias, for example—hyperparameters cannot be learned during the training process.

Research reveals that the chosen value of hyperparameters can affect both the quality of the model training as well as the time and memory requirements of the training algorithm. Therefore, hyperparameters must be tuned to be optimal for model training. Nowadays, HPO has become a standard step in the deep learning model development process.

As one of the deep learning components, HPO is very important to software engineers. This is because HPO doesn't require a deep understanding of deep learning algorithms, so engineers are often assigned to this task. Most of the time, HPO can run like a black box, and the training code does not need to be modified. Furthermore, engineers have the capability of building an automatic HPO mechanism, making HPO possible. As there are so many hyperparameters to tune (learning rate, number of epochs, data batch size, and more) and so many values to try, it is simply impractical to manually adjust each hyperparameter value. Software engineers are well-suited to create an automated system because of their expertise in microservices, distributed computing, and resource management.

In this chapter, we will focus on the engineering of automatic HPO. We first introduce the background information necessary to feel comfortable working with HPO. We delve into a deeper understanding of hyperparameters and the process of tuning or optimizing them. We'll also meet some popular HPO algorithms and compare two common approaches to automating HPO: using a library and building a service.

Then we'll start designing. We will look at how to design an HPO service, including five design principles for creating an HPO service, as well as one general design proposal that is particularly important at this stage. Finally, we show you three popular open source HPO frameworks that would be a perfect fit if you want to optimize your training code locally.

Unlike previous chapters, we will not be building a brand new sample service in this chapter. Instead, we suggest you use the open source Kubeflow Katib (discussed in appendix C). Katib is a well-designed, extensible, and highly portable HPO service that can be used for almost any HPO project. Thus, we do not have to build one if it is a low-hanging fruit for you.

This chapter should give you a holistic view of the HPO domain while also providing you with a practical understanding of how to run HPO for your specific needs. Whether you decide to run HPO with a remote service or at your local machine with libraries/frameworks like Hyperopt, Optuna, or Ray Tune, we've got you covered.

5.1 Understanding hyperparameters

Before we look at how to tune hyperparameters, let's get a clearer understanding of what hyperparameters are and why they are important.

5.1.1 What is a hyperparameter?

The process of training deep learning models uses two types of parameters, or values: *model parameters* and *hyperparameters*. Model parameters are trainable—that is, their values are learned during model training—and they change as the model iterates. Hyperparameters, in contrast, are static; these configurations are defined and set before the training starts. For example, we can set the training epoch as 30 and the activation function of the neural network as ReLU (rectified linear unit) in the input parameters to kick off a model training process.

In other words, any model training configuration that affects model training performance but can't be estimated from data is a hyperparameter. There can be hundreds of hyperparameters in a model training algorithm, including, for example, the choice of model optimizer—ADAM (see "Adam: A Method for Stochastic Optimization," by Diederik P. Kingma and Jimmy Ba; https://arxiv.org/abs/1412.6980) or RMSprop (see "A Look at Gradient Descent and RMSprop Optimizers," by Rohith Gandhi; http://mng.bz/xdZX)—the number of layers in the neural network, the embedding dimensions, the minibatch size, and the learning rate.

5.1.2 *Why are hyperparameters important?*

The choice of values for hyperparameters can have a tremendous effect on model training results. Typically set manually, the values control the behavior of training algorithm execution and determine the speed of model training and the model accuracy.

To see this effect for yourself, you can experiment with hyperparameter values by running model training in the TensorFlow playground (https://playground.tensorflow .org). In this online playground, you can design your own neural network and train it to recognize four types of graphic patterns. By setting different hyperparameters, such as learning rate, regularization method, activation function, neural network layer count, and neuron count, you will see not only how the model performance varies but also how the learning behavior, such as training time and learning curve, can differ. To train a model to recognize a complicated data pattern like a spiral shape in this playground, we need to select the hyperparameters very carefully. For example, try setting the hidden layer count to 6, the neuron count per layer to 5, the activation function to ReLU, the data batch size to 10, and the regularization method to L1. After nearly 500 epochs of training, you'll see that the model can make an accurate classification prediction on a spiral-shaped graph.

In the research field, the effect of hyperparameter selection on model performance has long been documented. Take natural language processing embedding training, for instance. One paper, "Improving Distributional Similarity with Lessons Learned from Word Embeddings," by Levy et al. (https://aclanthology.org/Q15-1016.pdf), reveals that much of the performance gains of word embeddings are due to certain system design choices along with the HPOs rather than the embedding algorithms themselves. In NLP embedding training, these authors found the selection of hyperparameters has more effect than the selection of the training algorithm! Because the hyperparameter selection is so crucial to model training performance, hyperparameter tuning has now become a standard step in the model training process.

5.2   *Understanding hyperparameter optimization*

Now that you have a solid idea of what hyperparameters are and why they are so important to model training, let's turn to the process of optimizing them for your model. In this section, we will walk you through the steps for HPO. We will also look at HPO algorithms, which are used to optimize hyperparameters, as well as common approaches to performing HPO.

5.2.1   *What is HPO?*

HPO, or tuning, is the process of discovering a set of hyperparameters that yields an optimal model. Optimal here means a model that minimizes a predefined loss function on a given dataset. In figure 5.1, you can see a high-level view of the generic workflow of HPO on the model training process.

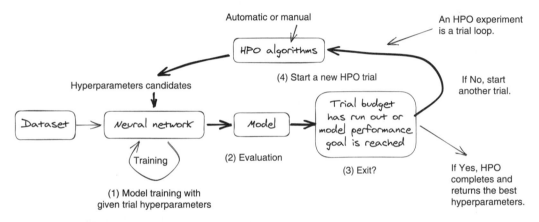

Figure 5.1   **This high-level view of the HPO workflow shows that the process is essentially an experiment to find the optimal hyperparameter values.**

From figure 5.1, we see that an HPO workflow can be visualized as a loop made with four steps. It shows us that the HPO process is a repetitive model training process, except that the neural network is trained each time with a different set of hyperparameters. The optimal set of hyperparameters will be discovered in this process. We normally call each run of the model training a *trial*. The whole HPO experiment is a trial loop in which we run one trial after another until the end criteria are met.

NOTE   To have a fair evaluation, the same dataset is used for each HPO trial.

Each trial has four steps, as shown in figure 5.1. Step 1 is training the neural network with a set of hyperparameter values. Step 2 is evaluating the training output (the model).

In step 3, the HPO process checks whether the end criteria have been met—for example, whether we have run out of our trial budget or whether the model produced in this trial has reached our performance evaluation target. If the trial result meets the end condition, the trial loop breaks and the experiment ends. The hyperparameter values that produced the best model evaluation result are considered the optimal hyperparameters.

If the end condition is not met, the process moves to step 4: the HPO process will produce a new set of hyperparameter values and start a new trial by triggering a model training run. The hyperparameter values used in each trial are generated either manually or automatically by an HPO algorithm. Let's look closer at these two approaches and the HPO algorithms in the next two sections.

MANUAL HPO

As data scientists, we often manually pick the hyperparameter values to run the HPO process shown in figure 5.1. Though, admittedly, choosing the optimal hyperparameter values manually is more like improvisation than science. But we are also drawing from our experience and the intuition that comes from that experience. We tend to start training a model with empirical hyperparameter values, such as the values used in a relevant published paper, and then make some small adjustments and test the model. After a few trials, we manually compare the model performance and choose the best-performing model from these trials. Figure 5.2 illustrates this workflow.

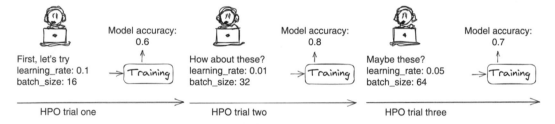

Figure 5.2   Manually picking hyperparameter values can be tedious and time-consuming.

The biggest problem with manual HPO is not knowing whether our hyperparameter values are optimal because we just choose some empirical values and tweak them. To get the optimal values, we need to try all possible hyperparameter values, aka search spaces. In the example of figure 5.2, we want to optimize two hyperparameters: learning rate and dataset batch size. In the HPO process, the goal is to find the pair of `batch_size` and `learning_rate` that produces the best model. Let's say we define a search space for `batch_size` as {8, 16, 32, 64, 128, 256} and define another search space for `learning_rate` as {0.1, 0.01, 0.001, 0.5, 0.05, 0.005}. Then the total number of hyperparameter values we need to verify is 36 (6^2).

Because we run the HPO manually, we have to run the model training process (HPO trial) 36 times and record the model evaluation result and the hyperparameters' values used in each trial. After completing all 36 trials and comparing the results, which is usually the model accuracy, we find the optimal `batch_size` and `learning_rate`.

Manually running HPO for the entire hyperparameter search space can be time-consuming, error prone, and tedious, as you can see. Moreover, deep learning hyperparameters usually have a complex configuration space, which often consists of a combination of continuous, categorical, and conditional hyperparameters as well as high dimensions. The deep learning industry is currently moving toward automatic HPO because manual HPO is simply not feasible.

AUTOMATIC HPO

Automatic HPO is the process of using compute power and algorithms to automatically find the optimal hyperparameters for a training code. The idea is to use an efficient search algorithm to discover the optimal hyperparameters without human intervention.

We also want the automatic HPO to run in a black-box fashion, so it is agnostic about the training code it is optimizing, and therefore we can easily onboard existing model training code to the HPO system. Figure 5.3 shows the automatic HPO workflow.

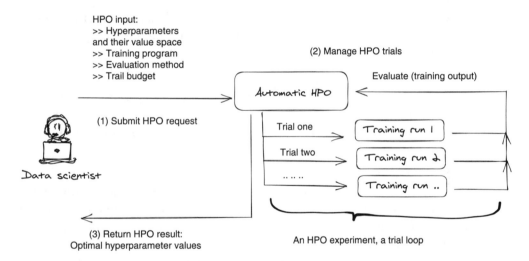

Figure 5.3 An automatic HPO workflow

In step 1, data scientists submit HPO requests to the automatic HPO system, which runs the HPO process in a black-box fashion (figure 5.3). They input the hyperparameters to be optimized and their value search space into the black box (the "automatic HPO" box in figure 5.3)—for example, the learning rate's search space may be [0.005, 0.1] and dataset batch size's search space may be {8, 16, 32, 64, 128, 256}. Data scientists also need to configure the training execution, such as the training code; an evaluation method; an exit objective; and a trial budget, such as 24 total trials for this experiment.

Once users submit the HPO request, the HPO experiment (step 2) starts. The HPO system schedules all the trials and manages their training executions; it also runs an HPO algorithm to generate hyperparameter values (picking values from the search space) for each trial. When the trial budget runs out or the training objective is met, the system returns a set of optimal hyperparameter values (step 3).

Automatic HPO relies on two key components: the HPO algorithm and trial training execution management. We can find the optimal hyperparameter values with fewer compute resources using an efficient HPO algorithm. By using a sophisticated training management system, data scientists can be hands-free for the entire HPO process.

> **NOTE** Because of the inefficiency of manual HPO, automatic HPO is the mainstream approach. To keep things concise, we will use the term *HPO* to refer to "automatic hyperparameter optimization" in the rest of this chapter.

5.2.2   *Popular HPO algorithms*

Most of the HPO algorithms can be categorized into three buckets: model-free optimization, Bayesian optimization, and multifidelity optimization.

> **NOTE** Because the main goal of this chapter is teaching HPO engineering, the HPO algorithms discussed here will stay at a high level. The goal of this section is to provide you with enough background knowledge on HPO algorithms to be able to build or set up an HPO system. If you want to know the mathematical reasoning behind the algorithms, please check out chapter 1, "Hyperparameter Optimization," by Matthias Feurer and Frank Hutter, of *AutoML: Methods, Systems, Challenges* (http://mng.bz/AlGx) and the paper "Algorithms for Hyper-Parameter Optimization," by Bergstra et al. (http://mng.bz/Zo9A).

MODEL-FREE OPTIMIZATION METHODS

In model-free methods, data scientists make no assumptions about training code, and the correlation between HPO trials is ignored. Grid search and random search are the most commonly used methods.

In grid search, users specify a limited set of values for each hyperparameter and then choose trial hyperparameters from the Cartesian product of those values. For example, we can first specify value sets (search space) for the learning rate as {0.1, 0.005, 0.001} and data batch size as {10, 40, 100} and then build the grid with Cartesian products (as grid value) of these sets, such as (0.1, 10), (0.1, 40), and (0.1, 100). After the grid is built, we can start the HPO trial with the grid values.

Grid search suffers when the number of hyperparameters becomes larger or the parameter's search space becomes bigger because the required number of evaluations will grow exponentially in this case. Another problem with grid search is its ineffectiveness. Because grid search treats each set of hyperparameter candidates equally, it will waste a lot of compute resources in the nonoptimal configuration space while not spending enough compute power on the optimal space.

Random search works by sampling the hyperparameter configuration space at random until a certain budget for the search is run out. For example, we can set the search space for the learning rate to [0.001, 0.1] and data batch size to [10, 100] and then set the search budget to 100, which means it will run up to a total of 100 HPO trials. In each trial, a random value is selected between 0.001 and 0.1 as the learning rate, and a random value is selected between 10 and 100 as the data batch size.

This approach has two advantages over grid search. First, random search can evaluate more values for each hyperparameter, which increases the chance of finding the optimal hyperparameter set. Second, random search has easier parallelization requirements; because all evaluation workers can run completely parallel, they don't need to communicate with each other, and a failed worker doesn't leave holes in the search space. But in grid search, a failed worker can skip the trial hyperparameters assigned to the worker in the HPO.

The downside of random search is uncertainty; there is no guarantee an optimal set of hyperparameters can be found within a finite computing budget. In theory, if we allow for enough resources, random search can add sufficient random points in the search, so it will, as expected, find the optimum hyperparameter set. In practice, random search is used as a baseline.

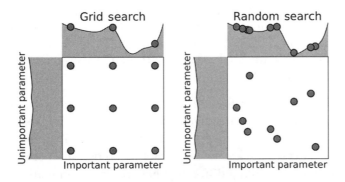

Figure 5.4   Comparison of grid search and random search for minimizing a function with one important and one unimportant parameter. (Source: Figure 1.1. of "Hyperparameter Optimization," by Matthias Feurer and Frank Hutter, in *AutoML: Methods, Systems, Challenges*, eds. Frank Hutter, Lars Kotthoff, and Joaquin Vanschoren; Springer, 2019. www.automl.org/ wp-content/uploads/2019/05/AutoML_Book_Chapter1.pdf)

Figure 5.4 illustrates the comparison between grid search and random search. The trial hyperparameter candidates (black dots) in grid search are Cartesian products of important parameter values (in rows) and unimportant value points (in columns). Their distribution can be seen as a grid in the search space (the white square canvas). The random search algorithm obtains the hyperparameter candidates randomly from the search space. When given enough of a search budget, its search point has a better chance of getting closer to the optimal position.

MODEL-BASED BAYESIAN OPTIMIZATION

Bayesian optimization is a state-of-the-art optimization framework for the global optimization of expensive black-box functions. It's used widely for various problem settings, such as image classification, speech recognition, and neural language modeling.

The Bayesian optimization methods can use different samplers, such as Gaussian process regression (see "An Intuitive Tutorial to Gaussian Processes Regression," by Jie Wang; https://arxiv.org/abs/2009.10862) and tree-structured Parzen estimator approach (TPE), to calculate hyperparameter candidates in the search space. In less rigorous words, the Bayesian optimization methods use statistical methods to calculate new hyperparameter value suggestions from the values used in past trials and their evaluation results.

> **NOTE**   Why is it called Bayesian optimization? Bayesian analysis (https://www
> .britannica.com/science/Bayesian-analysis) is a widely used statistical inference method, named after English mathematician Thomas Bayes (https://
> www.britannica.com/biography/Thomas-Bayes), that allows you to combine
> prior information about a population parameter with evidence from information contained in a sample to guide the statistical inference process. Based
> on this method, Jonas Mockus introduced the term Bayesian optimization (see
> "Bayesian Linear Regression," Bruna Wundervald; https://www.researchgate
> .net/publication/333917874_Bayesian_Linear_ Regression) in his 1970s and
> 1980s work on global optimization.

The concept behind Bayesian optimization methods is that the optimal hyperparameters search would be more efficient if the algorithm could learn from past trials. In practice, the Bayesian optimization method can find the optimal hyperparameters set with fewer evaluation runs (trials) and is more stable than the other search methods. Figure 5.5 shows the data sampling difference between random search and the Bayesian approach.

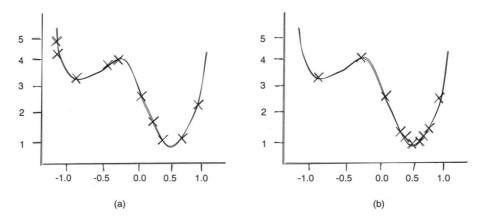

(a)   (b)

Figure 5.5   A data sampler comparison of random search (a) and Bayesian approach (b) using 10 trials

Let's assume the optimal hyperparameter value is at (x,y) = (0.5, 1), and we try to use random search and Bayesian search to find it. In figure 5.5 (a), we see the data is randomly sampled in the search space where x := [–1.0, 1.0] and y := [1, 5]. In figure 5.5 (b), we see that the data is sampled heavily in the area (x := [0.3, 0.7] and y := [1,1.5]), where the optimal value is located. This comparison shows that the Bayesian search is more likely to find the optimal hyperparameters in the given search space, and with a limited execution budget, the selected (sampled) hyperparameter values become closer and closer to the optimal value after each experiment in the search process.

There are other advanced HPO algorithms, such as Hyperband (http://mng.bz/Rlwv), TPE (http://mng.bz/2a6a), and covariance matrix adaptation evolution strategy (CMA-ES; http://mng.bz/1M5q). Although they do not follow the exact same mathematical theory as the Bayesian–Gaussian process method, they share the same hyperparameter selection strategy: calculating the next suggested value by considering the historical evaluation results.

MULTIFIDELITY OPTIMIZATION

Multifidelity methods improve the efficiency of model-free and Bayesian optimization methods. Nowadays, tuning hyperparameters on large datasets can take several hours and even days. To speed up the HPO, multifidelity methods were developed. With this approach, we minimize the loss function using so-called low-fidelity approximations of the actual loss function. As a result, we can skip a lot of computations during HPO.

> **NOTE** In the machine learning context, the loss function (https://www.datarobot.com/blog/introduction-to-loss-functions/) is a method of evaluating how well a training algorithm models your dataset. If the model output (predictions) is far off from the expected results, the loss function should output a higher number; otherwise, it should output a lower number. The loss function is a key component of ML algorithm development; the design of the loss function directly affects model accuracy.

Although the approximation introduces a tradeoff between optimization performance and run time, in practice, the speedups often outweigh the approximation errors. For more details, refer to "Hyperparameter Optimization," by Matthias Feurer and Frank Hutter (www.automl.org/wp-content/uploads/2019/05/AutoML_Book_Chapter1.pdf).

WHY DOES THE BAYESIAN-LIKE HPO ALGORITHM WORK?

The blog post "Intuition behind Gaussian Processes," by Michael McCourt (https://sigopt.com/blog/intuition-behind-gaussian-processes/) gives an excellent explanation for why the Bayesian-like optimization algorithm can find the optimum hyperparameter set without checking every possible value in the search space. In some settings, the experiments we observe are independent, such as flipping a coin 50 times; knowledge of one does not imply knowledge of others. But, fortunately, many settings have a more helpful structure from which previous observations provide insight into unobserved outcomes.

In the machine learning context, we assume there is some relationship between historical experiment (training trial) results and future experiment results. More specifically, we believe there is a math model for this relationship. Although using the Bayesian approach—for example, in the Gaussian process—to model this relationship is a very strong assumption, we are given great power to make provable optimal predictions. A side bonus is we now have a way to handle the uncertainty of the model prediction result.

> **NOTE** If you are interested in applying Bayesian optimization to deep learning projects, Quan Nguyen's book *Bayesian Optimization in Action* (Manning, 2022; https://www.manning.com/books/bayesian-optimization-in-action) is a good resource.

WHICH HPO ALGORITHM WORKS THE BEST?

No single HPO algorithm works best. Different optimization algorithms may fit different tuning tasks under different constraints. Some of those variables might include how the search space looks (e.g., hyperparameter types, value ranges), how the trial budget looks, and what the goal is (eventual optimality or optimal anytime performance). Figure 5.6 shows an HPO algorithm selection guideline from the Optuna (https://optuna.org/) HPO framework.

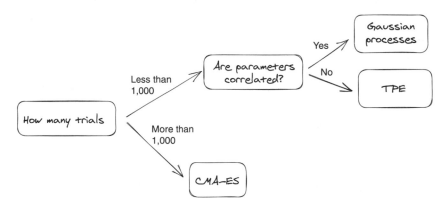

Figure 5.6   A HPO algorithm selection cheat sheet from the Optuna HPO framework

In figure 5.6, we see a decision graph for when to use the following three HPO algorithms: Gaussian process, TPE, and CMA-ES. Because HPO is a fast-developing field, new efficient algorithms can be published at any time, so algorithm selection cheat sheets like this will quickly become outdated. For example, FLAML (https://github .com/microsoft/FLAML) is a newly developed Python HPO library that checks the hyperparameter correlation during the HPO process; it is definitely worth a try. So please check with your data science team for the latest HPO algorithm selection guideline.

NOTE The HPO algorithm is not the primary focus of HPO engineering. The math behind the HPO algorithm can be intimidating, but luckily, it is not the engineer's focus. Normally, it's the data scientist's job to determine which HPO algorithm to use for a certain training job. As engineers, our role is to build a flexible, extensible, black-box–fashion HPO system, so data scientists can run their model training code with arbitrary HPO algorithms easily.

5.2.3   Common automatic HPO approaches

Fortunately, many mature frameworks and systems already exist today for conducting HPO. Depending on the usage, they fall into two different categories: the HPO library approach and the HPO service approach. Figure 5.7 illustrates the two approaches. Let's now discuss them one by one.

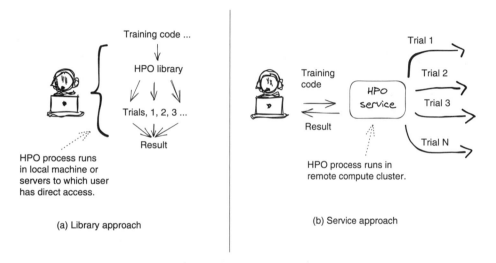

Figure 5.7   Two different HPO approaches: library vs. service. (a) HPO libraries can run HPO experiments (training) on a local machine or a group of servers with preconfiguration; (b) HPO service can run HPO experiments in a fully remote and automatic fashion.

HPO LIBRARY APPROACH

In figure 5.7 (a), the library approach, we see that data scientists manage the HPO process themselves, from coding to execution. They code the entire HPO flow by using an HPO library, such as Hyperopt—an open source Python HPO library—and integrate it with the training code together in one training application. Next, data scientists run this application on their local machine or on the servers to which they have direct access. The HPO library inside the application will execute the HPO workflow that we see in figure 5.3.

Flexibility and agility are the biggest advantages of the library approach; you can choose any HPO algorithm/libraries you like, integrate them into your training code, and start the HPO process right away because everything (training plus hyperparameter calculation) happens on your local machine. Some HPO libraries—for example, Ray Tune (section 5.4.3)—also support parallel distributed execution but not in a fully automatic manner. This requires setting up a distributed computing group with specific software that allows cross-machine communication, and it also requires manually kicking off the parallel process on each server.

The biggest challenges for the library approach are scalability, reusability, and stability. HPO requires lots of compute resources to execute its trials, so a single server is often not capable of HPO. Even with the distributed functionality, it still can't scale. Imagine we want to use 20 servers for an HPO task that requires 10,000 trial runs; we need to manually set up the HPO process on 20 servers and redo the setup every time the training or HPO code changes. Also, if 1 of the 20 parallel workers fails, the entire HPO work group comes to a halt. To address these problems, the HPO service approach is introduced.

HPO SERVICE APPROACH

Now let's take a closer look at the HPO service approach; we repeat figure 5.7 for clarity, presented here as figure 5.8. In figure 5.8 (b), the service approach, we see that the HPO happens in a remote compute cluster, managed by a service—the HPO service. A data scientist only provides training code and a selected HPO algorithm configuration to the service and starts the HPO job. The service manages both compute resource allocation and the HPO workflow (figure 5.3) execution; it tracks each trial's result (model performance metric, such as accuracy) and returns the final optimal hyperparameters to the data scientist when all trials are complete.

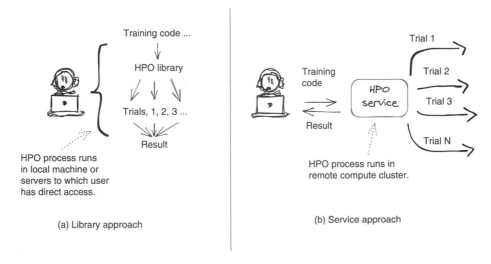

Figure 5.8   Two different HPO approaches: library vs. service

The service approach provides a real black-box experience. Data scientists don't need to worry about managing their own servers, setting up trial workers, and learning how to modify training code to work with different HPO algorithms. The HPO service takes care of all of these tasks. As the HPO service user, we just pass parameters into the service, and then the service runs the HPO automatically and returns the optimal hyperparameters at the end. The service also takes care of autoscaling and failure recovery of failed trial jobs. Because of these advantages, the service approach is now the dominant HPO approach in the deep learning production environment. Because you are now familiar with HPO concepts and approaches, let's look at how to design an HPO service and how to use HPO libraries in the next two sections.

> **NOTE** HPO is *not* a one-time job. If training with a different dataset, you need to redo the HPO even if the model architecture didn't change. If the dataset changes, the optimal set model weights that fit best with the given data change as well, so you need a new HPO searching effort.

5.3 Designing an HPO service

Now that you have a good understanding of the HPO library approach, let's review the HPO service approach. In this section, we will look at how to design an HPO service to support HPO for arbitrary model training in an automatic and black-box fashion.

5.3.1 HPO design principles

Before we look at the concrete design proposal, let's first check out the five design principles for building an HPO service.

PRINCIPLE 1: TRAINING CODE AGNOSTIC

The HPO service needs to be agnostic to training code and model training frameworks. In addition to supporting arbitrary machine learning frameworks like TensorFlow, PyTorch, and MPI, we would like the service to be able to tune hyperparameters of training code written in any programming language.

PRINCIPLE 2: EXTENSIBILITY AND CONSISTENCY IN SUPPORTING DIFFERENT HPO ALGORITHMS

From the HPO algorithms discussion in section 5.2.2, we know the hyperparameters search algorithm is the brain of the HPO process. The efficiency of the hyperparameter search decides the HPO performance. A good HPO algorithm can find optimal hyperparameters with a large hyperparameter number and arbitrary search spaces in a small number of trials.

Because HPO algorithm research is an active field, a new effective algorithm is published every few months. Our HPO service needs to integrate with these new algorithms easily and expose them as algorithm options to customers (data scientists). Also, the newly added algorithm should behave consistently with the existing algorithms in terms of user experience.

PRINCIPLE 3: SCALABILITY AND FAULT TOLERANCE

Besides HPO algorithms, another important responsibility of an HPO service is to manage the computing resources used for HPO—the model training with various hyperparameter values. From an HPO experiment perspective, we want distributed execution at both the experiment level and trial level. More specifically, we want to not only run trials in a distributed and parallel manner but also be able to run a single training trial distributedly—for example, running distributed training for the model training in one trial. From a resource utilization perspective, the system needs to support autoscaling, which allows the compute cluster size to be automatically adjusted to the current workload, so there is no under- or overutilization of resources.

Fault tolerance is also another important aspect of HPO trial execution management. Fault tolerance is important because some HPO algorithms are required to execute trials sequentially. For example, trial 2 must happen after trial 1 because the algorithm needs the past hyperparameter values and results to deduce the hyperparameters before the next trial starts. In this case, when one trial fails unexpectedly—for example, because of a node restart or a network problem—the entire HPO process fails. The system should recover from the previous failure automatically. The common approach is to record the latest state of each trial, so we can resume from the last recorded checkpoint.

PRINCIPLE 4: MULTITENANCY

An HPO process is essentially a set of model training executions. Similar to model training, HPO services must provide resource isolation for various users or groups. This will ensure that different user activities stay within their boundaries.

PRINCIPLE 5: PORTABILITY

Nowadays, the concept of "cloud neutral" has become very popular. People want to run their model training job in different environments—Amazon Web Services, Google Cloud Platform, and Azure—so the HPO service we build needs to decouple from the underlying infrastructure. Running HPO service on Kubernetes is a good choice here.

5.3.2 A general HPO service design

Because the HPO workflow (figure 5.3) is quite standard and there are not many variations, the HPO service system design (figure 5.9) can be applied to most of the HPO scenarios. It consists of three main components: an API interface, HPO job manager, and hyperparameter (HP) suggestion maker. (They are marked as A, B, and C in figure 5.9.)

The API interface (component A) is the entrance point for users to submit HPO jobs. To start an HPO experiment, users submit an API request (step 1) to the interface; the request provides model training code, such as a Docker image; hyperparameters and their search space; and an HPO algorithm.

The HP suggestion maker (component C) is a wrapper/adapter for different HPO algorithms. It provides a unified interface for users to run each different HPO algorithm, so users can select an algorithm without worrying about the execution details.

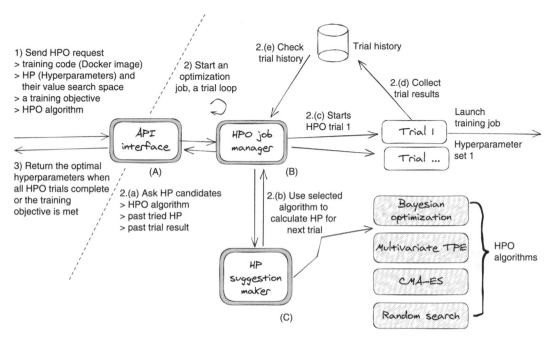

Figure 5.9   A general system design of an HPO service

To add a new HPO algorithm, it must be registered in this suggestion-maker component to become an algorithm option for users.

The HPO job manager (component B) is the core component of the HPO service;
it manages the HPO experiments for customer requests. For each HPO request, the
job manager starts an HPO trial loop (step 2). Within the loop, it first calls the HP
suggestion maker to obtain a set of suggested hyperparameter values (step 2.a) and
then creates a trial to run model training with these hyperparameter values (steps 2.b
and 2.c).

For each training trial, the HPO job manager creates a trial object. This object has
two responsibilities: first, it collects the output of a trial execution, such as the training
progress, model metrics, model accuracy, and tried hyperparameters; second, it manages the training process. It handles the training process launching, distributed training setup, and failure recovery.

HPO SERVICE END-TO-END EXECUTION WORKFLOW

Let's walk through the end-to-end user workflow, as shown in figure 5.9. For your convenience, we repeat figure 5.9, shown here as figure 5.10.

First, the user submits an HPO request to the API interface (step 1). The request
defines the training code, a list of hyperparameters and their value search space, the
training objective, and an HPO algorithm. Then, the HPO job manager starts an HPO
trial loop for this request (step 2). This loop launches a set of trials to determine
which set of hyperparameter values works the best. In the end, when the trial budgets

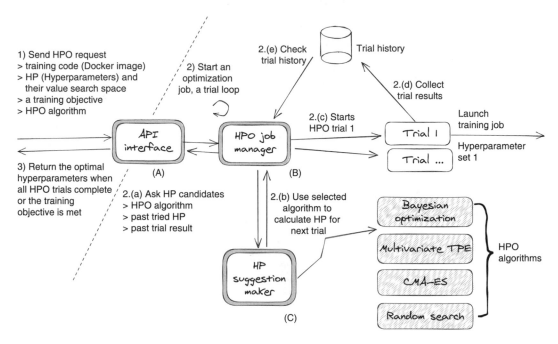

Figure 5.10   A general system design of an HPO service

run out or one trial meets the training objective, the trial loop breaks, and the best hyperparameters are returned (step 3).

Within a trial loop, the job manager first queries the HP suggestion maker to recommend hyperparameter candidates (step 2.a). The suggestion maker will run the selected HPO algorithm to calculate a set of hyperparameter values and return it to the job manager (step 2.b). The job manager then creates a trial object that launches a model training process with the suggested hyperparameter values (step 2.c). The trial object will also monitor the training process and continue reporting training metrics to the trial history database until the training completes (step 2.d). When the job manager notices the current trial is complete, it pulls the trial history (trial metrics and hyperparameter values used in past trials) and passes it to the HP suggestion maker to obtain a new set of HP candidates (step 2.e).

Because the HPO use cases are quite standard and generic and there are already multiple open source HPO projects that work out of the box, we think it's better to learn how to use them instead of rebuilding a new system that has no added value. So in appendix C, we will introduce you to a powerful and highly portable Kubernetes-based HPO service—Kubeflow Katib.

5.4   *Open source HPO libraries*

The HPO service might seem like too much overhead for a small data scientist team, especially if all their models are trained on a few servers they manage themselves. In this case, using HPO libraries to optimize model training in local machines or managed clusters (small scale, 1–10 servers) is a better option.

In this section, we will introduce three useful HPO open source libraries: Optuna, Hyperopt, and Ray Tune. They all run as HPO libraries, and they are easy to learn and simple to use. Because Optuna, Hyperopt, and Ray Tune all have clear onboarding docs and suitable examples, we will focus on the general overview and feature introduction so you can decide which one to use based on your own circumstances.

In the following discussion about different HPO libraries, especially in the "How to Use" sections, you will see the term *objective function* a lot. What is an objective function? Figure 5.11 demonstrates the process.

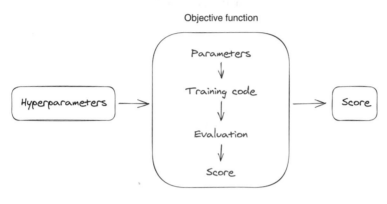

Figure 5.11   An objective function receives the hyperparameters as input and returns a score.

For an HPO algorithm, such as Bayesian search, to generate a hyperparameter suggestion so that the next trial works better, it needs to know how well the previous HPO trial operated. Therefore, the HPO algorithm requires that we define a function to score each training trial and continue minimizing or maximizing the return value of the function (score) in the subsequent trials. We named this the objective function.

In figure 5.11, we see that an objective function receives hyperparameters as input and returns a float value, or score. The objective function executes the model training with given hyperparameters and evaluates the output model when the training completes.

5.4.1   *Hyperopt*

Hyperopt (http://hyperopt.github.io/hyperopt/#getting-started) is a lightweight and easy-to-use Python library for serial and parallel HPO. Random search, TPE, and adaptive TPE are the three HPO algorithms implemented in Hyperopt. Bayesian optimization algorithms (based on Gaussian processes) and regression trees have been designed to accommodate but were not yet implemented at the time this book was written.

HOW TO USE

Let's say you want to know which classifiers work best for your deep learning case. We can use Hyperopt to obtain the answer in three steps.

First, we create an objective function that is basically a wrapper function of the actual training code but reads the hyperparameter values from the args variable. Second, we define search space for the selected hyperparameter. Third, we choose an HPO algorithm, which selects hyperparameter values from the search space and passes them to the objective function to start the optimization process. Listing 5.1 implements this scenario.

In this example, we want to determine which classifier leads to the best model accuracy, so we choose to optimize the classifier_type hyperparameter among three candidates: naive_bayes, svm, and dtree. You may also notice that each classifier has its own value search space, such as hp.lognormal('svm_rbf_width', 0, 1) for the svm classifier. In the fmin function (in step 3), we specify TPE as the HPO algorithm with 10 max trials and pass in the objective function and search space as the required parameters.

Listing 5.1 Getting started with Hyperopt

```
# Step 1: define an objective function
def objective(args):
  model = train(args)          Trains the model with the passed in
  return evaluate(model)       hyperparameters and evaluates the result

# Step 2 define search space for hyperparameters
space = hp.choice('classifier_type', [        Declares three
  {                                            classifier candidates
    'type': 'naive_bayes',
  },
  {
    'type': 'svm',
    'C': hp.lognormal('svm_C', 0, 1),
    'kernel': hp.choice('svm_kernel', [        Defines search
      {'ktype': 'linear'},                     space for the
      {'ktype': 'RBF',                         parameters of the
       'width': hp.lognormal('svm_rbf_width', 0, 1)},   SVM classifier
    ]),
  },
  {
    'type': 'dtree',
    'criterion': hp.choice('dtree_criterion',
      ['gini', 'entropy']),
    'max_depth': hp.choice('dtree_max_depth',
      [None, hp.qlognormal('dtree_max_depth_int', 3, 1, 1)]),
    'min_samples_split': hp.qlognormal(
      'dtree_min_samples_split', 2, 1, 1),
```

```
  },
  ])

# Step 3 start the hpo process execution
best = fmin(objective, space, algo=tpe.suggest,
      ➡ max_evals=100)
```

> The fmin function minimizes the objective over the space with the selected algorithm.

PARALLELIZATION

Although Hyperopt is a standalone library, we can run it parallelly in a cluster of machines. The basic idea is to run Hyperopt workers on different machines and let them talk to a central database for coordination. Hyperopt can also use Spark computing to run HPO parallelly. You can check out the following two articles for more details: "On Using Hyperopt: Advanced Machine Learning," by Tanay Agrawal (http://mng.bz/PxwR) and "Scaling Out Search with Apache Spark" (http://hyperopt.github.io/hyperopt/scaleout/spark/).

WHEN TO USE

Hyperopt is a good option for small or early-phase model training projects. First, it's easy to use. You can run HPO in three steps on a local machine or on servers to which you have direct access. Second, it's friendly to modification. Because it takes a library approach, the HPO code is placed with training code in the same code project. So, trying different optimization plans, such as choosing various hyperparameters to tune, is very convenient.

5.4.2 Optuna

Similar to Hyperopt, Optuna is also a lightweight Python library designed to automate hyperparameter searches. It supports large space search and early pruning on the unpromising trials, as well as parallelization on multiple threads or processes without modifying code.

In our opinion, Optuna is an advanced version of Hyperopt, and its visualization capabilities are much better. By examining the interactions between parameters in a graph, the visualization in hyperparameter search gives you a lot of insight, so you can easily determine which parameters are more effective than others. Optuna's visualization is beautiful and interactive.

Optuna has another advantage over Hyperopt concerning its documentation. Optuna's documentation is excellent. In addition to its detailed API doc and well-organized tutorials, it has well-maintained source code. If you look at its GitHub project issue section, you will find a very active and growing community, and great features and GitHub pull requests are still to come.

HOW TO USE

Listing 5.2 shows a quick three-step example of how to use Optuna: step 1, define the objective function; step 2, create a study object to represent the HPO process; and step 3, start the HPO process with a max trials quota.

Compared to Hyperopt, Optuna requires most of the HPO logic to be defined in the objective function. The general code pattern is as follows. First, define the search space and generate the hyperparameter values by `trial.suggest_xxx` function. Next, start the model training with the sampled hyperparameter values. Then run the evaluation method to calculate model performance and return the objective value. In the following example, the evaluation score is calculated by `mean_squared_error`. You can find more Optuna examples at https://github.com/optuna/optuna-examples.

Listing 5.2 Getting started with Optuna

```
# Step 1: define an objective function
def objective(trial):

  regressor_name = trial.suggest_categorical(        Sets classifier
    'classifier', ['SVR', 'RandomForest'])           candidates
  if regressor_name == 'SVR':
    svr_c = trial.suggest_float(                      Invokes suggest_XXX
      'svr_c', 1e-10, 1e10, log=True)                 methods to generate
    regressor_obj = sklearn.svm.SVR(C=svr_c)          the hyperparameters
  else:
    rf_max_depth = trial.suggest_int('rf_max_depth', 2, 32)   ◁─┐ Chooses
    regressor_obj = sklearn.ensemble                               max_depth in the
      .RandomForestRegressor(max_depth=rf_max_depth)               range of 2 and 32

  X_train, X_val, y_train, y_val = \
    sklearn.model_selection.train_test_split(X, y, random_state=0)

  regressor_obj.fit(X_train, y_train)        ◁─┐ Runs model training with
  y_pred = regressor_obj.predict(X_val)           the Optuna regressor

  error = sklearn.metrics
    .mean_squared_error(y_val, y_pred)       Sets mean square error as the objective
  return error                              value and links to the trial object

# Step 2: Set up HPO by creating a new study.
study = optuna.create_study()

# Step 3: Invoke HPO process
study.optimize(objective, n_trials=100)
```

PARALLELIZATION

We can run distributed HPO on one machine or a cluster of machines with Optuna. The distributed execution setup is fairly simple and can be done in three steps: first, start a relational database server, such as MySQL; second, create a study with storage argument; and third, share the study among multiple nodes and processes. Compared to Hyperopt, Optuna's distributed execution setup is simpler, and it can scale up from a single machine to multiple machines without code modifications.

WHEN TO USE

Optuna can be seen as the successor of Hyperopt; it has better documentation, visualization, and parallel execution. For any deep learning model training project that can run on one or more machines, you can use Optuna to find the optimal hyperparameters.

Optuna will hit its limit with a large data science team or multiple HPO projects to support because it requires managing a central machine cluster to provide the computing resource. But Optuna's parallel/distributed execution is manual; people need to distribute the code to each server and execute it one server at a time, manually. To manage distributed computing jobs in an automatic and programmatic fashion, we can use Kubeflow Katib (appendix C) or Ray Tune.

5.4.3   *Ray Tune*

Ray (https://docs.ray.io/en/latest/index.html) provides a simple, universal API for building distributed applications. Ray Tune (https://docs.ray.io/en/latest/tune/index .html) is a Python library built on top of Ray for HPO at any scale.

The Ray Tune library supports almost any machine learning framework, including PyTorch, XGBoost, MXNet, and Keras. It also supports state-of-the-art HPO algorithms such as Population Based Training (PBT), BayesOptSearch, and HyperBand/ ASHA. In addition, Tune provides a mechanism to integrate HPO algorithms from other HPO libraries, such as Hyperopt integration.

By using Ray as its distributed executing support, we can launch a multinode HPO experimentation in a few lines of code. Ray will take care of code distribution, distributed computing management, and fault tolerance.

HOW TO USE

Using Ray Tune to execute an HPO task is very straightforward. First, define an objective function. In the function, read hyperparameter values from the `config` variable, start model training, and return the evaluation score. Second, define hyperparameters and their value search space. Third, start the HPO execution by linking the objective function and search space together. Listing 5.3 implements the aforementioned three steps.

Listing 5.3   Getting started with Ray Tune

```
# Step 1: define objective_function
def objective_function(config):            ConvNet is a self-
  model = ConvNet()             ◁──────    defined neural
  model.to(device)                         network.

  optimizer = optim.SGD(                    Reads the
    model.parameters(), lr=config["lr"],    hyperparameter value
    momentum=config["momentum"])            from the input config
  for i in range(10):
    train(model, optimizer, train_loader)   ◁──  Starts model
    acc = test(model, test_loader)               training

    tune.report(mean_accuracy=acc)   ◁──────────  Sends the evaluation
                                                  result (accuracy) back
# Step 2: define search space for each hyperparameter   to Tune
search_space = {
  "lr": tune.sample_from(lambda spec:
    10**(-10 * np.random.rand())),
```

```
    "momentum": tune.uniform(0.1, 0.9)
}
```

◁ Samples a float value uniformly between 0.1 and 0.9 for "momentum"

```
# Uncomment this to enable distributed execution
# `ray.init(address="auto")`

# Step 3: start the HPO execution
analysis = tune.run(
    objective_function,
    num_samples=20,
    scheduler=ASHAScheduler(metric="mean_accuracy", mode="max"),
    config=search_space)

# check HPO progress and result
# obtain a trial dataframe from all run trials
# of this `tune.run` call.
dfs = analysis.trial_dataframes
```

You may notice a scheduler object, ASHAScheduler, is passed to the tune.run function in step 3. ASHA (http://mng.bz/JlwZ) is a scalable algorithm for principled early stopping (see "Massively Parallel Hyperparameter Optimization," by Liam Li; http://mng.bz/wPZ5). At a high level, ASHA terminates trials that are less promising and allocates time and resources to more promising trials. By properly adjusting the parameter num_samples, the search can be much more efficient, and it can support a larger search space.

PARALLELIZATION

Distributed execution is Ray Tune's biggest advantage compared with Optuna. Ray Tune allows you to transparently parallelize across multiple GPUs and multiple nodes (see Ray documentation at http://mng.bz/qdRx). Tune even has seamless fault tolerance and cloud support. Unlike Optuna and Hyperopt, we don't need to manually set up a distributed environment and execute worker scripts one machine after another. Ray Tune takes care of these steps automatically. Figure 5.12 shows how Ray Tune distributes HPO Python code to a cluster of machines.

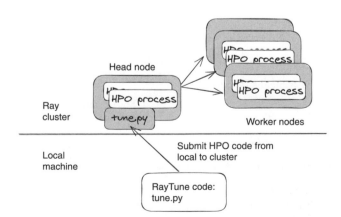

Figure 5.12   Ray Tune running distributed HPO on a cluster of machines

First, we set up a Ray cluster with the command `"ray up tune-cluster.yaml"`; the `tune-cluster.yaml` is a cluster configuration that declares the computing resources for the cluster. Then we run the following command to submit the HPO code from the local machine to the head node of the cluster: `"ray submit tune-cluster.yaml tune_script.py --start -- --ray-address={server_address}"`. Next, Ray assigns resources, copies the HPO code to the servers, and starts the distributed execution. For further details, please see "Tune Distributed Experiments" (http://mng.bz/71QQ).

Besides distributed HPO execution, Ray Tune also supports running distributed training for single-trial, automatic checkpoint management and TensorBoard logging. These features add great value to Ray Tune for their high fault tolerance and simple troubleshooting.

WHEN TO USE

Compared with other HPO libraries, is Ray Tune the way to go for HPO? Provisionally, yes. As this book is being written, Ray provides integration between the underlying training framework (such as TensorFlow and PyTorch) and the cutting-edge HPO algorithm (such as Bayesian search and TPE), as well as early stopping (ASHA). It allows us to run HPO searches distributedly in a straightforward and reliable manner.

For most of the data science team, who don't want to own an HPO service, Ray Tune is the suggested approach. It's simple to use, and it meets almost every model training project's HPO requirement: great documents, cutting-edge HPO algorithms, and efficient and simple distributed execution management.

> **NOTE** We recommend using Ray Tune over other HPO libraries for the following five reasons: (1) it is simple to use; (2) it has great documents and examples; (3) its distributed execution is automatic and programmatic; (4) Ray Tune supports distributed training for a single trial; and (5) Ray Tune has a scheduler feature (for example, `ASHAScheduler`) that can greatly reduce computing cost by terminating unpromising trials earlier.

THE LIMITATION OF RAY TUNE

Ray Tune and other HPO libraries will hit their limits when we need to support different teams and different deep learning projects in one shared HPO system. Ray Tune is missing computing isolation, which leads to two big problems.

First, package versions of different training codes can cause conflicts between Ray workers. When performing distributed HPO in Ray Tune, we submit the HPO code to the Ray cluster's head server and then run this code in the cluster workers in parallel. This means every Ray worker server needs to install the dependent libraries for every training code that it needs to run. Imagine how we manage the package installation and potential version conflicts when you have to run 10 different HPO tasks in one Ray cluster; the worker machine needs to install hundreds of packages for these 10 different training codes and also resolve their version conflicts. Second, Ray Tune doesn't enforce user segregation. It's very difficult to build a virtual boundary in Ray Tune for different data science teams to limit their computing resource usage.

5.4.4   *Next steps*

When you encounter the aforementioned problems with HPO libraries, it's time to switch to an HPO service. We strongly recommend you read appendix C before you consider building your own HPO. It introduces a solid open source HPO service called Kubeflow Katib, which is a well-designed, general-purpose HPO service.

Summary

- A hyperparameter is a parameter whose value is used to control the learning process. This type of parameter is not learnable in model training; therefore, we need to tune it.
- HPO is a process to discover a set of hyperparameters that yields an optimal model, which minimizes a predefined loss function on a given dataset.
- Automatic HPO is the process of using compute power and algorithms (HPO algorithms) to automatically find the optimal hyperparameters for a training code.
- Automatic HPO now is a standard step for model training.
- Most HPO algorithms can be categorized into one of three buckets: model-free optimization, Bayesian optimization, or multifidelity optimization.
- There is no single best HPO algorithm. Different optimization algorithms may fit different HPO tasks under different constraints.
- HPO can run with a library or in a remote service. The library approach is simple, flexible, and suitable for small teams and projects in the prototyping phase whereas the service approach is for large organizations and production use cases.
- The HPO service approach provides a fully automatic black-box HPO experience, including computing resource management; therefore, we recommend taking a service approach if you are building a deep learning system for large teams.
- The five design principles for building an HPO service are training code agnostic, high extensibility, high scalability and reliability, HPO execution and resource consumption segregation, and high portability.
- To expedite an HPO experiment, we can parallelize training executions of different trials, introduce distributed training, and stop the unpromising trials early.
- We encourage you to adopt Kubeflow Katib as your HPO service instead of building a new service yourself.
- Among three commonly used open source HPO libraries—Optuma, Hyperopt, and Ray tune—Ray Tune has so far proven to be the best.

Model serving design

This chapter covers

- Defining model serving
- Common model serving challenges and approaches
- Designing model serving systems for different user scenarios

Model serving is the process of executing a model with user input data. Among all the activities in a deep learning system, model serving is the closest to the end customers. After all the hard work of dataset preparation, training algorithm development, hyperparameter tuning, and testing results in models is completed, these models are presented to customers by model serving services.

Take speech translation as an example. After training a sequence-to-sequence model for voice translation, the team is ready to present it to the world. For people to use this model remotely, the model is usually hosted in a web service and exposed by a web API. Then we (the customers) can send our voice audio file over the web API and get back a translated voice audio file. All the model loading and execution happens at the web service backend. Everything included in this user workflow—service, model files, and model execution—is called *model serving*.

Building model serving applications is another special deep learning domain for which software engineers are particularly well suited. Model serving uses request latency, scalability, availability, and operability—all areas that engineers know inside and out. With some introduction to the concepts of deep learning model serving, developers who have some experience with distributed computing can play a significant role in building the model serving element.

Serving models in production can be challenging because models are trained by various frameworks and algorithms, so the methods and libraries to execute the model vary. Also, the terminology used in the model serving field is confusing, with too many terms, like *model prediction* and *model inference*, that sound different but mean the same thing in the serving context. Furthermore, there are many model serving options from which to choose. On the one hand, we have black-box solutions like TensorFlow Serving, TorchServe, and NVIDIA Triton Inference Server. On the other, we have customized approaches like building your own predictor service or embedding models directly into your applications. These approaches all seem very similar and capable, so it is hard to select one over another. Therefore, if you are new to this domain, you can quickly become lost.

Our goal here is to help you find your way. We hope to empower you to design and build the model serving solution that best fits your situation. To achieve this goal, we have lots of content to cover, from the conceptual understanding of model serving and service-design considerations to concrete examples and model deployment workflow. To avoid exhausting you with a super-long chapter, we divide this content into two chapters: chapter 6 focuses on concepts, definitions, and design, and chapter 7 puts those concepts into practice, including building a sample prediction service and addressing open source tools as well as deploying and monitoring model production.

In this chapter, we start by clarifying the terminology and providing our own definitions of the elements used in model serving. We also describe the main challenges facing us in the model serving field. Then we will move to the design aspect, explaining the three common strategies of model serving and designing a model serving system that fits different use cases.

By reading this chapter, you will not only gain a solid understanding of how model serving works, but you will also know the common design patterns that can address most of the model serving use cases. With the concepts and terminology clear in your mind, you should be comfortable joining any model serving–related discussion or reading articles and papers on the topic. And, of course, this chapter builds the foundation so you can follow the practical work addressed in the next chapter.

6.1   *Explaining model serving*

In the engineering of model serving, the terminology is a major problem. For example, *model, model architecture, inference graph, prediction,* and *inference* are all terms people use without clearly defining them, so they can have the same meaning or refer to different concepts depending on the context (model serving or model training). When we work with data scientists to build model serving solutions, the confusion around model serving terms causes a lot of miscommunication. In this section, we will explain the core concepts of model serving and interpret commonly used terminologies from an engineering perspective to help you avoid falling into the terminology trap.

6.1.1 What is a machine learning model?

There are multiple definitions of machine learning models in academia, from distilled representations of learnings of datasets to mathematical representations for recognizing certain patterns or making decisions based on previously unseen information. Nevertheless, as model serving developers, we can understand a model simply as a collection of files that are produced during training.

The idea of a model is simple, but many people misunderstand that models are just static files. Although models are saved as files, they aren't static; they're essentially executable programs.

Let's take apart that statement and determine what it means. A model consists of a machine learning algorithm, model data, and a model executor. A *model executor* is a wrapper code of the machine learning algorithm; it takes user input and runs the algorithm to compute and return prediction results. A *machine learning algorithm* refers to the algorithm used in model training, sometimes also called *model architecture*. Using speech translation as an example again, if the translation model is trained by a sequence-to-sequence network as its training algorithm, the machine learning algorithm in the model is the same sequence-to-sequence network. *Model data* is the data required to run the machine learning algorithm, such as the neural network's learned parameters (weights and biases), embeddings, and label classes. Figure 6.1 illustrates a generic model structure.

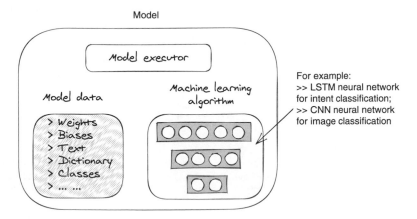

Figure 6.1 A model is composed of a machine learning algorithm, model executor, and model data.

NOTE We often refer to machine learning algorithms as *model algorithms* in this chapter for simplicity.

The most important takeaway in this section is that the output of a model training execution—or simply, a model—isn't just a set of static data. In contrast, deep learning models are executable programs that include a machine learning algorithm and its dependent data, so the models can make predictions based on input data at run time.

NOTE Models are not only weights and biases. Sometimes data scientists save a neural network's trained parameters—weights and biases—to a file and name it "model file." This confuses people into thinking a model is just a data file that contains only weights and biases. Weights and biases are the model *data*, but we also need the algorithm and the wrapper code to run the prediction.

6.1.2 *Model prediction and inference*

Academics may consider model inference and prediction to be two separate concepts. A model inference can refer to learning about how data is generated and understanding its causes and effects, whereas a model prediction might refer to predicting future events.

A sample model prediction scenario might include using sales records to train a model to predict which individuals are likely to respond to the next marketing campaign. And a sample model inference scenario would include using sales records to train a model to understand the sales effect from the product price and customer income. The predictive accuracy on previously unseen data for model inference is not very important because the main focus is on learning the data generation process. Model training is designed to fit the full dataset.

From an engineering perspective, model prediction and model inference mean the same. Although models can be built and used for different purposes, both model prediction and model inference in the context of model serving refer to the same action: executing the model with given data points to obtain a set of output values. Figure 6.2 illustrates the model serving workflow for the prediction model and the inference model; as you can see, there is no difference between them.

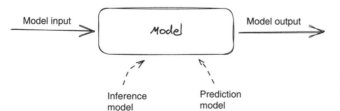

Figure 6.2 **Model prediction and model inference are the same in model serving engineering.**

To simplify the text in the illustrations of this chapter, starting from figure 6.2, we use the word *model* to represent model data, model executor, and machine learning (model) algorithm. This is not only to keep the text short but also to emphasize that the machine learning model is an executable program.

6.1.3   What is model serving?

Model serving simply means executing a model with input data to make predictions, which includes fetching the expected model, setting up the model's execution environment, executing the model to make a prediction with given data points, and returning the prediction result. The most used method for model serving is to host models in a web service and expose the model's predict function through a web API.

Suppose we build an object detection model to detect sharks in seacoast images; we can build a web service to host this model and expose a shark detection web API. This web API can then be used by beach hotels anywhere in the world to detect sharks with their own coast images. Conventionally, we call the model serving web service the prediction service.

A typical model prediction workflow in a prediction service has four steps: receiving a user request; loading the model from an artifact store to memory or GPU; executing the model's algorithm; and, finally, returning the prediction results. Figure 6.3 shows this workflow.

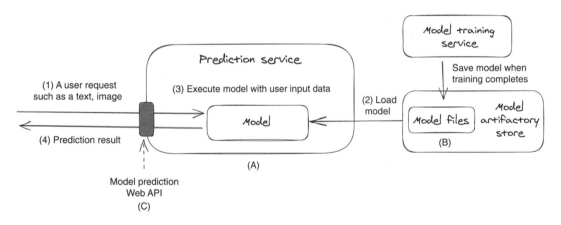

Figure 6.3   A typical model prediction workflow in a prediction service

Besides the four-step prediction workflow, figure 6.3 also mentions three main components of the model serving: the prediction service (A), the model artifactory store (B), and the prediction web API (C). The model artifactory store (component B) holds all the models produced by the model training. The web API (component C) receives prediction requests. The prediction service (component A) responds to the prediction request, loads the model from the artifactory store, runs the model, and returns the prediction result.

Although the four steps of the prediction workflow are generally applicable to all kinds of models, the actual implementation of the steps depends on the business needs, model training algorithm, and model training framework. We will discuss design options for prediction services in section 6.3, and we will present two sample prediction services in chapter 7.

> ## Model serving runs machine learning algorithms in a special mode
>
> Model training and model serving execute the same machine learning algorithm but in two different models: learning mode and evaluation mode.
>
> In the learning mode, we run the algorithm in an *open loop*, meaning in each training iteration, we first run the neural network (algorithm) with an input data sample to calculate prediction results. Based on the difference between the prediction results and the expected results, the network's parameters (weights and bias) are updated to fit the dataset closer.
>
> In the evaluation model, the neural network (algorithm) is run in a closed loop, which means that the network's parameters will not be updated. The neural network is run solely to obtain the prediction results. So from a code implementation perspective, model serving is essentially running the machine learning algorithm (neural network) in the evaluation mode.

6.1.4 *Model serving challenges*

Building a web service to serve models cost-effectively is a lot more complicated than running models locally on our laptops. Following are the six common challenges for serving models in web services.

The model prediction API differs per model algorithm. Different deep learning algorithms (such as recurrent neural networks and convolutional neural networks [CNN]) require different input data formats, and their output format can also vary. When designing the web prediction API, it's quite challenging to design a unified web API that meets the input data requirements for every model algorithm.

Model executing environments are different per training framework. Models can be trained in different frameworks, such as TensorFlow and PyTorch. And each training framework has its special setup and configuration to execute its models. The prediction service should encapsulate the model execution environment setup at its backend, so customers can focus on using the model prediction API, not the framework with which this model is trained.

There are too many model serving tools, libraries, and systems from which to choose. If we decide to use existing open source approaches to model serving, the immediate question becomes which approach we should choose. There are 20+ different options, such as TorchServe, TensorFlow Serving, NVIDIA Triton Inference Server, Seldon Core, and KFServing. How do we know which approach works best for our situation?

There is no universal, most cost-effective model serving design; we need to tailor a model serving approach that fits our own use case. Unlike model training and hyperparameter tuning service, which both have a one-fits-all approach—prediction service design heavily depends on concrete user scenarios. For example, designing a prediction service that supports just one model, such as a flower recognition model, is a lot different than designing a prediction service that supports 10 different types of models, such as PDF scanning, text intent classification, and image classification.

Reduce model prediction latency while maintaining resource saturation. From a cost-efficiency perspective, we want our compute resources to be fully saturated with model prediction workloads. In addition, we would like to provide our customers with a real-time model prediction experience, so we don't want the prediction latency to drop because of the rigid infrastructure budget. To accomplish this, we need to reduce the time cost at every step of the prediction workflow innovatively, such as loading the model faster or preheating the model before serving.

Model deployment and post-deployment model monitoring are things we should consider on day one. Model deployment—progressing a model from training to production—is critical for successful model development. We want to advance the model to production quickly, and we want to have multiple versions of the model in production, so we can evaluate different training algorithms quickly and choose the best model. Post-deployment model monitoring can help detect model performance regression; it's a crucial protection mechanism for models in fraud detection and loan approval, for instance.

The good news is that these six challenges are all engineering problems, so you will be able to handle them! We will discuss how to address them here and in the next chapter.

6.1.5 *Model serving terminology*

As we proceed through the chapter, we'd like to refresh your memory of the model serving terms. Many terms have various definitions in academia but are interchangeable in practice when talking about model serving. The following definitions should help you and your colleagues avoid confusion when they are mentioned.

- *Model serving, model scoring, model inference,* and *model prediction* are interchangeable terminologies in the deep learning context. They all refer to executing a model with given data points. In this book, we will use *model serving*.
- *Prediction service, scoring service, inference service,* and *model serving service* are interchangeable; they refer to the web service that allows remote model execution. In this book, we use the prediction service.
- *Predict* and *inference* are interchangeable in the model serving context; they are the entry function related to running the model algorithm. In this book, we use *predict*.
- *Prediction request, scoring request,* and *inference request* are interchangeable; they refer to the web API request that executes a model to make a prediction. In this book, we use *prediction request*.
- *Machine learning algorithm, training algorithm,* and *model algorithm* are interchangeable, as we state in section 6.1.3; the algorithm that runs in model training and

serving is the same machine learning algorithm (same neural network) but in a different execution mode.

- *Model deployment* and *model release* are interchangeable; they indicate the process of deploying/copying a trained model (files) to the production environment where the business is running, so the customer can benefit from this new model. Typically, this refers to loading the model files into the prediction service.

6.2   Common model serving strategies

Before we review the concrete model serving use cases and prediction service designs in section 6.3, let's first check out the three common model serving strategies: direct model embedding, model service, and model server. No matter what you need to do for your specific use cases, you can usually take one of the following three approaches to build your prediction service.

6.2.1   Direct model embedding

Direct model embedding means loading the model and running model prediction inside the user application's process. For example, a flower identity–check mobile app can load an image classification model directly in its local process and predict plant identity from the given photos. The entire model loading and serving happen within the model app locally (on the phone), without talking to other processes or remote servers.

Most user applications, like mobile apps, are written in strongly typed languages, such as Go, Java, and C#, but most deep learning modeling code is written in Python. It is therefore difficult to embed model code into application code, and even if you do, the process can take a while. To facilitate model prediction across non-Python processes, deep learning frameworks such as PyTorch and TensorFlow provide C++ libraries. Additionally, TensorFlow offers Java (https://github.com/tensorflow/ java) and JavaScript (https://github.com/tensorflow/tfjs) libraries for loading and executing TensorFlow models directly from Java or JavaScript applications.

Another disadvantage of direct embedding is resource consumption. If the model runs on client devices, users without high-end devices may not have a good experience. Running big deep learning models requires a lot of computation, and this can cause slower apps.

Lastly, direct embedding involves mixing model serving code with application business logic, which poses a challenge for backward compatibility. Therefore, because it is rarely used, we only describe it briefly.

6.2.2   Model service

Model service refers to running model serving on the server side. For each model, each version of a model, or each type of model, we build a dedicated web service for it. This web service exposes the model prediction API over HTTP or gRPC interfaces.

The model service manages the full life cycle of model serving, including fetching the model file from the model artifact store, loading the model, executing the model algorithm for a customer request, and unloading the model to reclaim the server resources. Using the documents classification use case as an example, to automatically sort documents in images and PDF by their content, we can train a CNN model for OCR (optical character recognition) to extract text from document images or PDF. To serve this model in a model service approach, we build a web service exclusively for this CNN model, and the web API is only designed for this CNN model's prediction function. Sometimes we build a dedicated web service for each major model version update.

The common pattern of model service is to build the model execution logic into a Docker image and use gRPC or HTTP interface to expose the model's predict function. For service setup, we can host multiple service instances and employ a load balancer to distribute customers' prediction requests to these instances.

The biggest advantage of the model service approach is simplicity. We can easily convert a model's training container to a model serving container because, essentially, a model prediction execution entails running the trained model neural network. The model training code can turn into a prediction web service quickly by adding an HTTP or gRPC interface and setting the neural network to evaluation mode. We will see a model service's design and use case in sections 6.3.1 and 6.3.2 and a concrete code example in chapter 7.

Because model service is specific to the model algorithm, we need to build separate services for different model types or versions. If you have several different models to serve, this one service-per-model approach can spawn many services, and the maintenance work for these services—such as patching, deploying, and monitoring—can be exhausting. If you are facing this situation, the model server approach is the right choice.

6.2.3 *Model server*

The model server approach is designed to handle multiple types of models in a black-box manner. Regardless of the model algorithm and model version, the model server can operate these models with a unified web prediction API. The model server is the next stage; we no longer need to make code changes or deploy new services with a new type of model or new version of the model. This saves a lot of duplicate development and maintenance work from the model service approach.

Yet, the model server approach is a lot more complicated to implement and manage than the model service approach. Handling model serving for various types of models in one service and one unified API is complicated. The model algorithms and model data are different; their predict functions are also different. For example, an image classification model can be trained with a CNN network, whereas a text classification model can be trained with a long short-term memory (LSTM) network. Their input data is different (text vs. image), and their algorithms are different (CNN vs.

LSTM). Their model data also varies; text classification models require embedding files to encode input text whereas CNN models don't require embedding files. These differences present many challenges to finding a low-maintenance, low-cost, and unified serving approach.

Although building a model server approach is difficult, it's definitely possible. Many open source model serving libraries and services—such as TensorFlow Serving, TorchServe, and NVIDIA Triton Inference Server—offer model server solutions. We simply need to build customized integration logic to incorporate these tools into our existing systems to solve business needs—for example, integrating TorchServe into our model storage, monitoring, and alerting system.

From a model deployment perspective, the model server is a black-box approach. As long as we save the model file following the model server standards, the model prediction should function when we upload the model-to-model server through its management API. The complexity of model serving implementation and maintenance can be greatly reduced. We will see a model server design and use case in section 6.3.3 and a code example with TorchServe in chapter 7.

> **NOTE** Should we always consider a model server approach? Not always. If we don't think of service development cost and maintenance cost, the model server approach is the most powerful because it's designed to cover all types of models. But if we care about model serving cost efficiency—and we should!—then the ideal approach depends on the use cases. In the next section, we will discuss the common model serving use cases and the applied design.

6.3 *Designing a prediction service*

A common mistake in software system design is aiming to build an omnipotent system without considering the concrete user scenario. Overdesign will redirect our focus from the immediate customer needs to the features that might be useful in the future. As a result, the system either takes an unnecessarily long time to build or is difficult to use. This is especially true for model serving.

Deep learning is an expensive business, both in terms of human and computational resources. We should build only the necessities to move models into production as quickly as possible and minimize the operation costs. To do so, we need to begin with user scenarios.

In this section, we will present three typical model serving scenarios, from simple to complex. For each use case, we explain the scenario and illustrate a suitable high-level design. By reading the following three subsections sequentially, you will see how the prediction service's design evolves when use cases become more and more complicated.

> **NOTE** The goal of prediction service design is not to build a powerful system that works for various models but to build a system that suits the circumstances in a cost-efficient manner.

6.3.1 Single model application

Imagine building a mobile app that can swap people's faces between two pictures. The consumer expects the app UI to upload photos, select sources and target pictures, and execute a deepfake model (https://arxiv.org/abs/1909.11573) for swapping faces between the two selected images. For an application like this that only needs to work with one model, the serving approach can be either model service (6.2.2) or direct model embedding (6.2.1).

MODEL SERVICE APPROACH

From the discussion in section 6.2.2, the model service approach involves building a web service for each model. So we can build the face-swap model app with the following three components: a front UI app (component A) that runs on our phone; an application backend to handle user operation (component B); and a backend service, or *predictor* (component C), to host a deepfake model and expose a web API to execute the model for each face-swap request.

When a user uploads a source image and a target image and clicks the face-swap button on the mobile app, the mobile backend application will receive the request and call the predictor's web API for face-swapping. Then the predictor preprocesses the user request data (the images), executes the model algorithm, and postprocesses the model output (the images) to the application backend. Ultimately, the mobile app will display the source and target images with swapped faces. Figure 6.4 illustrates a general design that suits the face-swap use case.

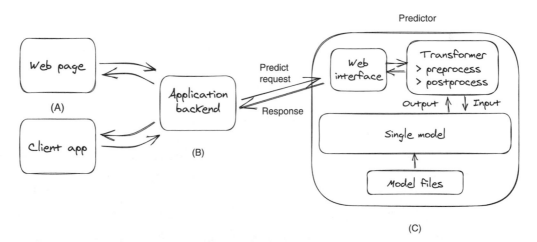

Figure 6.4 A single model predictor design in a client/server setup

If we zoom into the predictor (component C), we see that the model serving logic works the same as the general model prediction workflow that we introduced in figure 6.3. The predictor (model serving service) loads the model file from the model artifactory and runs the model to respond to the request received by the web interface.

HL 692 9417

The design in figure 6.4 generally works for any application that has a web back-end and only one model. The key component in this design is the predictor; it is a web service and often runs as a Docker container. We can implement this approach quickly because this predictor container can be easily converted from the model training container that builds the model. The two main work items that transform a training container to a predictor container are the web predict API and the evaluation mode in the training neural network. We will present a concrete predictor container example in section 7.1.

DIRECT MODEL EMBEDDING APPROACH

Another design approach for building a single model application is combining the model execution code with the application's user logic code. There is no server back-end, so everything happens locally on the user's computer or phone. Using the face swap app as an example, the deepfake model file is in the application's deployment package, and when the application starts, the model is loaded into the application's process space. Figure 6.5 illustrates this concept.

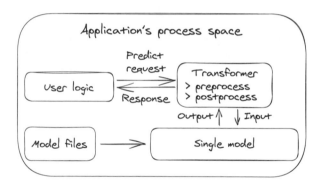

Figure 6.5   In the direct model embedding design, the model is executed in the same process as the application logic.

Model serving doesn't have to run in a separate service. In figure 6.5, we see that the model serving code (the single model box) and the data transformation code can run with the user logic code in the same application. Nowadays, many deep learning frameworks provide libraries to run models in non-Python applications. For example, TensorFlow offers Java, C++, and JavaScript SDK to load and execute models. With SDK's help, we can train and execute models directly in Java/C++/JavaScript applications.

> **NOTE** Why should we consider direct model embedding? By using model embedding, we can directly integrate model serving logic with application logic and run them together in the same process space. This provides two advantages over the predictor service approach in figure 6.4. First, it reduces one network hop; there is no web request to the predictor, and model execution happens locally. Second, it improves service debuggability because we can run the application as one piece locally.

WHY IS THE MODEL SERVICE APPROACH MORE POPULAR?

Although the direct model embedding approach looks simple and saves one network hop, it is still not a popular choice for building model serving. Here are the four reasons:

- The model algorithm has to be reimplemented in a different language. A model's algorithm and execution code is usually written in Python. If we choose a model service approach, implementing the model serving as a web service (predictor in figure 6.4), we can reuse most of the training code and build it quickly. But if we choose to embed model serving in a non-Python application, we must reimplement model loading, model execution, and data process logic in the application's language (such as Java or C++). This work is nontrivial, and not many developers have the depth of knowledge to rewrite the training algorithms.

- The ownership boundary is blurred. When embedding a model into an application, the business logic code can mingle with the serving code. When the codebase becomes complicated, it's difficult to draw a boundary between the serving code (owned by the data scientist) and other application code (owned by the developer). When data scientists and developers are from two different teams but work on the same code repo, the shipping velocity will drop significantly because the cross-team code review and deployment takes longer than usual.

- Performance problems can occur on the client's devices. Usually, apps are run on the customer's mobiles, tablets, or lower-end laptops. On these devices, capturing features from raw user data and then preprocessing model input data and running model prediction can lead to performance problems such as CPU usage spikes, app slowdown, and high memory usage.

- A memory leak can occur easily. For example, when executing a TensorFlow model in Java, the algorithm execution and input/output parameter objects are all created in the native space. These objects won't be recycled by Java GC (Garbage Collection) automatically; we have to manually depose them. It's very easy to overlook recycling the native resources claimed by the model, and because the native objects' memory allocations are not tracked in Java heap, their memory usage is difficult to observe and measure. So the memory leak can happen and is hard to fix.

NOTE   To troubleshoot native memory leaks, Jemalloc (https://github.com/ jemalloc/jemalloc/wiki/Background) is a very handy tool. You can check out my blog post "Fix Memory Issues in Your Java Apps" (http://mng.bz/lJ8o) for further details.

For the previously listed reasons, we highly recommend you adopt the model service approach for single model application use cases.

6.3.2   *Multitenant application*

We will use a chatbot application as an example to explain multitenant use cases. First, let's set the context. A *tenant* is a company or organization (such as a school or a retail store) that uses the chatbot application to communicate with its customers. The tenants use the same software/service—the chatbot application—but have separate accounts with their data segregated. A *chat user* is the customer of a tenant and uses the chatbot to do business with the tenant.

By design, the chatbot application relies on an intent classification model to identify the user's intention from his conversation, and then the chatbot redirects the user request to the correct service department of the tenant. Currently, this chatbot is taking a single model application approach, meaning it's using a single intent classification model for every user and tenant.

Now, because of customer feedback from tenants on the low prediction accuracy of the single intent classification model, we decide to let tenants use our training algorithm to build their own model with their own dataset. This way, the model can fit better with each tenant's business situation. For model serving, we will let tenants use their own model for intent classification prediction requests. When a chatbot user now speaks to the chatbot application, the application will find the tenant's specific model to answer the user's question. The chatbot is changed to a multitenant application.

In this chatbot multitenant use case, although the models belong to different tenants and are trained with different datasets, they are the same type of model. Because these models are trained with the same algorithm, their model's algorithm and predict function are all the same. We can extend the model service design in figure 6.4 to support multitenancy by adding a model cache. By caching model graphs and their dependent data in memory, we can perform multitenancy model serving in one service. Figure 6.6 illustrates this concept.

Compared with the model service design in figure 6.4, the design in figure 6.6 adds a model cache (component A) and a model file server (component B). Because we want to support multiple models in one service, we need a model cache in memory to host and execute different models. The model file server stores the model files that can be loaded into the prediction service's model cache. The model server can also be shared among prediction service instances.

To build a good model cache, we need to consider model cache management and memory resource management. For the model cache, we need to assign a unique model ID as a cache key to identify each model in the cache. For example, we can use the model training run ID as the model ID; the benefit is, for each model in the cache, we can trace which training run produced it. Another more flexible way of constructing the model ID is combining the model name (a customized string) and the model version. No matter which model ID style we choose, the ID has to be unique, and it must be provided in the prediction request.

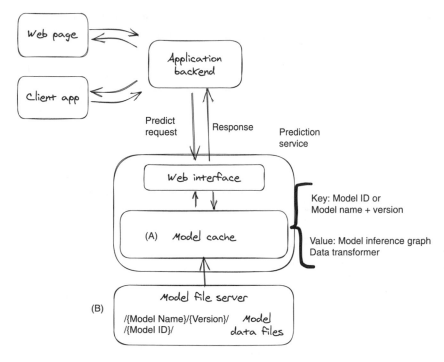

Figure 6.6   A prediction service with model caching for multitenant applications

For memory resource management, because each server has limited memory and GPU resources, we can't load all the required models into memory. So we need to build model-swapping logic to the model cache. When the resource capacity is reached—for instance, the process is about to run out of memory—some models need to be evicted from the model cache to free some resources for new model prediction requests. Methods like LRU (least recently used) algorithm and model partition across different instances can help reduce the cache missing rate (the request model is not in the cache) and make model swapping less disruptive. The sample intent classification prediction service we build in section 7.1 demonstrates the model caching concept; you can explore the details there.

CAN WE EXTEND THE MODEL CACHING DESIGN TO MULTIPLE MODEL TYPES?
We don't recommend extending the model caching design to multiple model types. The input/output data format and data process logic of various model types, such as the image classification model and intent classification model, are very different, so it's hard to host and execute different types of models in the same model cache. To do that, we would need to build separate web interfaces and separate data preprocess and postprocess code for each type of model. At this point, you will find it's easier to build separate prediction services for each model type—with each service having its own type of web interface and data process logic and managing the model cache for

its own model type. For example, we can build an image classification prediction service and an intent classification prediction service for these two different model types separately.

This one service per model type approach works well when you only have a few model types. But if you have 20+ types of models, then it can't scale. Building and maintaining web services—such as setting up a CI/CD pipeline, networking, and deployment—is costly. Also, the work of monitoring a service is nontrivial; we need to build monitoring and alerting mechanisms to ensure the service is running 24/7. Consider the costs of onboarding and maintenance work if we follow this design to support 100+ model types for the entire company. To scale up and serve lots of different model types in one system, we need to take the model server approach (section 6.2.3), which we will discuss further in the next section.

6.3.3   *Supporting multiple applications in one system*

You have successfully built multiple model serving services to support different applications, such as multitenant chatbot, face-swapping, flower recognition, and PDF document scanning. Now, you are given two more tasks: (1) building the model serving support for a new application that uses a voice recognition model and (2) reducing model serving costs for all applications.

So far, all the model serving implementations have been built with the model service approach. From previous discussions in sections 6.3.1 and 6.3.2, we know this approach can't scale when we have more and more model types. When many products and applications have model serving requirements, it's better to build just one centralized prediction service to address all the serving needs. We name this type of prediction service a *prediction platform*. It takes the model server approach (section 6.2.3) and handles all kinds of model serving in one place. This is the most cost-efficient approach for multiple application situations because the model onboarding and maintenance cost is limited to one system, which is much less than one prediction service per application approach (section 6.2.2).

To build such an omnipotent model serving system, we need to consider lots of elements, such as model file format, model libraries, model training frameworks, model caching, model versioning, model flow execution, model data processing, model management, and a unified prediction API that suits all model types. Figure 6.7 illustrates the design and workflow of the prediction platform.

The prediction platform design in figure 6.7 is much more complicated than the model service approach in figure 6.6. This is because we need to combine multiple components and services to support arbitrary models. Let's look at each component of the system and then the model prediction workflow.

UNIFIED WEB API

To support arbitrary models, we expect the public prediction APIs to be generic. No matter which model is called, the API's spec—for instance, its payload schema of the prediction request and response—should be generic enough to satisfy the model's

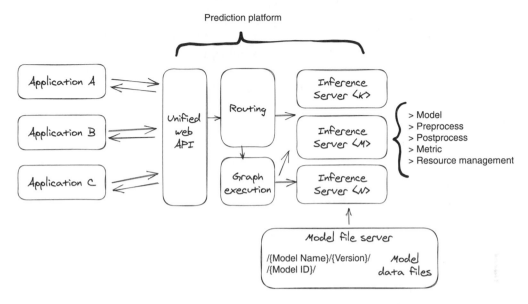

Figure 6.7   A general prediction service (platform) design that works with arbitrary model types

algorithm requirement. One example of this kind of unified API is the KFServing predict protocol (http://mng.bz/BlB2), which aims to standardize the prediction protocol that works for any models and various prediction backends.

The web APIs are also expected to be simple, so we can reduce the customer onboarding and maintenance effort. The prediction APIs can be categorized into three buckets: model prediction requests API, model metadata fetching API, and model deployment API. The model metadata fetching API and deployment API are very useful because they are agnostic about the model they are serving. We need these methods to check the model metadata, such as the model version and algorithm info, and to check the model deployment status.

ROUTING COMPONENT
Normally, each type of serving backend can only handle a few types of models. To support arbitrary models, we need to have different kinds of serving backends, such as TensorFlow Serving backend for TensorFlow models and TorchServe backend for PyTorch models. When receiving a model prediction request, the system needs to know which backend can handle it. This is done with the routing component.

The routing component responds to route the prediction request to the correct backend inference server. For a given request, the routing component first fetches the model's metadata; the metadata includes the model algorithm name and version, the model version, and the training framework. Then, by matching the model metadata with the routing config, it determines to which inference backend it should route the prediction request.

GRAPH EXECUTION COMPONENT

The graph execution component handles the type of prediction that needs to execute a series of model predictions. For example, to automate the mortgage approval process, we have to run a loan approval prediction request following three models in a sequence: a PDF scanning model to parse the text from the PDF loan application, a named entity recognition model to recognize the keywords, and a loan-scoring model to score the loan application. To support such requirements, we can define a directed acyclic graph (DAG) to describe the model execution chain and build a graph execution engine to execute in one go.

INFERENCE SERVER

The inference (model) server does the actual work to compute model prediction by managing model caching and model prediction execution. It's similar to the prediction service shown in figure 6.6 but more sophisticated because it needs to support arbitrary model algorithms. Besides the predict API, the inference server should also offer model management API to register new models and remove models programmatically.

Building an inference server is much more complicated than building a predictor service; not many engineers want to try that. But luckily, there are multiple black-box, open source approaches that work out of the box, such as TensorFlow Serving, Torch-Serve, and NVIDIA Triton Inference Server. In practice, we often reuse these existing open source inference servers and integrate them into our own routing component and graph execution component. We will discuss more on the open source model server tools in chapter 7.

APPLICATIONS

In figure 6.7, we see applications A, B, and C are sharing the same model serving backend. The model serving for different applications occurs at the same place. Compared with the model service design in figure 6.6, the prediction platform is more scalable and more cost-efficient because there is almost no onboarding cost to add new application D.

For example, if we want to onboard new application D—a voice-to-text scripting application—we just need to upload the voice scripting model to the model file server and then let the application use the unified prediction web API of the prediction platform. There is no code change on the prediction platform side for supporting a new application.

MODEL PREDICTION WORKFLOW

After explaining each key component, let's look at a typical model prediction workflow (figure 6.7). First, we publish our model files to the model file server and update the config in the routing component, so the routing component knows to which inference server it should route the prediction request for this type of model. Second, applications send prediction requests to the prediction system's web APIs, and then the request is routed by the routing component to the correct inference server. Third, the inference server will load the model from the model file server, convert the request payload to model input, run the model algorithm, and return the prediction result with a postprocess.

> **NOTE** Prediction platform design is not always the best serving approach! In theory, the design in figure 6.7 can work for any model, but it does come with some extra cost. Its setup, maintenance, and debugging are way more complicated than the model service approach. This design is overkill for scenarios introduced in sections 6.3.1 and 6.3.2. Because each design has its merits, we recommend not adhering to one serving approach but choosing the serving method based on your actual user scenarios.

6.3.4 *Common prediction service requirements*

Although we state that designing prediction services should start from concrete use cases, different situations lead to different designs. Three common requirements exist among all model serving designs:

- *Model deployment safety*—No matter what model rollout strategy and version strategy we choose, we must have a way to roll back a model to the previous state or version.
- *Latency*—Web request latency is a crucial factor in the success of many online businesses. Once we build the model serving support, the next step is to try our best to reduce the average prediction response time.
- *Monitoring and alerting*—Model serving is the most critical service in a deep learning system; if it goes down, the business stops. Remember, actual businesses run on top of the model prediction in realtime. Customers are affected immediately if the service is down or serving latency increases. Prediction service should be the most-equipped service among other deep learning services in monitoring and alerting.

In this chapter, we have reviewed concepts, definitions, and abstract high-level system designs of model serving. We hope you gain a clear picture of what model serving is and what to consider when designing model serving systems. In the next chapter, we will demo two sample prediction services and discuss the commonly used prediction open source tools. These examples will show you how the design concepts in this chapter are applied in real life.

Summary

- A model can be several files; it is composed of three elements: machine learning algorithm, model executor (wrapper), and model data.
- Model prediction and model inference have the same meaning in the model serving context.
- Direct model embedding, model service, and model server are the three common types of model serving strategies.

- The model service approach involves building a prediction service for each model, each version of a model, or each type of model.
- The model server approach consists of building only one prediction service, but it can run models trained with different algorithms and frameworks and can run different versions of each model.
- When designing a model serving system, the first component to understand is the use case, so we can decide which serving approach is most appropriate.
- Cost efficiency is the primary goal for designing model serving systems; the cost includes service deployment, maintenance, monitoring, infrastructure, and service development.
- For single model applications, we recommend the model service approach.
- For multitenant applications, we recommend the model service approach with an in-memory model cache.
- For supporting multiple applications with different types of models, the model server and prediction platform are the most suitable approaches. They include a unified prediction API, a routing component, a graph execution component, and multiple model server backends.

Model serving in practice

This chapter covers

- Building a sample predictor with the model service approach
- Building a sample service with TorchServe and the model server approach
- Touring popular open source model serving libraries and systems
- Explaining the production model release process
- Discussing postproduction model monitoring

In the previous chapter, we discussed the concept of model serving, as well as user scenarios and design patterns. In this chapter, we will focus on the actual implementation of these concepts in production.

As we've said, one of the challenges to implementing model serving nowadays is that we have too many possible ways of doing it. In addition to multiple black-box solutions, there are many options for customizing and building all or part of it from scratch. We think the best way to teach you how to choose the right approach is with concrete examples.

In this chapter, we implement two sample services to demo two of the most commonly used model serving approaches: one uses a self-build model serving container, which demonstrates the model service approach (section 7.1), and the other uses TorchServe (a model server for the PyTorch model), which demonstrates the model server approach (section 7.2). Both of these serve the intent classification model trained in chapter 3. Once you work through the examples, we provide (in section 7.3) a tour of the most popular open source model serving tools to help you understand their features, best uses, and other factors important to your decision on which to use. In the rest of the chapter, we will focus on the model serving operation and monitoring, including shipping models to production and monitoring the model performance.

By reading this chapter, you will not only have a concrete understanding of different model serving designs but also have the acumen to choose the right approach for your own situation. More importantly, this chapter will present a holistic view of the model serving field, not just *building* model serving but also *operating* and *monitoring* it after the model serving system is built.

> **NOTE**   In this chapter, the terms *model serving*, *model inference*, and *model prediction* are used interchangeably. They all refer to executing a model with given data points.

7.1   *A model service sample*

In this section, we will show you the first sample prediction service. This service takes the model service approach (section 6.2.2), and it can be used for both single-model (section 6.3.1) and multitenant applications (section 6.3.2).

This sample service follows the single model application design (section 6.3.1), which has a frontend API component and a backend predictor. We also made some enhancements in the predictor so it can support multiple intent classification models. We will tour this sample service by following these steps:

1. Running the sample prediction service locally
2. Discussing the system design
3. Looking at the implementation details of its subcomponents: frontend service and backend predictor

7.1.1   *Play with the service*

Listing 7.1 shows how to run the sample prediction service on your local machine. The following scripts first run the backend predictor and then the frontend service.

> **NOTE**   Setting up a prediction service is a bit tedious; we need to run the metadata and artifactory store service and prepare the models. To demonstrate the idea clearly, listing 7.1 highlights the main setup steps. To make model serving work on your local machine, please complete the lab (section A.2) in appendix A and then use the code ./scripts/lab-004-model-serving.sh {run_id} {document} to send the model prediction requests.

Listing 7.1   Starting a prediction service

```
# step 1: start backend predictor service
docker build -t orca3/intent-classification-predictor:latest \     ◁──┐  Builds the
    -f predictor/Dockerfile predictor                                   │  predictor
                                                                        │  Docker image

docker run --name intent-classification-predictor \
    --network orca3 --rm -d -p "${ICP_PORT}":51001 \        Runs the predictor
    -v "${MODEL_CACHE_DIR}":/models \                        service container
    orca3/intent-classification-predictor:latest

# step 2: start the prediction service (the web api)      Builds the prediction
docker build -t orca3/services:latest -f \          ◁──    service image
    services.dockerfile .
                                                            Runs the prediction
                                                            service container
docker run --name prediction-service --network orca3 \   ◁──
    --rm -d -p "${PS_PORT}":51001 -v "${MODEL_CACHE_DIR}":/tmp/modelCache \
    orca3/services:latest prediction-service.jar
```

Once the service starts, you can send prediction requests to it; the service will load the intent classification model trained in chapter 3, run the model prediction with the given text, and return the prediction results. In the following example, a text string "merry christmas" is sent to the service and is predicted to the "joy" category:

```
#./scripts/lab-004-model-serving.sh 1 "merry christmas"
grpcurl -plaintext
    -d "{                              Specifies the model
       "runId": "1",         ◁──      ID to the response
       "document": "merry christmas"    ◁──    Prediction
  }"                                           payload
localhost:"${PS_PORT}"
prediction.PredictionService/Predict
```

```
model_id is 1
document is hello world                Prediction response,
{                                      the predicted
    "response": "{\"result\": \"joy\"}"    category
}
```

7.1.2   Service design

This sample service consists of a frontend interface component and a backend predictor. The frontend component does three things: hosts the public prediction API, downloads model files from the metadata store to a shared disk volume, and forwards the prediction request to the backend predictor. The backend predictor is a self-built predictor container that responds to load intent classification models and executes these models to serve prediction requests.

This prediction service has two external dependencies: the metadata store service and a shared disk volume. The metadata store keeps all the information about a model, such as the model algorithm name, the model version, and the model URL, which points to the cloud storage of real model files. The shared volume enables model file sharing between the frontend service and the backend predictor. You can see an end-to-end overview of the model serving process in figure 7.1.

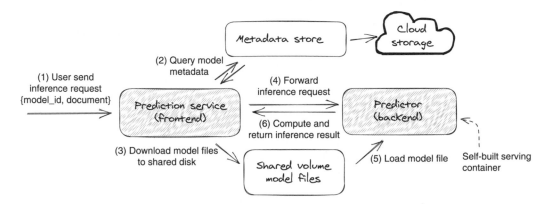

Figure 7.1   A system overview and model serving end-to-end workflow

Going through the system design of the sample model serving service shown in figure 7.1, you can see it takes six steps to complete a prediction request. Let's go through each step numbered in the figure:

1. The user sends a prediction request to the prediction service (frontend component) with a specified model ID and a text string—namely, `document`. The model ID is a unique identifier produced by the training service to identify each model it produces.

2. The frontend service fetches the model metadata from the metadata store by searching the model ID. For each successful model training, the training service will save the model files to cloud storage and also save the model metadata (model ID, model version, name, and URL) to the metadata store; this is why we can find the model information in the metadata store.

3. If the model file is not already downloaded, the frontend component will download it to the shared disk volume.

4. The frontend component forwards the inference request to the backend predictor.

5. The backend predictor loads the intent classification model to memory by reading model files from the shared disk volume.

6. The backend predictor executes the model to make a prediction on the given text string and returns the prediction result to the frontend component.

7.1.3 The frontend service

Now, let's focus on the frontend service. The frontend service has three main components: a web interface, a predictor management, and a predictor backend client (`CustomGrpcPredictorBackend`). These components respond to the host public gRPC model serving the API and manage the backend predictors' connection and communication. Figure 7.2 shows the internal structure of the frontend service and its inner workflow when receiving a prediction request.

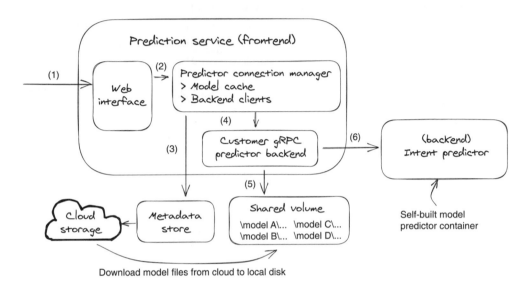

Figure 7.2 The frontend service design and the model serving workflow

Let's consider the intent prediction scenario in the model serving workflow described in figure 7.2, applying the six steps we just reviewed:

1 The user sends an intent prediction request with model ID A to the web interface.
2 The web interface calls the predictor connection manager to serve this request.
3 The predictor connection manager queries the metadata store to get model metadata by searching model IDs that equal A; the returned model metadata contains the model algorithm type and model file URL.
4 Based on the model algorithm type, the predictor manager picks the right predictor backend client to handle the request. In this case, it chooses `Custom-GrpcPredictorBackend` because we are demoing a self-built model serving container for intent classification.
5 The `CustomGrpcPredictorBackend` client first checks the existence of the model file in the shared model file disk for model A. If the model hasn't been downloaded before, it uses the model URL (from model metadata) to download model files from cloud storage to the shared file disk.

6 The `CustomGrpcPredictorBackend` client then calls the model predictor that is preregistered with this backend client in the service configuration file. In this example, the `CustomGrpcPredictorBackend` will call our self-built predictor, the intent predictor, which will be discussed in section 7.1.4.

Now that we have reviewed the system design and workflow, let's consider the actual code implementation of the main components, including the web interface (prediction API), predictor connection manager, predictor backend clients, and intent predictor.

FRONTEND SERVICE MODEL SERVING CODE WALKTHROUGH

The following code listing highlights the core implementation of the prediction workflow mentioned in figure 7.2. You can also find the full implementation at `src/main/java/org/orca3/miniAutoML/prediction/PredictionService.java`.

Listing 7.2   Frontend service prediction workflow

```
public void predict(PredictRequest request, .. .. ..) {
  .. .. ..
  String runId = request.getRunId();            ←─┤ Obtains the
                                                    required model ID

  if (predictorManager.containsArtifact(runId)) {          ←
    artifactInfo = predictorManager.getArtifact(runId);      Fetches the model
  } else {                                                   metadata from the
    try {                                                    metadata store
      artifactInfo = msClient.getArtifact(          ←
              GetArtifactRequest.newBuilder()
            .setRunId(runId).build());
    } catch (Exception ex) {
      .. .. ..
    }
  }


  # Step 4, pick predictor backend client by model algorithm type
  PredictorBackend predictor;
  if (predictorManager.containsPredictor(
        artifactInfo.getAlgorithm())) {        Chooses the backend
                                               predictor based on the
                                               model algorithm type
    predictor = predictorManager.getPredictor(  ←─┘
        artifactInfo.getAlgorithm());
  } else {
    .. .. ..
  }


  # Step 5, use the selected predictor client to download the model files
  predictor.downloadModel(runId, artifactInfo);      ←─┐
                                                        Downloads
  # Step 6, use the selected predictor client to call   the model file
  # its backend predictor for model serving
  String r = predictor.predict(                  Calls the backend predictor to
     artifactInfo, request.getDocument());       run model inference
  .. .. ..
}
```

PREDICTION API

The frontend service offers only one API—Predict—for issuing a prediction request. The request has two parameters, runId and document. The runId not only is used for referencing a model training run in the training service (chapter 3), but it also can be used as the model ID to reference a model. The document is the text on which the customer wants to run predictions.

By using the Predict API, users can specify an intent model (with runId) to predict the intent of a given text string (document). The following listing shows the gRPC contract of the Predict API (grpc-contract/src/main/proto/prediction_service .proto).

Listing 7.3   Prediction service gRPC interface

```
service PredictionService {
 rpc Predict(PredictRequest) returns (PredictResponse);
}

message PredictRequest {
 string runId = 3;
 string document = 4;
}

message PredictResponse {
 string response = 1;
}
```

PREDICTOR CONNECTION MANAGER

One important role of the frontend service is routing prediction requests. Given a prediction request, the frontend service needs to find the right backend predictor based on the model algorithm type required in the request. This routing is done in the PredictorConnectionManager. In our design, the mapping of model algorithms and predictors is predefined in environment properties. When the service starts, PredictorConnectionManager will read the mapping, so the service knows which backend predictor to use for which model algorithm type.

Although we are only demoing our self-built intent classification predictor in this example, PredictorConnectionManager can support any other type of backend predictors. Let's look at the following listing (config/config-docker-docker.properties) to see how the model algorithm and predictor mapping are configured.

Listing 7.4   Model algorithm and predictor mapping configuration

```
# the algorithm and predictor mapping can be defined in
# either app config or docker properties

# enable algorithm types
ps.enabledPredictors=intent-classification

# define algorithm and predictors mapping
# predictor.<algorithm_type>.XXX = predictor[host, port, type]
```

```
predictors.intent-classification.host= \
  Intent-classification-predictor
predictors.intent-classification.port=51001
predictors.intent-classification.techStack=customGrpc
```

> **Maps the intent-classification predictor to the intent-classification algorithm**

Now, let's review code listing 7.5 to see how the predictor manager reads the algorithm and predictor mapping and uses that information to initialize the predictor backend client to send prediction requests. The full implementation is located at `prediction-service/src/main/java/org/orca3/miniAutoML/prediction/PredictorConnectionManager.java`.

> **Listing 7.5   Predictor manager load algorithm and predictor mapping**

```java
public class PredictorConnectionManager {
  private final Map<String, List<ManagedChannel>>
    channels = new HashMap<>();

  private final Map<String, PredictorBackend>
    clients = new HashMap<>();

  private final Map<String, GetArtifactResponse>
    artifactCache;

  // create predictor backend objects for
  // the registered algorithm and predictor
  public void registerPredictor(String algorithm,
      Properties properties) {

    String host = properties.getProperty(
      String.format("predictors.%s.host", algorithm));

    int port = Integer.parseInt(properties.getProperty(
      String.format("predictors.%s.port", algorithm)));

    String predictorType = properties.getProperty(
      String.format("predictors.%s.techStack", algorithm));

    ManagedChannel channel = ManagedChannelBuilder
      .forAddress(host, port)
      .usePlaintext().build();

    switch (predictorType) {
      .. ..
      case "customGrpc":
      default:
        channels.put(algorithm, List.of(channel));
        clients.put(algorithm, new CustomGrpcPredictorBackend(
          channel, modelCachePath, minioClient));
      break;
    }
  }

  .. .. ..
}
```

Annotations:
- **The algorithm for the predictor backend mapping** (points to `clients = new HashMap<>();`)
- **The model metadata cache; the key string is the model ID.** (points to `artifactCache;`)
- **Reads the algorithm and predictor mapping from the configuration** (points to the `String host`, `int port`, and `String predictorType` reads)
- **Creates the predictor backend client and saves it in the memory** (points to the `switch` and `case "customGrpc":`)

In listing 7.5, we see the `PredictorConnectionManager` class offers the `register-Predictor` function to register predictors. It first reads the algorithm and predictor mapping information from the properties, and then it creates the actual predictor backend client—`CustomGrpcPredictorBackend`—to communicate with the backend intent predictor container.

You may also notice `PredictorConnectionManager` class has several caches, such as the model metadata cache (`artifactCache`) and the model backend predictor clients (`clients`). These caches can greatly improve the model serving efficiency. For example, the model metadata cache (`artifactCache`) can reduce the serving request response time by avoiding calling the metadata store service for the model that has already been downloaded.

PREDICTOR BACKEND CLIENTS

Predictor clients are the objects that the frontend service uses to talk to different predictor backends. By design, each type of predictor backend supports its own kind of model, and it has its own client for communication, which is created and stored in `PredictorConnectionManager`. Every predictor backend client inherits an interface `PredictorBackend`, as in the following listing.

> Listing 7.6   Predictor backend interface

```
public interface PredictorBackend {
    void downloadModel(String runId,
            GetArtifactResponse artifactResponse);

    String predict(GetArtifactResponse artifact, String document);

    void registerModel(GetArtifactResponse artifact);
}
```

The three methods, `downloadMode`, `predict`, and `registerModel`, are self-explanatory. Each client implements these methods to download models and send prediction requests to its registered backend service. The parameter `GetArtifactResponse` is a model's metadata object that is fetched from the metadata store.

In this (intent predictor) example, the predictor backend client is `CustomGrpc-PredictorBackend`. You can find the detailed implementation in `prediction-service/src/main/java/org/orca3/miniAutoML/prediction/CustomGrpcPredictorBackend.java`. The following code snippet shows how this client sends prediction requests to the self-built intent predictor container by using gRPC protocol:

```
// calling backend predictor for model serving
public String predict(GetArtifactResponse artifact, String document) {
    return stub.predictorPredict(PredictorPredictRequest
        .newBuilder().setDocument(document)        ⟵——  Text input for
        .setRunId(artifact.getRunId())     ⟵—┐           the model
        .build()).getResponse();              │
}                                     Model ID ┘
```

7.1.4   *Intent classification predictor*

We have seen the frontend service and its internal routing logic, so now let's look at the last piece of this sample prediction service: the backend predictor. To show you a complete deep learning use case, we implement a predictor container to execute the intent classification models trained in chapter 3.

We can see this self-built intent classification predictor as an independent microservice, which can serve multiple intent models simultaneously. It has a gRPC web interface and a model manager. The model manager is the heart of the predictor; it does multiple things, including loading model files, initializing the model, caching the model in memory, and executing the model with user input. Figure 7.3 shows the predictor's design graph and the prediction workflow within the predictor.

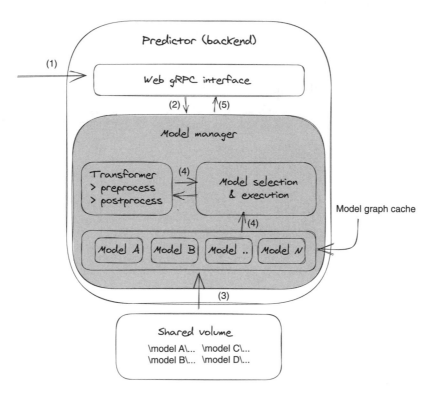

Figure 7.3   The backend intent predictor design and prediction workflow

Let's use an intent prediction request for model A to consider the workflow in figure 7.3. It runs in the following steps:

1 The predictor client in the frontend service calls the predictor's web gRPC interface to run an intent prediction with model A.
2 The model manager is invoked for the request.

3   The model manager loads the model files of model A from the shared disk volume, initializes the model, and puts it into the model cache. The model file should be placed at the shared disk volume by the frontend service already.

4   The model manager executes model A with the transformer's help to preprocess and postprocess the input and output data.

5   The predicted result is returned.

Next, let's look at the actual implementation of the components mentioned in the workflow.

PREDICTION API

Intent predictor has one API—`PredictorPredict` (see code listing 7.7). It accepts two parameters, `runId` and `document`. The `runId` is the model ID, and the `document` is a text string. You can find the full gRPC contract at `grpc-contract/src/main/proto/prediction_service.proto`.

Listing 7.7   Intent predictor gRPC interface

```
service Predictor {
 rpc PredictorPredict(PredictorPredictRequest) returns
     (PredictorPredictResponse);
}

message PredictorPredictRequest {
 string runId = 1;
 string document = 2;
}

message PredictorPredictResponse {
 string response = 1;
}
```

You may notice the predictor API is the same as the frontend API (code listing 7.2); this is for simplicity. But in real-world applications, they are normally different, mostly because they are designed for different purposes. The predictor's predict API is designed in favor of model execution, whereas the frontend predict API is designed in favor of the customer's and business's requirements.

MODEL FILES

Each intent classification model produced in our model training service (chapter 3) has three files. The `manifest.json` file contains both model metadata and dataset labels; the predictor needs this information to translate the model prediction result from an integer to a meaningful text string. The `model.pth` is the model's learned parameters; the predictor will read these network parameters to set up the model's neural network for model serving. The `vocab.pth` is the vocabulary file used in model training, which is also necessary for serving because we need it to transform user input (string) to model input (decimal number). Let's review the sample intent model:

```
                 Model metadata
                 and dataset labels
├──  manifest.json      ◁──┐         Model
├──  model.pth     ◁────┐   │         weights file
└──  vocab.pth   ◁──┐    │   │
                     │    Vocabulary file

// A sample manifest.json file
{
  "Algorithm": "intent-classification",    ◁──┐     Model
  "Framework": "Pytorch",                         │     metadata
  "FrameworkVersion": "1.9.0",
  "ModelName": "intent",
  "CodeVersion": "80bf0da",
  "ModelVersion": "1.0",
  "classes": {              ◁──┐       Dataset
    "0": "cancel",                │       labels
    "1": "ingredients_list",
    "2": "nutrition_info",
    "3": "greeting",
    .. .. ..
}
```

When saving a PyTorch model, there are two choices: serialize the entire model or serialize only the learned parameters. The first option serializes the entire model object, including its classes and directory structure, whereas the second option only saves the learnable parameters of the model network.

From Matthew Inkawhich's article "PyTorch: Saving and Loading Models" (http://mng.bz/zm9B), the PyTorch team recommends only saving the model's learned parameters (a model's state_dict). If we save the entire model, the serialized data is bound to the specific classes and the exact directory structure used when the model is saved. The model class itself is not saved; rather, the file containing the class is saved. Consequently, during loading time, the serialized model code can break in various ways when used in other projects or after refactors.

For this reason, we only save the model state_dict (learned parameters) as the model file after training; in this example, it is the model.pth file. We use the following code to save it: torch.save(model.state_dict(), model_local_path). As a result, the predictor needs to know the model's neural network architecture (see code listing 7.8) to load the model file because the model file is just state_dict—the model network's parameters.

Listing 7.8 (predictor/predict.py) shows the model architecture that we use to load the model file—model.pth (parameters only)—in the predictor. The model execution code in serving is derived from the model training code. If you compare the model definition in the following listing with the TextClassificationModel class in our training code (training-code/text-classification/train.py), you will find they are identical. This is because model serving is essentially a model training run.

Listing 7.8   The model's neural network (architecture)

```
class TextClassificationModel(nn.Module):

  def __init__(self, vocab_size, embed_dim,          Defines model
      fc_size, num_class):                           architecture

    super(TextClassificationModel, self).__init__()
    self.embedding = nn.EmbeddingBag(vocab_size, embed_dim, sparse=True)
    self.fc1 = nn.Linear(embed_dim, fc_size)
    self.fc2 = nn.Linear(fc_size, num_class)
    self.init_weights()

  def forward(self, text, offsets):
    embedded = self.embedding(text, offsets)
    return self.fc2(self.fc1(embedded))
```

You might wonder whether the training code and the model serving code are now combined. When the training code changes, it seems the model serving code in the predictor also needs to be adjusted. This is only partially true; the context tends to dictate how model serving is affected by changes to the model training algorithm. The following are some nuances of that relationship.

First, the training code and the serving code will only need to sync on the neural network architecture and input/output data schema. Other model training changes, such as training strategy, hyperparameter tuning, dataset splitting, and enhancements, will not affect serving because they result in model weights and bias files. Second, model versioning should be introduced when neural network architecture changes in training. In practice, every model training or retraining assigns a new model version to the output model. So the problem to address is how to serve different versions of a model.

This sample service does not handle model version management. However, in section 7.5 and chapter 8, we will discuss metadata management for the model version in depth. We just describe the rough idea here.

If you are using a similar model service approach with a customized predictor backend, you need to prepare multiple versions of the predictor backend to match the models that are trained with different neural network architectures. When releasing a model, the versions of the training code, serving code, and model file need to be related as part of the model metadata and saved in the metadata store. So, at the serving time, the prediction service (frontend service) can search the metadata store to determine which predictor version it should route a request to for the given model.

If you are using a model server approach, serving models with different versions becomes a lot easier because this approach breaks the dependency between the serving code (model execution code) and training code. You can see a concrete example in section 7.2.

> **NOTE** As we mentioned in chapter 6 (section 6.1.3), model training and serving both utilize the same machine learning algorithm but in different execution modes: learning and evaluation. However, we would like to clarify this concept once more. Understanding the relationship between training code, serving code, and model files is the foundation of a serving system design.

MODEL MANAGER

The model manager is the key component of this intent predictor. It hosts a memory model cache, loads the model file, and executes the model. The following listing (`predictor/predict.py`) shows the core code of the model manager.

Listing 7.9 Intent predictor model manager

```
class ModelManager:
  def __init__(self, config, tokenizer, device):
    self.model_dir = config.MODEL_DIR
    self.models = {}                          ◁── Hosts the model
                                                  in memory

  # load model file and initialize model
  def load_model(self, model_id):
    if model_id in self.models:
      return

    # load model files, including vocabulary, prediction class mapping.
    vacab_path = os.path.join(self.model_dir, model_id, "vocab.pth")
    manifest_path = os.path.join(self.model_dir, model_id, "manifest.json")
    model_path = os.path.join(self.model_dir, model_id, "model.pth")

    vocab = torch.load(vacab_path)
    with open(manifest_path, 'r') as f:
    manifest = json.loads(f.read())
    classes = manifest['classes']

    # initialize model graph and load model weights
    num_class, vocab_size, emsize = len(classes), len(vocab), 64
    model = TextClassificationModel(vocab_size, emsize,
      self.config.FC_SIZE, num_class).to(self.device)
    model.load_state_dict(torch.load(model_path))
    model.eval()

    self.models[self.model_key(model_id)] = model
self.models[self.model_vocab_key(model_id)]          Caches model graph;
    ➡ = vocab                                        dependencies and
self.models[self.model_classes(model_id)]            classes in memory
    ➡ = classes

  # run model to make prediction
  def predict(self, model_id, document):
    # fetch model graph, dependency and
    # classes from cache by model id
```

```
model = self.models[self.model_key(model_id)]
vocab = self.models[self.model_vocab_key(model_id)]
classes = self.models[self.model_classes(model_id)]

def text_pipeline(x):
  return vocab(self.tokenizer(x))

# transform user input data (text string)
# to model graph's input
processed_text = torch.tensor(text_pipeline(document), dtype=torch.int64)
offsets = [0, processed_text.size(0)]
offsets = torch.tensor(offsets[:-1]).cumsum(dim=0)

val = model(processed_text, offsets)        ←──┤ Runs the model to obtain
                                                 prediction results
# convert prediction result from an integer to
# a text string (class)
res_index = val.argmax(1).item()
res = classes[str(res_index)]
print("label is {}, {}".format(res_index, res))
return res
```

INTENT PREDICTOR PREDICTION REQUEST WORKFLOW

You've met the main components of the intent predictor, so let's see an end-to-end workflow inside this predictor. First, we expose the prediction API by registering `PredictorServicer` to the gRPC server, so the frontend service can talk to the predictor remotely. Second, when the frontend service calls the `PredictorPredict` API, the model manager will load the model into memory, run the model, and return the prediction result. Code listing 7.10 highlights the aforementioned workflow's code implementation. You can find the full implementation at `predictor/predict.py`.

Listing 7.10   Intent predictor prediction workflow

```
def serve():
  .. .. ..
  model_manager = ModelManager(config,
    tokenizer=get_tokenizer('basic_english'), device="cpu")
  server = grpc.server(futures.
    ThreadPoolExecutor(max_workers=10))        ←──┤ Starts the
                                                    gRPC server

  prediction_service_pb2_grpc.add_PredictorServicer_to_server(
    PredictorServicer(model_manager), server)   ←──┐ Registers the model serving
  .. .. ..                                          │ logic to the public API

class PredictorServicer(prediction_service_pb2_grpc.PredictorServicer):
  def __init__(self, model_manager):
    self.model_manager = model_manager

  # Serving logic
  def PredictorPredict(self, request, context: grpc.ServicerContext):

    # load model
    self.model_manager.load_model(model_id=request.runId)
```

Makes the
prediction
```
class_name = self.model_manager.
    predict(request.runId, request.document)
return PredictorPredictResponse(response=json.dumps({'res': class_name}))
```

7.1.5   *Model eviction*

The sample code did not cover model eviction—that is, evicting infrequently used model files from the prediction service's memory space. In the design, for every prediction request, the prediction service will query and download the request model from the metadata store and then read and initialize the model from the local disk to memory. For some models, these operations are time-consuming.

To reduce the latency for each model prediction request, our design caches model graphs in the model manager component (in memory) to avoid model loading a used model. But imagine that we could continue training new intent classification models and running predictions on them. These newly produced models will keep loading into the model manager's model cache in memory. Eventually, the predictor will run out of memory.

To address such problems, the model manager needs to be upgraded to include a model eviction feature. For example, we could introduce the LRU (least recently used) algorithm to rebuild the model manager's model cache. With the help of the LRU, we can keep only the recently visited model in the model cache and evict the least visited models when the currently loaded model exceeds the memory threshold.

7.2   *TorchServe model server sample*

In this section, we will show you an example of building a prediction service with the model server approach. More specifically, we use the TorchServe backend (a model serving tool built for the PyTorch model) to replace the self-built predictor discussed in the previous section (7.1.4).

To make a fair comparison to the model service approach in section 7.1, we develop this model server approach example by reusing the frontend service shown in the previous section. More precisely, we add only another predictor backend and still use the frontend service, gRPC API, and intent classification models to demo the same end-to-end prediction workflow.

There is one big difference between the intent predictor in section 7.1.4 and the TorchServe predictor (model server approach). The same predictor can serve any PyTorch model, regardless of its prediction algorithm.

7.2.1   *Playing with the service*

Because this model server sample is developed on top of the previous sample service, we interact with the prediction service in the same way. The only difference is we launch a TorchServe backend (container) instead of launching a self-built intent predictor container. Code listing 7.11 shows only the key steps to starting the service and sending intent prediction requests. To run the lab locally, please complete the lab in appendix A (section A.2), and refer to the `scripts/lab-006-model-serving-torchserve.sh` file (http://mng.bz/0yEN).

Listing 7.11 Starting the prediction service and making a prediction call

```
# step 1: start torchserve backend
docker run --name intent-classification-torch-predictor\
 --network orca3 --rm -d -p "${ICP_TORCH_PORT}":7070 \
 -p "${ICP_TORCH_MGMT_PORT}":7071 \
 -v "${MODEL_CACHE_DIR}":/models \
 -v "$(pwd)/config/torch_server_config.properties": \
     /home/model-server/config.properties \
 pytorch/torchserve:0.5.2-cpu torchserve \
 --start --model-store /models
```

Starts TorchServe

Mounts local dir to the TorchServe container

Sets TorchServe to load the model from /models dir

```
# step 2: start the prediction service (the web frontend)
docker build -t orca3/services:latest -f services.dockerfile .
docker run --name prediction-service --network orca3 \
  --rm -d -p "${PS_PORT}":51001 \
  -v "${MODEL_CACHE_DIR}":/tmp/modelCache \
 orca3/services:latest \
 prediction-service.jar
```

Sets local model dir for the prediction service to download the model

```
# step 3: make a prediction request, ask intent for "merry christmas"
grpcurl -plaintext
  -d "{
    "runId": "${MODEL_ID}",
    "document": "merry christmas"
  }"
  localhost:"${PS_PORT}" prediction.PredictionService/Predict
```

7.2.2 Service design

This sample service follows the same system design in figure 7.1; the only difference is the predictor backend becomes the TorchServe server. See figure 7.4 for the updated system design.

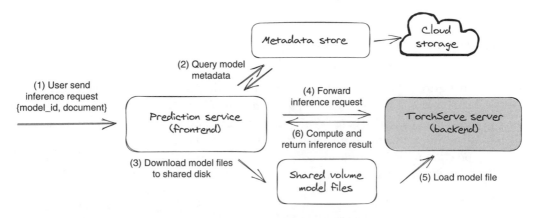

Figure 7.4 The system overview and model serving end-to-end workflow

From figure 7.4, we see the model serving workflow remains the same as the model service sample in figure 7.1. The user calls the prediction service's frontend API to send model serving requests; the frontend service then downloads the model files and forwards the prediction request to the TorchServe backend.

7.2.3   *The frontend service*

In section 7.1.3, we established that the frontend service can support different predictor backends by registering predictors in the predictor connection manager. When a prediction request comes in, the predictor connection manager will route the request to the proper predictor backend by checking the model algorithm type of the request.

Following the previous design, to support our new TorchServe backend, we add a new predictor client (`TorchGrpcPredictorBackend`) to the frontend service to represent the TorchServe backend; see figure 7.5 for the updated system design.

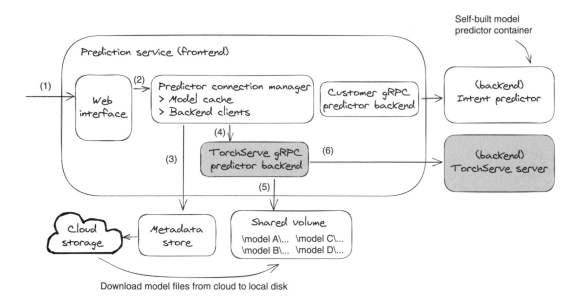

Figure 7.5   The frontend service design and the model serving workflow

In figure 7.5, two gray boxes are added; they are the TorchServe gRPC predictor backend client (`TorchGrpcPredictorBackend`) and the backend TorchServe server. `TorchGrpcPredictorBackend` responds by downloading the model files and then sending prediction requests to the TorchServe container. The TorchServe backend will be chosen by the predictor connection manager in this example because the requested model's metadata (in the metadata store) defines TorchServe as its predictor.

7.2.4 *TorchServe backend*

TorchServe is a tool built by the PyTorch team to serve PyTorch models. TorchServe runs as a black box, and it provides HTTP and gRPC interfaces for model prediction and internal resource management. Figure 7.6 visualizes the workflow for how we use TorchServe in this sample.

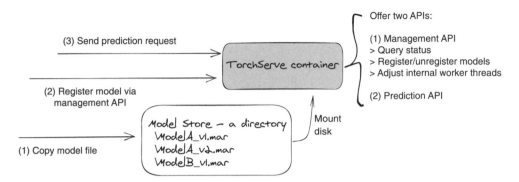

Figure 7.6   The model serving workflow in the TorchServe backend: the TorchServe application runs as a black box.

In our sample code, we run TorchServe as a Docker container, which is provided by the PyTorch team, and then mount a local file directory to the container. This file directory runs as the model store for the TorchServe process. In figure 7.6, we take three steps to run a model prediction. First, we copy PyTorch model files to the model store directory. Second, we call the TorchServe management API to register the model to the TorchServe process. Finally, we call the TorchServe API to run the model prediction for the model—in our case, the intent classification model.

Compared to the self-built intent predictor in section 7.1.4, TorchServe is much simpler. We can make the model serving work without writing any code; we just need to set up a Docker container with disk sharing. Also, unlike the intent predictor that only works for intent classification algorithms, TorchServe is not tied to any specific training algorithm; it can serve any model as long as it's trained with the PyTorch framework.

The great flexibility and convenience offered by TorchServe come with requirements. TorchServe requires operators to use their own set of APIs to send model serving requests, and it also requires that the model files are packaged in the TorchServe format. Let's look at these mandates in the next two subsections.

7.2.5 *TorchServe API*

TorchServe offers many types of APIs, such as health checks, model explanation, model serving, worker management, and model registration. Each API has two types of implementations: HTTP and gRPC. Because TorchServe has very detailed explanations of its API contract and usage on its official website (https://pytorch.org/serve/) and

GitHub repo (https://github.com/pytorch/serve), you can find the details there. In this section, we will focus on the model registration and model inference APIs that we use in our sample service.

MODEL REGISTRATION API

Because TorchServe takes a black-box approach to model serving, it requires a model to be registered first before using it. More specifically, after we place model files in TorchServe's model store (a local file directory), TorchServe won't load the model automatically. We need to register the model file and the model's execution method to TorchServe, so TorchServe knows how to work with this model.

In our code example, we use the TorchServe's gRPC model registration API to register our intent model from the prediction service, as in the following snippet:

```
public void registerModel(GetArtifactResponse artifact) {
  String modelUrl = String.format(MODEL_FILE_NAME_TEMPLATE,
        artifact.getRunId());

  String torchModelName = String.format(TORCH_MODEL_NAME_TEMPLATE,
          artifact.getName(), artifact.getVersion());
  ManagementResponse r = managementStub.registerModel(        ◁——┐ Registers the
          RegisterModelRequest.newBuilder()                           model to
            .setUrl(modelUrl)                                         TorchServe by
            .setModelName(torchModelName)                             providing the
            .build());                                                model file and
                                                                      model name
  # Assign resource (TorchServe worker) for this model
  managementStub.scaleWorker(ScaleWorkerRequest.newBuilder()
            .setModelName(torchModelName)
            .setMinWorker(1)
            .build());
}
```

The TorchServe model file already contains the model's metadata—including the model version, model runtime, and model serving entry point. So when registering models, we normally just set the model file name in the `registerModel` API. In addition to model registration, we can also use the `scaleWorker` API to control how much compute resources we allocate to this model.

MODEL INFERENCE API

TorchServe provides a unified model serving API for diverse models; this makes TorchServe simple to use. To run predictions for the default version of a model, make a REST call to POST `/predictions/{model_name}`. To run predictions for a specific version of a loaded model, make a REST call to POST `/predictions/{model_name}/{version}`. The content to be predicted in the prediction request is entered in binary format. For example,

```
# prediction with single input on model resnet-18
curl http://localhost:8080/predictions/resnet-18 \
 -F "data=@kitten_small.jpg"
```

```
# prediction with multiple inputs on model squeezenet1_1
curl http://localhost:8080/predictions/squeezenet1_1 \
 -F 'data=@docs/images/dogs-before.jpg' \
 -F 'data=@docs/images/kitten_small.jpg'
```

In our sample service, we use the gRPC interface to send prediction requests to Torch-Serve. Code listing 7.12 shows the `TorchGrpcPredictorBackend` client translating a prediction request from a frontend API call to a TorchServe backend gRPC call. You can find the full source ode of `TorchGrpcPredictorBackend` at `prediction-service/src/main/java/org/orca3/miniAutoML/prediction/TorchGrpcPredictorBackend.java`.

Listing 7.12   Calling the TorchServe prediction API from the frontend service

```
// call TorchServe gRPC prediction api
public String predict(GetArtifactResponse artifact, String document) {
  return stub.predictions(PredictionsRequest.newBuilder()
          .setModelName(String.format(TORCH_MODEL_NAME_TEMPLATE,
              artifact.getName(), artifact.getVersion()))
          .putAllInput(ImmutableMap.of("data",          ◁──────────┐
              ByteString.copyFrom(document, StandardCharsets.UTF_8)))
              .build()).getPrediction()                Converts text input to binary
          .toString(StandardCharsets.UTF_8);            format for calling TorchServe
}
```

7.2.6   *TorchServe model files*

So far, you have seen the TorchServe model serving workflow and API. You may wonder how model serving works in TorchServe when it knows nothing about the model it serves. In chapter 6, we learned that to serve a model, the prediction service needs to know the model algorithm and model input/output schema. Counterintuitively, TorchServe runs model serving without knowing the model algorithm and model input/output data format. The trick lies in the TorchServe model file.

TorchServe requires models to be packed into a special .mar file. We can use the `torch-model-archiver` CLI or `model_archiver` Python library to package PyTorch model files into a .mar file.

To archive a TorchServe .mar file, we need to provide the model name, model files (.pt or .pth), and a handler file. The handler file is the key piece; it is a Python code file that defines the logic for handling custom TorchServe inference logic. Because TorchServe's model package (.mar file) contains the model algorithm, model data, and model execution code and the model execution code follows TorchServe's prediction interface (protocol), TorchServe can execute any model (.mar file) by using its generic prediction API without knowing the model algorithm.

When TorchServe receives a prediction request, it will first find the internal worker process that hosts the model and then trigger the model's handler file to process the request. The handler file contains four pieces of logic: model network initialization, input data preprocess, model inference, and prediction result postprocess. To make the previous explanation more concrete, let's look at our intent model file as an example.

INTENT CLASSIFICATION .MAR FILE

If we open the .mar file of an intent model in our sample service, we will see that two additional files—MANIFEST.json and torchserve_handler.py—are added, compared with the model files we see in section 7.1.4. The following is the folder structure of an intent .mar file:

```
                        TorchServe .mar          Contains label
                        file metadata            information

# intent.mar content
├── MAR-INF                                   Model weights file
│   └── MANIFEST.json      ◁
├── manifest.json          ◁                  Model architecture and
├── model.pth              ◁                  model serving logic
├── torchserve_handler.py  ◁
└── vocab.pth              ◁                  Vocabulary file, required
                                              by the intent algorithm

# MANIFEST.json, TorchServe .mar metadata
{
  "createdOn": "09/11/2021 10:26:59",
  "runtime": "python",
  "model": {
    "modelName": "intent_80bf0da",
    "serializedFile": "model.pth",
    "handler": "torchserve_handler.py",
    "modelVersion": "1.0"
  },
  "archiverVersion": "0.4.2"
}
```

The MANIFEST.json file defines the metadata of a model, including the model version, model weights, model name, and handler file. By having a MANIFEST.json file, TorchServe knows how to load and run prediction on arbitrary models without knowing their implementation details.

TORCHSERVE HANDLER FILE

Once a model is registered in TorchServe, TorchServe will use the handle(self, data, context) function in the model's handler file as the entry point for model prediction. The handler file manages the entire process of model serving, including model initialization, preprocess on input request, model execution, and postprocess on the predicted outcome.

Code listing 7.13 highlights the key pieces of the handler file defined for the intent classification .mar file used in this sample service. You can find this file in our Git repository at training-code/text-classification/torchserve_handler.py.

> **Listing 7.13 Intent model TorchServe handler file**

```
class ModelHandler(BaseHandler):
    """
    A custom model handler implementation for serving
    intent classification prediction in torch serving server.
    """
```

```
# Model architecture
class TextClassificationModel(nn.Module):
    def __init__(self, vocab_size, embed_dim, fc_size, num_class):
        super(ModelHandler.TextClassificationModel, self)
._init__()
        self.embedding = nn.EmbeddingBag(vocab_size,
embed_dim, sparse=True)
        self.fc1 = nn.Linear(embed_dim, fc_size)
        self.fc2 = nn.Linear(fc_size, num_class)
        self.init_weights()

    def init_weights(self):
        .. .. ..

    def forward(self, text, offsets):
        embedded = self.embedding(text, offsets)
        return self.fc2(self.fc1(embedded))

# Load dependent files and initialize model
def initialize(self, ctx):

    model_dir = properties.get("model_dir")
    model_path = os.path.join(model_dir, "model.pth")
    vacab_path = os.path.join(model_dir, "vocab.pth")
    manifest_path = os.path.join(model_dir, "manifest.json")

    # load vocabulary
    self.vocab = torch.load(vacab_path)

    # load model manifest, including label index map.
    with open(manifest_path, 'r') as f:
        self.manifest = json.loads(f.read())
    classes = self.manifest['classes']

    # intialize model
    self.model = self.TextClassificationModel(
        vocab_size, emsize, self.fcsize, num_class).to("cpu")
    self.model.load_state_dict(torch.load(model_path))
    self.model.eval()
    self.initialized = True

# Transform raw input into model input data.
def preprocess(self, data):

    preprocessed_data = data[0].get("data")
    if preprocessed_data is None:
        preprocessed_data = data[0].get("body")

    text_pipeline = lambda x: self.vocab(self.tokenizer(x))

    user_input = " ".join(str(preprocessed_data))
    processed_text = torch.tensor(text_pipeline(user_input),
        dtype=torch.int64)
    offsets = [0, processed_text.size(0)]
    offsets = torch.tensor(offsets[:-1]).cumsum(dim=0)
```

```
        return (processed_text, offsets)

    # Run model inference by executing the model with model input
    def inference(self, model_input):
        model_output = self.model.forward(model_input[0], model_input[1])
        return model_output

    # Take output from network and post-process to desired format
    def postprocess(self, inference_output):
        res_index = inference_output.argmax(1).item()
        classes = self.manifest['classes']
        postprocess_output = classes[str(res_index)]
        return [{"predict_res":postprocess_output}]

    # Entry point of model serving, invoke by TorchServe
    # for prediction request
    def handle(self, data, context):

        model_input = self.preprocess(data)
        model_output = self.inference(model_input)
        return self.postprocess(model_output)
```

By starting from the handle function in listing 7.13, you will have a clear view of how model serving is executed by the handler file. The initialize function loads all the model files (weights, labels, and vocabulary) and initializes the model. The handle function is the entry point of model serving; it preprocesses the binary model input, runs the model inference, postprocesses the model output, and returns the result.

PACKAGING .MAR FILE IN TRAINING

When we decide to use TorchServe for model serving, it's better to produce the .mar file at training time. Also, because the TorchServe handler file contains the model architecture and model execution logic, it is usually a part of the model training code.

There are two methods of packaging a .mar file. First, when model training completes, we can run the torch-model-archiver CLI tool to package model weights as serialized files and dependent files as extra files. Second, we can use the model_archiver Python library to produce the .mar file as the last step of the model training code. The following code snippets are the examples we used for packaging intent classification models:

```
## Method one: package model by command line cli tool.
torch-model-archiver --model-name intent_classification --version 1.0 \
 --model-file torchserve_model.py --serialized-file \
    workspace/MiniAutoML/{model_id}/model.pth \
 --handler torchserve_handler.py --extra-files \
workspace/MiniAutoML/{model_id}/vocab.pth,
➥ workspace/MiniAutoML/{model_id}/manifest.json

## Method two: package model in training code.
model_archiver.archive(model_name=archive_model_name,
  handler_file=handler, model_state_file=model_local_path,
  extra_files=extra_files, model_version=config.MODEL_SERVING_VERSION,
  dest_path=config.JOB_ID)
```

7.2.7   Scaling up in Kubernetes

In our sample service, for demo purposes, we run a single TorchServe container as the prediction backend, but this is not the case for the production environment. The challenges for scaling up TorchServe are as follows:

- The load balancer makes TorchServe model registration difficult. In Torch-Serve, model files need to be registered to the TorchServe server first before they can be used. But in production, the TorchServe instances are put behind a network load balancer, so we can only send prediction requests to the load balancer and let it route the request to a random TorchServe instance. In this case, it's difficult to register models because we can't specify which TorchServe instance serves which model. The load balancer hides the TorchServe instances from us.
- Each TorchServe instance needs to have a model store directory for loading models, and model files need to be put in the model store directory before they can be registered. Having multiple TorchServe instances makes model file copying difficult to manage because we need to know every TorchServe instance's IP address or DNS to copy the model files.
- We need to balance the models among the TorchServe instances. Letting every TorchServe instance load every model file is a bad idea; it would be a great waste of compute resources. We should spread the load evenly across different TorchServe instances.

To address these challenges and scale up the TorchServe backend, we can introduce the "sidecar" pattern in Kubernetes. Figure 7.7 illustrates the overall concept.

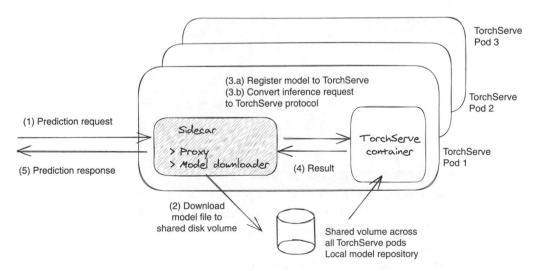

Figure 7.7   Add a proxy container in the TorchServe pod to scale up TorchServe in Kubernetes.

The proposal in figure 7.7 is to add a proxy container (as a sidecar) along with the TorchServe container in each TorchServe pod. Instead of calling the TorchServe API directly, we send the prediction requests to the proxy container. The proxy API in the proxy container will hide the TorchServe model management details, including model downloading and model registration. It will prepare the TorchServe container to serve arbitrary models.

After adding a proxy container, the model serving workflow (figure 7.7) occurs as follows. First, the prediction request lands on the proxy container. Second, the proxy downloads the model file and inputs the shared disk (model store). Third, the proxy registers the model to the TorchServe container and converts the inference request to the TorchServe format. Fourth, the TorchServe container runs model serving and returns the result to the proxy. Finally, the proxy container returns the prediction response to the user.

By having a proxy container, we don't need to worry about sending a prediction request to a TorchServe instance that doesn't have that model registered. The proxy container (sidecar) will get the TorchServe container ready for any prediction request by copying model files to the model store and registering the model. It also simplifies the resource management effort because now we can simply rely on the load balancer to spread the prediction workload (models) across the TorchServe pods. Also, by sharing a disk across all TorchServe pods, we can share the model store for all the TorchServe instances, which reduces model downloading time and saves network bandwidth.

> **The sidecar pattern: A common approach to running the model server**
>
> In section 7.4, we will introduce several other model server approaches, such as Tensor-Flow serving and Triton. Although the implementation of these model servers is different, their design ideas are similar. They all take a black-box approach and require certain model formats and some model management to enable model serving.
>
> The sidecar pattern in figure 7.7 is a common solution to running these different model server containers in a Kubernetes pod. The proxy container encapsulates all the special requirements of the model server and only exposes a general model serving API.

7.3   *Model server vs. model service*

Choosing between the model server approach and the model service approach is the first decision we need to make when designing a model serving application. When we choose improperly, our serving application either is hard to use and maintain or takes an unnecessarily long time to build.

We've already reviewed the differences between these two approaches in chapter 6 (sections 6.2 and 6.3), but this is such a crucial choice that it's worth examining again.

Now that you've seen concrete examples of each approach in action, these ideas may make more intuitive sense.

From working through the two sample services in sections 7.1 and 7.2, it's clear that the model server approach avoids the effort of building dedicated backend predictors for specific model types. Instead, it works out of the box and can serve arbitrary models regardless of which algorithm the model is implementing. So, it might seem like the model server approach should always be the best choice. But this is not true; the choice between the model server or model service should depend on the use case and business requirements.

For single-application scenarios, the model service approach is simpler to build and maintain in practice. Model service backend predictors are quite straightforward to build because model serving code is a simplified version of the training code. This means we can easily convert a model training container to a model serving container. Once it is built, the model service approach is easier to maintain because we own the code end to end and the workflow is simple. For the model server approach, whether we choose open source, prebuilt model servers, or build our own server, the process of setting up the system is complicated. It takes a lot of effort to learn the system well enough to operate and maintain it.

For model serving platform scenarios, where the system needs to support many different types of models, the model server approach is unquestionably the best. When you are building a model serving system for 500 different types of models, if you choose the model server approach, you only need to have one single type of predictor backend for all the models. In contrast, using the model service approach, you would need to have 500 different model predictors! It is incredibly hard to manage the compute resources and perform the maintenance work for all those predictors.

Our recommendation is to use the model service approach when you are first learning because it is simpler and easier. You can move to the model server approach when you need to support more than 5 to 10 types of models or applications in your serving system.

7.4   Touring open source model serving tools

There are plenty of open source model serving tools available. It's great to have options, but having so many of them can be overwhelming. To help make that choice easier for you, we will introduce you to some popular model serving tools, including TensorFlow Serving, TorchServe, Triton, and KServe. All of these can work out of the box and are applicable to production use cases.

Because each of the tools we describe here has thorough documentation, we will keep the discussion at a general level, looking just at their overall design, main features, and suitable use cases. This information should be enough to act as a starting point from which to explore further on your own.

7.4.1   *TensorFlow Serving*

TensorFlow Serving (https://www.tensorflow.org/tfx/guide/serving) is a customizable, standalone web system for serving TensorFlow models in production environments. TensorFlow Serving takes a model server approach; it can serve all types of TensorFlow models with the same server architecture and APIs.

FEATURES

TensorFlow Serving offers the following features:

- Can serve multiple models or multiple versions of the same model
- Has out-of-the-box integration with TensorFlow models
- Automatically discovers new model versions and supports different model file sources
- Has unified gRPC and HTTP endpoints for model inference
- Supports batching prediction requests and performance tuning
- Has an extensible design, which is customizable on version policy and model loading

HIGH-LEVEL ARCHITECTURE

In TensorFlow Serving, a model is composed of one or more servables. A servable is the underlying object to perform computation (for example, a lookup or inference); it is the central abstraction in TensorFlow Serving. Sources are plugin modules that find and provide servables. Loader standards are the API for loading and unloading a servable. The manager handles the full lifecycle of servables, including loading, unloading, and serving servables.

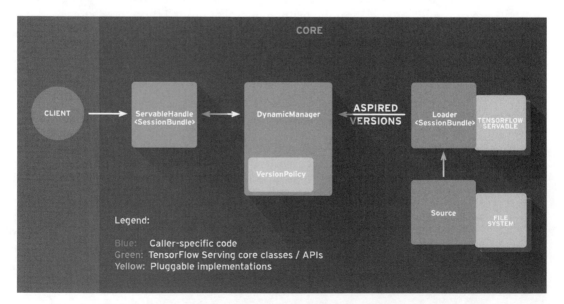

Figure 7.8   TensorFlow Serving architecture and model serving life cycle. Blue = darkest gray; green = lighter gray; yellow = lightest gray. (Source: TensorFlow; http://mng.bz/KINj)

Figure 7.8 illustrates the workflow of presenting a servable to the customer. First, the source plugin creates a loader for a specific servable; the loader contains the metadata to load the servable. Second, the source finds a servable in the filesystem (a model repository); it notifies the servable's version and loader to DynamicManager. Third, based on the predefined version policy, DynamicManager determines whether to load the model. Finally, the client sends a prediction request for a servable, and Dynamic-Manager returns a handle, so the client can execute the model.

TENSORFLOW SERVING MODEL FILE

TensorFlow Serving requires models to be saved in SavedModel (http://mng.bz/9197) format. We could use the `tf.saved_model.save(model, save_path)` API for this purpose. A saved model is a directory containing serialized signatures and the state needed to run them, including variable values and vocabularies. For example, a saved model directory has two subdirectories, `assets` and `variables`, and one file, `saved_model.pb`.

The assets folder contains files used by TensorFlow graphs, such as text files for initializing vocabulary tables. The variables folder contains training checkpoints. The `saved_model.pb` file stores the actual TensorFlow program, or model, and a set of named signatures, each identifying a function that accepts tensor inputs and produces tensor outputs.

MODEL SERVING

Because TensorFlow's SavedModel files can be directly loaded into the TensorFlow Serving process, running model serving is straightforward. Once the serving process starts, we can copy model files to TensorFlow Serving's model directory and then send gRPC or REST prediction requests right away. Let's review the following prediction example:

```
# 1. Save model in training code
MODEL_DIR='tf_model'
version = "1"
export_path = os.path.join(MODEL_DIR, str(version))
model.save(export_path, save_format="tf")


# 2. Start tensorflow serving service locally as a docker container
docker run -p 8501:8501
--mount type=bind,source=/workspace/tf_model,target=/models/model_a/
-e MODEL_NAME=model_a -t tensorflow/serving
--model_config_file_poll_wait_seconds=60
--model_config_file=/models/model_a/models.config


# 3. Send predict request to local tensorflow serving docker container
# The request url pattern to call a specific version of a model is
    /v1/models/<model name>/versions/<version number>
json_response = requests.post('http://localhost:8501/
  ➥ v1/models/model_a/versions/1:predict',
  data=data, headers=headers)
```

For loading multiple models and multiple versions of the same model into the serving server, we can configure the model's versions in the model config as follows:

```
model_config_list {
  config{
    name: 'model_a'
    base_path: '/models/model_a/'
    model_platform: 'tensorflow'
    model_version_policy{
      specific{
        versions:2          ◁─────┐ Finds model v2 at
        versions:3          ◁──┐  │ /models/model_a/versions/2
      }                         │
    }                           │   Finds model v3 at
  }                             └── /models/model_a/versions/3
  config{
    name: 'model_b'
    base_path: '/models/model_b/'
    model_platform: 'tensorflow'
  }
}
```

In this config, we defined two models, model_a and model_b. Because model_a has a model_version_policy, both the two versions (v2 and v3) are loaded and can serve requests. By default, the latest version of the model will be served, so when a new version of model_b is detected, the previous one will be replaced by the new one.

REVIEW

TensorFlow Serving is a production-level model serving solution for TensorFlow models; it supports REST, gRPC, GPU acceleration, minibatching, and model serving on edge devices. Although TensorFlow Serving falls short on advanced metrics, flexible model management, and deployment strategies, it's still a good choice if you only have TensorFlow models.

The main disadvantage of TensorFlow Serving is that it's a vendor lock-in solution; it only supports TensorFlow models. If you are looking for a training framework agnostic approach, TensorFlow Serving wouldn't be your choice.

7.4.2   *TorchServe*

TorchServe (https://pytorch.org/serve/) is a performant, flexible, and easy-to-use tool for serving PyTorch eager mode and torchscripted models (an intermediate representation of a PyTorch model that can be run in a high-performance environment such as C++). Similar to TensorFlow Serving, TorchServe takes a model server approach to serving all kinds of PyTorch models with a unified API. The difference is TorchServe provides a set of management APIs that makes model management very convenient and flexible. For example, we can programmatically register and unregister models or different versions of a model. And we can also scale up and scale down serving workers for models and different versions of a model.

HIGH-LEVEL ARCHITECTURE

A TorchServe server is composed of three components: the frontend, backend, and model store. The frontend handles TorchServe's request/response. It also manages the life cycles of the models. The backend is a list of model workers that are responsible for running the actual inference on the models. The model store is a directory in which all the loadable models exist; it can be a cloud storage folder or a local host folder. Figure 7.9 shows the high-level architecture of a TorchServing instance.

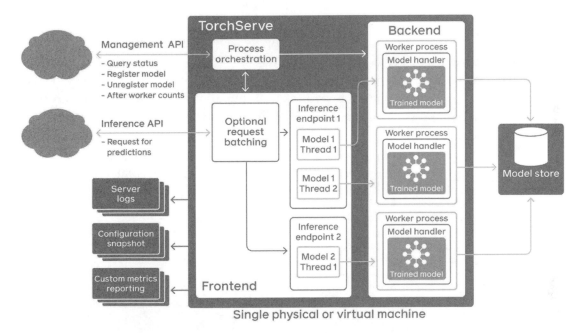

Figure 7.9   A TorchServe architecture diagram (Source: Kuldeep Singh, "Deploying Named Entity Recognition model to production using TorchServe," Analytics Vidhya, 2020)

Figure 7.9 draws two workflows: model inference and model management. For model inference, first, the user sends a prediction request to the inference endpoint of a model, such as /predictions/{model_name}/{version}. Next, the inference request is routed to one of the worker processes that already loaded the model. Then, the worker process will read model files from the model store and let the model handler load the model, preprocess the input data, and run the model to obtain a prediction result.

For model management, a model needs to be registered before users can access it. This is done by using the management API. We can also scale up and down the worker process count for a model. We will see an example in the upcoming sample usage section.

FEATURES

TorchServe offers the following features:

- Can serve multiple models or multiple versions of the same model
- Has unified gRPC and HTTP endpoints for model inference
- Supports batching prediction requests and performance tuning
- Supports workflow to compose PyTorch models and Python functions in sequential and parallel pipelines
- Provides management API to register/unregister models and scale up/down workers
- Handles model versioning for A/B testing and experimentation

TORCH SERVING MODEL FILE

Pure PyTorch models cannot be loaded to the Torch serving server directly. Torch-Serve requires all its models to be packaged into a .mar file. Please refer to section 7.2.6 for a detailed example of how a .mar file is created.

MODEL SERVING

The following code snippet lists five general steps to running model inference with TorchServe. For a concrete example, you can check out the README doc of our sample intent classification predictor (http://mng.bz/WA8a):

```
# 1. Create model store directory for torch serving
# and copy model files (mar files) to it
mkdir -p /tmp/model_store/torchserving
cp sample_models/intent.mar /tmp/model_store/torchserving    ◁─── Creates local
                                                                  model dir and
                                                                  copies the intent
                                                                  classification
                                                                  model
# 2. Run the torch serving container
docker pull pytorch/torchserve:0.4.2-cpu
docker run --rm --shm-size=1g \
        --ulimit memlock=-1 \
        --ulimit stack=67108864 \
        -p8080:8080 \
        -p8081:8081 \
        -p8082:8082 \
        -p7070:7070 \
        -p7071:7071 \
        --mount type=bind,source=/tmp/model_store/torchserving,target=/tmp/models
pytorch/torchserve:0.4.2-cpu torchserve --model-store=/tmp/models
```

Binds local model dir as the model store dir for TorchServe

```
# 3. Register intent model through torchserving management api
curl -X POST  "http://localhost:8081/models?url=
⮕ intent_1.mar&initial_workers=1&model_name=intent"
```

Intent_1.mar contains the model file and model metadata, such as the model version.

```
# 4. Query intent model in torch serving with default version.
curl --location --request GET 'http://localhost:8080/predictions/intent' \
--header 'Content-Type: text/plain' \
--data-raw 'make a 10 minute timer'

# 5. Query intent model in torch serving with specified version - 1.0
curl --location --request GET 'http://localhost:8080/predictions/intent/1.0' \
```

```
--header 'Content-Type: text/plain' \
--data-raw 'make a 10 minute timer'
```

Besides using management API to register models, we can also use the scale worker API to dynamically adjust the number of workers for any version of a model to better serve different inference request loads, as in the following example:

```
# 1. Scale up the worker number for the intent model. Default number is 1.
# Set minimum worker count to 3 and maximum worker count to 6
# for version 1.0 of the intent model
curl -v -X PUT "http:/ /localhost:8081/models/intent/1.0?min_worker=3&max_worker=6"

# 2. Use the describe model API to get detail runtime status of
# default version of the intent model.
curl http:/ /localhost:8081/models/intent

# 3. Use the describe model API to get detail runtime status of
# specific version (1.0) of the intent model.
curl http:/ /localhost:8081/models/intent/1.0
```

REVIEW

TorchServe is a production-level model serving solution for PyTorch models; it's designed for high-performance inference and production use cases. TorchServe's management API adds a lot of flexibility for customizing model deployment strategy, and it allows us to manage compute resources at the per-model level.

Similar to TensorFlow Serving, the main disadvantage of TorchServe is that it's a vendor lock-in solution; it only supports PyTorch models. So, if you are looking for a training framework agnostic approach, TorchServe wouldn't be your choice.

7.4.3   *Triton Inference Server*

Triton Inference Server (https://developer.nvidia.com/nvidia-triton-inference-server) is an open source inference server developed by NVIDIA. It provides a cloud and edge inferencing solution optimized for both CPUs and GPUs. Triton supports an HTTP/ REST and gRPC protocol that allows remote clients to request inferencing for any model being managed by the server. For edge deployments, Triton is available as a shared library with a C API that allows the full functionality of Triton to be included directly in an application.

Training framework compatibility is one of Triton's main advantages when compared with other serving tools. Unlike TensorFlow Serving, which only works with the TensorFlow model, and Torch serving, which only works with the PyTorch model, the Triton server can serve models trained from almost any framework, including Tensor-Flow, TensorRT, PyTorch, ONNX, and XGBoost. Triton server can load model files from local storage, Google Cloud Platform, or Amazon Simple Storage Service (Amazon S3) on any GPU- or CPU-based infrastructure (cloud, data center, or edge).

Inference performance is also an advantage for Triton. Triton runs models concurrently on GPUs to maximize throughput and utilization; supports x86 and ARM

CPU-based inferencing; and offers features like dynamic batching, model analyzer, model ensemble, and audio streaming. These features make model serving memory efficient and robust.

HIGH-LEVEL ARCHITECTURE

Figure 7.10 shows the Triton Inference Server's high-level architecture. All the inference requests are sent as REST or gRPC requests, and then they are converted to C API calls internally. Models are loaded from the model repository, which is a filesystem-based repository that we can see as folders/directories.

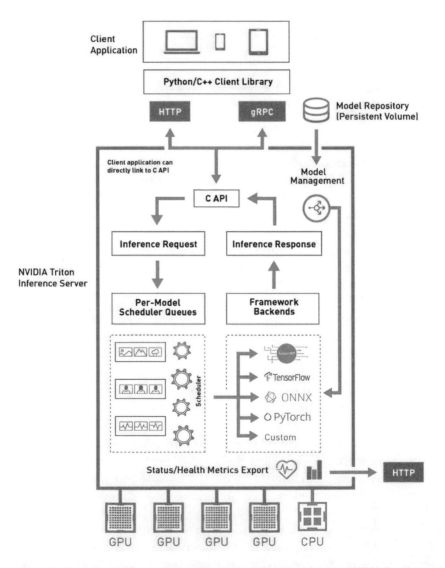

Figure 7.10   Triton Inference Server high-level architecture (Source: NVIDIA Developer, https://developer.nvidia.com/nvidia-triton-inference-server)

For each model, Triton prepares a scheduler. The scheduling and batching algorithms are configurable on a model-by-model basis. Each model's scheduler optionally performs batching of inference requests and then passes the requests to the backend corresponding to the model type, such as PyTorch backend for the PyTorch model. A Triton backend is the implementation that executes a model. It can be a wrapper around a deep learning framework, like PyTorch, TensorFlow, TensorRT, or ONNX Runtime. Once the backend performs inferencing using the inputs provided in the batched requests to produce the requested outputs, the outputs are returned.

One thing worth noting is that Triton supports a backend C API that allows Triton to be extended with new functionality, such as custom pre- and postprocessing operations or even a new deep learning framework. This is how we can extend the Triton server. You can check out the triton-inference-server/backend GitHub repo (https://github.com/triton-inference-server/backend) to find all Triton backend implementations. As a bonus, the models being served by Triton can be queried and controlled by a dedicated model management API that is available by HTTP/REST, gRPC protocol, or the C API.

FEATURES

Triton offers the following features:

- Supports all major deep learning and machine learning framework backends.
- Runs multiple models from the same or different frameworks concurrently on a single GPU or CPU. In a multi-GPU server, Triton automatically creates an instance of each model on each GPU to increase utilization.
- Optimizes inference serving for real-time inferencing, batch inferencing to maximize GPU/CPU utilization, and streaming inference with built-in support for audio streaming input. Triton also supports model ensembles for use cases that require multiple models to perform end-to-end inference, such as conversational AI.
- Handles dynamic batching of input requests for high throughput and utilization under strict latency constraints.
- Updates models live in production without restarting the inference server or disrupting the application.
- Uses model analyzer to automatically find the optimal model configuration and maximize performance.
- Supports multi-GPU, multinode inference of large models.

TRITON MODEL FILE

Each model in Triton must include a model configuration that provides required and optional information about the model. Typically, it's a config.pbtxt file specified as ModelConfig protobuf (http://mng.bz/81Kz). See a simple model config (config.pbtxt) for a PyTorch model as follows:

```
platform: "pytorch_libtorch"              ◁─────  Specifies the PyTorch
pytorch_libtorch                   ◁─────         serving backend for
  max_batch_size: 8              ◁─────           this model
  input [                      ◁─────
    {                                             Indicates this is a
      name: "input0"                              PyTorch backend config
      data_type: TYPE_FP32
      dims: [ 16 ]                                Defines the maximum
    },                                            batch size that the
    {                                             model supports
      name: "input1"
      data_type: TYPE_FP32
      dims: [ 16 ]                        Models input
    }                                     data schema
  ]
  output [          ◁─────  Models output
    {                       data schema
      name: "output0"
      data_type: TYPE_FP32
      dims: [ 16 ]
    }
  ]
```

Normally, the training application creates this config.pbtxt file when training completes at the training service and then uploads this config as part of the model files to the model repository. For more detail on Triton model configs, please check out the Triton model configuration documentation at http://mng.bz/Y6mA.

Besides a unified config file, the Triton model file format is different per training framework. For example, TensorFlow models in SavedModel format (http://mng.bz/El4d) can be loaded with Triton directly. But PyTorch models need to be saved by the TorchScript program.

TORCHSCRIPT

TorchScript is a way to create serializable and optimizable models from PyTorch code. The reason Triton requires PyTorch models to be serialized as TorchScript is that TorchScript can be used as an intermediate representation of a PyTorch model. It can run independently from Python, such as in a standalone C++ program. See the following code snippet for creating a TorchScript model from a PyTorch model:

```
#### Pytorch training code

# 1. Define an instance of your model.
Model = ...TorchModel()

# 2. Switch the model to eval model
model.eval()

# 3. Build an example input of the model's forward() method.
Example = torch.rand(1, 3, 224, 224)

# 4. Use torch.jit.trace to generate a torch.jit.ScriptModule via tracing.
Traced_script_module = torch.jit.trace(model, example)
```

```
# 5. Save the TorchScript model
traced_script_module.save("traced_torch_model.pt")
```

For the model format requirement of other training frameworks, please check out the triton-inference-server/backend GitHub repo (http://mng.bz/NmOn).

MODEL SERVING

Model serving in Triton involves the following three steps: first, copy the model file to the model repository; second, call the management API (POST v2/repository/models/${MODEL_NAME}/load) to register the model; and third, send an inference request (POST v2/models/${MODEL_NAME}/versions/${MODEL_VERSION}). For more information on the Triton management API, you can check the Triton HTTP/REST and gRPC protocol documentation (http://mng.bz/DZvR). For inference API, you can check the KServe community standard inference protocols documentation (https://kserve.github.io/website/0.10/modelserving/data_plane/v2_protocol/).

REVIEW

As we write this book, we consider Triton the best model serving approach for three reasons. First, Triton is training-framework agnostic; it provides a well-designed and extensible backend framework, which allows it to execute the models built by almost any training framework. Second, Triton offers better model serving performance, such as serving throughput. Triton has multiple mechanisms to improve its serving performance, such as dynamic batching, GPU optimization, and model analyzing tools. Third, Triton supports advanced model serving use cases such as model ensembles and audio streaming.

> **WARNING**   Be cautious! Triton may not be free. Triton is under BSD 3-Clause "new" or "revised" licensing, meaning it can be modified and distributed for commercial purposes for free. But what about troubleshooting and bug fixing? The project is complex, with a large code base, so you'll have a hard time debugging and fixing performance concerns, such as memory leaks. If you look for the NVIDIA AI-enterprise license to get the support, as this book is being written, it would cost you several thousand dollars per GPU per year. So be sure that you understand the Triton codebase before signing up.

7.4.4   *KServe and other tools*

The list of open source serving tools is extensive and includes KServe (https://www.kubeflow.org/docs/external-add-ons/kserve/), Seldon Core (https://www.seldon.io/solutions/open-source-projects/core), and BentoML (https://github.com/bentoml/BentoML). Each of these tools has some unique strengths. They either run lightweight and are easy to use, like BentoML, or they make model deployment easy and fast in Kubernetes, as do Seldon Core and KServe. Despite the diversity of the serving tools, they have a lot in common: they all need to pack models in a certain format, define a model wrapper and configuration file to execute the model, upload models to a repository, and send prediction requests via a gRPC or HTTP/REST endpoint. By reading the TorchServe, TensorFlow, and Triton examples in this chapter, you should be able to explore other tools on your own.

Before we end the serving tools discussion, we want to call out KServe specifically. KServe is a collaboration on model serving between several established high-tech companies, including Seldon, Google, Bloomberg, NVIDIA, Microsoft, and IBM. This open source project is worth your attention because it is designed to create a standardized solution for common machine learning serving problems.

KServe aims to provide a serverless inference solution on Kubernetes. It provides an abstract model serving interface that works for common machine learning frameworks like TensorFlow, XGBoost, scikit-learn, PyTorch, and ONNX.

From our point of view, KServe's main contribution is that it creates a standard serving interface that works for all major serving tools. For example, all the serving tools we mentioned previously now support the KServe model inference protocol. This means we can use only one set of inference APIs (the KServe API) to query any model hosted by different serving tools, such as Triton, TorchServe, and TensorFlow.

Another strength of KServe is that it is designed to provide a serverless solution natively on Kubernetes. KServe uses Knative to take care of the network routing, model worker autoscaling (even to zero), and model revision tracking. With a simple config (see the following example), you can deploy a model to your Kubernetes cluster and then use the standardized API to query it:

```
apiVersion: serving.kserve.io/v1beta1      ◁────  A sample model
kind: InferenceService                            deployment config
metadata:                                         for KServe
 name: "torchserve"
spec:                                        A backend
 predictor:                                  server type
   pytorch:                            ◁────
     storageUri: gs://kfserving-examples/models     A model file
            ➡ /torchserve/image_classifier          location
```

Behind the scenes, KServe uses different serving tools to run inference, such as TensorFlow Serving and Triton. KServe provides the benefit of hiding all the details behind a simple Kubernetes CRD config. In the previous example, the `InferenceSer-vice` CRD config hides the work, including prediction server setup, model copy, model version tracking, and prediction request routing.

As the book is being written, KServe's newer version (v2) is still in beta. Although it's not quite mature, its unique advantage of a standardized inference protocol across platform support and serverless model deployment makes it stand out among other approaches. If you want to set up a large serving platform that works for all major training frameworks on Kubernetes, KServe is worth your attention.

7.4.5 *Integrating a serving tool into an existing serving system*

In many cases, replacing an existing prediction service with a new serving backend is not an option. Each serving tool has its own requirements for model storage, model registration, and inference request format. These requirements sometimes conflict with the existing system's prediction interface and the internal model metadata and file systems. To introduce new technology without disrupting the business, we usually take an integration approach instead of completely replacing it.

Here, we use the Triton server as an example to show how to integrate a serving tool into an existing prediction service. In this example, we assume three things: first, the existing prediction service runs in Kubernetes; second, the existing prediction service's web inference interface is not allowed to change; and third, there is a model storage system that stores model files in cloud storage, such as Amazon S3. Figure 7.11 shows the process.

Figure 7.11 (A) illustrates the system overview. A list of Triton server Kubernetes pods is added behind the existing prediction API. With the Kubernetes load balancer, a prediction request can land on any Triton pod. We also add a shared volume that all Triton pods can access; this shared volume acts as a shared Triton model repository for all Triton instances.

Figure 7.11 (B) shows what's inside a Triton server Kubernetes pod. Each Triton pod has two Docker containers: a Triton Server Container and a sidecar container. The Triton server container is the Triton inference server we discussed in section 7.4.3. The model prediction happens in this container, and we can simply treat this container as a black box. The sidecar container acts as an adapter/proxy to prepare what Triton needs before forwarding the prediction request to the Triton container. This sidecar container downloads the model from cloud storage to the Triton local model repository (the shared volume), calls Triton to register the model, and converts the prediction request to the Triton API call.

By using this integration approach, all the changes happen inside the prediction service. The public prediction API and the external model storage system remain untouched, and our users won't be affected when we switch to a Triton backend. Although we use a specific tool (Triton) and a specific infrastructure (Kubernetes) to demo the idea, you can apply this pattern to any other system as long as they use Docker.

> **NOTE** Because the Triton server supports major training frameworks and KServe provides a standardized serving protocol, we can combine them to produce a serving system that works for all kinds of models trained by different frameworks.

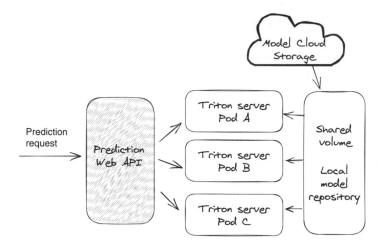

(A) Integrate Triton Server to an existing web API

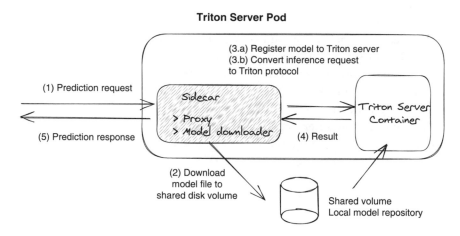

(B) A Sidecar acts as an adapter for Triton server

Figure 7.11   A proposal to integrate a list of Triton server instances into an existing serving system

7.5   *Releasing models*

Releasing a model is the act of deploying the newly trained model to the prediction service and exposing it to users. Automating the model deployment and supporting model evaluation are the two main problems we need to address when building model serving systems in production.

First, when the training service finishes the model building, the model should be published to the prediction service in the production environment automatically.

Second, the newly published model and its previous versions should all be accessible in the prediction service, so we can evaluate them in the same environment and make a fair comparison. In this section, we propose a three-step model release process to address these challenges.

First, the data scientist (Alex) or training service registers the recently produced model (consisting of the model's files and its metadata) to a metadata store—a cloud metadata and artifact storage system that will be discussed in the next chapter. Second, Alex runs the model evaluation on the newly registered models. He can test the performance of these models by sending prediction requests with their specific model versions to the prediction service. The prediction service has a built-in mechanism to load any specific version of a model from the metadata store.

Third, Alex sets the best-performing model version as the release model version in the metadata store. Once this is set, the selected version of the model will go public! Customer applications will unknowingly start using the new release version of the model from the prediction service. Figure 7.12 illustrates this three-step process.

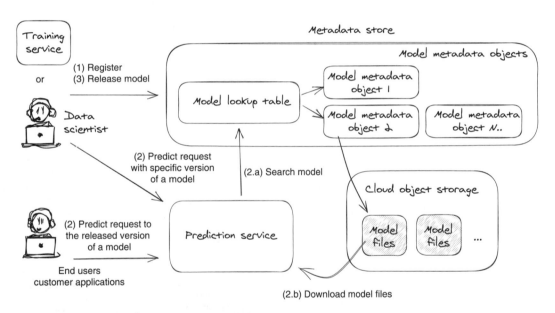

Figure 7.12   The model release process workflow: (1) registers models in the model metadata store; (2) loads arbitrary versions of a model to serve prediction requests; and (3) releases the model in the metadata store

In the next three sections, we will delve into the three model release steps (pictured in figure 7.12) one by one. As we do this, we will also explore the details of the metadata store and its interactions with storage and with the prediction service. Let's get started!

7.5.1   *Registering a model*

In most deep learning systems, there is a storage service to store models. In our example, this service is called the *metadata store*; it is used to manage the metadata of the artifacts produced by the deep learning system, such as models. The metadata and artifact store service will be discussed in detail in the next chapter.

To register a model to the metadata store, we usually need to provide model files and model metadata. Model files can be model weights, embeddings, and other dependent files to execute the model. Model metadata can be any data that describes the fact of the model, such as the model name, model ID, model version, training algorithm, dataset info, and training execution metrics. Figure 7.13 illustrates how metadata stores model metadata and model files internally.

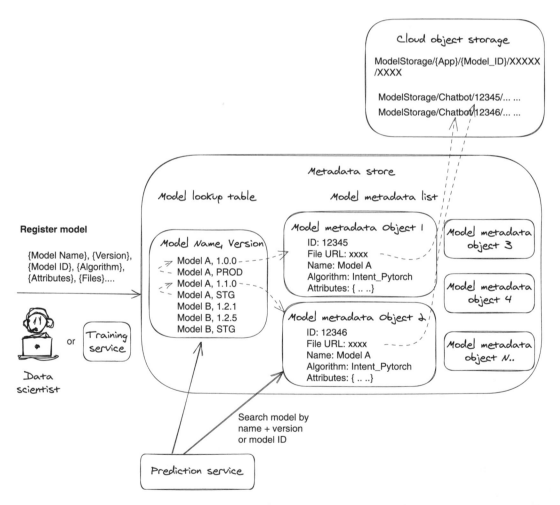

Figure 7.13   The internal storage design of the metadata store; model metadata are stored as object files with lookup tables in front of them.

In figure 7.13, we can see the metadata store has two sections: the model lookup table and the model metadata list. The model metadata list is just pure metadata storage; all the model metadata objects are stored in this list. The model lookup table is used as an index table for quick searches. Each record in the lookup table points to an actual metadata object in the metadata list.

Training service can register models automatically to the metadata store after training completes. Data scientists can also register models manually, which often happens when data scientists want to deploy the model they build locally (without using the deep learning system).

When the metadata store receives a model register request, first, it creates a metadata object for this model. Second, it updates the model lookup table by adding a new search record; the record enables us to find that model metadata object by using the model name and version. Besides searching the lookup table by using the model name and version, the metadata store also allows a model metadata search by using the model ID.

The actual model files are stored in the artifact store—a cloud object storage, such as Amazon S3. A model's storage location in the artifact store is saved in the model's metadata object as a pointer.

Figure 7.13 shows two search records in the model lookup table for model A: versions 1.0.0 and 1.1.0. Each search record maps to a different model metadata object (respectively, ID = 12345 and ID = 12346). With this storage structure, we can find any model metadata by using the model name and model version; for example, we can find model metadata object ID = 12346 by searching "model A" and version "1.1.0."

Using the model's canonical names and versions to find the actual metadata and model files is foundational to the prediction service's ability to serve different model versions at the same time. Let's see how the metadata store is used in the prediction service in the next section.

7.5.2 Loading an arbitrary version of a model in real time with a prediction service

To make decisions on which model version to use in production, we want to evaluate the model performance of each model version fairly (in the same environment) and easily (using the same API). To do so, we can call the prediction service to run prediction requests with different model versions.

In our proposal, the prediction service loads a model in real time from the metadata store when it receives a prediction request. Data scientists can allow the prediction services to use any model version to run the prediction by defining the model name and version in the prediction request. Figure 7.14 illustrates the process.

Figure 7.14 shows the prediction service loads models specified in the serving request in real time. When receiving a prediction request, the routing layer first finds the requested model in the metadata store, downloads the model files, and then

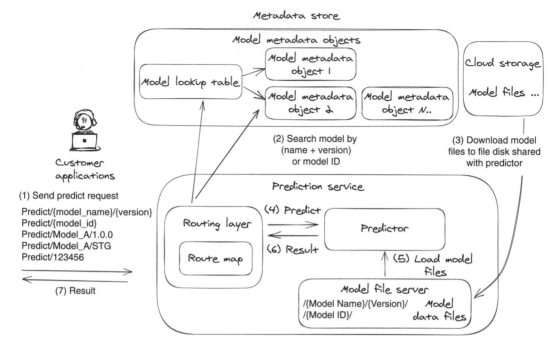

Figure 7.14   Model serving in prediction service with the metadata store

passes the request to the backend predictor. Here is a detailed explanation of the seven steps of the runtime model loading and serving process:

1 The user sends prediction requests to the prediction service. In the request, they can specify which model to use by providing the model name and version (/predict/{model_name}/{version}) or model ID (/predict/{model_id}).
2 The routing layer inside the prediction service searches the metadata store and finds the model metadata object.
3 The routing layer then downloads the model files to a shared disk that all the predictors can access.
4 By checking the model metadata, such as the algorithm type, the routing layer routes the prediction request to the correct backend predictor.
5 The predictor loads the model from the shared disk.
6 The predictor handles data preprocessing, executes the model, performs post-processing, and returns the result to the routing layer.
7 The routing layer returns prediction results to the caller.

7.5.3   *Releasing the model by updating the default model version*

After model evaluation, the last step of the model release is letting the customers consume the newly verified model version in the prediction service. We want the model release process to happen unknowingly, so customers aren't aware of the underlying model version changes.

In step 1 of the previous section (7.5.2), users can request a model serving on any specified model version by using the /predict/{model_name}/{version} API. This capability is crucial to evaluating multiple versions of the same model, so we can prevent model performance regression.

But in the production scenario, we don't expect our customers to track the model versions and model IDs. Alternatively, we can define a few static version strings as variables to represent the newly released models and let customers use them in the prediction request instead of using the real model version.

For example, we can define two special static model versions or tags, such as STG and PROD, which represent the preproduction and production environments, respectively. If the model version associated with the PROD tag for model A is 1.0.0, a user can call /predict/model_A/PROD and the prediction service will load model A and version 1.0.0 to run model serving. When we upgrade the newly released model version to 1.2.0—by associating the PROD tag to version 1.2.0—the /predict/model_A/PROD request will land on model version 1.2.0.

With the special static version/tag strings, prediction users don't need to remember model ID or versions; they can just use /predict/{model_name}/PROD to send prediction requests to consume the newly released model. Behind the scenes, we (data scientists or engineers) maintain the mapping between these special strings and the actual version in the metadata store's lookup table, so the prediction service knows which model version to download for a /STG or /PROD request.

In our proposal, we named the operation of mapping a specific model version to the static model version the *model release operation*. Figure 7.15 illustrates the model release process.

In figure 7.15, data scientists first register model A, version 1.0.0 to model A, version PROD in the metadata store. Then in the model lookup table, the (Model A, PROD) record changes to point to the actual model object record (ModelA, version: 1.0.0). So when users call /predict/ModelA/PROD in the prediction service, they are actually calling /predict/ModelA/1.0.0.

Next, when the prediction service receives a prediction request with a model version equal to STG or PROD, the service will search the lookup table in the metadata store and use the actual model version, which is registered to PROD, to download model files. In figure 7.15, the prediction service will load model ModelA, version: 1.0.0 for the /ModelA/PROD request, and it will load model ModelA, version: 1.1.0 for the /ModelA/STG request.

For future model releases, data scientists only need to update the model records to map the latest model version to STG and PROD in the metadata store's lookup table. The prediction service will load the new model version automatically for new prediction requests. All of these operations happen automatically and are imperceptible to users.

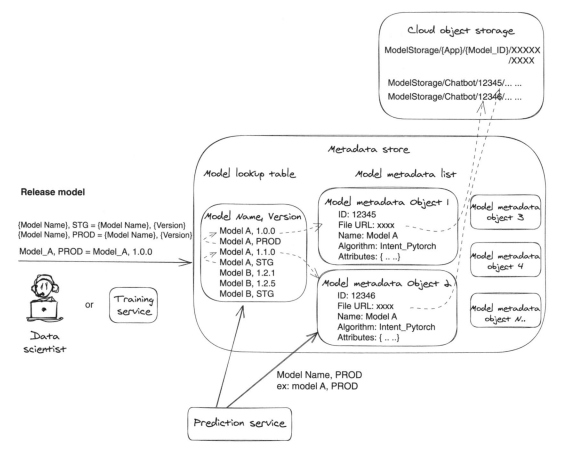

Figure 7.15   Model serving in prediction service with the metadata store

NOTE   The proposed release workflow is not the only way to release models. Model release approaches are highly dependent on a company's internal DevOps process and the prediction service design, so there is no single best design on this topic. We hope by reading the problem analysis and the proposed solution in section 7.5, you can derive a model release process that suits your situation.

7.6   *Postproduction model monitoring*

Compared with monitoring other services, such as data management, in machine learning systems, the job is still not complete after the model goes into production. We need not only to monitor and maintain the prediction service itself but also look at *the performance of models* that the service serves. Model drifting is a shift in the knowledge domain distribution that no longer matches the training dataset and leads to the deterioration of the model performance. This can happen while the prediction service is completely healthy because model inference runs independently from the prediction service.

To battle model drifting, data scientists need to retrain the model with new data or rebuild the model with an improved training algorithm. This sounds like a data science project on the surface, but it requires a lot of underlying engineering work, such as collecting and analyzing the model metrics from the prediction service to detect model drifting. In this section, we discuss model monitoring from an engineering perspective and look at the role that engineers can play in the monitoring process.

7.6.1 Metric collection and quality gate

The two most important areas where engineers can contribute are *model metric collection* and *model quality gate setup*. Let us explain.

To run an analysis to detect model drift, data scientists need data to analyze, and engineers can find ways to deliver the necessary data (metrics). Although engineers would have to create a separate data pipeline to collect model performance metrics, it would be overkill in most cases. Normally, model performance metrics can be collected and visualized with the existing telemetry system (like Datadog) and logging system (like Sumo and Splunk). So do yourself a favor and try to fully utilize the existing logging and metric systems you already have, instead of doing the heavy lifting of building a new metric system.

Engineers can also help with building model-quality gates. Engineers can work with data scientists to automate their troubleshooting steps, such as checking data quality and generating model inference analysis reports. With a given threshold, these checks will eventually form a model quality gate.

7.6.2 Metrics to collect

Theoretically, we need to collect at least five kinds of metrics to support model performance measurements. They are prediction tracing, the date of the prediction, model versions, observation, and observation rate and date. Let's look at them one by one:

- *Prediction tracing*—We normally track each prediction request by assigning it a unique request ID, but this is not enough. For some complicated scenarios, such as PDF scanning, we composite different types of model predictions together to produce a final result. For example, we first send a PDF doc to an OCR (optical character recognition) model to extract text information and then send the text to an NLP (natural language processing) model to recognize the targeted entities. In this case, besides assigning a unique request ID for a parent prediction request, we can also assign a `groupRequestID` to each sub/child prediction request, so we can group all the associated prediction requests when troubleshooting.

- *Date of the prediction*—Normally, a prediction request completes within a second. To track the date of a prediction, we can either use prediction start time or complete time because there is not much difference. But for cases like fraud detection, the prediction's completion timestamp might be a lot different from the prediction start timestamp because it can take multiple days of user activities as input.

- *Model version*—To map model performance data to the exact model file, we need to know the model version. Furthermore, when we combine multiple models to serve one prediction request, the version of every model needs to be tracked in logs.
- *Observation*—The prediction result needs to be logged along with prediction input for future comparison. Additionally, we can provide a feedback or investigation API for customers to report model performance concerns. By using the feedback API, customers can report the model ID, expected prediction result, and current prediction result.
- *Observation date and rate*—Many times, observations are collected manually, and the frequency of observation needs to be logged as well. Data scientists need the date and rate to decide whether the data can statistically represent the model's overall performance.

It is great that you have read this far! Model serving is an essential component of a machine learning system because external business applications depend on it. As types of models, numbers of prediction requests, and types of inference (online/offline) increase, many model serving frameworks/systems are invented, and they become increasingly complex. If you follow the serving mental model introduced in chapters 6 and 7, starting with how a model is loaded and executed, you can easily navigate these serving systems, regardless of how large the codebase or the number of components is.

Summary

- The model service sample in this chapter is made of a frontend API component and a backend model predictor container. Because the predictor is built on top of the intent model training code in chapter 3, it can only serve intent classification models.
- The model server sample is composed of the same frontend API as in chapter 3 and a different backend—TorchServe predictor. The TorchServe backend is not limited to intent classification models; it can serve arbitrary PyTorch models. This is a great advantage for the model server approach over the model service approach.
- For implementing model server approaches, we recommend using existing tools—for example, the Triton server—instead of building your own.
- The model service approach works for single application scenarios; it can be implemented quickly, and you have full control of the code implementation of the end-to-end workflow.
- The model server approach fits platform scenarios; it can greatly reduce development and maintenance efforts when the serving system needs to support five or more different types of models.
- TorchServe, TensorFlow Serving, and Triton are all solid open source model serving tools, and they all take a model server approach. If applicable, we

recommend Triton because it is compatible with most model training frameworks and has a performance advantage in terms of GPU acceleration.

- KServe provides a standard serving interface that works for all major serving tools, including TensorFlow Serving, TorchServe, and Triton. KServe can greatly improve the compatibility of our serving system because we can use a single set API to run model serving with different backends.

- Releasing a new model or new version of the model serving system in production shouldn't be an afterthought; we need to consider it properly in the design phase.

- Model metric collection and model quality gates are the two areas on which engineers need to focus for model performance monitoring.

Metadata and artifact store

8

This chapter covers

- Understanding and managing metadata in the deep learning context

- Designing a metadata and artifact store to manage metadata

- Introducing two open source metadata management tools: ML Metadata and MLflow

To produce a high-quality model that fits business requirements, data scientists need to experiment with all kinds of datasets, data processing techniques, and training algorithms. To build and ship the best model, they spend a significant amount of time conducting these experiments.

A variety of *artifacts* (datasets and model files) and *metadata* are produced from model training experiments. The metadata may include model algorithms, hyperparameters, training metrics, and model versions, which are very helpful in analyzing model performance. To be useful, this data must be persistent and retrievable.

When data scientists need to investigate a model performance problem or compare different training experiments, is there anything we, as engineers, can do to facilitate these efforts? For example, can we make model reproducing and experiment comparison easier?

The answer is yes. As engineers, we can build a system that retains the experimental metadata and artifacts that data scientists need to reproduce and compare models. And if we design this storage and retrieval system well, with proper metadata management, data scientists can easily select the best model from a series of experiments or figure out the root cause of a model degradation quickly without a deep understanding of the metadata system.

In previous chapters, we've learned about designing services to produce and serve models. Here, we turn our attention to the metadata and artifacts management system that facilitates two more key operations: troubleshooting and comparing experiments.

We will start this chapter with an introduction to *artifacts* and *metadata* and the meaning of these concepts in the context of deep learning. Then we will show you how to design metadata management systems using examples and emphasizing design principles. Finally, we will discuss two open source metadata management systems: MLMD (ML Metadata) and MLflow. By reading this chapter, you will gain a clear vision of how to manage metadata and artifacts to facilitate experiment comparison and model troubleshooting.

8.1 Introducing artifacts

People often assume that an artifact in deep learning is the model file produced by the model training process. This is partially true. Artifacts are actually the files and objects that form both the inputs and outputs of the components in the model training process. This is a crucial distinction, and it is important to keep this broader definition in mind if you want to engineer a system that supports model reproducibility.

Under this definition, artifacts can include datasets, models, code, or any other number of objects used in a deep learning project. For example, the raw input training data, the labeled dataset produced from a labeling tool, and the results data of a data processing pipeline are all considered artifacts.

In addition, artifacts must be preserved with metadata that describes their facts and lineage to allow performance comparisons, reproducibility, and troubleshooting. In practice, artifacts are stored as raw files on a file server or cloud storage service, such as Amazon Simple Storage Service or Azure Blob Storage. And we associate artifacts with their metadata in a *metadata store* on a separate storage service. See figure 8.1 for a diagram of what this arrangement typically looks like.

Figure 8.1 displays the common practice of managing artifacts. The artifact files are saved to a file storage system, and their file URLs are saved with other related metadata (such as model training execution ID and model ID) in the metadata store. This setup allows us—or data scientists—to search for a model in the metadata store and easily find all the input and output artifacts of the corresponding model training process.

8.2 Metadata in a deep learning context

In general terms, metadata is structured reference data that provides information about other data or objects, such as the nutrition facts label on packaged food. In

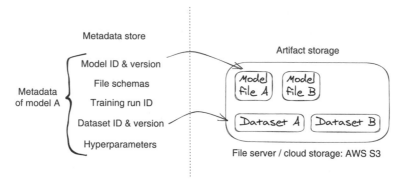

Figure 8.1   Artifacts are associated with their metadata in the metadata store.

machine learning (ML) and deep learning, however, metadata is more specific to models; it's the data that describes model training executions (runs), workflows, models, datasets, and other artifacts.

For any distributed system, we track service metadata in the form of logs and metrics at a service level. For example, we might track metrics such as CPU rate, number of active users, and number of failed web requests. We use these metrics for system/service monitoring, troubleshooting, and observation purposes.

In deep learning systems, beyond the service-level metric, we collect metadata for model troubleshooting, comparison, and reproduction purposes. You can think of deep learning metadata as a special subset of logs and metrics that we use to monitor and track every deep learning activity in the system. These activities include data parsing, model training, and model serving.

8.2.1   *Common metadata categories*

Although we've just defined metadata, the term is actually somewhat arbitrary; there is no set guideline on which data should be considered metadata. For engineers of deep learning systems, we recommend defining metadata in the following four categories: model training run, general artifact, model file, and orchestration workflow. To give you a concrete feel for these categories, let's look at each category and some examples of metadata that go into each one.

METADATA FOR A MODEL TRAINING RUN

To reproduce models, analyze model performance, and facilitate model troubleshooting, we need to track all the input and output data and artifacts of a model training run. This includes

- *Dataset ID and version*—The unique identity of the dataset used in model training.
- *Hyperparameters*—The hyperparameters used in the training, such as learning rate and number of epochs.
- *Hardware resources*—CPU, GPU, TPU, memory, and disk size allocated in the training and the actual consumption of these resources.

- *Training code version*—The unique identity of the training code snapshot used in model training.

- *Training code configuration*—The configuration for recreating the training code execution environment, such as conda.yml, Dockerfile, and requirement.txt.

- *Training metrics*—The metrics show how model training progresses, for example, the loss value at each training epoch.

- *Model evaluation metrics*—The metrics show the model performance, such as F-score and root-mean-squared error (RMSE).

METADATA FOR GENERAL ARTIFACTS

Artifacts can be any arbitrary files, such as datasets, models, and prediction results. To be able to find the artifact in artifact storage, we want to track below metadata for artifacts:

- *File location*—The path to the place where the artifact is stored, for example, Amazon S3 file path or internal file system path

- *File version*—The unique identity to distinguish different file updates

- *Description*—The additional information to describe what's inside the artifact file

- *Audit history*—The information about who created the artifact version, when the artifact was created, and how it was created

METADATA FOR MODEL FILE

Models are one kind of artifact, but because models are the main product of every deep learning system, we recommend tracking model metadata separately from other artifacts. When we define model metadata, it's best to consider two perspectives: model training and model serving.

For model training, to have model lineage, we want to keep a mapping between a model and the model training run that produced it. Model lineage is important for model comparison and reproduction. For example, when comparing two models, by having the link of model training run and model, data scientists can easily determine all the details of how the model is produced, including the input datasets, training parameters, and training metrics. The model training metrics are very useful for understanding model performance.

For model serving, we want to track the model execution data for future model performance analysis. These execution data, such as model response latency and prediction miss rate, are very useful for detecting model performance degradation.

The following are a few recommended model metadata categories besides the aforementioned general artifact metadata:

- *Resource consumption*—Memory, GPU, CPU, and TPU consumption for model serving

- *Model training run*—The model training run ID, which is used to find the code, dataset, hyperparameters, and environments that create the model

- *Experiment*—Tracking the model experiment activities in production, for example, customer traffic distribution for different model versions

- *Production*—Model usage in production, such as query per second and model prediction statistics
- *Model performance*—Tracking model evaluation metrics for drift detection, such as concept drift and performance drift

> **NOTE** Models will, unavoidably, start performing worse once they are shipped to production. We call this behavior *model degradation*. As the statistical distribution of the target group changes over time, model prediction becomes less accurate. New popular slogans, for example, can affect the accuracy of voice recognition.

METADATA FOR PIPELINE

A pipeline or workflow is needed when we want to automate a multiple-step model training task. For example, we can use workflow management tools like Airflow, Kubeflow, or Metaflow to automate a model training process that contains multiple functional steps: data collection, feature extraction, dataset augmentation, training, and model deployment. We will discuss workflow in detail in the next chapter.

For pipeline metadata, we usually track the pipeline execution history and the pipeline input and output. This data can provide audit information for future troubleshooting.

> **NOTE** Deep learning projects vary a lot. The model training code is dramatically different for voice recognition, natural language processing, and image generation. There are many factors specific to the project, such as the size/type of the dataset, type of the ML model, and input artifacts. Besides the sample metadata mentioned previously, we recommend you define and collect the metadata based on your project. When you are looking for data that helps model reproducing and troubleshooting, the metadata list will come to you naturally.

8.2.2   Why manage metadata?

Because metadata is normally instrumented or recorded in the form of logs or metrics, you may wonder why we need to manage deep learning metadata separately. Can we simply fetch the deep learning metadata from log files? Log management systems like Splunk (https://www.splunk.com/) and Sumo Logic (https://www.sumologic.com/) come in very handy because they allow developers to search and analyze logs and events produced by distributed systems.

To better explain the necessity of having a dedicated component for managing metadata in a deep learning system, we will convey a story. Julia (data engineer), Ravi (data scientist), and Jianguo (system developer) work together on a deep learning system to develop intent classification models for a chatbot application. Ravi develops intent classification algorithms, Julia works on data collection and parsing, and Jianguo develops and maintains the deep learning system.

During the project development and test phases, Julia and Ravi work together to build an experimental training pipeline to produce intent models. After the models are built, Ravi passes them to Jianguo to deploy the experiment models to the prediction service and test them with real customer requests.

When Ravi feels good about the experimentation, he promotes the training algorithm from the experimental pipeline to an automated production training pipeline. This pipeline runs in the production environment and produces intent models with customer data as input. The pipeline also deploys the models to the prediction service automatically. Figure 8.2 illustrates the whole story setting.

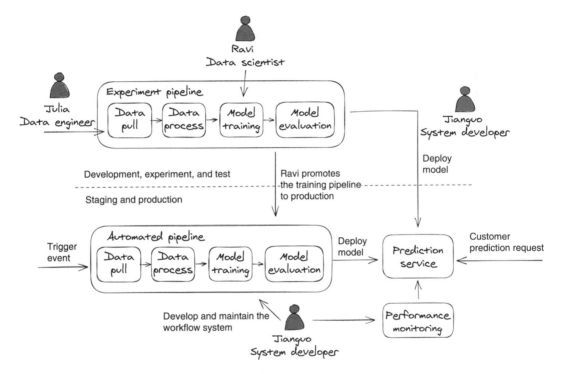

Figure 8.2   Model development without metadata management

A few weeks later, after Ravi released the latest intent classification algorithm, one chatbot customer—BestFood Inc.—reported a model performance degradation problem to Ravi. In the investigation request, BestFood mentioned that their bot's intent classification accuracy dropped 10% after using a new dataset.

To troubleshoot the reported model performance degradation problem, Ravi needs to verify lots of information. He first needs to check which model version is currently being used by BestFood in the prediction service and then check the model lineage of the current model, such as the dataset version and code version used in the training pipeline. After that, Ravi may also need to reproduce the model for local debugging. He needs to compare the current model and the previous model to test the data distribution effect (current new dataset vs. previous dataset).

Ravi is a natural language process (NLP) expert, but he has very little knowledge about the deep learning system on which his training code runs. To continue his investigation, he has to ask Jianguo and Julia to obtain the relevant model, dataset, and code information. Because everyone has only a fragment of knowledge about the model training application and underlying deep learning system/infrastructure, for each model performance troubleshooting, Ravi, Julia, and Jianguo have to work together to grasp the full context, which is time-consuming and inefficient.

This story, of course, is oversimplified. In practice, deep learning project development is made of data, algorithms, system/runtime development, and hardware management. The whole project is owned by different teams, and there is seldom one person who knows everything. Relying on cross-team collaboration to troubleshoot model-related problems is unrealistic in a corporate setting.

The key factor missing in figure 8.2 is an effective method for searching and connecting deep learning metadata in a centralized place so that Julia, Ravi, and Jianguo can obtain the model metadata easily. In figure 8.3, we add the missing piece—a metadata and artifact store (the gray box in the middle)—to improve the debuggability.

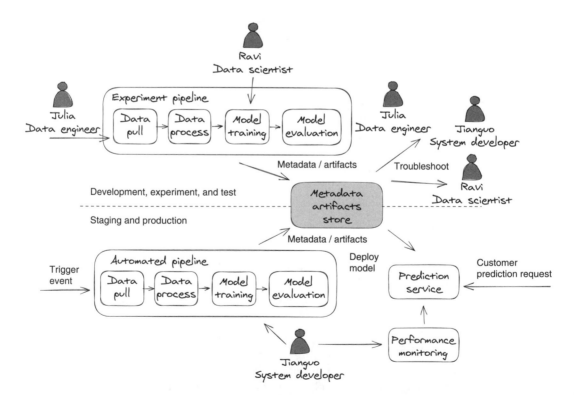

Figure 8.3   Model troubleshooting with metadata management

If you compare figure 8.3 to figure 8.2, you'll see a new component (the metadata and artifact store) is introduced in the middle of figure 8.3. All the deep learning metadata we described in section 8.2.1, regardless of whether they are from the experiment pipeline or production pipeline, are collected and stored in this metadata store.

The metadata store provides a holistic view of metadata for every data science activity in the deep learning system. Metadata of the model, pipeline/training run, and artifacts are not only saved but also correlated inside this store, so people can obtain related information easily. For example, because model files and model training runs are linked in the store, people can easily determine the model lineage of a given model.

Now, Ravi, the data scientist, can use the metadata store UI to list all the models and training runs in the system. Then he can dive deep into the metadata store to find the input parameters, datasets, and training metric used in the past training run, which are super helpful in evaluating the model. More importantly, Ravi can retrieve the metadata quickly and completely on his own, without knowing the underlying infrastructure of model training and serving.

8.3 Designing a metadata and artifacts store

In this section, we will first discuss the design principles for building a metadata and artifact store and then introduce a general design proposal that follows those principles. Even if you prefer to use open source technology to manage metadata, the discussion in this section will still benefit you; understanding the design requirements and solutions will help you choose the right tool for your needs.

NOTE To keep things short, we use *metadata and artifact store* and *metadata store* interchangeably in this chapter. When we mention *metadata store*, it includes the artifacts management as well.

8.3.1 Design principles

A metadata and artifact store is designed to facilitate model performance troubleshooting and experiment comparison. It stores all kinds of metadata and aggregates it around models and training runs, so data scientists can obtain the correlated model lineage and model training metadata quickly for an arbitrary model. A good metadata store should address the following four principles.

PRINCIPLE 1: SHOWING MODEL LINEAGE AND VERSIONING
When receiving a model name, a metadata store should be able to determine the versions of that model and the lineage for each model version, such as which training run produced the model and what the input parameters and dataset are. Model version and lineage are essential to model troubleshooting. When a customer reports a problem on a model, such as model performance degradation, the first questions we ask are: When is the model produced? Has the training dataset changed? Which version of training code is used, and where can we find the training metric? We can find all the answers in the model lineage data.

PRINCIPLE 2: ENABLING MODEL REPRODUCIBILITY

A metadata store should track all the metadata required to reproduce a model, such as the training pipeline/run configuration, input dataset files, and algorithm code version. Being able to reproduce a model is crucial for model experiment evaluation and troubleshooting. We need a place to capture the configuration, input parameters, and artifacts to kick off a model training run to reproduce the same model. The metadata store is the ideal place to retain such information.

PRINCIPLE 3: EASY ACCESS TO PACKAGED MODELS

A metadata store should let data scientists access model files easily, without having to understand the complex backend system. The store should have both manual and programmatic methods, as data scientists need to be able to run both manual and automated model performance testing.

For example, by using a metadata store, data scientists can quickly identify the model file that is currently used in production service and download it for debugging. Data scientists can also write code to pull arbitrary versions of models from the metadata store to automate the model comparison between the new and old model versions.

PRINCIPLE 4: VISUALIZING MODEL TRAINING TRACKING AND COMPARING

Good visualization can greatly improve the efficiency of the model troubleshooting process. Data scientists rely on a huge range of metrics to compare and analyze model experiments, and the metadata store needs to be equipped with visualization tools that can handle all (or any type of) metadata queries.

For example, it needs to be able to show the differences and trending behavior on the model evaluation metrics for a set of model training runs. It also needs to be able to show model performance trends on the latest 10 released models.

8.3.2   *A general metadata and artifact store design proposal*

To address the design principles in section 8.3.1, a deep learning metadata store should be a metric storage system, and it needs to store all kinds of metadata and the relationships between them. This metadata should be aggregated around model and training/experiment executions, so we can find all model-correlated metadata quickly during troubleshooting and performance analysis. Therefore, the data schema of the internal metadata storage is the key to the metadata store design.

Although a metadata store is a data storage system, data scaling is usually not a concern because the data volume of metadata for a deep learning system is not high. Because the metadata size depends on the number of model training executions and models and we don't expect to have more than 1,000 model training runs each day, a single database instance should be good enough for a metadata store system.

For user convenience, a metadata store should offer a web data ingestion interface and logging SDK, so deep learning metadata can be instrumented in a similar way as application logs and metrics. Based on the design principles and this analysis of the system requirements, we have come up with a sample metadata store design for your reference. Figure 8.4 shows the overview of this component.

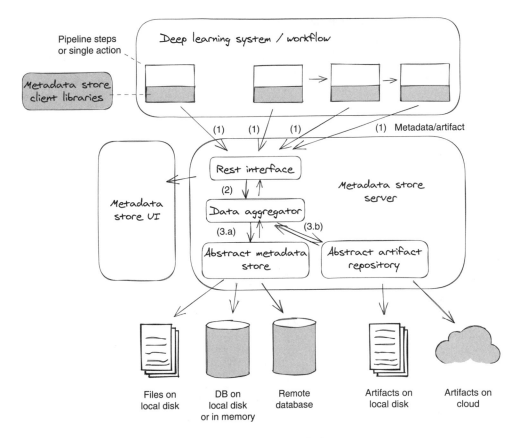

Figure 8.4   A general metadata and artifact store system design

In figure 8.4, the sample metadata store system is composed of four components: a client SDK, a web server, backend storage, and a web UI. Each component and step in a deep learning workflow uses the client SDK to send metadata to the metadata store server. The metadata store exposes a RESTful interface to metadata ingestion and querying. The web UI visualizes the metadata store server's RESTful interface. Besides the basic metadata and artifact organizing and searching, it can also visualize the model performance metrics and model differences for various model training runs.

The metadata store server is at the center of this design. It has three layers—a RESTful web interface, a data aggregator, and storage. The data aggregator component knows how the metadata is organized and interlinked, so it knows where to add new metadata and how to serve different kinds of metadata-searching queries. In terms of storage, we recommend building an abstract metadata and artifact storage layer. This abstract layer works as an adapter that encapsulates the actual metadata and filestoring logic. So the metadata store can run on top of different types of storage backends, such as cloud object storage, local files, and a local or remote SQL server.

THE METADATA STORAGE SCHEMA

Now let's look at the data schema of the metadata storage. Whether we save the metadata in an SQL or noSQL database or plain files, we need to define a data schema for how the metadata is structured and serialized. Figure 8.4 shows the entity relationship diagram of our metadata storage.

In figure 8.5, the model training run (`Training_Runs` object) is at the central stage of the entity relationship map. This is because model performance troubleshooting always starts from the process (training runs or workflow) that produced the model, so we want to have a dedicated data object to track the training executions that produce model files.

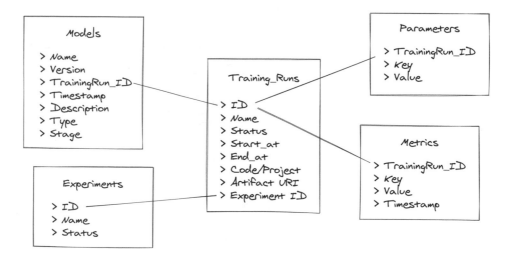

Figure 8.5   An entity relationship diagram of the data schema of the metadata storage

The detailed metadata for model training is saved in the `Metrics` and `Parameters` objects. The `Parameters` object stores the input parameters of the training run, such as dataset ID, dataset version, and training hyperparameters. The `Metrics` object stores the training metrics produced during training, such as model F2 score.

The `Experiments` objects are used to organize and group model training runs. One experiment can have multiple training runs. For example, we could define our intent classification model development project as one training experiment and then associate all the intent classification model training execution with this experiment. Then, on the UI, we can group training executions by different experiments.

The `Models` objects store the metadata of model files, such as model version, type, and stage. A model can have multiple stages, such as test, preproduction, and production, and all of these can be preserved as well.

Notice also that each of the entities in figure 8.5 is linked (noted by lines in the diagram) to the specific training run that produces them, so they will all share a common `training_run_id`. By leveraging this data link, you can start with any training run object and find its output model, training input data, and model training metrics.

Earlier we said we may call it the metadata store for short, but it also stores artifacts. So where is the artifact in this design? We store the artifact URL in the `Training_Runs` object as the training run's output. If we query the model or training execution, we will get the artifacts' URL.

Model focus vs. pipeline focus

There are two schools of thought on designing metadata systems: model focus and pipeline focus. The model focus method correlates metadata around model files, whereas the pipeline focus method aggregates metadata around the pipeline/training run, like what we proposed in figure 8.4.

We think model focus and pipeline focus are equally useful to the end users (data scientists), and they are not mutually exclusive. We can support both of them.

You can implement the metadata store's storage layer by using the pipeline focus method, similar to our sample in figure 8.5, and then build search functionality on the web UI to support both pipeline search and model search.

8.4   Open source solutions

In this section, we will discuss two widely used metadata management tools, MLMD and MLflow. Both systems are open source and free to use. We will first give an overview of each of the tools and then provide a comparison to determine which one to use and when.

8.4.1   ML Metadata

MLMD (https://github.com/google/ml-metadata) is a lightweight library for recording and retrieving metadata associated with ML developer and data scientist workflows. MLMD is an integral part of TensorFlow Extended (TFX; https://www .tensorflow.org/tfx) but is designed so that it can be used independently. For example, Kubeflow (https://www.kubeflow.org/) uses MLMD to manage metadata produced by its pipeline and notebook service. For more details, see the Kubeflow metadata documentation (http://mng.bz/Blo1). You can consider MLMD a logging library and use it to instrument metadata in each step of your ML pipeline, so you can understand and analyze all the interconnecting parts of your workflow/pipeline.

SYSTEM OVERVIEW

The metadata instrumentation with the MLMD library can be set up with two different backends: an SQL or gRPC server. See figure 8.6 for the concept.

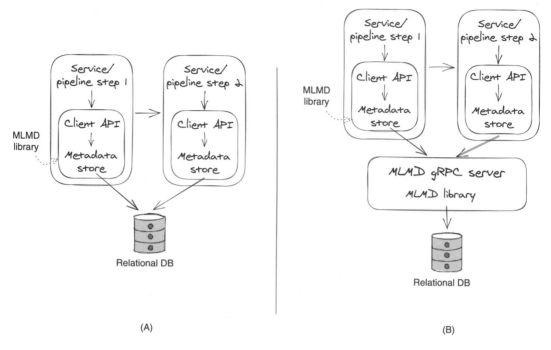

Figure 8.6 Two different setups for instrumenting metadata with MLMD: (A) directly report metadata to the backend database and (B) report metadata to the gRPC server DB, database.

In figure 8.6, we see that each step of an ML pipeline/workflow uses MLMD library (MLMD client API) to instrument metadata. On the backend, MLMD will save the metadata in a relational database, such as mySQL or PostgreSQL.

You can choose to let each MLMD library talk directly to an SQL server (figure 8.5, A) or use the server setup code in the MLMD library to set up a gRPC server and let the client libraries talk to the server (figure 8.5, B). Approach A is simple; you don't need to host a dedicated logging server, but approach B is recommended because it avoids exposing the backend database.

You can check out the following two docs for detailed metadata storage configuration: "Metadata Storage Backends and Store Connection Configuration" (http://mng.bz/dJMo) and "Use MLMD with a Remote gRPC Server" (http://mng.bz/rd8J).

LOGGING API

The metadata store in MLMD uses the following data structures to record metadata in the storage backend. An *execution* represents a component or a step in a workflow; an *artifact* describes an input or output object in an execution; and an *event* is a record of relationships between artifacts and executions. A *context* is a logic group that is used to correlate artifacts and executions together in the same workflow.

With this concept in mind, let's look at some sample metadata instrumentation code:

```
# define a dataset metadata
data_artifact = metadata_store_pb2.Artifact()          ◁────┐  A dataset is recorded
data_artifact.uri = 'path/to/data'                          │  as an artifact.
data_artifact.properties["day"].int_value = 1
data_artifact.properties["split"].string_value = 'train'
data_artifact.type_id = data_type_id                  ┌──────────────────
[data_artifact_id] = store                            │ Saves the metadata
    .put_artifacts([data_artifact])                   │ to storage

# define a training run metadata
trainer_run = metadata_store_pb2.Execution()           ◁────┐  A model training
trainer_run.type_id = trainer_type_id                       │  run is recorded as
trainer_run.properties["state"].string_value = "RUNNING"    │  an execution.
[run_id] = store.put_executions([trainer_run])

# define a model metadata
model_artifact = metadata_store_pb2.Artifact()         ◁────┐  A model is recorded
model_artifact.uri = 'path/to/model/file'                   │  as an artifact.
model_artifact.properties["version"].int_value = 1
model_artifact.properties["name"].string_value = 'MNIST-v1'
model_artifact.type_id = model_type_id
[model_artifact_id] = store.put_artifacts([model_artifact])

# define an experiment metadata
my_experiment = metadata_store_pb2.Context()           ◁────┐  Defines the logic group
my_experiment.type_id = experiment_type_id                  │  for the metadata of
# Give the experiment a name                                │  model training
my_experiment.name = "exp1"
my_experiment.properties["note"].string_value = \
    "My first experiment."
[experiment_id] = store.put_contexts([my_experiment])

# declare relationship between model, training run
# and experiment
attribution = metadata_store_pb2.Attribution()
attribution.artifact_id = model_artifact_id
attribution.context_id = experiment_id

association = metadata_store_pb2.Association()
association.execution_id = run_id
association.context_id = experiment_id

# Associate training run and model with the          ┌─────────────
# same experiment                                    │ Saves the
store.put_attributions_and_associations( \           │ relationship
  [attribution], [association])              ◁────────│ between
                                                      │ metadata
```

Check out the MLMD "Get Started" doc (http://mng.bz/VpWy) for the detailed code sample and local setup instructions.

SEARCHING METADATA

MLMD doesn't provide a UI to show the metadata it stores. So, for querying metadata, we need to use its client API. See the following code example:

```
                      artifacts = store.get_artifacts()                    ◁──┐  Queries all
                                                                              │  registered
              ┌─▷    [stored_data_artifact] = store                          │  artifacts
Queries       │         .get_artifacts_by_id([data_artifact_id])
artifact      │
by ID         │
                      artifacts_with_uri = store                         ◁──┐  Queries
                         .get_artifacts_by_uri(data_artifact.uri)          │  artifact by uri

                      artifacts_with_conditions = store
                         .get_artifacts(
                            list_options=mlmd.ListOptions(               ◁──┐  Queries artifact
                               filter_query='uri LIKE "%/data"              │  by using a filter
                               AND properties.day.int_value > 0'))
```

The MLMD "Get Started" doc (http://mng.bz/VpWy) provides lots of query examples for fetching metadata of artifacts, executions, and context. If you are interested, please take a look.

The best way to learn the data model of MLMD is to look at its database schema. You can first create an SQLite database and configure the MLMD metadata store to use that database and then run the MLMD sample code. At the end, all the entities and tables are created in the local SQLite database. By looking at the table schema and content, you will gain a deep understanding of how the metadata is organized in MLMD, so you can build a nice UI on top of it yourself. The following sample code shows how to configure the MLMD metadata store to use a local SQLite database:

```
connection_config = metadata_store_pb2.ConnectionConfig()
connection_config.sqlite.filename_uri =                            ◁──┐  Local files path of
  '{your_workspace}/mlmd-demo/mlmd_run.db'                            │  the SQLite database
connection_config.sqlite.connection_mode = 3                       ◁──┐  Allows read,
store = metadata_store.MetadataStore(connection_config)               │  write, and create
```

8.4.2 *MLflow*

MLflow (https://mlflow.org/docs/latest/tracking.html) is an open source MLOps platform. It is designed to manage the ML lifecycle, including experimentation, reproducibility, deployment, and central model registry.

Compared to MLMD, MLflow is a whole system, not a library. It's composed of four main components:

- *MLflow Tracking (a metadata tracking server)*—For recording and querying metadata
- *MLflow Projects*—For packaging code in a reusable and reproducible way
- *MLflow Models*—For packaging ML models that can be used for different model serving tools
- *MLflow Model Registry*—For managing the full life cycle of MLflow models with a UI, such as model lineage, model versioning, annotation, and production promotion

In this section, we focus on the tracking server, since that's most relevant to metadata management.

SYSTEM OVERVIEW

MLflow provides six different setup approaches. For example, the metadata of MLflow runs (training pipeline) can be recorded to local files, an SQL database, a remote server, or a remote server with proxied storage backend access. For details about these six different setup methods, you can check out the MLflow doc "How Runs and Artifacts Are Recorded" (https://mlflow.org/docs/latest/tracking.html#id27).

In this section, we focus on the most commonly used setup approach: remote server with proxied artifact storage access. See figure 8.7 for the system overview diagram.

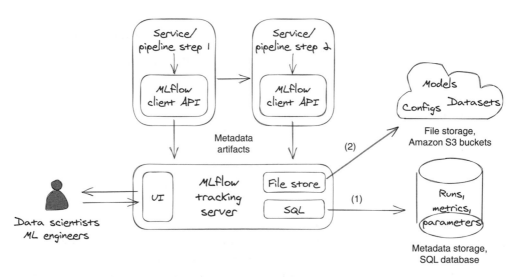

Figure 8.7 Setting up MLflow tracker server for metadata ingestion and query

From figure 8.7, we see that each step/action of a deep learning pipeline (workflow) uses the MLflow client to instrument metadata and artifact to the MLflow tracking server. The tracking server saves metadata, such as metrics, parameters, and tags, in a specified SQL database; artifacts, such as models, images, and documents, are saved in a configured object storage, such as Amazon S3.

MLflow offers two ways to upload artifacts: (1) direct upload from the client and (2) proxy upload through the tracking server. In figure 8.6, we illustrated the latter method: utilizing the tracking server as a proxy server for any operations involving artifacts. The advantage is the end users can have a direct path to access the backend remote object store without providing access credentials.

Another nice thing about MLflow is that it offers a nice UI; data scientists can check and search metadata thru the website hosted in the tracking server. The UI allows users not only to view metadata from a pipeline execution perspective but also to search and operate models directly.

LOGGING API

Sending metadata to the MLflow tracking server is straightforward. We can start by creating an active run as a context manager and then call the log function to log artifacts or a single key-value parameter, metric, and tag. See the sample code as follows:

```
import mlflow
remote_server_uri = "..."                          ◁────┐  Defines the
mlflow.set_tracking_uri(remote_server_uri)              │  MLflow server
                                                        │  URL
mlflow.set_experiment("/my-experiment")

with mlflow.start_run():
  mlflow.log_param("parameter_a", 1)          Logs metadata in Python
  mlflow.log_metric("metric_b", 2)            context manager made by
  mlflow.log_artifact("features.txt")         the MLflow ActiveRun object
```

Automatic logging

If you are tired of specifying lots of metadata yourself, MLflow supports automatic logging. By calling `mlflow.autolog()` or a library-specific autolog function before your training code, such as `mlflow.tensorflow.autolog()`, `mlflow.keras.autolog()`, or `mlflow.pytorch.autolog()`, MLflow will log metadata, even artifacts, automatically without the need for an explicit log statement. If you want to learn more about MLflow logging, check out the MLflow logging functions doc (http://mng.bz/xd1d).

SEARCHING METADATA

The tracking UI hosted by the MLflow tracking server lets you visualize, search, and compare runs, as well as download run artifacts or metadata for analysis in other tools. The UI contains the following key features: experiment-based run listing and comparison, searching for runs by parameter or metric value, visualizing run metrics, and downloading run results. Besides UI, you can also achieve all the operations provided in the tracking UI programmatically, as in the following examples:

```
from mlflow.tracking import MlflowClient

client = MlflowClient()               ◁────┐  Initializes
.. .. ..                                    │  client

# Fetch the run metadata from the backend store,
# which contains a list of  metadata
active_run = client.get_run(run_id)
print("run_id: {}; lifecycle_stage: {}"\       ◁────┐  Prints out the
  .format(run_id, active_run.info.lifecycle_stage))  │  execution stages
                                                     │  of a run

# Retrieve an experiment by
# experiment_id from the backend store
experiment = client.get_experiment(exp_id)

# Get a specific version of a model
mv = client.get_model_version(model_name, mv_version)
```

The programmatic metadata access is not only helpful when using your analysis tool (for example, pandas) to query and compare the model performance of different training runs, but also for integrating models with your model serving system since it allows you to fetch models from the MLflow model registry programmatically. For full `MLflowClient` API usage, you can check out the MLflow Tracking API doc (http://mng.bz/GRzO).

8.4.3 MLflow vs. MLMD

From the descriptions in the previous sections, we see that MLMD is more of a lightweight library while MLflow is an MLOps platform. Both tools can run independently, offer metadata ingestion and search functionality, and track metadata on the basis of model training runs. But MLflow offers much more.

In addition to MLMD's functionality, MLflow supports automatic metadata logging and a well-designed UI to visualize experiment metadata (including experiment comparison), model registry, artifact management, code reproducibility, model package, and more.

If you need to introduce a complete, new metadata and artifact store to your system, MFflow is your first choice. It's supported by an active open source community, and it covers most of the user requirements of ML metadata management. As a bonus, MLflow has a great support on MLOps, such as MLflow project management and model deployment.

If you already have an artifact registry and a metric visualization website and you want to integrate metadata functionality into your existing system, then MLMD is a good choice. MLMD is lightweight, easy to use, and simple to learn. For example, the Kubeflow (https://www.kubeflow.org/) deep learning platform integrates MLMD as the metadata tracking tool into its components, such as Kubeflow pipeline (https://www.kubeflow.org/docs/components/pipelines/).

Summary

- Machine learning metadata can be categorized into four buckets: model training runs, general artifacts, model artifacts, and pipelines.
- A metadata and artifact store is designed to support model performance comparison, troubleshooting, and reproducing.
- A good metadata management system can help to show model lineage, enable model reproducibility, and facilitate model comparison.
- MLMD is a lightweight metadata management tool, which originated from the TensorFlow pipeline, but it can be used independently. For example, Kubeflow uses MLMD to manage ML metadata in its pipeline component.
- MLMD is good for integrating metadata management into an existing system.
- MLflow is an MLOps platform; it's designed to manage the ML lifecycle, including experimentation, reproducibility, deployment, and a central model registry.
- MLflow is applicable if you want to introduce a completely independent metadata and artifact management system.

Workflow orchestration 9

This chapter covers

- Defining workflow and workflow orchestration
- Why deep learning systems need to support workflows
- Designing a general workflow orchestration system
- Introducing three open source orchestration systems: Airflow, Argo Workflows, and Metaflow

In this chapter, we will discuss the last but critical piece of a deep learning system: workflow orchestration—a service that manages, executes, and monitors workflow automation. Workflow is an abstract and broad concept; it is essentially a sequence of operations that are part of some larger task. If you can devise a plan with a set of tasks to complete a work, this plan is a workflow. For example, we can define a sequential workflow for training a machine learning (ML) model. This workflow can be composed of the following tasks: fetching raw data, rebuilding the training dataset, training the model, evaluating the model, and deploying the model.

Because a workflow is an execution plan, it can be performed manually. For instance, a data scientist can manually complete the tasks of the model training workflow we just described. For example, to complete the "fetching raw data" task, the data scientist can craft web requests and send them to the dataset management (DM) service to fetch a dataset—all with no help from the engineers.

However, executing a workflow manually is not ideal. We want to automate the workflow execution. When there are numerous workflows developed for different purposes, we need a dedicated system to handle the complexity of workflow executions. We call this kind of system a *workflow orchestration system.*

A workflow orchestration system is built to manage workflow life cycles, including workflow creation, execution, and troubleshooting. It provides not only the pulse to keep all the scheduled code running but also a control plane for data scientists to manage all the automation in a deep learning system.

In this chapter, we will discuss workflow orchestration system design and the most popular open source orchestration systems used in the deep learning field. By reading this chapter, you will not only gain a solid understanding of the system requirements and the design options, but you will also learn how to choose the right open source orchestration system that works best for your own situation.

9.1 Introducing workflow orchestration

Before we dive into the details of designing workflow orchestration systems, let's have a quick discussion on the basic concept of workflow orchestration, especially about the special workflow challenges from a deep learning/ML perspective.

NOTE Because the requirements of using workflow orchestration for deep learning projects and ML projects are almost identical, we will use the word *deep learning* and *machine learning* interchangeably in this chapter.

9.1.1 What is workflow?

In general, a workflow is a sequence of operations that are part of some larger task. A workflow can be viewed as a directed acyclic graph (DAG) of steps.

A step is the smallest resumable unit of computation that describes an action; this task could be fetching data or triggering a service, for example. A step either succeeds or fails as a whole. In this chapter, we use the word *task* and *step* interchangeably.

A DAG specifies the dependencies between steps and the order in which to execute them. Figure 9.1 shows a sample workflow for training natural language processing (NLP) models.

From the sample DAG in figure 9.1, we see a workflow that consists of many steps. Every step depends on another, and the solid arrows show the dependencies between steps. These arrows and steps form a workflow DAG with no loops.

If you follow the arrows in the DAG (from left to right) and complete the tasks, you can train and release an NLP model to production. For example, when an incoming request triggers the workflow, the auth (authorization) step will be executed first, and then the dataset-building step and the embedding fetching step will both be executed

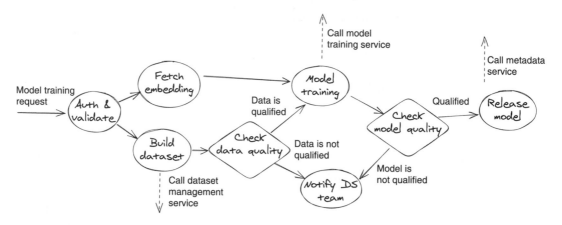

Figure 9.1   A DAG of a sample model training workflow with multiple steps. Both ovals and diamonds are steps, but different types. The solid arrows indicate the dependencies between steps, and the dotted-line arrows represent the external web requests sent from steps.

simultaneously. The steps on the other side of the arrows will be executed after these two steps have been completed.

Workflows are used everywhere in the IT industry. As long as you can define a process as a DAG of single tasks/steps, this process can be considered a workflow. Workflows are critical to deep learning model development. In fact, in production environments, most of the deep learning model–building activities are presented and executed as workflows.

> **NOTE**   A workflow should not have a loop. To guarantee a workflow can be completed under any condition, its execution graph needs to be a DAG, which prevents the workflow execution from falling into a dead loop.

9.1.2   *What is workflow orchestration?*

Once we define a workflow, the next step is to run the workflow. Running a workflow means executing the workflow steps based on the sequence defined in the workflow's DAG. *Workflow orchestration* is the term we use to describe the execution and monitoring of the workflow.

The goal of workflow orchestration is to automate the execution of tasks defined in workflows. In practice, the concept of workflow orchestration often extends to workflow management as a whole—that is, creating, scheduling, executing, and monitoring multiple workflows in an automated manner.

Why do deep learning systems need workflow orchestration? Ideally, we should be able to code an entire deep learning project as one piece. And that's exactly what we do in the prototyping phase of a project, putting all the code in a Jupyter notebook. So, why do we need to transform the prototyping code into a workflow and run it in a workflow orchestration system? The answer is twofold: automation and work sharing. To understand these reasons, let's look at three sample training workflows in figure 9.2.

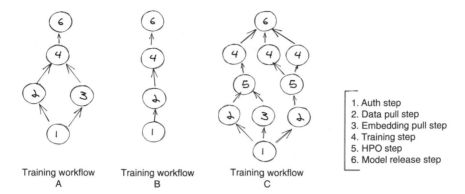

Figure 9.2   Deep learning workflows are composed of many reusable tasks.

A great benefit of using a workflow is that it turns a large chunk of code into a group of sharable and reusable components. In figure 9.2, we imagined three data scientists working on three model training projects (A, B, and C). Because each project's training logic is different, data scientists developed three different work-flows (A, B, and C) to automate their model training processes. Although each workflow has different DAGs, the steps in each DAG are highly overlapped. The total six steps are sharable and reusable. For example, the auth step (step 1) is the first step for all three workflows.

Having reusable steps can greatly improve data scientists' productivity. For exam-ple, to pull data from a DM service (step 2 in figure 9.2), data scientists need to learn how the DM web API works. But if someone already built a DM data pull method as a step function, scientists can just reuse this step in their workflow without learning how to interact with the DM service. If everyone writes their project in the form of a work-flow, we will have lots of reusable steps, which will save lots of duplicate effort at an organizational level!

Another reason that a workflow is well adapted to deep learning development is that it facilitates collaboration. Model development requires teamwork; a dedicated team might work on data while another team works on the training algorithm. By defining a complex model-building process in the workflow, we can dispatch a big complex project in pieces (or steps) and assign them to different teams while still keeping the project organized and the components in proper order. The workflow DAG shows the task dependencies clearly for all the project participants to see.

In short, a good workflow orchestration system encourages work sharing, facili-tates team collaboration, and automates complicated development scenarios. All these merits make workflow orchestration a crucial component of deep learning project development.

9.1.3 The challenges for using workflow orchestration in deep learning

In the previous section, we saw how a workflow system can provide a lot of benefits to deep learning project development. But there is one caveat: using workflows to prototype deep learning algorithm ideas is cumbersome.

To understand how and why it is cumbersome, let's look at a deep learning development process diagram (figure 9.3). This diagram should set the foundation for you to understand the challenges that workflow presents in the deep learning context.

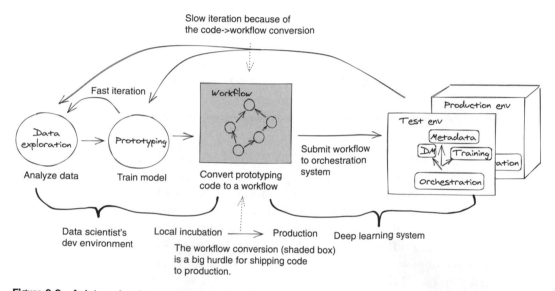

Figure 9.3   A data scientist's view of deep learning project development

In figure 9.3, we see a typical deep learning project development process from a data scientist's perspective. The process can be divided into two phases: the local incubation phase and the production phase.

In the local incubation phase, data scientists work on data exploration and model training prototyping at their local/dev environment. When the prototyping is done and the project looks promising, data scientists start to work on production onboarding: moving the prototyping code to the production system.

In the production phase, data scientists convert the prototyping code to a workflow. They break the code down into multiple steps and define a workflow DAG and then submit the workflow to the workflow orchestration system. After that, the orchestration system takes over and runs the workflow based on its schedule.

GAPS BETWEEN PROTOTYPING AND PRODUCTION

If you ask an engineer who works on workflow orchestration systems how they feel about the development process in figure 9.3, the answer most likely is: It's pretty good! But in practice, this process is problematic for data scientists.

From the data scientists' point of view, once an algorithm is tested locally, its prototyping code should be shipped to production right away. But in figure 9.3, we see the prototyping phase and production phase are *not* smoothly connected. Shipping incubation code to production is not straightforward; data scientists have to do extra work to construct a workflow to run their code in production. The gap between prototyping code and production workflow jeopardizes development velocity for two reasons:

- *Workflow building and debugging aren't straightforward*—Data scientists normally face a huge learning curve when authoring model training workflows in orchestration systems. Learning the workflow DAG syntax, workflow libraries, coding paradigms, and troubleshooting is a huge burden to data scientists. The workflow troubleshooting is the most painful part. The majority of the orchestration system doesn't support local execution, which means data scientists have to test their workflow in the remote orchestration system. This is hard because both the workflow environment and workflow execution logs are remote, so data scientists cannot easily figure out the root cause when a workflow execution goes wrong.

- *Workflow construction happens not once but frequently*—The common misperception is that because workflow construction only happens once, it's fine if it is time-consuming and cumbersome. But the fact is, workflow construction happens continuously because deep learning development is an iterative process. As figure 9.3 shows, data scientists work on prototyping and production experimentation iteratively, so the workflow needs to be updated frequently to test new improvements from local to production. Therefore, the unpleasant and time-consuming workflow construction happens repeatedly, which hinders the development velocity.

SMOOTHING THE TRANSITION FROM PROTOTYPING TO PRODUCTION

Although there are gaps, the process in figure 9.3 is good. Data scientists start prototyping locally with a straightforward script, and then they keep working on it. If the results after each iteration seem promising enough, the "straightforward local script" is converted to a workflow and runs in the orchestration system in production.

The key improvement is to make the transition step from prototyping code to a production workflow seamless. If an orchestration system is designed for deep learning use cases, it should provide tools to help data scientists build workflows from their code with minimum effort. For example, Metaflow, an open source library that will be discussed in section 9.3.3, allows data scientists to authorize workflow by writing Python code with Python annotations. Data scientists can obtain a workflow from their prototyping code directly without making any changes. Metaflow also provides a unified user experience on model execution between local and cloud production environments. This eliminates the friction in workflow testing because Metaflow operates workflows the same way in both local and production environments.

A deep learning system should be humancentric

When we introduce a general-purpose tool—like workflow orchestration—to deep learning systems, don't be satisfied with only enabling the functionality. Try to reduce human time in the system. Customization work is always possible to help our users be more productive.

Metaflow (section 9.3.3) is a good example of what happens when engineers aren't satisfied with just building an orchestration system to automate deep learning workflows. Instead, they went a step further to optimize the workflow construction and management to address the way data scientists work.

9.2   *Designing a workflow orchestration system*

In this section, we will approach the design of workflow orchestration systems in three steps. First, we use a typical data scientist user scenario to show how an orchestration system works from a user perspective. Second, we learn a generic orchestration system design. Third, we summarize the key design principles for building or evaluating an orchestration system. By reading this section, you will understand how orchestration systems work, in general, so you can be confident evaluating or working on any orchestration system.

9.2.1   *User scenarios*

Although the process of workflows varies a lot from one scenario to another, the user scenarios for data scientists are quite standard. Most workflow usage can be divided into two phases: the development phase and the execution phase. See figure 9.4 for a

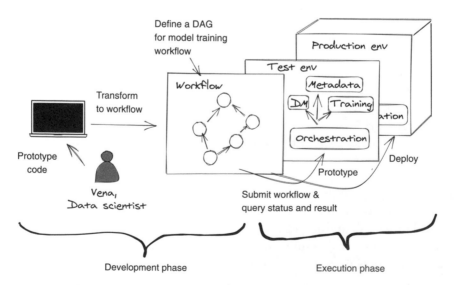

Figure 9.4   A general deep learning user scenario of a workflow orchestration system

data scientist's (Vena's) workflow user experience. Let's follow through with Vena's user scenario in figure 9.4 step by step.

DEVELOPMENT PHASE
During the development phase, data scientists convert their training code into a workflow. See Vena's example as follows:

1 Vena, a data scientist, prototypes her model training algorithm in a Jupyter notebook or pure Python in her local environment. After local testing and evaluation, Vena thinks it's time to deploy the code to production for online experiments with real customer data.

2 Because everything running in production is a workflow, Vena needs to convert her prototype code to a workflow. So Vena uses the syntax provided by the orchestration system to rebuild her work into a DAG of tasks in a YAML (a text configuration) file. For example, data parsing -> data augmentation -> dataset building -> training -> [online evaluation, offline evaluation] -> model release.

3 Vena then sets the input/output parameters and actions for each step in the DAG. Using the training step as an example, Vena sets the step action as a RESTful HTTP request. This step will send a RESTful request to the model training service to start a training job. The payload and parameters of this request come from the step input parameters.

4 Once the workflow is defined, Vena sets the workflow's execution schedule in the DAG YAML file. For example, Vena can schedule the workflow to run on the first day of every month, and she also sets the workflow to be triggered by an external event.

5 Vena runs the workflow local validation and submits the workflow to the orchestration service.

To give you an idea of what a workflow means in reality, the following code shows a pseudo workflow for Vena (in section 9.3, we will discuss the actual workflow systems):

```
# define workflow DAG
with DAG(
  description='Vena's sample training workflow',
  schedule_interval=timedelta(months=1),
  start_date=datetime(2022, 1, 1),
) as dag:
```
◄——— DAG definition; defines the body of the workflow, including steps and dependencies

```
  # define execution logic for each step
  data_parse_step = BashOperator( .. .. ..)
  data_augment_step = BashOperator( .. .. ..)
  dataset_building_step = BashOperator( .. .. ..)
  training_step = BashOperator( .. .. ..)
```
◄— Executes a bash command for data augmentation

```
  # Declares step dependencies
  data_parse_step >> data_augment_step
  >> dataset_building_step >> training_step
```
A sequential execution flow

EXECUTION PHASE

In the execution phase, the orchestration service executes the model training workflow, as illustrated by Vena's example:

1 Once Vena's workflow is submitted, the orchestration service saves the workflow DAG into a database.

2 The orchestration service's scheduler component detects Vena's workflow and dispatches the tasks of the workflow to backend workers. The scheduler will make sure the tasks are executed in the sequence that is defined in the workflow DAG.

3 Vena uses the orchestration service's web UI to check the workflow's execution progress and results in real time.

4 If the workflow produces a good model, Vena can promote it to the staging and production environments. If not, Vena starts another iteration of prototyping.

A critical indicator of whether an orchestration system is a good fit for deep learning is how easy it is to convert the prototyping code into a workflow. In figure 9.4, we see that Vena needs to transform her training code into a workflow every time she prototypes a new idea. We can imagine how much human time it would save if we eased the friction of converting the deep learning code to a workflow.

> **NOTE** A workflow should always be lightweight. The workflow is used to automate a process; its goal is to group and connect a series of tasks and execute them in a defined sequence. The great benefit of using a workflow is that people can share and reuse the tasks, so they can automate their process faster. Therefore, the workflow itself shouldn't do any heavy computation, the real work should be done by the tasks of the workflow.

9.2.2 A general orchestration system design

Let's now turn to a generic workflow orchestration system. To help you understand how an orchestration system works and how to research open source orchestration systems, we prepared a high-level system design. By zooming out of the detailed implementation and only keeping the core components, this design is applicable to most orchestration systems, including open source systems, which will be discussed in section 9.3. See figure 9.5 for the design proposal.

A workflow orchestration system generally consists of the following five components:

- *Web server*—The web server presents a web user interface and a set of web APIs for users to create, inspect, trigger, and debug the behavior of a workflow.
- *Scheduler and controller*—The scheduler and controller component does two things. First, the scheduler watches every active workflow in the system, and it schedules the workflow to run when the time is right. Second, the controller dispatches the workflow tasks to workers. Although the scheduler and controller are two different function units, they usually are implemented together because they are all related to workflow execution.

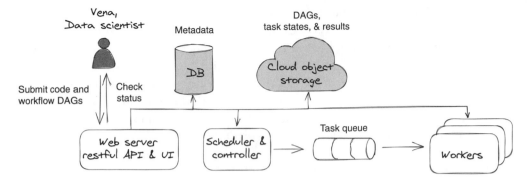

Figure 9.5 **A design overview for a generic workflow orchestration service**

- *Metadata database*—The metadata database stores the workflows' configuration, DAG, editing and execution history, and the tasks' execution state.
- *Worker group*—The worker group provides the compute resource to run workflow tasks. The worker abstracts the infrastructure and is agnostic to the task that's running. For example, we might have different types of workers, such as a Kubernetes worker and an Amazon Elastic Compute Cloud (EC2) worker, but they can all execute the same task, albeit on different infrastructures.
- *Object store*—The object store is shared file storage for all other components; it's normally built on top of cloud object storage, such as Amazon Simple Storage Service (S3). One usage of an object store is task output sharing. When a worker runs a task, it reads the output value of the previous task from the object store as the task input; the worker also saves the task output to the object store for its successor tasks.

Both the object store and the metadata database are accessible to all the components of the orchestration system, including the scheduler, web server, and workers' components. Having centralized data storage decouples the core components, so the web server, scheduler, and workers can work independently.

HOW IS A WORKFLOW EXECUTED?

First, Vena defines the DAG for the workflow. Inside the DAG, Vena declares a set of tasks and defines the control flow of the task execution sequence. For each task, Vena either uses the system's default operator, such as a Shell command operator or Python operator, or builds her own operator to execute tasks.

Second, Vena submits the workflow—DAG with dependent code—to the web server through the web UI or command line. The workflow is saved in the metadata database.

Third, the scheduler periodically (every few seconds or minutes) scans the metadata database and detects the new workflow; it then kicks off the workflow at the scheduled time. To execute a workflow, the scheduler calls the controller component to dispatch the workflow's tasks to the worker queue based on the task sequence defined in DAG.

Fourth, a worker picks up a task from the shared job queue; it reads the task definition from the metadata database and executes the task by running the task's operator. During the execution, the worker saves the task's output value to the object store and reports the task's execution status back to the metadata database.

Last but not least, Vena uses the web UI hosted on the web server component to monitor the workflow execution. Because both the scheduler/controller components and the workers report the status to the metadata database in real time, the web UI always displays the latest workflow status.

9.2.3   *Workflow orchestration design principles*

Because we have seen how a workflow orchestration system works internally and externally, now it's time to examine the design principles that make an orchestration system outstanding for deep learning scenarios. We hope you can use the principles here as a guide to evolving your system or for evaluating open source approaches.

> **NOTE** The workflow orchestration system is one of the most complicated components in a deep learning system in terms of engineering effort, so don't worry too much about making your system match perfectly with these principles in the first few versions.

PRINCIPLE 1: CRITICALITY

Workflow orchestration is essentially a job scheduling challenge, so the bottom line for any orchestration system is to provide a solid workflow execution experience. A valid workflow should always be executed correctly, repeatedly, and on schedule.

PRINCIPLE 2: USABILITY

The usability measurement of an orchestration system in a deep learning context is whether it optimizes data scientists' productivity. Most data scientist interactions in an orchestration system are workflow creation, testing, and monitoring. So a user-friendly orchestration system should let users create, monitor, and troubleshoot workflows easily.

PRINCIPLE 3: EXTENSIBILITY

To cater to the wide variety of deep learning infrastructures, people should easily define their own task operators and executors without worrying about where they are deployed to. The orchestration system should provide the level of abstraction that suits your environment, whether if it's Amazon EC2 or Kubernetes.

PRINCIPLE 4: ISOLATION

Two types of isolations can occur that are critical: workflow creation isolation and workflow execution isolation. Workflow creation isolation means people can not interfere with each other when creating workflows. For example, if Vena submits an invalid workflow DAG or releases a new version of a common shared library that's referenced in other workflows, the existing workflows shouldn't be affected.

Workflow execution isolation means that each workflow is running in an isolated environment. There should be no resource competition between workflows, and failure of a workflow won't affect other workflow's executions.

PRINCIPLE 5: SCALING

A good orchestration system should address the following two scaling problems: handling large numbers of concurrent workflows and handling large expansive workflows. Concurrent workflow scaling generally means that given enough compute resources—for example, adding more workers to the worker group—the orchestration system can cater to an infinite concurrent number of workflow executions. Also, the system should always keep the service-level agreement (SLA) for every workflow. For example, a workflow should be executed at its scheduled time and no later than 2 seconds, regardless of how many other workflows are executing.

For single, large workflow scaling, the system should encourage users not to worry about performance, so they can focus on readable, straightforward code, and easy operations. When the workflow execution hits a limit—for example, the training operators take too long to execute—the orchestration system should provide some horizontal parallelism operators, such as distributed training operators, to address single workflow performance problems.

The main scaling idea for deep learning orchestration is that we should solve the performance problem at the system level and avoid asking users to write code with scalability in mind. This can lead to worse readability, harder debuggability, and increased operational burden.

PRINCIPLE 6: HUMAN-CENTRIC SUPPORT FOR BOTH PROTOTYPING AND PRODUCTION

The capability of connecting the data scientist's local prototyping code to the production workflow is a requirement specific to deep learning. It's a key indicator that we use to evaluate whether an orchestration system is a good fit for deep learning systems.

An orchestration system designed for deep learning will respect that deep learning project development is an iterative, ongoing effort from prototyping to production. Therefore, it will make a dedicated effort to help data scientists convert their local prototype code to production workflow in a seamless fashion.

9.3 *Touring open source workflow orchestration systems*

In this section, we will introduce three battle-tested workflow orchestration systems: Airflow, Argo Workflows, and Metaflow. These three open source systems are widely adopted in the IT industry and backed by active communities. In addition to introducing them generally, we also evaluate these workflow systems from the perspective of deep learning project development.

To make a fair comparison, we implement pseudocode for the same workflow in Airflow, Argo Workflows, and Metaflow. Basically, if there is new data, we initially transform the data and save it to a new table in the database, and then we notify the data science team. Also, we expect the workflow to run daily.

9.3.1 *Airflow*

Airflow (https://airflow.apache.org/docs/apache-airflow/stable/index.html) was created in 2014 at Airbnb and is now a part of the Apache Foundation. Airflow is a platform to programmatically author, schedule, and monitor workflows. Airflow is not designed for deep learning use cases; it was originally built to orchestrate the increasingly complex ETL (extract, transform, load) pipelines (or data pipelines). But because of Airflow's good extensibility, production quality, and GUI support, it's widely used in many other domains, including deep learning. As this book is written, Airflow is the most adopted orchestration system.

A TYPICAL USE CASE

Building a workflow in Airflow takes two steps. First, define the workflow DAG and tasks. Second, declare the task dependencies in the DAG. An Airflow DAG is essentially Python code. See the following listing for how our sample workflow is implemented in Airflow.

> **Listing 9.1   A sample Airflow workflow definition**

```
# declare the workflow DAG.
with DAG(dag_id="data_process_dag",
        schedule_interval="@daily",
        default_args=default_args,
        template_searchpath=[f"{os.environ['AIRFLOW_HOME']}"],
        catchup=False) as dag:

    # define tasks of the workflow, each code section below is a task

    is_new_data_available = FileSensor(
        task_id="is_new_data_available",
        fs_conn_id="data_path",
        filepath="data.csv",
        .. .. ..
    )

    # define data transformation task
    transform_data = PythonOperator(
        task_id="transform_data",
        python_callable=transform_data
    )

    # define table creation task
    create_table = PostgresOperator(
        task_id="create_table",
        sql='''CREATE TABLE IF NOT EXISTS invoices (
                .. .. ..
                );''',
        postgres_conn_id='postgres',
        database='customer_data'
    )

    save_into_db = PythonOperator(
        task_id='save_into_db',
```

Checks whether a new file arrives

The actual logic is implemented in the "transform_data" function.

The PostgresOperator is a predefined airflow operator for interacting with postgres db.

```
        python_callable=store_in_db
    )

    notify_data_science_team = SlackWebhookOperator(
        task_id='notify_data_science_team',
        http_conn_id='slack_conn',
        webhook_token=slack_token,
        message="Data Science Notification \n"
        .. .. ..
    )


# Step two, declare task dependencies in the workflow
    is_new_data_available >> transform_data
    transform_data >> create_table >> save_into_db
    save_into_db >> notify_data_science_team
    save_into_db >> create_report

# The actual data transformation logic, which is referenced
# in the "transform_data" task.
def transform_data(*args, **kwargs):
    .. .. ..
```

In code listing 9.1, we see the sample workflow DAG consists of multiple tasks, such as create_table and save_into_db. A task in Airflow is implemented as an operator. There are lots of predefined and community-managed operators, such as MySql-Operator, SimpleHttpOperator, and Docker operator.

Airflow's predefined operators help users implement tasks without coding. You can also use the PythonOperator to run your customized Python functions. Once the workflow DAG is constructed and all the code is deployed to Airflow, we can use the UI or the following CLI command to check workflow execution status; see some sample shell commands as follows:

```
airflow dags list                ⊲――|  Prints all
                                       active DAG

airflow tasks list data_process_dag         |  Prints the list of tasks in the
                                       ⊲――|  "data_process_dag" DAG

airflow tasks list data_process_dag --tree      ⊲―|  Prints the hierarchy of tasks in
                                                    the "data_process_dag" DAG
```

If you want to learn more about Airflow, you can check out its architecture overview doc and tutorials (http://mng.bz/Blpw).

KEY FEATURES

Airflow offers the following key features:

- *DAGs*—Airflow abstracts complex workflow using DAGs, and the workflow DAG is implemented through a Python library.
- *Programmatic workflow management*—Airflow supports creating tasks on the fly and allows the creation of complex dynamic workflows.

- *Great built-in operators to help build automation*—Airflow offers lots of predefined operators that help users achieve tasks without coding.
- *Solid task dependency and execution management*—Airflow has an auto-retry policy built into every task, and it provides different types of sensors to handle runtime dependencies, such as detecting task completion, workflow run status change, and file presence.
- *Extensibility*—Airflow makes its sensors, hooks, and operators fully extendable, which allows it to benefit from a large amount of community-contributed operators. Airflow can also be easily integrated into different systems by adding customized operators.
- *Monitoring and management interface*—Airflow provides a powerful UI so users can get a quick overview of workflow/task execution status and history. Users can also trigger and clear tasks or workflow runs from the UI.
- *Production quality*—Airflow provides many useful tools for maintaining the service in production environments, such as task log searching, scaling, alerting, and restful APIs.

LIMITATIONS

Although Airflow is a great workflow orchestration, we still see several disadvantages when using it for deep learning scenarios:

- *High upfront cost for data scientists to onboard*—Airflow has a steep learning curve to achieve tasks that are not supported by the built-in operators. Also, there is no easy way to do workflow local testing.
- *High friction when moving deep learning prototyping code to production*—When we apply Airflow to deep learning, data scientists have to convert their local model training code into Airflow DAG. This is extra work, and it's an unpleasant experience for data scientists, especially when considering that this is avoidable if we build workflow DAG from the model training code directly.
- *High complexity when operating on Kubernetes*—Deploying and operating Airflow on Kubernetes is not straightforward. If you are looking to adopt an orchestration system to run on Kubernetes, Argo Workflows is a better choice.

9.3.2 *Argo Workflows*

Argo Workflows is an open source, container-native workflow engine for orchestrating parallel workflows/tasks on Kubernetes. Argo Workflows solves the same problem that Airflow addresses but in a different way; it takes a Kubernetes-native approach.

The biggest difference between Argo Workflows and Airflow is that Argo Workflows is built natively on Kubernetes. More specifically, the workflows and tasks in Argo Workflows are implemented as Kubernetes custom resource definition (CRD) objects, and each task (step) is executed as a Kubernetes pod. See figure 9.6 for a high-level system overview.

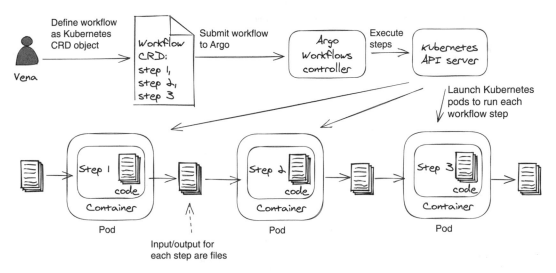

Figure 9.6   The workflow and its steps in Argo Workflows are executed as Kubernetes pods.

In figure 9.6, Vena (the data scientist) first defines a workflow and its steps/tasks as a Kubernetes CRD object, which is usually presented as a YAML file. Then she submits the workflow to Argo Workflows, and its controller creates CRD objects inside the Kubernetes cluster. Next, Kubernetes pods are launched dynamically to run the workflow steps/tasks in the workflow sequence.

You may also notice that each step's execution is completely isolated by container and pod; each step uses files to present its input and output values. Argo Workflows will magically mount the dependent file into the step's container.

The task isolation created by the Kubernetes pod is a great advantage of Argo Workflows. Simplicity is also another reason people choose Argo Workflows. If you understand Kubernetes, Argo's installation and troubleshooting are straightforward. We can use either Argo Workflows commands or the standard Kubernetes CLI commands to debug the system.

A TYPICAL USE CASE

For a better understanding, let's look at an Argo Workflows example. In this section, we use Argo Workflows to automate the same data processing work we saw in the previous Airflow section. The workflow includes checking new data first, transforming the data, saving it to a new table in the database, and then notifying the data scientist team by Slack. See the following code listing for the Argo Workflows definition.

> **Listing 9.2   A sample workflow for Argo Workflows with a series of steps**

```
apiVersion: argoproj.io/v1alpha1
kind: Workflow          ◁──── Claims the CRD
metadata:                      object type as
 generateName: data-processing-   workflow
spec:
```

```
entrypoint: argo-steps-workflow-example
templates:
  - name: argo-steps-workflow-example
    Steps:                                    ◁——————  Declares the steps
      - - name: check-new-data                         of the workflow
          template: data-checker
      - - name: transform-data              ◁——————  The step body is defined
          template: data-converter                   as another template,
          arguments:                                 similar to a function.
            artifacts:
              - name: data-paths
                from: "{{steps.check-new-data.outputs.
                          artifacts.new-data-paths}}"   ◁——
      - - name: save-into-db                                 This is how steps
          template: postgres-operator                        pass parameters.
      - - name: notify-data-science-team
          template: slack-messenger
                                          The actual step definition, similar
  - name: data-checker          ◁————————  to a function implementation
    container:
      image: docker/data-checker:latest
      command: [scan, /datastore/ds/]
    outputs:
      artifacts:
        - name: new-data-paths
          path: /tmp/data_paths.txt

  - name: data-converter
    inputs:
      artifacts:
        - name: data_paths
          path: /tmp/raw_data/data_paths.txt
    container:
      image: docker/data-checker:latest
      command: [data_converter, /tmp/raw_data/data_paths.txt]

  - name: save-into-db
    .. .. ..
  - name: notify-data-science-team
    .. .. ..
```

Declares the data-paths artifact is from the new-data-paths artifact generated by the check-new-data step

Declares an output artifact (generates new-data-paths) for this step; the artifact is from /tmp/data_paths.txt, which can also be a directory.

Unpacks the data_paths input artifact and puts it at /tmp/raw_data/data_paths.txt

The most fundamental concepts in Argo Workflows are the workflow and template. A workflow object represents a single instance of a workflow; it contains the workflow's definition and execution state. We should treat a workflow as a "live" object. A template can be thought of as *functions*; they define instructions to be executed. The entrypoint field defines what the main function will be, meaning the template that will be executed first.

In code listing 9.2, we see a four-step sequential workflow: check-new-data -> transform_data -> save-into-db -> notify-data-science-team. Each step can reference a template, and steps pass parameters via artifacts (files). For example, the check-new-data references the data-checker template, which defines the Docker image for checking whether there is new data. The data-checker template also declares that the step output—the newly arrived data file path—will be saved to /tmp/data_paths.txt as its output value.

Next, the step transform_data binds the output of the check-new-data to the input of the data-converter template. This is how variables move around between steps and templates. Once you submit the workflow—for example, argo submit -n argo sample_workflow.yaml—you can either use the Argo Workflows UI or the following commands to review the details of the workflow run:

```
# list all the workflows
argo list -n argo

# get details of a workflow run
argo get -n argo {workflow_name}
```

Besides using the argo command, we can also use the Kubernetes CLI command to check the workflow execution because Argo Workflows runs natively on Kubernetes; see the following example:

```
# list all argo customer resource definitions
kubectl get crd -n argo

# list all workflows
kubectl get workflows -n argo

# check specific workflow
kubectl describe workflow/{workflow_name} -n argo
```

To learn more about Argo Workflows, you can check out Argo Workflows user guide (http://mng.bz/WAG0) and Argo Workflows architecture graph (https://argoproj .github.io/argo-workflows/architecture).

CODE DOCKERIZATION: EASY PRODUCTION DEPLOYMENT

Argo Workflows is essentially a Kubernetes pod (Docker images) scheduling system. Although it forces people to write their code into a series of Docker images, it creates great flexibility and isolation inside the orchestration system. Because the code is in Docker form, it can be executed by any worker without worrying about configuring the worker environments.

Another advantage to Argo Workflows is its low cost of production deployment. When you test your code locally in Docker, the Docker image (prototyping code) can be used directly in Argo Workflows. Unlike Airflow, Argo Workflows has almost no conversion effort from prototyping code to production workflow.

KEY FEATURES

Argo Workflows offers the following key features:

- *Low cost of installation and maintenance*—Argo Workflows runs natively on Kubernetes, so you can just use the Kubernetes process to troubleshoot any problems;

no need to learn other tools. Also, its installation is very straightforward; with a few `kubectl` commands, you can get Argo Workflows running in a Kubernetes environment.

- *Robust workflow execution*—The Kubernetes pod creates great isolation for Argo Workflows' task execution. Argo Workflows also supports cron workflow and task retry.

- *Templating and composability*—Argo Workflows templates are like functions. When building a workflow, Argo Workflows supports composing different templates (step functions). This composability encourages sharing the common work across teams, thus greatly improving productivity.

- *Fully featured UI*—Argo Workflows offers a convenient UI to manage the entire life cycle of a workflow, such as submitting/stopping a workflow, listing all workflows, and viewing workflow definitions.

- *Highly flexible and applicable*—Argo Workflows defines REST APIs to manage the system and add new capabilities (plugins), and workflow tasks are defined as Docker images. These features make Argo Workflows highly customizable and used widely in many domains, such as ML, ETL, batch/data processing, and CI/CD (continuous integration and continuous delivery/continuous deployment).

- *Production quality*—Argo Workflows is designed to run in a serious production environment. Kubeflow pipeline and Argo CD are great examples of productionizing Argo Workflows.

LIMITATIONS

The downsides of using Argo Workflows in deep learning systems are as follows:

- *Everyone will write and maintain YAML files*—Argo Workflows demands that the workflow is defined as a Kubernetes CRD in a YAML file. A short YAML file for a single project is manageable, but once the number of workflows starts increasing and workflow logic becomes more complex, the YAML file can become long and confusing. Argo Workflows offers templates to keep the workflow definition simple, but it's still not very intuitive unless you are accustomed to working with Kubernetes YAML configurations.

- *Must be an expert on Kubernetes*—You will feel like it's second nature if you are an expert on Kubernetes. But a novice user may need to spend quite some time learning Kubernetes concepts and practices.

- *Task execution latency*—In Argo Workflows, for every new task, Argo will launch a new Kubernetes pod to execute it. The pod launching can introduce seconds or minutes to every single task execution, which limits Argo when supporting time-sensitive workflows. For example, Argoflow is not a good fit for real-time model prediction workflow, which runs model prediction requests with millisecond SLAs.

9.3.3   *Metaflow*

Metaflow is a human-friendly Python library that focuses on MLOps. It was originally developed at Netflix and open-sourced in 2019. Metaflow is special in that it follows a humancentric design; it's not only built for automating workflows but also aims to reduce the human time (operational cost) spent in deep learning project development.

In section 9.1.3, we pointed out that the conversion from prototyping code to production workflow generates a lot of friction in ML development. Data scientists have to construct and test a new version of the workflow for each model development iteration. To bridge the gap between prototyping and production, Metaflow made two improvements: first, it simplifies workflow construction, and second, it unifies the workflow execution experience between the local and production environments (see figure 9.7).

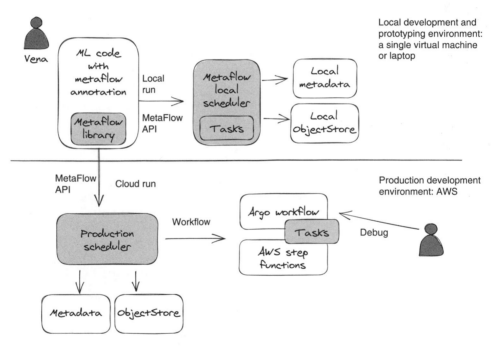

Figure 9.7   Metaflow offers a unified development experience between prototyping and production.

In figure 9.7, we can see that Metaflow treats both prototyping and production environments as first-class execution environments. Because the Metaflow library offers a set of unified APIs to abstract the actual infrastructure, a workflow can be executed in the same way regardless of which environment it runs on. For example, a workflow can be run by both a local scheduler and a production scheduler without any change. The local scheduler executes workflows locally whereas the production scheduler integrates into other production orchestration systems, such as AWS Step Functions or Argo Workflows.

Metaflow lets users annotate a Python code—a DAG Python class—to define the workflow. The Metaflow library then creates/packages the workflow automatically from the Python annotations. With Metaflow Python annotation, Vena can build a workflow without changing any of her prototyping code.

Besides seamless workflow creation and testing, Metaflow offers other useful features that are key to model reproducibility, such as workflow/steps versioning and step input/output saving. To learn more about Metaflow, you can check out Metaflow's official website (https://docs.metaflow.org/) and a great Metaflow book, *Effective Data Science Infrastructure*, written by Ville Tuulos (Manning, 2022; https://www.manning.com/books/effective-data-science-infrastructure).

A TYPICAL USE CASE

Let's use Metaflow to automate the same data process work we saw in sections 9.3.1 and 9.3.2. See the following listing for the pseudocode.

Listing 9.3   A sample Metaflow workflow

```python
# define workflow DAG in a python class
class DataProcessWorkflow(FlowSpec):

  # define "data source" as an input parameter for the workflow
  data_source = Parameter(
     "datasource_path", help="the data storage location for data process"
     , required=True
  )

  @step
  def start(self):
    # The parameter "self.data_source" are available in all steps.
    self.newdata_path = dataUtil.fetch_new_data(self.data_source)

    self.next(self.transform_data)

  @step
  def transform_data(self):
    self.new_data = dataUtil.convert(self.newdata_path)

    # fan out to two parallel branches after data transfer.
    self.next(self.save_to_db, self.notify_data_science_team)

  @step
  def save_to_db(self):
    dataUtil.store_data(self.new_data)
    self.next(self.join)

  @step
  def notify_data_science_team(self):
    slackUtil.send_notification(messageUtil.build_message(self.new_data))

    self.next(self.join)

  # join the two parallel branches steps:
  # notify_data_science_team and save_to_db
```

```
@step
def join(self, inputs):

   self.next(self.end)

@step
def end(self, inputs):
   # end the flow.
   pass


if __name__ == "__main__":
  DataProcessWorkflow()
```

In code listing 9.3, we see Metaflow takes a novel approach to building a workflow by using code annotations. By annotating `@step` on the functions and using `self.next` function to connect steps, we can easily construct a workflow DAG (figure 9.8) from our prototyping code.

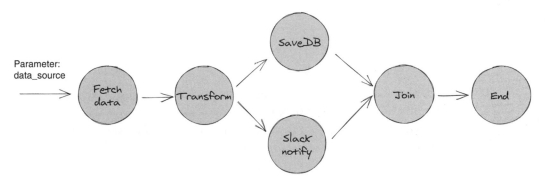

Figure 9.8   Workflow DAG constructed from listing 9.3

One of the beauties here is that we don't have to define the workflow DAG in a separate system and repackage code to a different format, such as a Docker image. The Metaflow workflow is immersed in our code. Workflow development and prototyping code development happen at the same place and can be tested together from the very beginning to the end of the entire ML development cycle.

Once the code is ready, we can validate and run the workflow locally. See the following sample commands:

```
# display workflow DAG
python data_process_workflow.py show

# run the workflow locally
python data_process_workflow.py run
```

Once we finish local development and testing, it's time to push the workflow to production, which can be achieved by the following two commands:

```
# push the workflow from local to AWS step functions
python data_process_workflow.py --with retry step-functions create

# push the workflow from local to Argo workflows
python data_process_workflow.py --with retry argo-workflows create
```

These commands will export our data process workflow defined in code listing 9.3 to AWS Step Functions and Argo Workflows. You can then also search for the flow by name within the AWS Step Functions UI or Argo Workflows UI and hence see the exported flow.

> **NOTE** Metaflow offers a unified development experience between local and production environments. Thanks to the unified API provided by Metaflow, we have a seamless experience when testing our code and workflow locally and in production. Regardless of the backend workflow orchestration system used, whether Metaflow local scheduler, Argo Workflows, or AWS Step Functions, the Metaflow user experience on the workflow development remains the same!

KEY FEATURES

Metaflow offers the following key features:

- *Structures code as workflow*—Metaflow lets users create a workflow by annotating Python code, which greatly simplifies workflow construction.
- *Reproducibility*—Metaflow preserves an immutable snapshot of the data, code, and external dependencies required to execute each workflow step. Metaflow also records the metadata of each workflow execution.
- *Versioning*—Metaflow addresses the version control requirement of an ML project by hashing all the code and data in a workflow.
- *Robust workflow execution*—Metadata provides dependency management mechanisms at both the workflow level and step level by using the @conda decorator. It also offers task retries.
- *Usability design for ML*—Metaflow treats prototyping and production as equally important. It provides a set of unified APIs to abstract the infrastructure, so the same code can run in both the prototyping environment and the production environment without any changes.
- *Seamless scalability*—Metaflow integrates with Kubernetes and AWS Batch, which allows users to define the required computing resource easily, and can parallel the workflow steps over an arbitrarily large number of instances. For example, by applying an annotation like @batch(cpu=1, memory=500) to a step function, Metaflow will work with AWS Batch to allocate the required resource to compute this step.

LIMITATIONS

The downsides of using Metaflow in deep learning systems are as follows:

- *No conditional branching support*—Metaflow step annotation doesn't support conditional branching (only executing a step when a condition is met). This is not a red flag, but it's a nice feature to have.
- *No job scheduler*—Metaflow itself doesn't come with a job scheduler, so you can't use a cron workflow. This is not a big problem because Metaflow can integrate with other orchestration systems that support job scheduling, such as AWS Step Functions and Argo Workflows.
- *Tightly coupled to AWS*—the most important features of Metaflow are tightly coupled to AWS—for example, Amazon S3 and AWS Batch. Luckily, Metaflow is an open source project, so it's possible to extend it to non-AWS alternatives.

9.3.4 *When to use*

If you are looking for an orchestration system to automate workflow execution for non-ML projects, both Airflow and Argo Workflows are great choices. They have excellent community support and have been used widely in the IT industry. If your system runs on Kubernetes and your team feels comfortable working with Docker, then Argo Workflows would be a good fit; otherwise, Airflow won't disappoint you.

If you are looking for a system to streamline your ML project development, Metaflow is highly recommended. Metaflow is not just an orchestration tool; it's an MLOps tool that focuses on saving data scientists' time in the ML development cycle. Because Metaflow abstracts the backend infrastructure part of a ML project, data scientists can focus on model development without worrying about production conversion and deployment.

Summary

- A workflow is a sequence of operations that are part of some larger task. A workflow can be viewed as a DAG of steps. A step is the smallest resumable unit of computation that describes what to do; a step either succeeds or fails as a whole. A DAG specifies the dependencies between steps and the order in which to execute them.
- Workflow orchestration means executing the workflow steps based on the sequence defined in the workflow's DAG.
- Adopting a workflow encourages work sharing, team collaboration, and automation.
- The main challenge of applying a workflow on deep learning projects is to reduce workflow construction costs and simplify workflow testing and debugging.
- The six recommended design principles for building/evaluating workflow orchestration systems are criticality, usability, extensibility, task isolation, scalability, and human centricity.

- When choosing an orchestration system for non-ML projects, both Airflow and Argo Workflows are great choices. Argo Workflows is a better option if the project runs on Kubernetes and Docker.
- When selecting an orchestration system for ML projects, Metaflow is so far the best option.

Path to production

This chapter covers

- Preliminary work and tasks before productionizing deep learning models
- Productionizing deep learning models with a deep learning system
- Model deployment strategies for experimentation in production

For the concluding chapter of the book, we think it makes sense to return to a high-level view and connect all the dots from previous chapters. We have now discussed in detail each service in a deep learning system. In this chapter, we will talk about how the services work together to support the deep learning *product development cycle* we introduced in chapter 1. That cycle, if you remember, brings the efforts of research and data science all the way through productionization to the end products that customers use.

As a reminder, figure 10.1, borrowed from chapter 1, shows the product development cycle. Our focus in this chapter will be on three phases that occur toward the end of the process: deep learning research, prototyping, and productionization. This focus means we'll ignore the cycles of experimentation, testing, training,

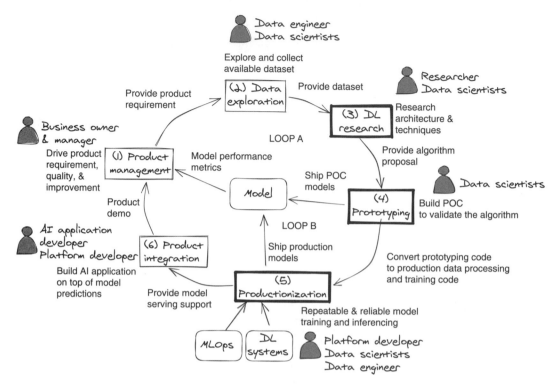

Figure 10.1 **This deep learning development cycle is a typical scenario for bringing deep learning from research to the finished product. Boxes (3), (4), and (5) are the focus of this chapter.**

and exploration and look at how to take a final product from the research phase to the end product, making it ready to be released to the public.

> **DEFINITION** Productionization is the process of producing a product that is worthwhile and ready to be consumed by its users. Production worthiness is commonly defined as being able to serve customer requests, withstand a certain level of request load, and gracefully handle adverse situations such as malformed input and request overload.

As we've said, this chapter focuses on the path of the production cycle from research, through prototyping, to productionization. Let's lift those three phases out of the typical development cycle shown in figure 10.1, so we can see them in greater detail. We've placed those phases in the next diagram, figure 10.2, and zoomed in on them to reveal the steps within each phase, as well as the ways the three phases connect to each other. Don't let the complexity of this diagram alarm you! We will walk you through each phase, and each step, in this chapter.

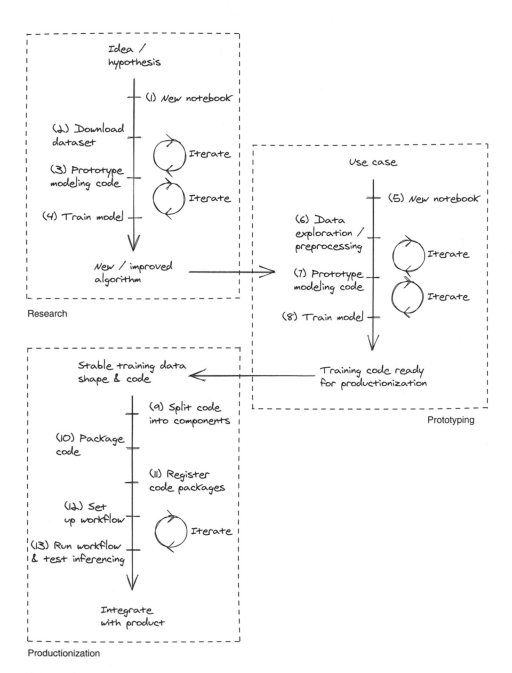

Figure 10.2 Three major stages in a sample path to production. Research and prototyping go through many iterations before productionization.

Let's briefly review this diagram, as it will provide a preview of the chapter. The first two phases in figure 10.2 are research and prototyping. Both of these efforts require rapid iteration and turnaround from model training and experimentation. The primary interaction point in these phases (steps 1–8) is a notebooking environment. Using notebooks, researchers and data scientists invoke the dataset management service for tracking training datasets (during steps 2 and 6) and may use the training service and hyperparameter optimization library/service for model training and experimentation (during steps 4 and 8). We go over these phases in section 10.1, ending at the point where training data shape and code become fairly stable and are ready to be productionized. In other words, the team has come up with the more-or-less final version, and it is ready to go through the final steps to release it to the public.

In section 10.2, we will pick up from the previous section and walk through the productionization of models, up to the point where models are served to production inference request traffic.

> **DEFINITION**   *Inference requests* are inputs generated by a user or an application against a trained model to produce inferences. Take visual recognition as an example. An inference request can be a picture of a cat. Using a trained visual recognition model, or an inference, a label in the form of the word *cat* can be generated.

This section corresponds to the third and final phase in figure 10.2. In productionization, pretty much every service in our system will come into play. The dataset management service manages training data; the workflow management service launches and tracks training workflows; the training service executes and manages model training jobs; the metadata and artifacts store contains and tracks code artifacts, trained models, and their metadata; and the model service serves trained models to inference request traffic.

From productionization, we move to deployment. In section 10.3, we look at a number of model deployment strategies that support updating models to new versions in production. These strategies also support experimentation in production. The main focus here will be on the model service because this is where all inference requests are served.

By walking through the full journey to production, we hope that you will be able to see how the first principles that we discussed in previous chapters affect the work of different parties that use the system to deliver deep learning features. The understanding that you gain from this chapter should help you adapt your own design to different situations. We will use the development of an image recognition product as an example to illustrate all the steps in action.

10.1   *Preparing for productionization*

In this section, we will look at the journey of a deep learning model from before its birth to when it is ready to be productionized. In figure 10.3, we highlight the phases

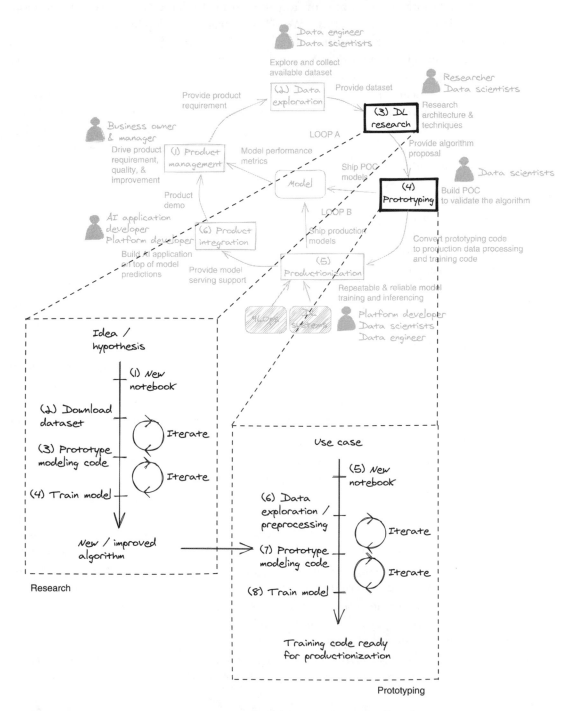

Figure 10.3 Excerpt of the path to production in the research and prototyping phases

of deep learning research and prototyping from the larger deep learning development cycle (shown in figure 10.1). We will start from the deep learning research step, where model training algorithms are born. Not every organization performs deep learning research—some use out-of-the-box training algorithms—so feel free to skip this step if it does not apply to your situation.

After deep learning research, we proceed to prototyping. At this stage, we assume algorithms are ready to use for training models. A rapid and iterative process of data exploration and experimental model training forms the central part of this step. The goal of this step is to find the appropriate training data shape and develop a stable codebase for model training.

10.1.1 *Research*

New deep learning algorithms are invented, and existing ones are improved through research. Because peer-reviewed research requires reproducible results, model training data needs to be publicly accessible. Many public datasets, such as ImageNet for example, are available for research teams to use.

The notebooking environment, such as JupyterLab, is a popular choice among researchers for prototyping model training due to its interactivity and flexibility. Let's go through some sample steps that a researcher may take during model training prototyping:

1 Alice, a deep learning researcher, is working on improving a visual recognition algorithm. After working on her theories, she is ready to start prototyping.
2 Alice creates a new notebook in JupyterLab.
3 Alice wants to use the ImageNet dataset for training and benchmarking her algorithm. She may
    a Write code to download the dataset to her notebook and store it in the dataset management service (chapter 2) for reuse.
    b Find that the dataset is already stored in the dataset management service and write code to use it as is.
4 Alice starts coding up improvements on an existing visual recognition algorithm until it can produce experimental models locally within the notebook.
5 Alice tries to change some hyperparameters, train and test a few experimental models, and compare the metrics that they generate.
6 Alice may further use hyperparameter optimization techniques (chapter 5) to run more experiments automatically to confirm that she has indeed made improvements to the existing algorithm.
7 Alice publishes her results and packages her training code improvement as a library for others to use.

By using a versioned dataset for training, Alice is sure that the input training data of all her experimental model training runs are the same. She also uses a source-control management system, such as Git, to keep track of her code so that all experimental models can be traced back to a version of her code.

Notice that model training at this stage usually takes place locally at the computing node where the notebooking environment is hosted, so it is a good idea to allocate sufficient resources to these nodes. If training data is stored over the network, make sure the read speed does not become a bottleneck for model training.

10.1.2 Prototyping

Prototyping is where research is bridged with real-world use cases. It is a practice of looking for the right combination of training data, algorithm, hyperparameter, and inference support to provide the right deep learning feature that meets product requirements.

At this stage, it is still very common to find notebooking environments to be the top choice for data scientists and engineers due to the rapid iterative nature of prototyping. A fast turnaround is expected. Let's walk through one possible scenario of prototyping:

1　The model development team receives product requirements to improve the motion detection of a security camera product.

2　Based on the requirements, the team finds that Alice's new vision recognition training algorithm may help improve motion detection.

3　The team creates a new notebook and begins exploring data that is relevant for model training, given the set of algorithms that they picked:

　　a　The team may be able to use existing, collected data for model training if they happen to fit the problem that is being solved.

　　b　In some cases, the team may need to collect new data for training.

4　In most cases, transfer learning is applied at this stage, and the team picks one or more existing models as source models.

5　The team develops modeling code with algorithms and trains experimental models with collected data and source models.

6　Experimental models are evaluated to see whether they yield satisfactory results. Steps 3 to 6 are repeated until the training data shape and code become stable.

We call steps 3 to 6 the exploratory loop. This loop corresponds to the iterate circles in the blow-up section of prototyping in figure 10.3. When prototyping begins, the loop is iterated rapidly. The focus at this stage is to narrow down the training data shape and code.

Once training data shape and code become stable, they will be ready for further tuning and optimization. The goal in this phase is to converge to a state where model training and inference code are ready to be packaged and deployed to production.

10.1.3 Key takeaways

We have walked through both the research and prototyping phases of our reference deep learning development cycle in figure 10.1. Even though they serve different purposes, we see quite a bit of overlap in how they work with the deep learning system:

- The notebooking environment is a common choice for both research and preproduction prototyping due to its high degree of interactivity and verbosity.
- Access to training data should be as wide and flexible as possible (to the limit of legality and compliance), which helps accelerate the data exploration process.
- Sufficient computing resources should be allocated for model training so that turnaround time is short.
- At a minimum, use a dataset management service and a source-control management system to keep track of the provenance of experimental models. In addition, use a metadata store to contain metrics and associate them with a training dataset and code for complete lineage tracking.

10.2 Model productionization

Before deep learning models can be integrated into an end product, they need to go through the process of productionization. There are certainly many interpretations of this term, but fundamentally:

- Models need to serve production inference requests either from end products or end users.
- Model serving should meet a predefined service level agreement, such as responding within 50 milliseconds or being available 99.999% of the time.
- Production problems related to models should be easy to troubleshoot.

In this section, we will look at how deep learning models transition from living in a rather dynamic environment, such as a notebook, to a production environment where they are hit by various harsh conditions. Figure 10.4 shows the productionization phase relative to the rest of the development cycle. Let's review the steps in this phase.

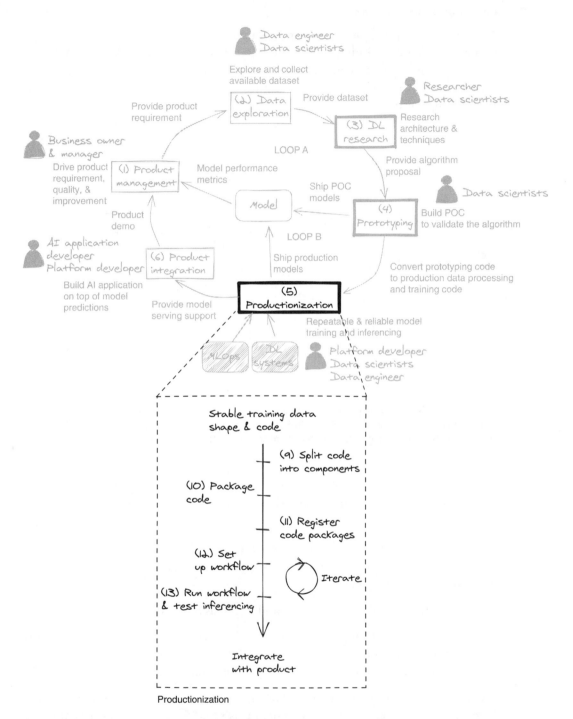

Figure 10.4   Excerpt of the path to production in the productionization phase

10.2.1 *Code componentization*

As shown in the previous section, it is common during prototyping for training data preparation, model training, and inference code to exist in a single notebook. To productionize them into a deep learning system, we need to split them apart as separate components. One approach to splitting the components, or *code componentization*, is shown in figure 10.5.

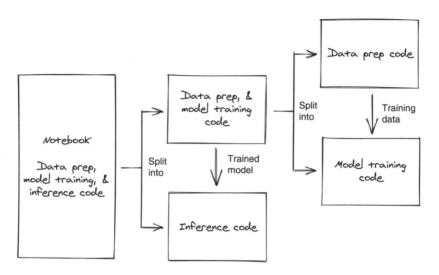

Figure 10.5 Componentizing code from a single notebook into multiple pieces that can be packaged separately. The first split happens where a trained model is the output. An optional second split happens where training data is the output.

Let's put the process in the figure into action. The first place to draw a line for separation in the code is where the model is the output. This should result in two pieces of code as follows:

- Model training code that outputs a model
- Model inference code that takes a model and an inference request as input to produce an inference

Optionally, the model training code can be split as follows:

- Training data transformation code, which takes raw data as input and output training data that can be consumed by model training code
- Model training code, which takes training data and trains a model as its output

If you have other model training code that will benefit from the same kind of prepared data, it is a good idea to perform this separation. Separation is also a good idea if your data preparation step needs to be executed on a different cadence from model training.

10.2.2 Code packaging

Once code components are separated cleanly, they are ready to be packaged for deployment. To be able to run them on a training service (chapter 3), model service (chapter 6), and workflow service (chapter 9), we first need to make sure they follow the conventions set by these services.

Model training code should be modified to fetch training data from the location indicated by an environment variable set by the training service. A similar convention should be followed in other components.

Model inference code should follow the convention of the model serving strategy of your choice:

- If you use direct model embedding, work with the team that embeds your model to make sure your inference code works.
- If you plan to serve your model with model service, make sure your inference code provides an interface with which the model service can communicate.
- If you use a model server, you may not need model inference code as long as the model server can serve the model properly.

We package these code components as Docker containers so that they can be launched, accessed, and tracked by their respective host services. An example of how this is done can be found in appendix A. If special data transformation is needed, we can integrate data transformation code into the data management service.

10.2.3 Code registration

Before training code and inference code can be used by the system, their packages must be registered and stored with the metadata and artifacts service. This provides the necessary link between the training code and the inference code. Let's look at how they are related (figure 10.6).

Once the training and inference codes are packaged as containers (the training container and inference container in the diagram), they can be registered with the metadata and artifacts store using a common handle, such as `visual_recognition` like in the example shown in figure 10.6. This helps system services find and use correct code containers when they receive requests that provide the same handle name. We will continue walking through the figure in the next few sections.

10.2.4 Training workflow setup

We recommend setting up a training workflow even if you do not regularly train your model. The main reason is to provide reproducibility of the same model training flow in production. This is helpful when someone other than you needs to train a model and can use the flow that you set up. In some cases, the production environment is

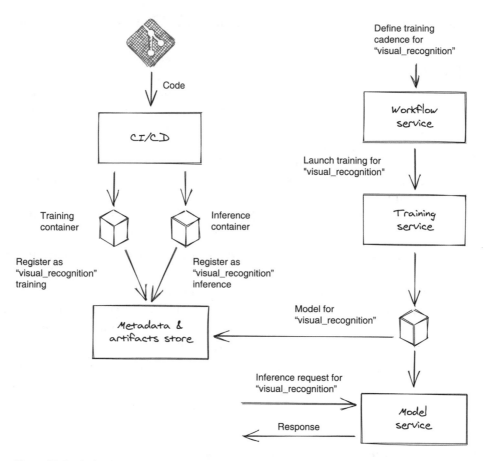

Figure 10.6   A simple training and inference execution flow in a production deep learning system

isolated, and going through a workflow that is set up in the production environment may be the only way to produce a model there. In figure 10.7, we've enlarged the model training portion of the previous diagram so you can see the details.

Referring to figure 10.7, once a training workflow for `visual_recognition` is set up, training can be triggered to the training service. The training service uses the handle to look up the training code container to execute from the metadata and artifacts store. Once a model is trained, it saves the model to the metadata and artifacts store with the handle name.

At this stage, it is also common to find hyperparameter optimization techniques being used to find optimal training hyperparameters during model training. If an HPO service is used, the workflow will talk to the HPO service instead of to the training service directly. If you need a reminder of how the HPO service works, refer to chapter 5.

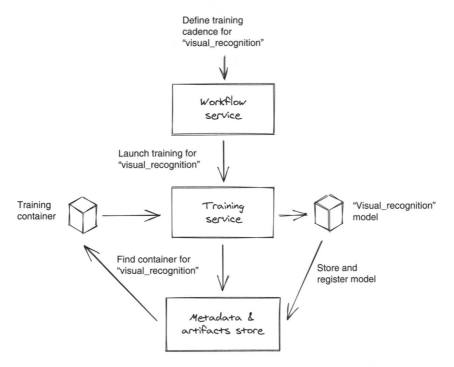

Figure 10.7 A typical production model training setup. The workflow service manages what, when, and how training flows are run. The training service runs model training jobs. The metadata and artifacts store provides training code, stores trained models, and associates them with metadata.

10.2.5 Model inferences

Once a model is trained and registered in the production environment, the next step is to make sure it can handle inference requests coming into our system at a certain rate and producing inferences within a certain latency. We can do so by sending inference requests to the model service. When the model service receives a request, it finds the handle name `visual_recognition` in the request and queries the metadata and artifacts store for the matching model inference container and model file. The model service can then use these artifacts together to produce an inference response. You can see this process in figure 10.8, which, again, is an enlarged version of the model serving portion of figure 10.6.

If you use a model server, you may need a thin layer in front of it so that it knows where to obtain the model file. Some model server implementations support custom model manager implementation, which can also be used to make queries against the metadata and artifacts store to load the correct model.

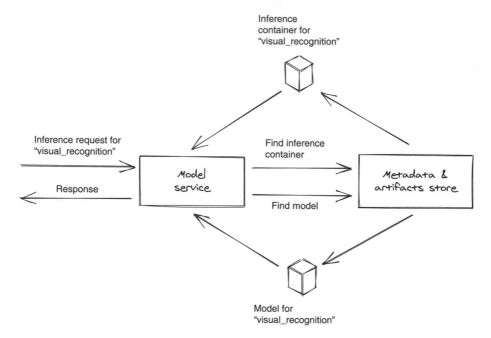

Figure 10.8 A typical production model serving setup. When inference requests arrive at the model service, the service looks for the inference container and model using the metadata and artifacts store to produce inference responses.

10.2.6 *Product integration*

Once you get a proper inference response back from the model service, it is time to integrate a model service client into the product that will use these inferences. This is the final step in productionization, and we should make sure to check a few things before launching it to the end customer. Because we are improving the motion detection of our security camera product, we must integrate a model service client in the security camera video-processing backend that will request inferences from the newly improved model:

- Make sure the inference response is consumable by the product using it.
- Stress test inferencing by sending inference requests at a rate that approximates the production traffic.
- Test inferencing with malformed inference requests to make sure they do not break the model inference code or the model service.

This is a very basic list of items to look for. Your organization may define more production readiness criteria that you need to fulfill before launching the integration. Besides system metrics that can tell us whether our model is serving inference requests properly, we should also set up business metrics that will tell us whether the model helps the business use case.

10.3   Model deployment strategies

In the previous section, we went through a sample path from prototyping to production. That process assumed that the model was deployed for the first time, without an existing version of the model to replace. Once a model is being used in production, unless there is a maintenance window allowance, we usually need to use a model deployment strategy to ensure production inference request traffic is not disrupted. In fact, these model deployment strategies can also double as performing experimentation in production by using business metrics that we set up in the previous section. We will look at three strategies: canary, blue-green, and multi-armed bandit.

10.3.1   Canary deployment

A canary deployment, similar to A/B testing, means deploying a new model to serve a small portion of production inference requests while keeping the old one to serve the remaining majority of requests. An example is shown in figure 10.9. This requires the model service to support segmenting and routing a small portion of inference request traffic to the new model.

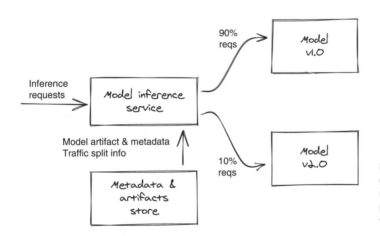

Figure 10.9   Canary deployment showing the redirection of a small portion of traffic to a new version of the model

With this strategy, any potential adverse effect from deploying a new model is contained within a small portion of end users. Rolling back is rather straightforward by routing all inference request traffic back to the old model.

A drawback to this approach is that you only get to know the performance of the model to a small portion of end users. Releasing the new model to serve all inference request traffic may have a different effect from what you observe serving only a small portion of the traffic.

10.3.2   Blue-green deployment

In our context, a blue-green deployment means deploying a new model, routing all inference request traffic to the new model, and keeping the old model online until we have

UN 890 8306

confidence that the new model's performance meets expectations. Implementation-wise it is the simplest among all three strategies because there is no traffic splitting at all. All the service needs to do is point to the new model internally to serve all inference requests. Blue-green deployment is depicted in figure 10.10.

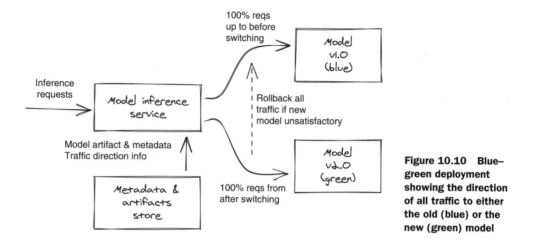

Figure 10.10   Blue–green deployment showing the direction of all traffic to either the old (blue) or the new (green) model

Not only is this strategy simple, but it also gives you a full picture of how the model performs when serving all end users. Rolling back is also straightforward. Simply point the model service back to the old model.

The obvious downside to this approach is if something goes wrong with the new model, it affects all end users. This strategy may make sense when you are developing a new product feature based on a new model. As you iterate on training a better model over time, you may want to move away from this strategy, as end users would have built their expectations on having a stable experience.

10.3.3   *Multi-armed bandit deployment*

Multi-armed bandit (MAB) is the most complex deployment strategy among the three. MAB refers to a technique that continuously monitors multiple models' performance and redirects more and more inference request traffic to the winning model over time. This uses the most elaborate implementation of the model service because it requires the service to understand model performance, which can be complicated depending on how your model performance metrics are defined. MAB deployment is illustrated in figure 10.11.

This strategy does come with an advantage, though, because it maximizes the benefits of the best-performing models within a set time frame, whereas with a canary deployment, you may only gain minimal benefits if the new model outperforms the old one. Notice that you should make sure the model service reports how the traffic split changes over time. This helps correlate with the models' performance.

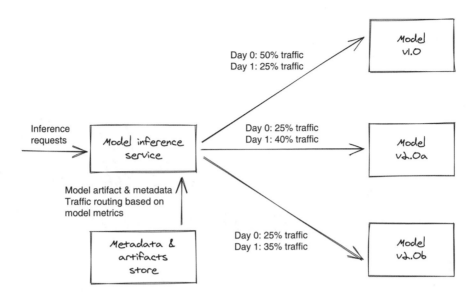

Figure 10.11 Multi-armed bandit deployment showing traffic patterns on day 0 and day 1. Notice that model v2.0a is leading in terms of model performance on day 1 as it is receiving the most traffic.

Summary

- Deep learning research teams invent and improve deep learning algorithms that are used to train models.
- Model development teams make use of existing algorithms and available data to train models that help solve a deep learning use case.
- Both research and prototyping require a high degree of interactivity with code development, data exploration, and visualization. Notebooking environments are popular choices for these teams.
- Dataset management service can be used during research and prototyping to help track training data used to train experimental models.
- Once training data and code are stable enough, the first step to productionization is to package model training code, model inference code, and any source models.
- These packages can be used by all services of the deep learning system to train, track, and serve models.
- Once a model training workflow is up and running and a satisfactory inference response is obtained, integration with the end-user product can begin.
- A model deployment strategy is required if serving inference requests cannot be interrupted.
- Multiple model deployment strategies are available, and they can double as performing experimentation in production.

appendix A
A "hello world"
deep learning system

This book is about teaching design principles for building a deep learning system that fits your own situation. But you may be wondering what a deep learning system even looks like. Or how, why, and when people can use a system like this in practice. These are all great questions at this stage.

We believe the best method for learning new ideas, skills, and approaches is by doing—by getting your hands on some examples and seeing what you can do with them. To help you, we built a mini deep learning system and a code lab for you to play with. Playing around in this "hello world" deep learning system should help you build the knowledge base for understanding the concepts and principles introduced in this book. To make this sample system easy to digest, we focus on the key components of a deep learning system, such as dataset management (DM) and model training and serving. The entire mini system can be set up easily on your local system with a bash script, and its components are discussed in detail in the later chapters.

In this appendix, we will first take a tour of our sample system and then run the lab exercise to let you experience the most common user activities in a deep learning system, including dataset ingestion, model training, and model serving. Although our sample system is extremely simplified, it covers all the basics of a deep learning system. By reading this appendix, you will not only gain a practical understanding of how a basic deep learning system is organized and how it functions, but you will also have a holistic view of the sample services that are discussed in the rest of the book.

A.1 Introducing the "hello world" deep learning system

The quickest way to understand a software system is from the user's perspective. So in this introduction section, we will first look at the users of a deep learning system: the personas and their responsibilities. Then we will dive into system design, the major components, and the user workflows.

A.1.1 Personas

To keep the complexity to a minimum, our sample mini deep learning system only has four *personas*, or *roles*: data engineer, data scientist/researcher, system developer, and deep learning application developer. We pick these four roles because they are the minimum personnel needed to keep a deep learning system functioning. The role definition and job description of each persona in this "hello world" system are listed in the following sections.

> **NOTE** The role responsibilities described here are oversimplified because we want to concentrate on the most fundamental workflows of a deep learning system. For more detailed definitions of the personas and roles involved in a deep learning system, please refer to section 1.1.

A.1.2 Data engineers

Data engineers are responsible for collecting, processing, and storing the raw data for deep learning training. We have a DM service in this mini system to store datasets for model training. Data engineers will use this service to upload the raw training data. In our lab exercise, we prepared some intent classification datasets for you to experience this process.

A.1.3 Data scientists/researchers

Data scientists or researchers develop training algorithms and produce models that meet business requirements. They are the *customers* of the model training infrastructure in a deep learning system.

Our example system contains a training service to run model training code. In the lab, we prebuilt an intent classification training code for you to experience the model training execution.

A.1.4 System developer

System developers build the entire deep learning system and maintain it to make sure all the machine learning activities are functioning well. Their activities include dataset uploading, model training, and model serving.

A.1.5   *Deep learning application developers*

Deep learning application developers utilize deep learning models to build commercial products, such as chatbots, self-driving software, and facial recognition mobile apps. These applications are the most important customers of any deep learning system because they create the business impact (revenue) for the models produced by the system. In our lab, you will have the opportunity to imagine yourself as a chatbot customer by running a script to send requests to the prediction service and categorize your message.

A.1.6   *Sample system overview*

Our mini deep learning system consists of four services and one storage system:

- *Data service*—Designed for storing and fetching dataset
- *Model training service*—Designed for running model training code
- *Metadata store service*—Designed for storing model metadata, such as model name, model version, and model algorithm
- *Prediction service*—Designed to execute models to process customer's prediction requests
- *MinIO storage*—Designed to run on your local computer as an object storage similar to Amazon S3

Almost all these services have their own chapters in this book, so we will be able to study them in more detail. For now, we just want to provide you with the high-level overview you'll need to comprehend the user scenarios and lab exercises later in the book. Figure A.1 illustrates the major components of the sample system (the four services and the storage system) along with their interdependencies.

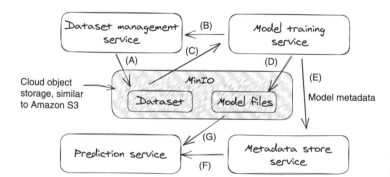

Figure A.1   The design overview of the sample deep learning system

Along with the four services and storage (in rectangular boxes), you'll notice lots of directed arrows between these boxes. These arrows show the interdependencies of the services inside the sample system. Here are the explanations for these dependencies:

- The DM service saves the dataset to MinIO storage.
- The model training service queries DM to prepare the training dataset and obtain the training data.
- The model training service downloads training data from MinIO.
- The model training service saves model files to MinIO.
- The model training service saves model metadata to the metadata store service.
- The prediction service queries the metadata store to determine which model to use.
- The prediction service downloads model files from MinIO to serve the prediction request.

A.1.7 User workflows

Now that we have introduced the personas and the main services, let's look at the user workflows. Figure A.2 illustrates the user workflow for each persona.

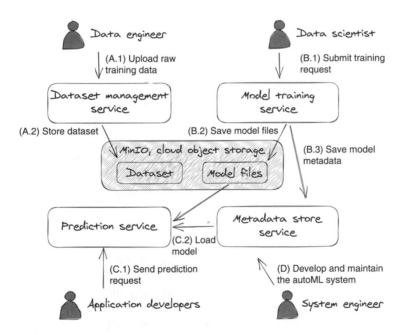

Figure A.2 Four different workflows are enabled in the system for DM, training, serving, and system maintenance.

Figure A.2 shows each persona using the mini deep learning system to perform its own task by utilizing the services introduced in figure A.1. Let's review each of these workflows:

- *Scenario A*—Data engineers call the DM service to upload raw data; DM ingests the data and saves it to MinIO storage in a training dataset format.
- *Scenario B*—Data scientists first write the training code and then submit a training request to the training service. The training service executes the training code and produces the model. It then saves model metadata to the metadata store and saves model files to MinIO storage.
- *Scenario C*—Application developers build applications to call the prediction service to consume the model trained in scenario B.
- *Scenario D*—System developers build and maintain this system.

A.2   Lab demo

Now it's time for you to start learning by doing. In this lab exercise, you will engage in the user scenarios mentioned in section A.1.3 on your local computer. To make this exercise more vivid, we introduced some characters so you will not only know how to work with a deep learning system but also understand who handles each different job. The fictitious characters include Ivan, a data scientist; Feng, a data engineer; Tang, a system developer; and Johanna, an application developer.

A.2.1   Demo steps

In this demo scenario, we will have Tang, Feng, Ivan, and Johanna work together to train an intent classification model and use the model to classify arbitrary text messages. This scenario simulates the four fundamental steps of a typical model development workflow: system setup, dataset building, model training, and model serving.

To make the lab easy to run, we Dockerized all the microservices and built shell scripts to automate the lab setup and demo scenarios. By following the instructions in the README file (https://github.com/orca3/MiniAutoML#lab) at our GitHub repo (https://github.com/orca3/MiniAutoML), you can complete the lab by running four shell scripts.

> **NOTE** You can find the lab demo scripts in the scripts folder (https://github .com/orca3/MiniAutoML/tree/main/scripts) at our GitHub repo (https:// github.com/orca3/MiniAutoML). The scripts folder contains the demo scripts for the entire book. The files starting with *lab-* are used in this demo—for example, the lab-001-start-all.sh (http://mng.bz/zmv1) can be set up on your local system. In the case of future updates, and to execute the lab scripts successfully, please always refer to the instructions in the GitHub repo.

Step 1 is the system setup. Run scripts/lab-001-start-all.sh (http://mng.bz/zmv1).

Tang (system developer) lights up the mini deep learning system by running the scripts/lab-001-start-all.sh script. The script will download the prebuilt Docker images of the demo services and execute them.

When the script finishes, the mini deep learning system is up and running. You can use the following command to list all the local running Docker containers to verify that all the services are running:

```
$ docker ps --format="table {{.Names}}\t{{.Image}}"
```

The Docker containers required to run the lab are provided in the following listing.

Listing A.1   Verifying all system components are running

```
NAMES                                     IMAGE
training-service                          orca3/services:latest
prediction-service                        orca3/services:latest
intent-classification-torch-predictor     pytorch/torchserve:0.5.2-cpu
intent-classification-predictor           orca3/intent-classification-predictor
metadata-store                            orca3/services:latest
data-management                           orca3/services:latest
minio                                     minio/minio
```

Once Tang verifies that all the microservices are running, the system is ready to use. He informs Ivan and Feng to start their work.

> **NOTE** If you read the `lab-001-start-all.sh`, you will find that most of the services—such as data management and model training—in the system (except predictors) are packaged into one Docker image (`orca3/services`). This is not a recommended pattern for production use cases, but it fits our demo needs here since it uses less disk space and it's simple to execute.

Step 2 is building a training dataset. Run `scripts/lab-002-upload-data.sh` (http://mng.bz/0yqJ).

Feng (data engineer) first downloads raw data from the internet and applies some modifications for training (see `scripts/prepare_data.py` at http://mng.bz/KlKX). Feng then uploads the processed data to the DM service. Once the dataset upload completes, DM returns a unique dataset ID for future reference.

We automated Feng's work in the `scripts/lab-002-upload-data.sh` script. After executing this script, a dataset is created. You can see a JSON object being printed out by the DM service in your terminal. This JSON object presents the metadata of a dataset; see the following example.

Listing A.2   A sample dataset metadata in DM service

```
# DM returns dataset metadata for a newly created dataset
{
    "dataset_id": "1",              ⟵———— Dataset identifier
    "name": "tweet_emotion",        ⟵——— Dataset name
    "dataset_type": "TEXT_INTENT",
    "last_updated_at": "2022-03-25T01:32:37.493612Z",
```

Dataset type ⟶

```
    "commits": [
      {
        "dataset_id": "1",
        "commit_id": "1",
        "created_at": "2022-03-25T01:32:38.919357Z",
        "commit_message": "Initial commit",
        "path": "dataset/1/commit/1",
        "statistics": {
          "numExamples": "2963",
          "numLabels": "3"
        }
      }
    ]
}
```

Dataset audit history

Dataset metadata is discussed in detail in chapter 2. For now, we can ignore most attributes of the metadata JSON object and only pay attention to the `dataset_id` attribute. *Dataset ID* is a unique identifier for a dataset; you need to pass this ID to the training service for model training in step 3. Once the dataset is ready, Feng informs Ivan to start model training with `dataset_id="1"`.

Step 3 is model training. Run `scripts/lab-003-first-training.sh` (http://mng .bz/vnra).

Ivan (the data scientist) first builds the intent classification training code (`training-code/text-classification` at http://mng.bz.jmKa) and packages it into a Docker image (http://mng.bz/WA5g). Next, Ivan submits a training request to the model training service to create a model training job. In the training request, he specifies which dataset (dataset ID) and training algorithm (Docker image name) to use in training.

> **NOTE** In this lab, we use a hardcoded dataset ID `"1"`. To test other datasets, please feel free to set any other dataset ID into the training request.

Once the training service receives the training request, it will launch a Docker container to run the intent classification training code provided by Ivan. In our demo, the Docker image is `orca3/intent-classification` (http://mng.bz/WA5g). See code listing A.3 for a sample gRPC training request. Please run the lab script (`scripts/lab-003-first-training.sh` at http://mng.bz/916j) to kick off a model training job, which sets up the dependencies and parameters.

Listing A.3   Submitting a training job to a training service

```
# send gRPC request to kick off a model training in training service.
function start_training() {
 grpcurl -plaintext \
   -d "{
   \"metadata\": {
     \"algorithm\":\"intent-classification\",
```

Training the Docker image name

```
Dataset          \"dataset_id\":\"1\",          ◁────    The ID of the
version          \"name\":\"test1\",                      dataset to train
          └─▷   \"train_data_version_hash\":$2,
                \"output_model_name\":\"twitter-model\",
                \"parameters\": {
                  \"LR\":\"4\",
                  \"EPOCHS\":\"15\",                               Training
                  \"BATCH_SIZE\":\"64\",                           hyperparameters
                  \"FC_SIZE\":\"128\"
                }
              }
          }" \
            localhost:"6003" training.TrainingService/Train
        }
```

Once the training job starts, the training service will keep monitoring the training
execution status and return a job ID for tracking purposes. With the job ID, Ivan can
fetch the latest training job status and training metadata by querying the `GetTrain-`
`ingStatus` API of the training service and the `GetRunStatus` API of the metastore service. See the sample query requests as follows.

Listing A.4 Querying the model training job status and model metadata

```
# query training job status from training service
grpcurl -plaintext \
 -d "{\"job_id\": \"1\"}" \
 localhost:"6003" training.TrainingService/GetTrainingStatus         ◁──      Model ID,
                                                                              also the
# query model training metrics from metadata store.                           training
grpcurl -plaintext \                                                          job ID
 -d "{\"run_id\": \"1\"}" \
 localhost:"6002" metadata_store.MetadataStoreService/GetRunStatus   ◁──
```

The training service can return training execution status in real time; see the sample
response as follows:

```
job 1 is currently in "launch" status, check back in 5 seconds
job 1 is currently in "running" status, check back in 5 seconds     Training
job 1 is currently in "succeed" status              ◁───────────    completes
```

Because the training Docker container reports real-time metrics, such as training
accuracy, to the metadata store during training execution, the metadata store service
can return real-time training metrics. See the sample model training metrics from the
metadata store service as follows:

```
              {
                "run_info": {
                  "start_time": "2022-03-25T14:25:44.395619",
Training          "end_time": "2022-03-25T14:25:48.261595",      The last message
status            "success": true,                               from the training
          └─▷     "message": "test accuracy 0.520",   ◁───────   container
```

```
        "run_id": "1",                              ◁──   The training job
        "run_name": "training job 1",                     ID, as well as the
        "tracing": {                                      model ID
The dataset     "dataset_id": "1",
identifier      "version_hash": "hashAg==",
            "code_version": "231c0d2"
        },
        "epochs": {
          "0-10": {
            "start_time": "2022-03-25T14:25:46.880859",
            "end_time": "2022-03-25T14:25:47.054872",
            "run_id": "1",                                        Training
            "epoch_id": "0-10",                                   metric per
            "metrics": {                                          epoch
              "accuracy": "0.4925373134328358"
            }
          },
          .. .. ..
        }
}
```

After training is completed, Ivan informs Johanna that the model is ready to consume. In our lab, he passes the model ID (job ID = "1") to Johanna so she knows which model to use.

> **NOTE** All the API requests described in code listings A.3 and A.4 are automated in `scripts/lab-003-first-training.sh`; you can execute them in one go. In chapters 3 and 4, we discuss in detail how the training service works.

Step 4 is model serving. Run `scripts/lab-004-model-serving.sh` (http://mng.bz/815K).

Johanna (application developer) is building a chatbot, so she wants to consume the newly trained intent classification model to categorize customers' questions. When Ivan tells Johanna that the model is ready to use, Johanna sends a prediction request to the prediction service to test the newly trained model.

In the prediction request, Johanna specifies the model ID (`runId`) and document, where the document is the text message that is being categorized. And the sample prediction service will load the model requested in the prediction request automatically. You can see a sample gRPC prediction request in the following listing.

Listing A.5   A sample model prediction gRPC request

```
grpcurl -plaintext \                                    Model ID, as well
  -d "{                                                 as the training
    \"runId\": \"1\",                           ◁──┘    job ID
    \"document\": \"You can have a certain arrogance,
      and I think that's fine, but what you should never
      lose is the respect for the others.\"       ◁──
  }" \                                                  Request
  localhost:6001 prediction.PredictionService/Predict   body (text)
```

After executing the query (code listing A.5) or `scripts/lab-004-model-serving.sh` in the terminal, you will see output—a predicted category (label) from the intent classification model for the given text—from the model serving service as follows:

```
{
    "response": "{\"result\": \"joy\"}"          ◁——|  The predict
}                                                     category is "joy."
```

NOTE If you encounter any issues while trying to complete the lab, please check the latest instructions in the lab section (https://github.com/orca3/MiniAutoML#lab) of our GitHub repo's README file. We aim to keep these instructions updated if the sample system is modified.

A.2.2 *An exercise to do on your own*

Now that we walked you through a completed model development cycle, it's homework time. Imagine after a successful chatbot release, Johanna's chatbot service needs to support a new category, *optimism*. This new requirement means the current intent classification model needs to be retrained to recognize the optimism type of text messages.

Feng and Ivan need to work together to build a new intent classification model. Feng needs to collect more training data with the "optimism" label and add it to the current dataset. Although Ivan doesn't need to change the training code, he does need to trigger a training job in the training service with the updated dataset to build a new model.

By following the sample queries and scripts in section A.2.1, you should be able to complete the tasks for Feng and Ivan. If you want to check your results or get help completing these tasks, you can find our solution in the `scripts/lab-005-second-training.sh` file. We encourage you to experiment—or play—with this problem yourself before checking our solution.

appendix B
Survey of existing solutions

Deep learning systems are huge undertakings when implemented from scratch. In some situations, special requirements may warrant spending the extra effort to build a deep learning system from scratch. In other cases, given finite resources and time, it may make sense to use existing components, or even systems as a whole, and tailor them to your own needs.

The purpose of this appendix is to examine a few deep learning systems that have been implemented by different cloud vendors and open source communities. These operations range from serverless deployment to custom service container deployment. You will gain a sense of which pieces of these operations you can use to design your own project by comparing them with our reference architecture and highlighting their similarities and differences.

If you want to see a quick summarized comparison of every solution that we will cover, feel free to skip ahead to section B.5. Also, for your convenience, the reference architecture introduced in section 1.2.1 is reposted in figure B.1.

B.1 Amazon SageMaker

Amazon SageMaker is the umbrella term for its collection of artificial intelligence products that can be used together to form a complete deep learning system. In this section, we will review the suite of products and see how they compare with our key components. As mentioned at the beginning of this section, we make these comparisons so that you will learn what product will best help to build your own system.

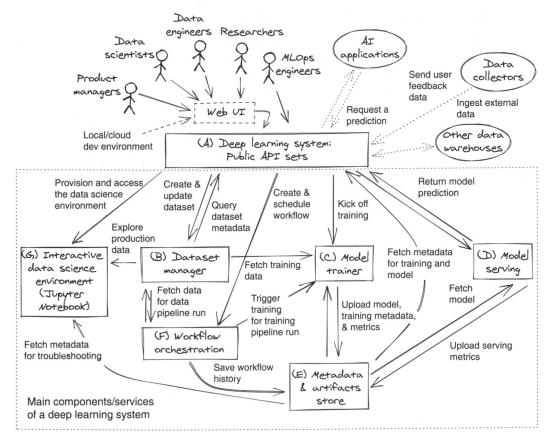

Figure B.1 An overview of a typical deep learning system that includes basic components to support a deep learning development cycle. This reference architecture can be used as a starting point and further tailored.

B.1.1 Dataset management

Amazon SageMaker does not offer a dataset management component that provides a unified interface to help manage the complex interaction of data preparation with the different types of users of a deep learning system. Amazon, however, does provide a collection of data storage, transformation, and querying solutions that can be used to build a data management component.

It is possible to build a data management component that collects raw data for Amazon S3, an object storage product. Metadata tagging can be backed by AWS Glue Data Catalog, which can be used by AWS Glue ETL for further processing into datasets that can be used for training. After reading chapter 2, you should be able to identify how you can use these Amazon products to build your own data management component.

B.1.2   Model training

Amazon SageMaker supports both built-in algorithms and externally provided custom code for training deep learning models. It also supports containers for training runs. It exposes an API that can be called to launch training jobs on demand. This is largely similar to the compute backend that powers the training component of a deep learning system, which is covered in this book. To implement the resource management portion of the training component, you may use the existing tools provided by Amazon, such as assigning resource limits and policies to different AWS Identity and Access Management (IAM) users or roles. If your organization requires extra control or sophistication or already has an identity provider implementation, you may need to spend more time building a custom solution. After reading chapters 3 and 4, you should be able to figure out how you can build your own training component with existing Amazon tools.

B.1.3   Model serving

Amazon SageMaker, in its most basic form, supports deploying trained models as web services that are accessible over the internet. For scaling out to host multiple models without deploying each of them to separate endpoints, SageMaker provides a multi-model endpoint that also comes with configurable model-caching behavior. These tools can come in handy if they fit your bill. As of the time of this writing, SageMaker supports multi-container endpoints and serial inference pipelines, which are similar to the serving architecture and DAG support described in this book. Chapters 6 and 7 review model-serving principles so that you will understand what existing tools you can use and how you can build your own when you encounter limitations with existing tools.

B.1.4   Metadata and artifacts store

As the component that centers around trained models, it is not surprising to see cloud vendors make products that do just that. The SageMaker Model Registry provides functionalities that map to many key concepts of the metadata and artifacts store of a deep learning system. For example, metadata, such as training metrics of a model and model versions, can be tracked using Model Registry. It does not, however, provide a storage solution for artifacts in the same component. You can easily build an interface on top of Model Registry and other Amazon storage products to provide the artifact storage aspect of this component.

Another important type of metadata that is tracked between artifacts is their lineage information. SageMaker provides ML Lineage Tracking as a separate feature that keeps tabs on this information automatically.

In chapter 8, we will discuss key concerns in building the metadata and artifacts store. After reading the chapter, you will understand the design principles behind this component and how existing products can help you to build your own quickly.

B.1.5 Workflow orchestration

On Amazon SageMaker, you can use the Model Building Pipelines product to manage your workflows, or *pipelines* (which is SageMaker terminology). Using this product, you can execute a set of actions, such as data preparation steps, training steps, and model validation steps, as one unit with a predefined order in an arbitrary fashion. To allow multiple types of users to work on the same problem, SageMaker also provides a Project product to help organize relationships between workflows, code versions, lineage information, and different access permissions for each user type.

In chapter 9, we review how to use a workflow manager to enable different modes of training. After reading the chapter, you will understand the reasoning behind the design and utility of a workflow manager in a deep learning system, as well as its role in an enterprise environment.

B.1.6 Experimentation

Amazon SageMaker provides a feature called Experiments that tags experimental runs with relevant tracking information and metrics. Indeed, this type of tracking information is also a kind of metadata, which is important to users of a deep learning system who need to evaluate the performance of different combinations of data input, training algorithms, and hyperparameters.

B.2 Google Vertex AI

Google Vertex AI, a combination of Google's AI platform offering and its AutoML product, provides a collection of tools and services that can be used as a deep learning system. In this section, we will review its offerings and compare them with key components introduced in this book.

B.2.1 Dataset management

Google Vertex AI provides a simple API to manage datasets, though you must first upload your object data to Google Cloud Storage and then upload metadata and annotation files that reference object data in Google Cloud Storage via the Vertex AI API. The dataset API is similar across different types of datasets (images, text, video, etc.) that provide a unified experience to developers. The API, however, does not provide versioning information and other lineage tracking information. In chapter 2, we explore core data management principles. After reading the chapter, you will be able to compare existing solutions and extend them or build from scratch for your own needs.

B.2.2 Model training

Google Vertex AI supports training with Docker containers. It provides prebuilt training containers for those who do not need further customization and also supports custom-built training containers for those who require more than what the prebuilt flavor provides. Its training service exposes an interface that allows the launching of training runs on either a single node or on multiple nodes for distributed training. When running distributed training, Vertex AI provides additional support with reduction to accelerate training. In chapters 3 and 4, we explore these features and the principles behind them. After reading these chapters, you will be able to determine what existing offerings you can use, how to extend them if you need more, and how to build it from scratch if you have more specific requirements.

B.2.3   Model serving

Google Vertex AI supports serving online inference requests to trained models, either with prebuilt inference containers or custom inference containers. Trained models are decoupled from containers and must be deployed with compute resources to form an endpoint that can serve online inference requests. Vertex AI supports deploying one model to multiple endpoints and supports deploying multiple models to a single endpoint. Different from other solutions that support various model types, deploying multiple models to a single endpoint in Vertex AI is primarily used for canarying new model versions using split traffic patterns. In Vertex AI, if you train a Vertex AI video model, it cannot be made to serve online inference requests.

In chapters 6 and 7, we learn the fundamental principles behind model serving. After completing these chapters, you will have a good understanding of model serving and will be able to decide whether existing solutions are sufficient for your needs. You will be able to build your own, as well as understand how to operate a model server efficiently and at scale.

B.2.4   Metadata and artifacts store

Vertex ML Metadata is Google's metadata store solution that can be used in a deep learning system. It uses a graph to describe relationships between artifacts such as datasets, training runs, and trained models. Each node and edge in the graph can be tagged with a list of key-value pairs to describe any metadata. When used properly, this can provide comprehensive lineage information for everything in a deep learning system.

Artifacts are not stored directly in Vertex ML Metadata. Artifacts are stored in Google Cloud Storage. Vertex ML Metadata uses a URI reference to point to these artifacts.

In chapter 8, we will explore a similar approach in building a metadata and artifacts store, where both can be managed through a single, unified interface. After reading the chapter, you will be able to tell how to leverage and extend existing solutions for your needs.

B.2.5   Workflow orchestration

With Google, you can use Vertex Pipelines to manage and operate your deep learning workflows. You can represent data preparation and training operations as steps in a pipeline. In Vertex Pipelines, steps are organized as nodes in a directed acyclic graph. Each step of the pipeline is implemented by a container. A run of a pipeline is in fact an orchestration of executions of containers.

In chapter 9, we review how to use a workflow manager to enable different modes of training. After reading the chapter, you will understand the reasoning behind the design and utility of a workflow manager in a deep learning system and its role in an enterprise environment.

B.2.6 Experimentation

Google Vertex AI Experiments provides a unified UI to create, track, and manage experiments. The Vertex AI SDK provides autologging support for model training code to record hyperparameters, metrics, and data lineage. When paired with Vertex ML Metadata, you can get a complete overview of all your model training experiment runs.

B.3 Microsoft Azure Machine Learning

Different from the classic ML Studio offering from Microsoft that focuses on a GUI approach to machine learning, Azure Machine Learning is a new suite of tools and services that also supports a wide variety of customization using code and established open source frameworks. In this section, we will compare their offerings to key components that are described in this book. After completing this section, you will gain a sense of what you can use as is, what you can extend, and what you need to build from scratch to fulfill your requirements.

B.3.1 Dataset management

On Azure Machine Learning, datasets are first-class objects that are inputs and outputs of data processing and training tasks. Datasets are defined as a collection of metadata associated with the raw data of the dataset. The dataset references its raw data via a URI reference to underlying data storage. Once a dataset is created, it becomes immutable. The underlying data, however, does not have the same guarantee, and it is up to you to manage its immutability.

Once datasets are defined, data processing and training codes can access them through a unified client API. Data can either be downloaded for local access or mounted as network storage for direct access. After reading chapter 2, you will be able to identify similarities between this paradigm and the one that is described in the book. You will learn how you can use this existing product as is and how you can extend it for your own needs.

B.3.2 Model training

Azure Machine Learning supplies prebuilt containers with Python distributions and allows users to define a custom-base image that conforms to specific requirements. As of this writing, only Python is supported for defining custom training code. To launch a training run, you need to specify a runtime container and a reference to training code that conforms to a certain convention. If you need something other than this setup, you will need to build your own training service. Chapters 3 and 4 will show you the key principles of a training service and an example that you can use as a starting point for your own training service.

B.3.3   *Model serving*

On Azure Machine Learning v2, an endpoint can be created to serve online inference requests. The endpoint can either be configured to load a certain model and use a Python script to produce inferences or be configured to use a completely custom container image—such as TensorFlow Serving—to produce inferences. Azure Machine Learning also integrates with NVIDIA Triton Inference Server, which provides additional performance gain when GPU is used to produce inferences.

If you need to deploy multiple models to a single endpoint or manage models and inference production on edge devices, you will need to build your own. In chapters 6 and 7, we discuss model serving in depth. After completing these chapters, you will be able to build your own model server should you require additional features that existing offerings do not support.

B.3.4   *Metadata and artifacts store*

In Azure Machine Learning, metadata can be tagged along many objects, such as models, training runs, etc., in the form of tags. While not a standalone product, the model registration capability supports additional metadata when registering a model. The interface receives the metadata as well as the model file (artifact) at the same time during registration, taking one less step when compared to other solutions that require models to be registered to already exist in their cloud storage.

As of this writing, a preview feature called registry can be used to centralize ML related metadata to one place. If you want to track lineage between different artifacts, though you may need to build your own solution.

After reading chapter 8, you will gain an in-depth understanding of the metadata and artifacts store. You will learn its fundamentals and will be able to quickly build one yourself.

B.3.5   *Workflow orchestration*

Azure Machine Learning provides a feature called *ML pipelines* that allows you to define data, training, and other tasks as steps. These steps are put together programmatically to form a pipeline that can be executed periodically based on a schedule or trigger or be launched once manually. Compute resources, execution environment, and access permissions can be configured programmatically when the pipeline is defined.

In chapter 9, we review how to use a workflow manager to enable different modes of training. After reading the chapter, you will understand the reasoning behind the design and utility of a workflow manager in a deep learning system and its role in an enterprise environment.

B.3.6 Experimentation

Azure Machine Learning provides a feature for defining and tracking experiments. When model training is being performed as part of an experiment, metrics can be logged from the training code and visualized through the web interface. It also supports arbitrary tagging and parent-child relationships between experiment runs for a hierarchical organization and lookup.

B.4 Kubeflow

Kubeflow is an open source suite of tools that provides many useful components for building a deep learning system without being locked into a particular cloud vendor. In this section, we walk through the list of key components that are introduced in this book and compare them with similar components provided by Kubeflow.

B.4.1 Dataset management

Kubeflow's vision is to not reinvent any existing tools, so it should not be a surprise that it does not come with a data management component, as other open source solutions exist. In chapter 2, we review some open source data management solutions and explore how they can be further extended to implement key principles described in that chapter.

B.4.2 Model training

Kubeflow, being a suite of tools that is based on Kubernetes, has the luxury of being backed by a sophisticated resource scheduler. Unlike cloud vendors that provide pre-built model training containers, you must build your own and manage their launches. In chapters 3 and 4, we talk about the principles of a training service and how it helps to abstract the complexity in resource assignment and scheduling. We go over a reference training service, and you learn how to build one yourself for your requirements.

B.4.3 Model serving

As of this writing, Kubeflow provides a KServe component that can be used to deploy trained models as an inference service, which serves inference requests over the network. It is an interface that sits on top of existing serving frameworks such as TensorFlow Serving, PyTorch TorchServe, and NVIDIA Triton Inference Server. The main benefit of using KServe is the additional abstraction of operational complexity such as autoscaling, health checks, and auto-recovery. Because it is an open source solution, it is possible to host either one model or multiple models with the same endpoint. In chapters 6 and 7, we will go through model serving principles so that you will understand the reason behind the design of popular serving interfaces and how you can customize them to fit your own needs.

B.4.4 Metadata and artifacts store

Starting with Kubeflow version 1.3, metadata and artifacts become an integral part of Kubeflow Pipelines. Kubeflow Pipelines consist of a graph of pipeline components.

Between each component, parameters and artifacts can be passed along. Similar to the description in this book, artifacts encapsulate any kind of data that is the side effect of a deep learning system, such as the model itself, training metrics, and data distribution metrics. Metadata is any data that describes pipeline components and artifacts. With these constructs, you can deduce the lineage between input training datasets, trained models, experiment results, and served inferences.

In chapter 8, we discuss key concerns for building the metadata and artifacts store. After reading the chapter, you will understand the design principles behind this component and how existing products can help you build your own quickly.

B.4.5   *Workflow orchestration*

Also described in the previous section, Kubeflow Pipelines can be used to help manage deep learning data preparation and training workflows. Metadata and versioning are built into pipelines, and native users and access permissions from Kubernetes can be used to restrict access.

In chapter 9, we review how a workflow manager enables different modes of training. After reading the chapter, you will understand the reasoning behind the design and utility of a workflow manager in a deep learning system.

B.4.6   *Experimentation*

Kubeflow Pipelines provides the Experiment construct in which multiple training runs can be organized into a logical group, where it provides additional visualization tools for differences between each experimental run. This fits well with offline experimentation. If you need to perform online experimentation, you will need to roll your own solution.

B.5   *Side-by-side comparison*

We think it will be handy to provide a summarized overview table of every solution grouped by components that we have covered previously. We hope that table B.1 will make it easier for you to pick the right solution.

Table B.1   Side-by-side comparison

	Amazon SageMaker	Google Vertex AI	Microsoft Azure Machine Learning	Kubeflow
Comparing dataset management solutions	AWS components, such as S3, Glue Data Catalog, and Glue ETL, can be used to build a dataset management component.	APIs for managing datasets are ready to use. Data content upload and metadata tagging are separate operations.	Datasets are first-class objects and are immutable once created. A unified client API is provided for training jobs to access training datasets.	Does not provide a dataset management solution. Other open source alternatives are readily available.

Table B.1   Side-by-side comparison *(continued)*

	Amazon SageMaker	Google Vertex AI	Microsoft Azure Machine Learning	Kubeflow
Comparing model training solutions	Supports built-in algorithms, externally provided custom code, and custom containers for training. Exposes an API for launching training jobs on demand.	Provides prebuilt training containers that can be used as is. Supports custom training containers. Exposes an API that supports launching training containers on multiple nodes.	Provides prebuilt training containers with Python that can be customized. Training containers must conform to a certain convention.	Has native access to Kubernetes scheduling capabilities. No prebuilt training containers are provided.
Comparing model serving solutions	Models can be deployed as web endpoints. Multiple models can be deployed to the same endpoint for better utilization, with some limitations when GPUs are used. Configurable model caching behavior.	Models and inference containers are decoupled. They must be deployed together to form a web endpoint for serving. Custom inference containers are supported. Multiple models per endpoint are primarily used for canarying new versions of models. Video models are not supported.	Endpoints can be deployed to serve models over the web. Endpoints are configured to use a particular model with a custom Python script for producing inferences. NVIDIA Triton Inference Server integration is available.	KServe is the Kubeflow component that serves models. It provides a serverless inferencing abstraction on top of popular serving frameworks such as TensorFlow Serving, PyTorch TorchServe, and NVIDIA Triton Inference Server.
Comparing metadata and artifacts store solutions	SageMaker Model Registry provides a central metadata store solution. Artifacts are stored separately in Amazon's object store.	Vertex ML Metadata provides a central metadata store solution. Metadata is stored as graphs that can describe complex relationships. Artifacts are stored in Google's object store.	A preview feature called registry can be used to centralize ML metadata. Metadata exists as tags of different objects (training runs, models, etc.), and objects can be artifacts. Lineage information can be deduced using these object tags.	Does not have a central repository of metadata or artifacts. Metadata and artifacts are integral parts of Kubeflow Pipelines. Each stage in the pipeline can be annotated with metadata and produce artifacts that can be tracked. Lineage information can be deduced from this information that can be retrieved from the Pipelines API.

Table B.1   Side-by-side comparison *(continued)*

	Amazon SageMaker	Google Vertex AI	Microsoft Azure Machine Learning	Kubeflow
Comparing workflow orchestration solutions	Model Building Pipelines can be used to build and manage deep learning workflows.	Vertex ML Metadata provides a central metadata store solution. Metadata is stored as graphs that can describe complex relationships. Artifacts are stored in Google's object store.	A preview feature called registry can be used to centralize ML metadata. Metadata exists as tags of different objects (training runs, models, etc.), and objects can be artifacts. Lineage information can be deduced using these object tags.	Does not have a central repository of metadata or artifacts. Metadata and artifacts are integral parts of Kubeflow Pipelines. Each stage in the pipeline can be annotated with metadata and produce artifacts that can be tracked. Lineage information can be deduced from the details that can be retrieved from the Pipelines API.
Comparing experimentation solutions	The Experiments feature provides grouping and tracking for training runs.	Provides Vertex AI Experiments for tracking and visualizing experiment setups and run results.	Provides features for defining and tracking experiments. Experiments can be associated with a parent-child relationship. The web interface supports visualization.	Provides an Experiment construct for logical grouping of Kubeflow Pipelines that belong to the same experiment group. Visualization tools are provided to highlight differences between each pipeline run in the same experiment.

appendix C
Creating an HPO service with Kubeflow Katib

We will introduce you to an open source hyperparameter optimization (HPO) service—Kubeflow Katib—that addresses virtually all the HPO requirements we discussed in chapter 5. We strongly recommend that you consider adopting Katib before building your HPO service. Along with showing you how to use Katib, we will also cover its system design and its codebase to make you comfortable with the open source service.

As a member of the Kubeflow family, Katib is a cloud-native, scalable, and production-ready hyperparameter optimization system. In addition, Katib is agnostic to the machine learning framework or programming language. Also, Katib is written in Go, takes a Kubernetes-native approach, and runs standalone in a Kubernetes cluster. In addition to hyperparameter optimization with early stopping support, Katib supports neural architecture search (NAS).

There are many advantages to Katib, including its ability to support multitenancy and distributed training, its cloud nativeness, and its extensibility, all of which distinguish it from other systems. No matter if you manage your server cluster using Kubernetes in the cloud or on your local server, Katib is the best choice. In this chapter, we will tour Katib in the following five steps: Katib overview, how to use Katib, Katib system design and code reading, expediting HPO execution, and adding customized HPO algorithms to Katib.

C.1 Katib overview

Katib manages HPO experiments and computing resources in a black-box fashion, so Katib users only need to provide training code and define the HPO execution plan, and then Katib will take care of the rest. Figure C.1 shows Katib's system overview.

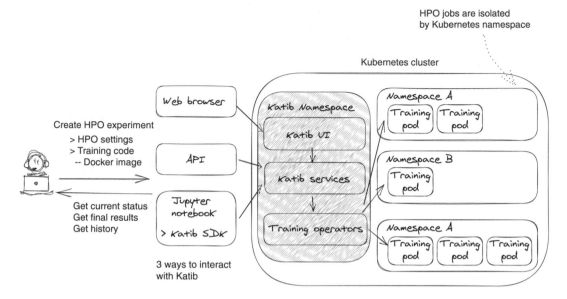

Figure C.1   Katib system overview. Katib components run as Kubernetes native services, and Katib supports three types of user interfaces: UI, API, and SDK.

In figure C.1, we see that Katib exposes three types of user interfaces for the user's convenience: a web UI, a Python SDK, and a set of APIs. Users can run HPO via a web page, a Jupyter notebook, Kubernetes commands, and an HTTP request.

From a user perspective, Katib is a remote system. To run HPO, a user submits an experiment request to Katib, and Katib executes the HPO experiment for them. To build the experiment request, users need to do two things: first, Dockerize the training code and expose the hyperparameters they want to optimize as external variables; second, create an experiment object that defines the spec of the HPO experiment, such as HPO algorithm, trial budget, or hyperparameters and their value search space. Once the experiment object is created inside Katib, Katib will allocate computing resources to start the HPO execution.

Katib runs inside a Kubernetes cluster. Katib service itself doesn't consume a lot of memory or disk space; it launches Kubernetes pod to run model training jobs (HPO trials) for testing different hyperparameter suggestions. Katib can run training jobs in different namespaces for different users to create resource segregation.

C.2   *Getting started with Katib*

In this section, we will look at how to operate Katib. First, we install Katib locally and then explain the terms, and finally, we show you a Katib end-to-end use case.

> ### Why talk about Katib operation and installation in a design book?
>
> Ideally, we don't want to include installation and user guides for software in a design book, because this information might become stale right after the book is published, and we can find the living doc on its official website. Here are two reasons why we violated our rules.
>
> First, because we recommend you use Katib instead of building your own service, we are obligated to show you the complete user experience, both from the perspective of a Katib user (a data scientist) and a Katib operator (an engineer). Second, to understand Katib's design and learn how to read its codebase, it's best to first explain its terminology and typical user workflow. Once you comprehend how Katib works, you'll have a much easier time reading its code.

C.2.1 Step 1: Installation

If you install the Kubeflow system (https://mng.bz/WAp4), then Katib is included. But if you are only interested in HPO, you can install Katib standalone. Katib is actively evolving and well maintained, so please check its official installation document "Getting Started with Katib: Installing Katib" (http://mng.bz/81YZ) for the up-to-date installation tips.

C.2.2 Step 2: Understanding Katib terms

For a Katib user, experiment, suggestion, and trial are the three most important entities/concepts with which to familiarize yourself. The definitions are as follows.

EXPERIMENT

An experiment is a single optimization run; it is an end-to-end HPO process. An experiment configuration contains the following main components: a Docker image for training code, an objective metric (aka target value) for what we want to optimize, hyperparameters to tune, and a value search space and HPO algorithm.

SUGGESTION

A suggestion is a set of hyperparameter values that the HPO algorithm has proposed. Katib creates a trial job to evaluate the suggested set of values.

TRIAL

A trial is one iteration of the experiment. A trial takes one suggestion, executes a training process (a trial job) to produce a model, and evaluates the model performance.

Each experiment runs a trial loop. The experiment keeps scheduling new trials until either the objective is met or the configured maximum number of trials is reached. You can see more of Katib concepts' explanation in Katib's official doc "Introduction to Katib" (http://mng.bz/ElBo).

C.2.3 Step 3: Packaging training code to Docker image

Compared to the HPO library approaches (section 5.4), the biggest difference is that the HPO service approach requires us to package model training code to a Docker image. This is because the HPO service needs to run the HPO training experiment in a remote cluster, and a Docker image is the ideal method to run the model training code remotely.

There are two things we need to pay attention to when preparing the Docker image: defining hyperparameters as command-line arguments of the training code and reporting training metrics to Katib. Let's look at an example.

First, we define the hyperparameters needed to be optimized as command-line arguments in the training code. Because Katib needs to execute the training code as a docker container for different hyperparameter values, the training code needs to take the hyperparameter value from the command-line arguments. In the next code example, we define two hyperparameters to tune: lr (learning rate) and batch size. During the HPO process, Katib will pass in the values at the training container launching time; see the code that follows:

```
def main():
  parser = argparse.ArgumentParser( \
    description="PyTorch MNIST Example")
  parser.add_argument("--batch-size", \          ◁─────┐   Parses the
    type=int, default=64, metavar="N", \                │   hyperparameter
    help="input batch size for training (default: 64)") │   value from the
  parser.add_argument("--lr", \                          │   command line
    type=float, default=0.01, metavar="LR", \    ◁─────┘   arguments
    help="learning rate (default: 0.01)")
```

Second, we let the training code report training metrics, especially the objective metrics, to Katib, so it can track the progress and result of each trial execution. Katib can collect metrics from the following three places: stdout (OS standard output location), an arbitrary file, and TensorFlow events. If you have special metric collection or storage requirements, you can also write your own metric collection container.

The simplest option is to print evaluation (objective) metrics to stdout from your training code and collect them with Katib's standard metrics collector. For example, if we define our objective metric as Validation-accuracy and want the HPO process to find optimal HP to minimize this value, we can write the following logs to stdout. Katib standard metric collector will detect Validation-accuracy=0.924463 in the stdout and parse the value. See a sample stdout output as follows:

```
2022-01-23T05:19:53Z INFO  Epoch[5] Train-accuracy=0.932769
2022-01-23T05:19:53Z INFO  Epoch[5] Time cost=31.698
2022-01-23T05:19:54Z INFO  Epoch[5] Validation-accuracy=0.924463
2022-01-23T05:19:58Z INFO  Epoch[6] Batch [0-100] Speed: 1749.16 ..
```

The default regex format Katib uses to parse objective metrics from the log is ([\w|-]+)\s*=\s*([+-]?\d*(\.\d+)?([Ee][+-]?\d+)?). You can define your own regex format at .source.filter.metricsFormat in the experiment configuration file. Please check out the Metrics Collector section (http://mng.bz/NmvN) of the Katib doc "Running an Experiment" for more details.

To get you started, Katib provides a list of sample training codes and sample Docker image files to show you how to package your training code. These examples are written for different training frameworks, such as TensorFlow, PyTorch, MXNet, and more. You can find these samples in the Katib GitHub repo (http://mng.bz/DZln).

C.2.4 *Step 4: Configuring an experiment*

Now that you have the training code ready, we can start to prepare an HPO experiment in Katib. We just need to create an Experiment CRD (customer resource definition) object in Katib.

By using Kubernetes API or the `kubectl` command, we can create the experiment CRD by specifying a YAML configuration. See the following config as an example. For ease of reading, we divided the sample config into three chunks. Let's go over each chunk individually.

FIRST SECTION: OBJECTIVE

The first section is to define the goal of an HPO experiment and determine how to measure the performance of each trial (training execution). Katib uses the value of `objectiveMetric` and `additionalMetric` as the objective value to monitor how the suggested hyperparameters work with the model. If the objective value in a trial reaches the goal, Katib will mark the suggested hyperparameters as the best value and stop further trials in the experimentation.

For the following configuration, the objective metric is set as `Validation-accuracy` and the goal is set to `0.99`:

```
apiVersion: kubeflow.org/v1beta1
kind: Experiment
metadata:
 namespace: kubeflow
 name: bayesian-optimization
spec:
  Objective:
    type: maximize
    goal: 0.99
    objectiveMetricName: Validation-accuracy      <┐  Defines the
    additionalMetricNames:                           │  objective
      - Train-accuracy                               ┘  metric
```

SECOND SECTION: THE HPO ALGORITHM AND HYPERPARAMETERS

After setting the HPO objective, we can configure the HPO algorithm and declare their search spaces and the hyperparameters that need to be tuned. Let's look at these configs separately.

The *algorithm config* specifies the HPO algorithm we want Katib to use for the experiment. In the current example, we chose the Bayesian optimization algorithm (http://mng.bz/lJw6). Katib supports many cutting-edge HPO algorithms; you can see them in the Katib official doc "Running an Experiment" in the section Search

Algorithm in Detail (http://mng.bz/BlV0). You can also add your own HPO algorithm to Katib, which we will discuss in section C.5.

ParallelTrialCount, maxTrialCount, and maxFailedTrialCount: are self-explanatory by their names, which define how the trials are scheduled for experimentation. In this example, we run three trials in parallel, with a total of 12 trials. The experiment stops if we have three failed trials.

The *parameters config* defines the hyperparameters to tune and their value search space. Katib selects hyperparameter values in the search space based on the hyperparameter tuning algorithm that you specified. See the following code:

```
algorithm:
  algorithmName: bayesianoptimization        ◁──── Uses the Bayesian
  algorithmSettings:                                optimization algorithm
    - name: "random_state"                          provided by Katib
      value: "10"
parallelTrialCount: 3
maxTrialCount: 12
maxFailedTrialCount: 3
Parameters:                    ◁──── Defines hyperparameters
  - name: lr                          to optimize and their
    parameterType: double             value search space
    feasibleSpace:
      min: "0.01"
      max: "0.03"
  - name: num-layers
    parameterType: int
    feasibleSpace:
      min: "2"
      max: "5"
  - name: optimizer
    parameterType: categorical
    feasibleSpace:
      list:
        - sgd
        - adam
        - ftrl
```

LAST SECTION: TRIAL CONFIGURATION

In this *trial template config*, we define what training code (Docker image) to execute and what hyperparameters are passed to the training code. Katib has built-in jobs for almost every model training framework—such as TensorFlow, PyTorch MXNet job types, and more—which takes care of the actual training execution in Kubernetes.

For example, if we want to run distributed training in an HPO trial for a PyTorch training code, which requires setting up a distributed group, we can define the trial as a PyTorch job type. Katib will run the distributed training for you.

In the following example, we define the trial as the default job type Kubernetes Job. In the experimentation, Katib will run the trial job as a Kubernetes pod, using no special customized configuration for the training code; see the code as follows:

```
trialTemplate:
  primaryContainerName: training-container
  trialParameters:                          ◁──┐ Declares hyperparameters
    - name: learningRate                        │ for the training code
      description: Learning rate for the training model
      reference: lr
    - name: numberLayers
      description: Number of training model layers
      reference: num-layers
    - name: optimizer
      description: Training model optimizer (sdg, adam or ftrl)
      reference: optimizer
  trialSpec:                      ◁──┐ Configures
    apiVersion: batch/v1              │ the training
    kind: Job                         │ container
    spec:
      template:
        spec:
          containers:
            - name: training-container
              image: docker.io/kubeflowkatib/mxnet-mnist:latest
              command:
                - "python3"
                - "/opt/mxnet-mnist/mnist.py"
                - "--batch-size=64"
                - "--lr=${trialParameters.learningRate}"
                - "--num-layers=${trialParameters.numberLayers}"
                - "--optimizer=${trialParameters.optimizer}"
          restartPolicy: Never
```

Configures how to execute the training code

Katib provides sample experiment configuration files for each HPO algorithm it supports; you can find them in the Katib GitHub repo: `katib/examples/v1beta1/hp-tuning/` (http://mng.bz/dJVN)

C.2.5   *Step 5: Start the experiment*

Once we define the experiment configuration and save it in a YAML file, we can run the following command to start the experiment:

```
% kubectl apply -f bayesian-optimization.yaml
experiment.kubeflow.org/bayesian-optimization created

% kubectl get experiment -n kubeflow
NAME                    TYPE      STATUS   AGE
bayesian-optimization   Created   True     46s
```

From the return message of the `kubectl get experiment -n kubeflow`, we see the experiment `bayesian-optimization` is created as an Experiment CRD resource. From now on, Katib will own the HPO experiment completely until a result is obtained.

> **NOTE**   Katib completely relies on Kubernetes CRD objects to manage the HPO experiments and trials. It also uses CRD objects to store metrics and status for its HPO activities, so we say Katib is a Kubernetes native application.

Besides the previous `kubectl` commands, we can also start an experiment by using Katib SDK, by using its web UI, or by sending HTTP requests.

C.2.6   Step 6: Query progress and result

You can check the experiment running status by using the following commands:

```
% kubectl describe experiment bayesian-optimization -n kubeflow
```

The `kubectl describe` command will return all the information about the experiment, such as its configuration, metadata, and status. From a progress tracking perspective, we are mostly interested in the status section. See the following example:

```
Status:
  Completion Time:   2022-01-23T05:27:19Z
  Conditions:                                          ⟵ ┤ Experiment
    .. .. ..                                               history
    Message:                Experiment is created
    Type:                   Created
    .. .. ..
    Message:                Experiment is running
    Reason:                 ExperimentRunning
    Status:                 False
    Type:                   Running
    .. .. ..
    Message:                Experiment has succeeded because max trial count
     has reached
    Reason:                 ExperimentMaxTrialsReached
    Status:                 True
    Type:                   Succeeded
  Current Optimal Trial:
    Best Trial Name:  bayesian-optimization-9h25bvq9
    Observation:
      Metrics:
        Latest:    0.979001
        Max:       0.979001
        Min:       0.955713
        Name:      Validation-accuracy
        Latest:    0.992621
        Max:       0.992621
        Min:       0.906333
        Name:      Train-accuracy
    Parameter Assignments:
      Name:     lr
      Value:    0.014183662191100063
      Name:     num-layers
      Value:    3
      Name:     optimizer
      Value:    sgd
    Start Time:  2022-01-23T05:13:00Z
  Succeeded Trial List:
    .. .. ..
    bayesian-optimization-5s59vfwc
    bayesian-optimization-r8lnnv48
```

Metadata of the current best trial ⟶ (points to `Current Optimal Trial:`)

The objective metrics of the current best trial ⟶ (points to `Metrics:`)

Hyperparameters' value used in the current best trial ⟵ (points to `Parameter Assignments:`)

The list of finished trials ⟵ (points to `Succeeded Trial List:`)

```
    bayesian-optimization-9h25bvq9
    .. .. ..
  Trials:            12
  Trials Succeeded:  12
```

Here are a few explanations of the previous sample response:

- *Status/conditions*—Shows current and previous states. In the previous example, we see that the experiment went through three states: created, ran, and succeeded. From the message, we know the experiment completes because it runs out the training budget—the max trial count.
- *Current optimal trial*—Displays the current "best" trial and the hyperparameter values the trial used. It also shows the statistics of the objective metrics. As the experiment progresses, these values will keep updating until all the trials in the experiment are completed, and then we take status.currentOptimalTrial .parameterAssignment (the hyperparameter value assignment) as the final result.
- *Succeeded trial lists/failed trial lists/trials*—Shows how the experiment is progressing by listing all the trials the experiment executes.

C.2.7 Step 7: Troubleshooting

If there are failed trials, we can run the following command to check the error message of the failed trial job. See the failed HPO example as follows:

```
-> % k describe trial bayesian-optimization-mnist-pytorch-88c9rdjx \
    -n kubeflow
Name:           bayesian-optimization-mnist-pytorch-88c9rdjx
.. .. ..
Kind:           Trial
Spec:
  .. .. ..
  Parameter Assignments:
    Name:             lr
    Value:            0.010547476197421666
    Name:             num-layers
    Value:            3
    Name:             optimizer
    Value:            ftrl

Status:
  Completion Time:  2022-01-23T06:23:50Z
  Conditions:
    .. .. ..
    Message:  Trial has failed. Job message: Job has reached the specified
      backoff limit
    Reason:   TrialFailed. Job reason: BackoffLimitExceeded     <-| Failure
    .. .. ..                                                      | message
```

From the return data, we can see the hyperparameter values used in the trial and the associated error message.

Besides the error message from the `describe` command, we can also find the root cause by checking the logs of the training container. If you choose to use the Katib standard metric collector, Katib will run a `metrics-logger-and-collector` container with your training code container in the same pod. That metric collector captures all the stdout logging from your training container; you can check these logs by using the following command: `kubectl logs ${trial_pod} -c metrics-logger-and-collector -n kubeflow`. See a sample command as follows:

```
% kubectl logs bayesian-optimization-mkqgq6nm--1-qnbtt -c \
    metrics-logger-and-collector -n kubeflow
```

The `logs` command outputs lots of valuable information, such as initial parameters to the training process, dataset download results, and model training metrics. In the following sample log output, we can see `Validation-accuracy` and `Train-accuracy`. Katib metric collector will parse these values out because they are defined as the objective metric in the experiment configuration:

```
Trial Name: bayesian-optimization-mkqgq6nm
2022-01-23T05:17:17Z INFO  start with arguments Namespace(
add_stn=False, batch_size=64, disp_batches=100,
 dtype='float32', gc_threshold=0.5, gc_type='none', gpus=None,
image_shape='1, 28, 28', … warmup_epochs=5,
warmup_strategy='linear', wd=0.0001)
I0123 05:17:20.159784    16 main.go:136] 2022-01-23T05:17:20Z INFO
    downloaded http://data.mxnet.io/data/mnist/t10k-labels-idx1-ubyte.gz
 ➥ into t10k-labels-idx1-ubyte.gz successfully
.. .. ..
I0123 05:17:26.711552      16 main.go:136] 2022-01-23T05:17:26Z INFO
    Epoch[0] Train-accuracy=0.904084
.. .. ..
I0123 05:17:26.995733      16 main.go:136] 2022-01-23T05:17:26Z INFO
    Epoch[0] Validation-accuracy=0.920482
I0123 05:17:27.576586      16 main.go:136] 2022-01-23T05:17:27Z INFO
   Epoch[1] Batch [0-100]  Speed: 20932.09 samples/sec  accuracy=0.926825
I0123 05:17:27.871579      16 main.go:136] 2022-01-23T05:17:27Z INFO
   Epoch[1] Batch [100-200]  Speed: 21657.24 samples/sec  accuracy=0.930937
```

Annotations on the log output:
- **Trial name** → `Trial Name: bayesian-optimization-mkqgq6nm`
- **Initial parameters of the training trial** → `start with arguments Namespace(`
- **Dataset download** → `into t10k-labels-idx1-ubyte.gz successfully`
- **Additional metric value** → `Epoch[0] Train-accuracy=0.904084`
- **Objective metric value** → `Epoch[0] Validation-accuracy=0.920482`

C.3   Expedite HPO

HPO is a time-consuming and expensive operation. Katib offers three methods to expedite the process: parallel trials, distributed training, and early stopping.

C.3.1   Parallel trials

By specifying `parallelTrialCount` in the experiment configuration, you can run trials parallelly. One thing we should be aware of is that some HPO algorithms don't support parallel trial execution. Because this type of algorithm has a linear requirement on the trial execution sequence, the next trial needs to wait until the current trial completes.

C.3.2   *Distributed trial (training) job*

To get trial jobs completed faster, Katib allows us to enable distributed training for running training code. As we explained in C.2 (step 4), Katib defines different job types in `trialTemplate` for different training frameworks, such as PyTorch, TensorFlow, and MXNet.

The following is an example of how to enable distributed training (one master, two workers) for a PyTorch training code in the Katib experiment:

```
trialTemplate:
  primaryContainerName: pytorch
  trialParameters:          ◀─┐
    - name: learningRate
      description: Learning rate for the training model
      reference: lr
    - name: momentum
      description: Momentum for the training model
      reference: momentum
  trialSpec:
      apiVersion: kubeflow.org/v1
      kind: PyTorchJob    ◀─┐
      spec:
        pytorchReplicaSpecs:
          Master:
            replicas: 1
            restartPolicy: OnFailure
            template:
              spec:
                containers:
                  - name: pytorch
                    image: docker.io/kubeflowkatib/pytorch-mnist:latest
                    command:
                      - "python3"
                      - "/opt/pytorch-mnist/mnist.py"
                      - "--epochs=1"
                      - "--lr=${trialParameters.learningRate}"
                      - "--momentum=${trialParameters.momentum}"
          Worker:
            replicas: 2
            restartPolicy: OnFailure
            template:
              spec:
                containers:
                  - name: pytorch
                    image: docker.io/kubeflowkatib/pytorch-mnist:latest
                    command:
                      - "python3"
                      - "/opt/pytorch-mnist/mnist.py"
                      - "--epochs=1"
                      - "--lr=${trialParameters.learningRate}"
                      - "--momentum=${trialParameters.momentum}"
```

Declares learning rate and momentum as hyperparameters

Sets the trial job type as PyTorch

Configures the master trainer

Configures the worker trainer

In the previous example, we see the only difference compared to the nondistributed experiment configuration in section C.2 (step 4) is the `trialSpec` section. The job type now changes to `PyTorchJob`, and it has separate settings, such as replicas numbers, for the master and worker trainer. You can find the details of the Katib training operator and their configuration examples in the following two GitHub repositories: Kubeflow training operator (https://github.com/kubeflow/training-operator) and Katib operator configuration examples (http://mng.bz/rdgB).

C.3.3 Early stopping

Another useful trick Katib offers is early stopping. Early stopping ends the trial when its objective metric(s) no longer improves. It saves computing resources and reduces execution times by cutting off the unpromising trials.

The advantage of using early stopping in Katib is that we only need to update our experiment configuration file without modifying our training code. Simply define `.earlyStopping.algorithmName` and `.earlyStopping.algorithmSettings` in the `.spec.algorithm` section and you are good to go.

The current early stopping algorithm Katib supports is median stopping rules, which stops a trial if the trial's best objective value is worse than the median value of the running averages of all other completed trials' objectives reported up to the same step. Please read more details in the Katib official doc "Using Early Stopping."

C.4 Katib system design

Finally, we can talk about our favorite topic—system design. By reading sections C.2 and C.3, you should have a clear sense of how Katib solves HPO problems from a user perspective. This builds a great foundation for understanding Katib's system design.

As we have seen, Katib is not only solving the HPO problem but also addressing it in production quality. Normally, such a powerful system has a large and complicated codebase, but Katib is an exception. Because the core Katib's components are all implemented in a sample design pattern—Kubernetes controller/operator pattern—if you understand one component, you understand almost the entire system. By following our introduction in this section, reading the Katib source code will be straightforward for you.

C.4.1 Kubernetes controller/operator pattern

We have discussed the controller design pattern in section 3.4.2. However, to help you remember, we reposted figure 3.10 as figure C.2 here. If figure C.2 doesn't look familiar, please revisit section 3.4.2.

C.4.2 Katib system design and workflow

Figure C.2 illustrates Katib's internal components and their interactions. The system has three core components: experiment controller (marked as A), suggestion controller (marked as B), and trial controller (marked as C).

The experiment controller manages HPO experiments throughout its lifecycle, such as scheduling HPO trials for an experiment and updating its status. The suggestion controller runs HPO algorithms to provide suggested values for given hyperparameters. And the trial controller runs the actual model training for a given set of hyperparameters.

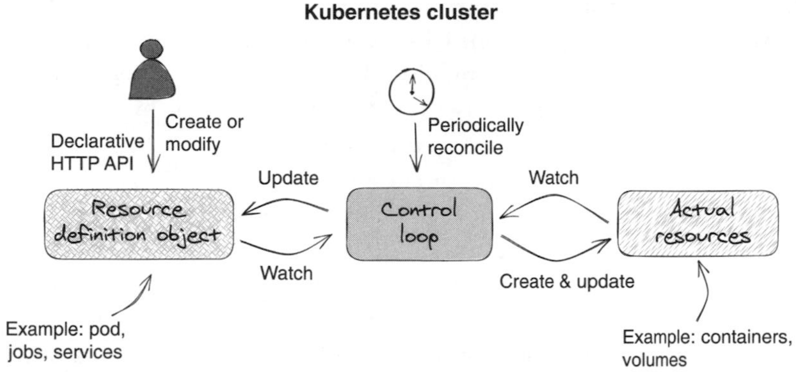

Kubernetes cluster

Resource
definition object

Control
loop

Actual
resources

Declarative
HTTP API

Create or
modify

Update

Watch

Periodically
reconcile

Watch

Create & update

Example: pod,
jobs, services

Example: containers,
volumes

**Figure C.2 The Kubernetes controller/operator pattern runs an infinite control
loop that watches the actual state (on the right) and desired state (on the left) of
certain Kubernetes resources and tries to move its actual state to the desired one.**

From the names of these core components, you know their implementations all follow
the Kubernetes controller pattern. Besides the controller, Katib defines a set of CRD
objects (spec) to work with these three controllers. For example, *experiment spec* is a
type of CRD that defines the desired state for an HPO experiment and works as an
input request to the experiment controller.

As shown in figure C.3, Alex, a data scientist, might follow a typical workflow when
interacting with Katib. The major steps are listed in the following sections.

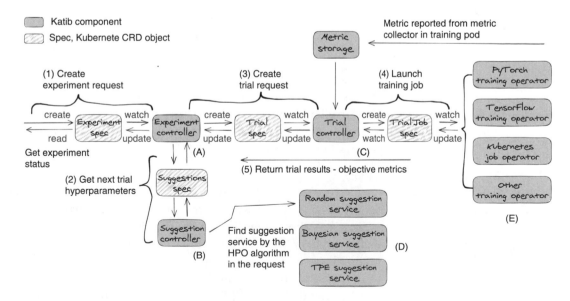

Figure C.3   A Katib system design graph and user workflow

STEP 1: CREATING AN EXPERIMENT REQUEST

In step 1, Alex creates an experiment CRD object by using client tools, such as Katib SDK, Katib web UI, or `kubectl` commands. This experiment object contains all the HPO experiment definitions, such as the training algorithm, hyperparameters and their search spaces, HPO algorithm, and trial budget.

The experiment controller (component A) periodically scans all the experiment CRD objects. For every experiment CRD object, it creates the declared suggestion CRD object and trial CRD object. In short, the experiment controller spawns the actual resources to achieve the desired state defined in the experiment CRD. Additionally, it keeps the experiment's runtime status updated in the experiment's CRD object, so Alex can see trial hyperparameters and the execution status of the experiment in real time.

Once Alex's experiment object has been created in step 1, Katib deploys an HPO algorithm suggestion service (component D) for Alex's experiment so that the required HPO algorithm can be run. In this suggestion service, the HPO search algorithm (library) defined in the experiment CRD object is loaded and exposed through a gRPC interface, allowing the suggestion controller to talk to it and ask for suggested hyperparameters.

STEP 2: GET THE NEXT TRIAL HYPERPARAMETERS

When the experiment controller finds Alex's experiment CRD object in step 2, it creates a suggestion CRD object as an input request for the suggestion controller (component B). Hyperparameters and their values are specified in this suggestion CRD object, as well as the search algorithm and the number of suggestions.

Afterward, the suggestion controller calls the suggestion algorithm service, created in step 1, to calculate the suggested hyperparameter values. Additionally, the suggestion controller maintains the history of the suggested hyperparameter values in the suggestion CRD objects.

STEP 3: CREATE A TRIAL REQUEST

As part of step 3, after the suggestion controller provides a set of trial hyperparameter values, the experiment controller (component A) creates a trial CRD object to kick off a model training trial. The trial trains the model using the set of hyperparameter values calculated by the suggestion service (component D).

STEP 4: LAUNCH TRAINING JOB

In step 4, the trial controller (component C) reads the newly created trial CRD objects (created in step 3) and creates a TrialJob CRD object. There are several types of Trial-Job CRD objects, including Kubernetes jobs, PyTorch jobs, TF jobs, and MXNet jobs. For each job type, Kubeflow (https://www.kubeflow.org/docs/components/training/) provides a dedicated training operator to execute it, such as a PyTorch training operator or TensorFlow training operator (component E).

Upon detecting a newly created TrialJob CRD object in its type, the training operator (component E) creates Kubernetes pods to execute the training image based on the hyperparameters defined in the trial job. The training trials for Alex's HPO experiment will be run by a PyTorch training operator because his training code is written in PyTorch.

STEP 5: RETURN TRIAL RESULT

As the model trial training begins, the metric collector sidecar (a Docker container in a Kubernetes training pod) collects training metrics and reports them to the Katib metric storage (a MySQL database) in step 5. Using these metrics, the trial controller (component C) updates the trial execution status to the trial CRD object. When the experiment controller notices the latest changes on the trial CRD object, it reads the change and updates the experiment CRD object with the latest trial execution information, so the experiment object has the latest status. The latest status is aggregated into the experiment object in this way.

The HPO workflow is essentially a trial loop. To work on Alex's HPO request in Katib, steps 2, 3, 4, and 5 in this workflow keep repeating until the exit criterion is met. Alex can check the experiment CRD object throughout the HPO execution process to obtain the timely execution status of the HPO, which includes the number of completed or failed trials, the model training metrics, and the current best hyperparameter values.

> **NOTE**   Simplicity and reliability are two major benefits of using CRD objects to store HPO execution data. First, the information on the experiment's latest status can be accessed easily. For example, you can use Kubernetes commands, such as `kubectl describe experiment|trial|suggestion`, to get the intermediate data and the latest status of experiments, trials, and suggestions in a few seconds. Second, CRD objects help improve the reliability of HPO experiments. When the Katib service is down or the training operator fails, we can resume the HPO execution from where it failed, because these CRD objects retain the HPO execution history.

C.4.3   Kubeflow training operator integration for distributed training

Katib's default training operator—Kubernetes job operator—only supports single-pod model training; it launches a Kubernetes pod for each trial in an experiment. To support distributed training, Katib works with Kubeflow training operators (https://www.kubeflow.org/docs/components/training/). You can see how this works in figure C.4.

An HPO experiment consists of trials. Katib creates a trial CRD object and a TrialJob CRD object for each trail. The trial CRD contains the HPO trial metadata, such as suggested hyperparameter values, worker numbers, and exit criteria. In the TrialJob CRD, trial metadata is reformatted so that Kubeflow training operators can understand it.

`PyTorchJob` and `TFJob` are two of the most commonly used CRD types for TrialJobs. They can be processed by TensorFlow training operators and PyTorch training operators, each of which supports distributed training. When Alex sets the number of

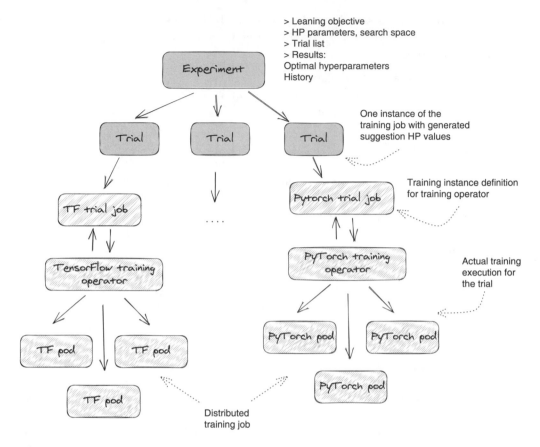

Figure C.4   Katib creates different trial jobs to trigger training operators to run distributed training for different training frameworks.

workers to three in the experiment CRD object, Katib creates a PyTorchJob trial CRD object, and the PyTorch trainer can conduct distributed training on this experiment.

This example also illustrates how flexible and extensible the Kubernetes controller pattern is. Two applications, Katib and KubeFlow training operators, can integrate easily if they are all implemented as controllers.

NOTE   We discussed Kubeflow training operator design in section 3.4.3. Please revisit it if you want to know more.

C.4.4   *Code reading*

Although Katib has a large code repository (https://github.com/kubeflow/katib), reading and debugging its code isn't too difficult.

WHERE TO START CODE READING

All Katib core components are written in controller pattern: `experiment_controller`, `trial_controller`, and `suggestion_controller`. It's a controller's job to ensure that, for any given object, the actual state of the Kubernetes world matches the desired state in the object. We call this process *reconciling*. For example, the reconcile function in `experiment_controller` reads the state of the cluster for an experiment object and makes changes (suggestion, trial) based on the state read. By following this thought, we can start with the reconcile function of each controller class to understand its core logic.

You can find the experiment controller at `pkg/controller.v1beta1/experiment/experiment_controller.go`, suggestion controller at `pkg/controller.v1beta1/suggestion/suggestion_controller.go`, and trial controller at `pkg/controller.v1beta1/trial/trial_ controller.go`. Remember to start with the reconcile function in these files.

DEBUGGING

The Katib core application (katib-controller) runs as a console application. There is no UI or web code in this console application, just pure logic code, so its local debugging setup is straightforward. To debug Katib, first set up your local Kubernetes cluster and run katib-controller locally with breakpoints, then you can start the HPO process by creating a test experiment request—for example, `kubectl apply -f {test_experiment.yaml}`. The breakpoint in the reconcile function will be hit, and you can start to debug and explore the code from there.

To set up a local development environment, please follow Katib's Developer Guide (http://mng.bz/VpzP). The entry point for katib-controller is at cmd/katib-controller/v1beta1/main.go.

> **NOTE** Katib is a production-quality HPO tool. It runs with high reliability and stability. But to operate it on a daily basis, we need to read its source code to understand its behavior so we know how to steer it when an HPO execution goes off the script. By following the workflow in figure C.2 and reading the reconcile function of each controller, you will gain a great understanding of Katib in a few hours.

C.5   Adding a new algorithm

From figure C.2, we know Katib runs different HPO algorithms as independent suggestion/algorithm services. Once an experiment is created, Katib creates a suggestion service for the selected HPO algorithm. This mechanism makes it easy to add a new algorithm to Katib and let the newly added algorithm work consistently with existing algorithms. To add a new algorithm to Katib, we need to carry out the following three steps.

C.5.1   Step 1: Implement Katib Suggestion API with the new algorithm

First, we need to implement the Katib `Suggestion` interface. This interface is defined in gRPC, so you can implement it in any language you prefer. The detailed definition of this interface can be found at http://mng.bz/xdzW; see the following code:

```
service Suggestion {
  rpc GetSuggestions(GetSuggestionsRequest)
```

```
      returns (GetSuggestionsReply);
  rpc ValidateAlgorithmSettings(ValidateAlgorithmSettingsRequest)
      returns (ValidateAlgorithmSettingsReply);
}
```

The following code snippet is one example of implementing the `Suggestion` interface. The hyperparameters and their value search spaces are defined in the `request` variable. The past trials and their metrics can also be found in the `request` variable, so you can run your algorithm to calculate the next suggestion by using these input data in the `GetSuggestions` method; see the following code:

```
class NewAlgorithmService(                          Defines a new algorithm
  api_pb2_grpc.SuggestionServicer,                  service and implements the
  HealthServicer):                                  GetSuggestions interface
  def ValidateAlgorithmSettings(self, request, context):
    # Optional, it is used to validate
    # algorithm settings defined by users.
    Pass                                            The Suggestion function
                                                    provides hyperparameters
                                                    to each trial.
  def GetSuggestions(self, request, context):     ◄
    search_space = HyperParameterSearchSpace.convert(request.experiment)

    trials = Trial.convert(request.trials)        ◄─  Obtains the
                                                      past trials
    # Implement the logic to use your algorithm
    # to generate new assignments
    # for the given current request number.
    list_of_assignments = your_logic(search_space,   Implements the actual
      trials, request.current_request_number)        HPO algorithm to provide
                                                      candidate values
    return api_pb2.GetSuggestionsReply(
      trials=Assignment.generate(list_of_assignments))
```

C.5.2   Step 2: Dockerize the algorithm code as a GRPC service

Once we implement the `Suggestion` interface, we need to build a gRPC server to expose this API to Katib and Dockerize it so Katib can launch the algorithm service and obtain hyperparameter suggestions by sending gRPC calls. The code would look as follows:

```
server = grpc.server(futures.ThreadPoolExecutor(max_workers=10))
service = YourNewAlgorithmService()
api_pb2_grpc.add_SuggestionServicer_to_server(service, server)
health_pb2_grpc.add_HealthServicer_to_server(service, server)
server.add_insecure_port(DEFAULT_PORT)
print("Listening...")
server.start()
```

C.5.3 Step 3: Register the algorithm to Katib

The last step is to register the new algorithm to Katib's starting configuration. Add a new entry in the `suggestion` section of the Katib service config; see an example as follows:

```
suggestion: |-
  {
    "tpe": {
      "image": "docker.io/kubeflowkatib/suggestion-hyperopt"
  },
    "random": {
      "image": "docker.io/kubeflowkatib/suggestion-hyperopt"
  },
+   "<new-algorithm-name>": {
+     "image": "new algorithm image path"
+ }
```

C.5.4 Examples and documents

Most of the previous content comes from the readme file—"Document about How to Add a New Algorithm in Katib" (http://mng.bz/Alrz)—at the Katib GitHub repo (https://github.com/kubeflow/katib). This is a very detailed and well-written doc that we highly recommend you read.

Because all of Katib's predefined HPO algorithms follow the same HPO algorithm registering pattern, you can use them as examples. This sample code can be found at katib/cmd/suggestion (http://mng.bz/ZojP).

C.6 Further reading

Good job on getting here! This is a lot to digest, but you made it this far. Although we have covered a good portion of Katib, there are still important pieces we didn't discuss because of page limits. In case you want to proceed further, we listed some useful reading materials for you to explore.

- To understand the thinking process behind the Katib design, please read "A Scalable and Cloud-Native Hyperparameter Tuning System" (https://arxiv.org/pdf/2006.02085.pdf).
- To check feature updates, tutorials, and code examples, please visit the Katib official website (https://www.kubeflow.org/docs/components/katib/) and Katib GitHub repo (https://github.com/kubeflow/katib).
- To use Python SDK to run an HPO from a Jupyter notebook directly, please read the SDK API doc (http://mng.bz/RlpK) and Jupyter notebook samples (http://mng.bz/2aY0).

C.7   *When to use it*

As we can see from this discussion, Katib satisfies all the design principles of an HPO service. It is agnostic to training frameworks and training code; it can be extended to incorporate different HPO algorithms and different metric collectors; and it is portable and scalable thanks to Kubernetes. Katib is the best option if you are seeking a production-level HPO service.

The only caveat for Katib is that its upfront costs are high. You need to build a Kubernetes cluster, install Katib, and Dockerize the training code to get started. You need to know Kubernetes commands to troubleshoot failures. It requires dedicated engineers to operate and maintain the system, as these are nontrivial tasks.

For production scenarios, these challenges are not major problems, because usually the model training system is set up in the same way as Katib in Kubernetes. As long as engineers have experience operating model training systems, they can manage Katib easily. But for small teams or prototyping projects, if you prefer something simpler, an HPO library approach—such as Ray Tune—is a better fit.

index

E

F

RELATED MANNING TITLES

Deep Learning with Python, Second Edition
by François Chollet

ISBN 9781617296864
504 pages, $59.99
October 2021

Effective Data Science Infrastructure
by Ville Tuulos
Foreword by Travis Oliphant

ISBN 9781617299193
352 pages, $59.99
July 2022

Deep Learning Patterns and Practices
by Andrew Ferlitsch

ISBN 9781617298264
472 pages, $59.99
August 2021

Acing the System Design Interview
by Zhiyong Tan

ISBN 9781633439108
275 pages *(estimated)*, $59.99
Summer 2023 *(estimated)*

For ordering information, go to www.manning.com